JEZEBEL & PROPHET

YOUR GUIDE TO UNDERSTANDING AND RECEIVING DELIVERANCE FROM THE NARCISSIST

Tiffany Buckner

Copyright

Jezebel & the Prophet
Your Guide to Understanding and Receiving Deliverance from the Narcissist
by Tiffany Buckner

© 2025, Tiffany Buckner
info@anointedfire.com

Published by Anointed Fire™ House
www.anointedfirehouse.com
Cover Design by Anointed Fire

978-1-955557-59-7

Table of Contents

This book covers the topic of narcissism from a practical, psychological, and a spiritual point of view, so prepare yourself to receive a wealth of information from each worldview. Some chapters are practical; some chapters are logical, and some chapters will give you in-depth information about the Jezebel spirit, which is the dragon or demon behind narcissism.

Introduction

Did you know that a lot of true science concurs with what we've read in the Bible? Some people genuinely believe that science and faith are at odds with one another when the truth is—science, if performed correctly, will always lead you back to the Word of God. For example, the church has been talking about the Jezebel spirit for thousands of years now, but the world at large was introduced to the term "narcissism" (in the psychological sense) in 1889 when Paul Näcke and Havelock Ellis used the term to describe a sexual phenomenon. De Gruyter Academic Publishing reported the following:

> "When he introduced the concept of narcissism into psychoanalytic theory in 1914, Freud drew on the works of the German psychiatrist Paul Näcke, who himself referred to the British physician and social reformer, Havelock Ellis. In 1899, Ellis published a study on "auto-erotism," which he understood as "the phenomena of spontaneous sexual emotion generated in the absence of an external stimulus proceeding, directly or indirectly, from another person" (Ellis 1942 [1899]: 161). Näcke, for his part, used the term "narcissism" ('Narcismus') in a narrower sense: his "narcissist" obtains sexual satisfaction solely by *looking* at himself – and not, for instance, by means of masturbation (Näcke 1899: 375). The reason for this narrower definition lies in the notion's eponym, the youth Narcissus from Ovid's *Metamorphoses*, who falls in love with his own reflection" (Source: www.degruyter.com/Narcissism in cultural theory: Perspectives on Christopher Lasch, Richard Sennett, and Robert Pfaller/Bernadette Grubner).

Narcissistic Personality Disorder was officially recognized in 1980 in the third edition of the Diagnostic and Statistical Manual, also known as DSM, and criteria started to be created for its diagnosis. It has since been revived, and it has gained a lot of popularity and traction since 2002, whereas, we have watched this pandemic continue to surge in numbers and in strength. However, the church has been talking about the spirit of Jezebel for thousands of years and the world is catching up, however, the world believes this to be nothing more than an incurable mental disorder when, in truth, it is a demon and a demonic system (stronghold).

Jezebel and the Prophet: A Biblical View of Narcissism was written to give readers insight into this spirit from both a spiritual and a natural (psychological) standpoint; this way, we can avoid the many traps that this particular demon commonly sets to ensnare prophets and prophetic people. This book is also designed for prophets and prophetic people to better understand their wiring and why they tend to attract narcissists and incredibly narcissistic people. Jezebel and the Prophet is revelatory, potent, life-altering, and information-rich! After reading this powerful book, you will no longer find yourself in the middle of an identity crisis; instead, you will know who you are and you will be better equipped to identify, reject, and overcome the advances of the narcissist in your life.

Note: in this guide, you will find several glossaries filled with terms commonly used in the world of psychology to describe Narcissistic Personality Disorder.

Before You Get Started (Important)

You're not a victim. You're a reaper. I'm sharing this with you because the way in which you approach this book or any book, including the Bible, will determine what you take from it. Am I saying that you've never been victimized? Absolutely not! More than likely, you have been victimized several times in your life, especially if you are a prophet or a highly prophetic person. Nevertheless, freedom is yours for the taking, and if you don't have it yet, it's because:
1. You didn't realize that you had access to it.
2. You're still convinced that you're a victim, and therefore, you're owed an apology before you can receive anything else.
3. You like being a victim because of the attention and/or the benefits you're extracting from that state of mind.
4. No one ever taught you your true identity, and therefore, you've been walking through life wearing a fake I.D.
5. You've never been taught how to truly take accountability for your role in your own adult-sized pain.
6. You're still looking at past events from the victim's viewpoint and not

God's vantage point.

7. You're afraid of freedom because you're accustomed to being bound.
8. You don't want to lose access to the bound people who've embraced you in your life, and you know that getting free from the devil means that you're going to simultaneously be freed from those people.
9. Your pain or your perversion has made you blind.
10. You're simply not interested in being free. You like your life as it is, and you don't want anything or anyone to disrupt it ... even God Himself.

Read this carefully. Even if you are in prison, freedom (in Christ) is yours *if you want it*. However, you have to want to be free more than the enemy wants to keep you bound. If Satan is more invested in your bondage than you are in your freedom, he holds the keys to your future. This is to say, once again, you're not a victim; you were supposed to leave that state of mind the moment you accepted Jesus Christ as your Lord and Savior. You are more than a conqueror in Christ Jesus. All the same, we reap what we sow. Therefore, if you sow idolatry, you will reap one of idolatry's favorite madams: the spirit of Jezebel, after all, Jezebel, also known today as the infamous narcissist, is your reward for idolatry. Peace, on the other hand, is your reward for seeking and putting God first. I'm saying this to say—please don't read this book from a victim's standpoint. Read it with the goal of being educated, corrected, and ultimately changed, understanding that the Bible tells us in Matthew 10:16, "Behold, I send you forth as sheep in the midst of wolves: be ye therefore wise as serpents, and harmless as doves." Your goal is to be wise as a serpent; you were never supposed to date and marry the serpent. But you may have found yourself entangled with a narcissist simply because you chose a partner before you fully and wholeheartedly chose God; you chose to love someone before your love for God had matured. This is the recipe for idolatry, and again, it is the very scent that attracts Jezebel. And this is why you're not a victim, and understanding this truth will help you to access your freedom, and it will also help you to sustain it.

"Be not deceived; God is not mocked: for whatsoever a man soweth, that shall he also reap. For he that soweth to his flesh shall of the flesh reap corruption; but he that soweth to the Spirit shall of the Spirit reap life everlasting. And let us not be weary in well doing: for in due season we shall reap, if we faint not" (Galatians 6:7-9).

Your state of mind is your status.
Your status is your state of mind.
When you want to change your status, you have to change your mind.
When you want to change your mind, you have to change what you take into it.

Remember this as you read this book:

- God **form**ed you.
- Sin de**form**ed you.
- The Bible tells us not to be con**form**ed to this world.
- We have to be trans**form**ed by the renewing of our minds.
- How do we renew our minds? Through good or, better yet, God in**form**ation. Our minds are renewed with the Truth!

"And ye shall know the truth, and the truth shall make you free" (John 8:32).

Mind Over Measure

There's a difference between a narcissist and a narcissistic person. While all narcissists are narcissistic, not all narcissistic people are narcissists. There's a difference between a prophet and a prophetic person. While prophets are prophetic, most prophetic people are not prophets. The reason these truths are necessary is because whenever we misidentify ourselves or others, we typically fight wars and take on assignments that we weren't supposed to burden ourselves with. For example, a woman who believes herself to be a prophetess may go around telling everyone that she is a prophet. She may even tell her pastor, believing that her pastor will ordain her as a prophet in that church. This could lead to a series of offenses, misunderstandings, and the potential severing of covenant relationships. She may come to believe that everyone is jealous of her and intimidated by her anointing when, in truth, God has not told her pastor that she is a prophet. This state of disillusionment could lead the woman to repeatedly challenge the leaders that God has put in place in her attempts to prove herself to be a true prophet of God when, in actuality, she may be a prophetic person. However, she's not called to the office of the prophet. All the same, I've heard people screaming at the top of their lungs that their friends, exes, parents, or pastors are narcissists when the people in question were simply narcissistic; they were immature, wounded souls that were in need of deliverance, counseling, and a strong spiritual community.

It's all on a spectrum. Prophetic people, just like prophets, are on a spectrum. Narcissists and narcissistic people are on a spectrum. You see, not all prophetic people have the same degree of sensitivity or prophetic ability. Let's backtrack for a bit. Every child of God, once he or she receives Holy Spirit, is prophetic, but not everyone taps into their prophetic abilities. In truth, many people intentionally avoid opening their God-given gifts because of their wayward desires to be "normal." This causes them to run from God by hiding in the congregation at their local assemblies, hiding in relationships, or hiding in religions where their gifting is not permitted because the people who make up that religion believe that certain gifts are demonic or outdated. And this is how many people find themselves being swallowed by pride and held captive by Jezebel. But let's start here. Not all prophets will surrender themselves to God. Many will find themselves in witchcraft, rebellion, ungodly marriages, and demonic lifestyles all the days of their lives, and when this happens, God will oftentimes raise up a prophetic person in their place. No, this does not mean that the prophetic person will graduate from being prophetic to being a prophet, after all, prophets are hardwired to be prophets before they are placed in their mothers' wombs. Consider what God said to Prophet Jeremiah in Jeremiah 1:5. He said, "Before I formed thee in the belly I knew thee; and before thou camest forth out of the womb I sanctified thee, and I ordained thee a prophet unto the nations." Jeremiah was ordained to be a prophet *before* he was even conceived in his mother's womb. This does mean that many prophets may find themselves being all the more prophetic or sensitive than their prophetic counterparts (in some instances). For example, there are some prophetic people who are more potent, more prophetic, and more in tune with God than some people who were called to the office of the prophet. This has everything to do with each person's capacity, understanding, and level of surrender. Your capacity is like your stomach; your stomach is a muscle that can expand or shrink, depending on how much you repeatedly put in it. The same is true with your faith. Your faith is your spiritual muscle; it is grown through Bible study and application. In other words, you have to practice what you hear, after all, faith comes by hearing, and hearing by the Word of God (see Romans 10:17), and faith without works is dead (see James 2:26). So, when a prophet chooses the world over the Word, or when a prophet repeatedly rebels against God, God can and sometimes will still use that prophet but not to his or her full capacity. Instead, He will raise someone up in that prophet's place. This is what happened to the prophet Elijah. When he went on the run from Jezebel, God raised up Elisha in his place, but Elisha was also a prophet. The point is that we are all replaceable regardless of whether we're prophets or prophetic people. Simply put, God will not allow His people to go to hell simply because some of His prophets got so distracted and mesmerized by the world and what it had to offer that they went off post to chase the temporal things.

Another note that's worth taking is this—the spectrum of narcissism is singular, but prophets and prophetic people are not on the same spectrum. Again, if you are truly saved, you are prophetic; I'm only noting this to keep down confusion because we are living in a time when everyone wants to be a prophet until it's time to be a prophet. For example, in the Bible, there were minor prophets and major prophets. What made some of the men minor prophets and what made some of them major prophets? The length of their books. Major prophets had significantly longer books than minor prophets. This is to say that not all prophets rank the same. Rank has everything to do with trust; you wouldn't promote someone in your organization that you could not trust, and if you did, you'd someday regret it. This is to say that God trusts some prophets more than He trusts others. He trusted Abraham to be the father of all nations. Please understand that there were other prophets in that time. He trusted Samuel to prophesy to kings, He trusted Nathan to speak to King David, and He trusted Elijah to address Ahab. He then transferred that trust to Elisha, and gave him the duty to take down Jezebel by appointing Jehu as her replacement. He trusted Joseph to walk alongside a pagan pharaoh named Zaphenath-Paneah. He trusted Daniel to serve under four kings:

1. King Nebuchadnezzar
2. King Belshazzar
3. King Darius
4. King Cyrus

Before David became king, God trusted him to minister, through music, to King Saul. He trusted Esther to marry a pagan king (King Xerxes, also known as King Ahasuerus) in order to save His people from the impending genocide that hell (and Haman) was plotting against them. He trusted Job with warfare and wealth. He trusted Noah to build the ark. These are just a few of the prophets and prophetic souls that God trusted to stand before kings and queens. Again, we are dealing with rank. This is to say that not all prophets are equal in rank. Those of higher rank are trusted with a greater depth, height, and worldview of information, while others are trusted with varying measures of revelation and information. This isn't to promote or provoke pride in anyone, nor is this designed to make one prophet feel inferior to another; this is simply to say that there is a spectrum and not all prophets rank the same on that spectrum, which means that one prophet may not be able to understand the assignment that God gives another prophet because he or she isn't necessarily wired for that particular mission. Howbeit, on the prophetic spectrum, there are degrees of sensitivity, and again, your movement on this spectrum has everything to do with how much God can trust you with; it has everything to do with your capacity. In other words, some people are far more prophetic than others; they were wired to be sensitive so that they can sense God's presence. And it is for this reason that some prophets and prophetic people tend to isolate themselves; this has everything to do with their degrees of sensitivity. It also has something to do with their traumas. For example, some prophetic people are so sensitive that they can feel the emotions of the people around them. Because of this, they will oftentimes self-isolate in an attempt to not feel those emotions. Consequently, many prophets and prophetic people identify as empaths and introverts, not realizing that they are simply sensitive to spiritual stimuli. This is why it is good for prophets and prophetic people to have mentors and prophetic communities; they need people who understand where they are, why they're feeling what they feel, and how to navigate the many seasons and emotions that they repeatedly and routinely experience. Furthermore, this is why it is not wise, as a prophet or prophetic person, to allow everyone to speak into your life. Remember, Peter didn't understand why Jesus had to go to the cross, so he tried to talk Him out of His destiny. Mark 8:31-33 reads, "And he began to teach them, that the Son of man must suffer many things, and be rejected of the elders, and *of* the chief priests, and scribes, and be killed, and after three days rise again. And he spake that saying openly. And Peter took him, and began to rebuke him. But when he had turned about and looked on his disciples, he rebuked Peter, saying, Get thee behind me, Satan: for thou savourest not the things that be of God, but the things that be of men." Sometimes, people have good intentions, but they are bound by wicked spirits. Why did Jesus refer to Peter as Satan? He didn't. He rebuked the spirit that was using Peter. This is to say that anointed people can misguide you, and they can do so with no malicious intent in their hearts, however, they can be bound by a lack of understanding, fear, or demons.

Last but not least, remember that there were thousands, if not millions of prophets from the biblical era, whose names we do not know. Some of them were used nominally by God, while some were used majorly by Him. Then again, some prophets never surrendered themselves to Him, so they weren't used at all. The same is still true today. Many of you are prophets, just like many of you are prophetic people, and you have yet to surrender yourself to God to be used by Him.

And finally, let's talk about the spectrum of narcissism. This is a single spectrum, with the narcissist being on the full left of this spectrum and the average person being on the right. This particular spectrum doesn't start at zero, since mankind is filled with iniquitous patterns. We start at 30-fold. What this means is that, in our day and age, there is a degree of narcissism that is considered normal. For example, what's been normalized today wasn't normal in 1985; what's been accepted as good today was considered evil yesterday. This is to say that the world is growing more and more evil as time transports us from our realities to our eternities.

Every generation represents a batch of humans; we are like bread in a baker's oven. If that baker was selling his bread at a cafe and people were repeatedly buying the bread, he'd have to keep making new batches. Not all batches would be equal. Most would look and taste the same if he had the right measuring tools and equipment. Then again, some bread batches would be softer than others, just like some batches would be browner and more firm than the batches that preceded them. Google's AI Overview reported the following:

> "According to many analyses, Generation X is often considered to have a stronger work ethic and greater resilience compared to Generation Z, with key strengths like independence, resourcefulness, and the ability to adapt to challenging situations, largely due to the different societal and economic conditions they grew up in; however, this is a generalization

and individual strengths can vary across both generations."

Baby Boomers, Generation X, Millennials, Generation Z … we're all batches. It doesn't mean that everyone in my generation, for example, all think the same; it does mean, however, that there are strengths that are common and pretty much necessary in my generation that aren't necessarily commonplace in the generations that followed. The same is true for weaknesses. There are weaknesses in my generation that are not commonplace with the generations that succeeded my own. There are strengths in Gen Z that many, if not most of the people in my generation do not have. Why? Because we didn't need them at the time. Strengths are oftentimes a response to a need or a demand.

Sin weakens people. Proverbs 14:34 says it this way: "Righteousness exalteth a nation: but sin is a reproach to any people." The following information was taken from the Berean Study Bible:

> "The word "disgrace" is derived from the Hebrew "חֶסֶד" (chesed), which in this context means shame or reproach. Sin brings disgrace to a nation by tarnishing its reputation and leading to negative consequences. Historically, nations that have embraced sinful practices have faced internal strife, economic decline, and loss of influence. From a conservative Christian viewpoint, sin not only dishonors God but also brings shame upon a nation, highlighting the urgent need for moral and spiritual renewal."

Sin sets the stage for cultures and traditions that break apart nations, destroy families, and usher in demons that become familiar to any given group of people. This is how narcissism is normalized. So, what's considered "normal" today, while relatively narcissistic, won't be the standard 10-15 years from now when the next generation takes the driver's seat. You see, Satan thinks in generations. He understands that the more he can normalize certain sins, the more he can introduce the people to even more sins; that is until the world and its inhabitants are filled to the brim with sin, rebellion, witchcraft, and a disdain for the Most High God. And this is how we end up with more narcissism and more narcissists.

Narcissism at its core is nothing but self-worship (more on this later). It means to exalt one's self over the Word of God; it means to be led by the flesh and the ungodly desires of the flesh. And understand this—believers are to consume and produce the fruits of the Spirit, meaning that we are spiritually vegan, but demons are meat eaters who love uncrucified flesh; they are carnivores with an appetite for the walking dead. The more sin we love, the more demons we'll have, and the more narcissistic we'll be. And on the spectrum of narcissism, there is constant movement.

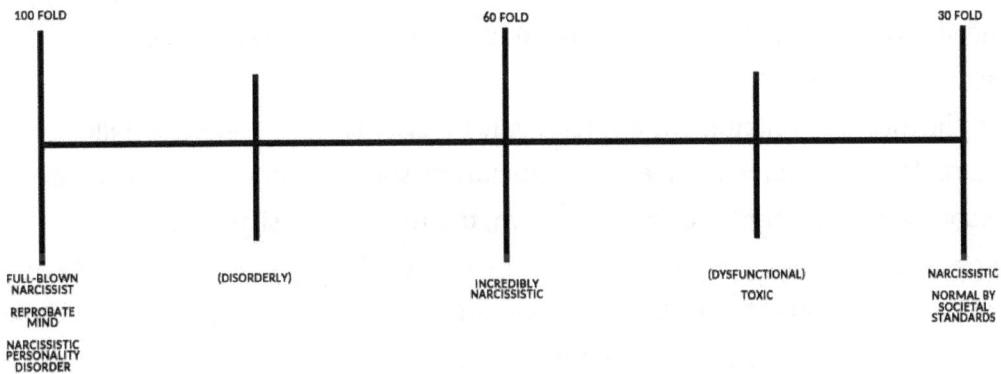

100 FOLD		60 FOLD		30 FOLD
FULL-BLOWN NARCISSIST	(DISORDERLY)	INCREDIBLY NARCISSISTIC	(DYSFUNCTIONAL) TOXIC	NARCISSISTIC
REPROBATE MIND				NORMAL BY SOCIETAL STANDARDS
NARCISSISTIC PERSONALITY DISORDER				

Some people are moving towards the center and left of the spectrum, meaning with every wound, every rejection, and every upset, they are becoming more and more narcissistic, while others are doing the work necessary to heal themselves. They are reading their Bibles, taking accountability, repenting of their sins, getting therapy, taking their bodies off the black market of fornication, and chasing God instead of chasing their dreams. Consequently, they are moving more towards the right of the spectrum in the direction of healing. And remember, the far right of the spectrum is 30-fold. Get this—once you move to the right of 30-fold, you begin to find God all the more; this is when you'll step into your God-given identity, and this is when you'll stand out from the crowd. The outskirts of this spectrum is, simply put, the will of God. This is when we've chosen the narrow path; this is when we've chosen to be more like Christ, not just through works, but in our minds. Howbeit, we are born on this spectrum, and we move towards the center of it as we grow up in the world. This is to say that as we mature in the world, we move further and further away from God, but as we mature in the things of God, we move further and further away from the world. And it is possible to come so far outside of the world that you find yourself at the edge of the spectrum feeling like you're about to lose yourself if you were to dive face-first into God's will and into your true identity. How do you know when you're in this space? It's when you learn to be unapologetically but humbly be the person that you were once afraid to be; it's when you stretch out your potential, and what you'll soon discover is that the more you embrace who you are, the less space people will have for you in their lives. That's because the true you is too big to fit into the tight spaces of someone's expectations and limitations of you.

The short of it is—all humans are relatively narcissistic because of our fallen nature. Howbeit, some people are more narcissistic than others, and the closer a person gets to the center of the spectrum, the more narcissistic that person is. Once an individual grazes the center of the spectrum, this is when the world of psychology will oftentimes diagnose that individual with a disorder, whether that disorder is Narcissistic Personality Disorder, Histrionic Personality Disorder, Bipolar Disorder, or any of the Cluster B personalities.

Prophets often confront and take down narcissists, whereas, prophetic people typically wrestle with and hopefully overcome narcissistic people. This isn't necessarily a rule of thumb, but what you'll come to discover is that there is rank in the spiritual realm, and nothing that outranks you can attack you without the angels assigned to you getting involved (more on this later). So, if you're prophetic, you'll know the rank that you walk in based on the level and the frequencies of the attacks that you find yourself under. You see, the devil has an odd way of telling on himself. You might not think that you have the measure of rank that you were graced with, but the attacks on your life may say otherwise. Consider Job. Satan himself was given the green light to attack Job. This indicates that Job had great rank in the realm of the spirit. And please understand that an attack is NOT you going into sin, and then reaping from that sin. That's not an attack, that's a harvest. By attack, I'm talking about demons waging war with you as you follow Christ AND the demons that waged war with you when you were a child. It's easier to measure your enemy when you aren't swollen with pride and blinded by iniquity.

This is to say ... mind your measure. But to know your measure, you have to follow God's instructions in Matthew 6:33, which reads, "But seek ye first the kingdom of God, and his righteousness; and all these things shall be added unto you." Stop trying to figure out who you are when you haven't fully grasped Whose you are. And that's why I wrote this book.

In this book, you will find information about the Jezebel spirit, along with information about prophets and prophetic people. You will learn the practical, psychological, and spiritual side of what you've been wrestling against; this way, you will be better equipped to deal with the devil when he throws another narcissist at you.

Stages and Ages

I've met, formed relationships with, and even mentored a lot of prophets; the same is true for prophetic people, and one thing I can truly say is that there are prophetic patterns that many prophets have. Some of these patterns only serve to hinder, muzzle, and destroy God's prophets. I don't necessarily see these patterns with prophetic people; I mainly see them in prophets, and I'll list those patterns below. But before I do, we have to discuss the fact that, just like prophets have varying degrees of rank, they also have stages of maturity. As a matter of fact, most prophets will never mature enough to be used by God, while others will only let Him use them in small measures. This is because most prophets, in their infancy, tend to be attracted to anyone or anything that takes them to the proverbial "cloud nine." In other words, they love oxytocin, dopamine, serotonin, adrenaline, and anyone who gives these drugs to them. With that said, if you are a prophet, you may not have experienced some of what I've posted on the list, but buyer beware—some of the issues mentioned are often experienced as the prophet starts maturing. Think of it this way. Let's create a character named Janice, and let's say, for example's sake, that Janice is a prophet. When Janice was young in her gifting, Satan would often tempt her with her ex-boyfriend, Nolan. Nolan would repeatedly reach out to Janice, pretend to be her friend, take advantage of the budding prophet, and then discard her. Over time, Janice got closer to God so her perspective began to shift. All of a sudden, she understood the word "narcissist," and Janice started to realize that the man who'd mastered pulling her strings was just that—a narcissist—a demon in the flesh. As Janice grew, she began to learn more about God, her wiring, and about the spirit of Jezebel, and this led her to cut Nolan off wholeheartedly. She changed her phone number, blocked Nolan on social media, threatened to call the cops on him when he'd used a temporary virtual number to contact her, and she slowly moved on with her life. During stage two of her gifting, Janice started having financial problems. It would seem as if hell had gotten the PIN to her bank account and was draining her of everything she'd worked for. No matter how much she prayed, fasted, sought wise counsel, or threatened to go back into the world, debt and poverty seemed to follow her wherever she went. During this phase, Janice started to wrestle with suicidal thoughts because she was more than convinced that God was mad at her about something, but she couldn't put her finger on what it was that she'd done wrong. She got laid off from her job, her hair care brand wasn't selling at all, and her bills continued to mount. What she didn't realize was that she was in a place that I like to call systematic deliverance; this is when we transition from one system to another, and yes, this happens without our permission. It's when that great fish that we've been eating from the inside out spits us out. It's when we can no longer rely on the people, the government, and the systems we once relied on for our sustenance. During this phase, every ounce of witchcraft that still resides in the prophet will begin to tempt the prophet more than ever. For example, the prophet will be tempted to burn sage, buy crystals, return to Nolan (or whatever Jezebel that the prophet has escaped) to get financial assistance, date someone who is better off than themselves financially, leave the people they feel aren't of any help to them, etc.

Next, there's phase or stage three. This is a teenage phase of the prophet; this is when the prophet's immaturity wages war against their maturity. This is when the prophet starts wrestling all the more with double-mindedness, but by double-mindedness, I don't mean that the prophet is lukewarm, not to God at least. During this stage, prophets tend to start feeling like they know more than their leaders, mentors, and wise counselors. Ask any leader who's ever had the opportunity to lead a true prophet for any measure of time and they will tell you about the many times they've been challenged, discarded, and attacked by teenage prophets. This is the phase when rebellion is at an all-time high with many prophets; this is when they begin to, as the old folks would say, "smell themselves." And again, a lot of prophets fall in the wilderness during this phase because a lot of them start thinking that they know more than the Lord Himself. During this phase, many prophets have memorized a lot of scriptures, started attending ministry schools, attaching themselves to prominent people in ministry by joining their programs, and busying themselves so much that they don't have time anymore to study their Bibles, pray, or even show up to the schools and programs that they are being raised in. I always liken this phase to puberty because, like teenagers, prophets tend to self-isolate during this phase; they also begin to wrestle with ungodly ambition. A great example of a prophet who entered this phase is Miriam. Miriam got to the space where she'd witnessed her gifting work; she'd witnessed God working miracles through her, and because of this, she started wanting to break away from Moses to start her own ministry. This story is found in Numbers 12; let's read the NIV version of this story for context:

> Miriam and Aaron began to talk against Moses because of his Cushite wife, for he had married a Cushite. 'Has the LORD spoken only through Moses?' they asked. 'Hasn't he also spoken through us?' And the LORD heard this. (Now Moses was a very humble man, more humble than anyone else on the face of the earth.) At once the LORD said to Moses, Aaron and Miriam, 'Come out to the tent of meeting, all three of you.' So the three of them went out. Then the LORD came down in a pillar of cloud; he stood at the entrance to the tent and summoned Aaron and Miriam. When the two of them stepped forward, he said, 'Listen to my words: When there is a prophet among you, I, the LORD, reveal myself to them in visions, I speak to them in dreams. But this is not true of my servant Moses; he is faithful in all my house. With him I speak face to face, clearly and not in riddles; he sees the form of the LORD. Why then

were you not afraid to speak against my servant Moses?' The anger of the Lᴏʀᴅ burned against them, and he left them. When the cloud lifted from above the tent, Miriam's skin was leprous—it became as white as snow. Aaron turned toward her and saw that she had a defiling skin disease, and he said to Moses, 'Please, my lord, I ask you not to hold against us the sin we have so foolishly committed. Do not let her be like a stillborn infant coming from its mother's womb with its flesh half eaten away.' So Moses cried out to the Lᴏʀᴅ, 'Please, God, heal her!' The Lᴏʀᴅ replied to Moses, 'If her father had spit in her face, would she not have been in disgrace for seven days? Confine her outside the camp for seven days; after that she can be brought back.' So Miriam was confined outside the camp for seven days, and the people did not move on till she was brought back. After that, the people left Hazeroth and encamped in the Desert of Paran."

Notice here that God first establishes Moses's rank with Miriam and Aaron. He distinguishes Moses from other prophets, saying that He reveals Himself to His prophets through visions and dreams, but with Moses, He has face-to-face meetings. In other words, Moses had direct access to God. Remember, rank is trust; this means that God likely trusted Moses more than He trusted any other prophet during that era and in that camp. All the same, Miriam and Aaron were both prophets as well, and they were now "smelling themselves," especially Miriam. We know this because God punished her and not Aaron. Aaron was rebuked, but Miriam had to suffer through an episode of leprosy for seven days, and in that time, she had to be put outside of the camp. This was because she'd made the oh-so-common Jezebelic move of trying to usurp the authority that God had granted to Moses.

After helping the two rogue prophets, God asked them why they weren't afraid to speak against Moses. Once again, we are witnessing God make a distinction between Moses and all other prophets, trying to get them to understand that they are NOT equal. With more trust comes more favor, and with more favor comes more power. With more power comes more positioning and a greater punishment. "But he that knew not, and did commit things worthy of stripes, shall be beaten with few stripes. For unto whomsoever much is given, of him shall be much required: and to whom men have committed much, of him they will ask the more" (Luke 12:48). You have to go outside of Western thinking to grasp this, but God is not a slave to our ideologies surrounding "fairness." He doesn't buy a toy for a crying child just because He gave that child's sibling a toy. He doesn't pacify our comparison, nor does He sow into mindsets that promote equality in spiritual matters because that's just not how the Kingdom works! If I had triplet sons, and one of them was incredibly mature, the second was mildly mature, and the third triplet was immature, I wouldn't give the immature child the keys to my car just because I let the mature one drive it. Why would I reward a behavior that I don't support? And I wouldn't withhold the keys from the mature one just because his brother is immature. I'm sharing this because in the American church lies the belief that we can say what we want to say, when we want to say it, and about whomever we want to say it with no repercussions. But if God put someone in place, and you start working to get people to question that person or walk away from that person's ministry, are you not directly waging war against a move of God? This is why we see so many prophets and believers altogether losing their minds. It's not just that the devil is attacking them. No, the issue is that they are allowing the devil to use them to attack someone else that God has placed in position for such a time as this. Consider how Jesus addressed His disciples in Mark 9:38-41 when they were more than ready to stop another man from ministering deliverance to His people. "And John answered him, saying, Master, we saw one casting out devils in thy name, and he followeth not us: and we forbad him, because he followeth not us. But Jesus said, Forbid him not: for there is no man which shall do a miracle in my name, that can lightly speak evil of me. For he that is not against us is on our part. For whosoever shall give you a cup of water to drink in my name, because ye belong to Christ, verily I say unto you, he shall not lose his reward." In this, Jesus warned His disciples by telling them to not come against the other guy's ministry simply because they did not understand it.

Lastly, in the story of Moses, God releases His judgment and His grace. You see,

Miriam was burdened with leprosy; this way, all of the camp would know that she'd sinned against God and there would be no green-room deliverance, meaning she wouldn't get a private pop on the hands. Instead, God made a public example out of Miriam; this was to dissuade anyone else from getting the not-so-bright idea that they could promote themselves at the expense of someone God had elected into a specific office; yes, even if they themselves were anointed. When God warned us to "touch not my anointed and do my prophets no harm," He was talking directly to the anointed. You see, the Bible wasn't written for the unbeliever; it was written for the believer. And because many believers read the Bible as if God is talking to those outside the camp, they commit the very crimes and sins that God warned us about, thus provoking God's wrath. What's sad and funny today is that whenever a saint steps into a chastening, they immediately think that the devil is attacking them, not realizing that we are NOT victims, we are reapers.

Please note that most prophets don't make it past stage three. Many of them get swallowed up by Jezebel and Leviathan because they don't seek the safety of wise counsel or they begin to challenge and attack their wise counselors. This is to say that many of them end up hosting the Jezebel spirit. This is what happened to Miriam. Miriam clearly displayed the signs and the symptoms of Jezebel, especially in the fact that she was willing and ready to usurp the authority that God had given to Moses, and she'd managed to entice her younger brother, Aaron, using the same method that Satan used to deceive one-third of God's angels; this was also the same method he'd used to deceive Eve. He made them feel as if God wasn't all-powerful, he led them to question God's motives by making them feel like God was withholding the truth from them, and then he convinced them that they could be "like God," knowing all things. In other words, they could be equal to God and independent of God; they could be their own gods and be just as powerful or even more powerful than the Most High God. Understand this—every single prophet and believer who steps into a position of power is tempted with this lie. Every single one! Remember, this is the temptation that Satan tried to ensnare Jesus with when He was in the wilderness. Check out the chart below.

14

Temptation	Jesus' Response
And when the tempter came to him, he said, If thou be the Son of God, command that these stones be made bread.	But he answered and said, It is written, Man shall not live by bread alone, but by every word that proceedeth out of the mouth of God.
Then the devil taketh him up into the holy city, and setteth him on a pinnacle of the temple, and saith unto him, If thou be the Son of God, cast thyself down: for it is written, He shall give his angels charge concerning thee: and in their hands they shall bear thee up, lest at any time thou dash thy foot against a stone.	Jesus said unto him, It is written again, Thou shalt not tempt the Lord thy God.
Again, the devil taketh him up into an exceeding high mountain, and sheweth him all the kingdoms of the world, and the glory of them; and saith unto him, All these things will I give thee, if thou wilt fall down and worship me.	Then saith Jesus unto him, Get thee hence, Satan: for it is written, Thou shalt worship the Lord thy God, and him only shalt thou serve.

After this, the devil fled. Matthew 4:11 reads, "Then the devil leaveth him, and, behold, angels came and ministered unto him." This is an example of James 4:7 in action; it reads, "Submit yourselves therefore to God. Resist the devil, and he will flee from you." If the devil doesn't flee from you, he will enter you; that's just how this works. This is why we are charged in Ephesians 4:26-27, "Be ye angry, and sin not: let not the sun go down upon your wrath: Neither give place to the devil." And remember this—if the devil is not mad at you, he must be proud of you. Choose your fight wisely.

After stage three, there's stage four. During this phase, many prophets run back into the congregation, hoping to hide from their assignments; this is oftentimes because they start to meet their Sauls. Many prophets discover that (some of) the people who were leading them, mentoring them, coaching them, or counseling them were not their supporters; these people served as monitoring spirits in their lives. Now, this is not true for ALL prophets, as many do have great counselors and leaders, but the majority of prophets, during this stage, will discover the many faces of Jezebel that have become familiar faces and familiar spirits in their lives. This is when the prophet has to choose between toxic and ungodly loyalty versus stepping outside of a bunch of man-made policies and politics, religion, and the expectations of the people that they once honored to step into their destinies. But get this—I'm not exclusively talking about (some of) their pastors or other religious leaders. I'm also talking about some of their parents, their friends, and their lovers! Again, many prophets have great leaders; I place emphasis on this because during phase three, some prophets will look for any excuse to deliver themselves from the authority figures in their lives in an attempt to hijack their next seasons, so many of them would swear on their pinky fingers that they are in stage four, their wise counselors are their Sauls, and that their escapes are justified. This may be true for some, but it isn't true for every single prophet. Remember, Jezebel killed off many of God's prophets during her era, but there were still a few on the loose. For example, Obadiah hid 100 prophets in two caves; Micaiah was free, and he'd been invited to the castle a few times to prophesy. And of course, there was Elijah. While he was elusive, he was still free. This is simply to say that not every prophet is headed by a Saul, however, every prophet has a Saul somewhere lingering in their lives, and during their infancy, they are likely a suckling, drinking from Saul's breast because prophets HATE pressure; this is why many of them are easily captured by Jezebel. A large number of them lean to the government, family members, and lovers to take care of them because they hate the pressures associated with:

1. Feeling the emotions of others in the workplace.
2. Dealing with Jezebels in the workplace.
3. Dealing with Jezebels in the church.
4. Paying bills and dealing with numbers (unless they are called to finance).
5. Growing up.

Jezebel will happily take on these roles in a prophet's life in exchange for the prophet's trust, alliance, allegiance, and complacency. Jezebel will take on these roles, all the while yelling and tearing the prophets down one day, one complaint, and one accusation at a time. Many prophets grow used to this behavior because they inwardly reason that it's far easier for them to deal with Jezebel's tantrums than it is to take responsibility for themselves, their children, and whatever it is that they want in life. This is why Satan loves to attack prophets in the area of finance; this way, the prophet can become a suckling of Jezebel. Over time, the prophet ends up becoming a house for Jezebel to live in, meaning they begin to host and have the Jezebel spirit, and when this transition is done, Satan then causes them to despise authority figures by using the authority figures in their lives to hurt or disappoint them, or by using Jezebel to take them on a tour of pain. For example, I remember ministering to a young woman whose mother had a strong or, better yet, high-ranking Jezebel spirit. She'd gone no-contact with her mother several times for months on end, but just like every Ahab I've ever met, she repeatedly returned to her mother when times got tough. This is because her mother had intentionally handicapped her in the financial realm; most narcissists do this to their children. They do this by creating a codependent relationship with their children, wherein they teach their children to see them as strong; they teach their children to see them as gods. They also teach their children that they (the children) are either too weak to take responsibility for themselves, or in many cases, they teach them that they are victims in need of a savior. This savior, of course, is Jezebel. This is how the spirit of Jezebel grooms Jezebel's children to become its next host. So, during phase four, the pressures begin to crush the prophet's dreams and plans as God prepares the prophet for his or her assignment all the more; this includes (for many) going before kings, queens, and notable people. This can be likened to the pressures that Esther felt when she was being massaged with myrrh for six months, and then massaged with spices and ointments for another six months. And get this—Esther wasn't massaged by Godly people; she was massaged by pagan people in preparation to marry a pagan king as part of her Kingdom assignment. What does this mean? Sometimes, the prophetic pressures that you experience aren't God's angels touching you; all too often, the pressures come from demons attacking you. This could be and often is the prophet's proverbial "thorn in the flesh." And please note that this is NOT done for you to go out and marry a Gomer or an unbeliever, after all, prophets tend to wrestle with idolatry, and it is common for them to get impatient and begin to reason with themselves that the men or women they're interested in are their God-established assignments. Consequently, they often come to engage in evangelistic dating, whereas they'll try to date, obsess over, and even marry the people they were charged to rebuke, warn, or point to Christ.

During phase four, the greatest temptation that a prophet suffers through is to quit or to become bitter, but if the prophet makes it past this stage, he or she will have accomplished a feat that most prophets will never accomplish. Also, it's worth mentioning that during this phase, the prophet has to learn to discern between a good idea and a God idea. This is because Satan will try to negotiate a deal with God's prophets during this era of their lives; he uses this time to present opportunities to them that they once dreamed of; these opportunities can be ministry-related, romantic in nature, or career-related. For example, I've seen a lot of ambitious prophets jumping around, connecting with one leader after another in an attempt to get their names out there. I've also witnessed them forsaking their calls to ministry to build their careers, not realizing that sometimes, their careers and their ministries are interlinked. In other words, you don't have to break up with one system to enjoy the benefits of another unless God says otherwise. The best practice is to pray, fast, and wait on God for your next set of instructions instead of chasing after a bunch of good ideas that lead you to tire yourself out. After all, those good ideas can lead you away from the God ideas and straight into the custody of Jezebel. This is what I call the prophet's bait, and sadly enough, we find many of God's prophets on the tail end of Jezebel's fishing pole holding onto Jezebel's lies. In this, we find them covered with the scales of Leviathan, jumping around excitedly, not realizing that they are about to enter into a dark season where there is weeping and gnashing of teeth; this, within itself, is one of the woes or judgments of God. This is what it looks like to be in the belly of the great fish, Leviathan. However, there's a beautiful side to this—many prophets repent, get spit out of Jezebel's system, and go on to be used by God in great and marvelous ways. Sadly enough, the rest find themselves in Jezebel's bed committing adultery with not just the spirit of Jezebel but the system of Jezebel; this is when they become tolerant of Jezebel and learn to coexist with a demon they were supposed to cast out. Consider God's rebuke to the Church at Thyatira in Revelation 2:19-23; He said, "I know thy works, and charity, and service, and faith, and thy patience, and thy works; and the last to be more than the first. Notwithstanding I have a few things against thee, because thou sufferest that woman Jezebel, which calleth herself a prophetess, to teach and to seduce my servants to commit fornication, and to eat things sacrificed unto idols. And I gave her space to repent of her fornication; and she repented not. Behold, I will cast her into a bed, and them that commit adultery with her into great tribulation, except they repent of their deeds. And I will kill her children with death; and all the churches shall know that I am he which searcheth the reins and hearts: and I will give unto every one of you according to your works." Understand that tribulation is a woe. Merriam Webster's online dictionary defines both tribulation and woe this way:

- **Tribulation:** a cause of great trouble or suffering.
- **Woe:** great sorrow or distress (often used hyperbolically); things that cause sorrow or distress; troubles.

This is to say that the weeping and gnashing of teeth starts here on Earth and climaxes in hell. This is why many prophets have found themselves lying next to Jezebel in a dark room trying to muffle or muzzle the sounds of their cries in an attempt to not further upset the narcissists that they won at Satan's Circus for Idolaters.

And finally, there is phase or stage five. This is when the prophet has given God a yes that he or she refuses to take back; this is when prophetic numbness takes over, whereas the prophet is delivered from emotional immaturity, emotional and relational witchcraft, and the systems of Jezebel. This is when the prophet regains all of his or her sanity back; I'm talking about the peace, clarity, and confidence that Satan once robbed them of. This is when the prophet will prophesy confidently and boldly; this is also when you'll start to notice wealth and favor following the prophet around. But in this, the prophet hasn't fully escaped the devil's snares because, during this phase, Satan has one more trick up his sleeves, and that trick is praise. This is when people, seeing how potent, accurate, and effective the prophet is, will begin to praise, follow, and idolize the prophet. If the prophet steals God's praise repeatedly and refuses to repent, their fall is inevitable. After all, praise is intoxicating, and remember, prophets love their wiring to be tantalized. So, during this stage, Satan will give the prophet a lot of narcissistic supply, and if the prophet does not have the safety of wise counselors or the prophet does not utilize the wise counselors in his or her life because of pride, rejection, or "not wanting to bother anyone," it will be easy for Satan to ensnare the prophet. He does this by repeatedly having people to praise the prophet, and those same people will get offended whenever the prophet returns the praise to God. They'll typically say things like:

"Don't be so heavenly minded that you're no earthly good."

"I know God did it, but it's okay for you to be celebrated as well because you obeyed God, right?!"

"I hate when people do that! Let some people celebrate you for a change! Don't be so religious that you become weird!"

If the prophet allows himself or herself to become subject or a slave of these people's emotions, the prophet will start holding God's praise with the intent of giving Him the glory privately. This people-pleasing behavior is ungodly, and it will always lead to the prophet getting high on God's praise and then getting addicted to it. Before long, the world would witness a spooky prophet running around in the churches, covered with glitter, adorned with excessive jewels, and decorated like a Christmas tree blowing dust and debris on God's people. This is when we start to see the emergence of:

- Magic-finger prophets who appear to play invisible keyboards.
- Fighting prophets who punch, shove, and jump in the faces of God's people while prophesying or ministering deliverance to them.
- Perverted prophets who accurately prophesy while wearing push-up bras, Brazilian butt-lifts, and muscle shirts. Then again, you will see some who are clearly wrestling with the spirit of homosexuality but again, they can and often do prophesy accurately, and this opens the door for confusion.

- Worldly prophets who start covering themselves in tattoos, hanging around some questionable people, and calling anyone who calls them out religious.

It is during this phase that everything the prophet has not been delivered from will make its way to the surface and start ministering alongside the prophet. So, you may find a prophet ministering deliverance and hope to God's people, all the while, the demonic spirit in that prophet will be cat-calling for other men in the church who are wrestling with same-sex attraction, or it'll be calling for women in the church who haven't fully been delivered from fornication, adultery, and spiritual prostitution.

During this phase, the prophet has to intentionally and consistently humble himself or herself. The prophet also needs to get plenty of rest, therapy, and deliverance during this stage. Prophets, like other leaders, need more deliverance than laymen, but when a prophet enters stage five of their gifting, they will especially need deliverance because they'll repeatedly come in contact with co-laborers who are jealous of them and people who will try to use them to platform themselves and their ministries. They will also deal quite a bit with betrayal, fight against religious systems and people, and they'll be on hell's hit list. Howbeit, the prophet can overcome the temptations and tests of this stage by:

1. Remaining accountable to their wise counselors.
2. Being all the more consistent with their Bible studies.
3. Praying often and interceding for others.
4. Fasting often.
5. Getting therapy.
6. Intentionally, aggressively, violently, and repeatedly forgiving the people who hurt, abandon, persecute, betray, and take advantage of them.
7. Having a made-up mind that they won't quit regardless of what it'll cost them.
8. Giving God His praise, even in the faces of His enemies; yes, even those enemies who identify as Christians, but are truly religious narcissists who

take pride in flattering or, better yet, love-bombing God's prophets until they become prideful and unhinged.

9. Refusing to latch onto the breasts of Jezebel when she offers them relief from the very systems she's created. This means that all money ain't good money, and every opportunity extended to you isn't from God.

10. By becoming more intentional with what he or she consumes. Mature prophets know that they can't eat from everybody's table.

11. By refusing some gifts that are extended to them, understanding that a gift with strings attached is not a gift. It's bait.

12. By remaining at the feet of Jesus, not just in prayer but in heart posture.

Prophetic Patterns

Once the prophet breaks through these five stages, we will find an uncompromising soul who fears and loves the Lord, is not willing to exploit their gifting for fame and fortune, and is remarkably accurate whenever they prophesy. But a few pages ago, I told you that I'd share a few prophetic patterns that tend to hinder God's prophets. As promised, here is that list:

1. Telling the devil God's plans. This happens a lot when the prophet is immature and is the result of the prophet being overstimulated. Prophets tend to get excited and tell everyone with a set of working ears what the Lord said to them. Consequently, they end up experiencing a lot of unnecessary warfare, delays, and cancellations because they're repeatedly calling and chasing the monitoring spirits assigned to them.

2. Prophetic zoomies; this is when the prophet rushes excitedly towards his or her assignment, thus bypassing God and every checkpoint that God has established for the prophet. What does this mean? Simply put, the prophet becomes more interested in his or her title and assignment than the prophet's relationship with God, thus causing many of them to rush towards platforms and opportunities. Consequently, many of them try to rush past the seasons they'll have to go through, the battles they'll have to fight, and the altars they'll have to confront and destroy, and straight into the pits of idolatry. This is where they find Jezebel, and this is when

we start hearing the wails and screams of prophets crying out, "Narcissist! Narcissist!"

3. Trying to connect their way to fame. God didn't design prophets to be famous; He designed them to make Him famous, but ungodly ambition is the psyche ward that many prophets check themselves into, and they never escape. Don't mistake what I'm saying—God can and does highlight some of His prophets; these are the ones He can trust with fame and fortune, but for others, He hides them from themselves so that they can find Him.

4. Staying connected to people who are jealous or envious of their wise counselors. Demons are sticky; please remember this. Souls are sticky as well. Satan can and often will send demonized people into organizations, group settings, and friendships with the sole intent of soul-tying themselves to immature and ambitious prophets. They'll go out of their way to become best-friends with the prophets of God, and in this, they will steal the prophet's loyalty away from God by making them question the assignments God gave them. Once they've stolen the prophet's loyalty, they will leave the organizations, friendships, or groups that they met the prophets in, and from there, they will pull them out of those settings. I've seen this firsthand on several occasions, and what's crazy is months, if not a year or two later, you'll find those prophets in a backslidden state, living in sin, being used by demons, and in many cases, having renounced the faith to practice witchcraft.

5. Falling in love with Jezebel. Let's face it. Prophets aren't just Jezebel or narcissist magnets, they are oftentimes attracted to Jezebel because Jezebel has mastered their wiring. Prophets can and do get bored in relationships with "regular people." They even get bored with anointed folks who love holiness, but they tend to like people who take them from high to low, cold to hot, joy to torment, and peace to chaos. Why is this, you ask? Because many of them deal with rejection. They are used to being discarded, so they learn to find a false sense of security in the emotional roller coasters that Jezebel repeatedly takes them on. They love the movie scenes when the hero or heroes show up to rescue the

good guys while they are losing their final fights with their enemies. This gives them their drug of choice, wherein they start experiencing "butterflies" in their stomachs, joy, sadness, anxiety, gratitude, fear, relief, anguish, excitement … all in one moment. This concoction of madness helps them to escape what they revere to be their arch-nemesis: boredom. They experience this same emotional whiplash whenever Jezebel takes them for a joy ride to hell, and then shows up to rescue them from the pits she pushed them in.

6. Monitoring the escaped narcissist. Prophets aren't that skilled with breaking soul ties; this is especially true during the infancy stage of their salvation. Because of this, many prophets make the mistake of repeatedly looking back when God has called them to move forward. Consequently, they become salty or, better yet, bitter.

7. Addiction. Prophets tend to have addictive personalities, and the enemy goes out of his way to lock them in one of his many demonic daycare centers when they are young in the faith. He does this by introducing them to sex, drugs, alcohol, pornography, gambling, video games, ungodly churches and leaders, gluttony, crime, gangs, careers that lead them away from God or busy them up, witchcraft, social media, TV shows (series) that are designed to kidnap their attention, etc.

8. Quitting and starting over. I can't tell you how many prophets I've met who live a dizzy life, whereas, they are constantly starting over with someone or something because they tend to get going when the going gets tough or, at minimum, boring. And every time they start over, they move faster and faster in their newfound relationships. This cycle repeats itself until the prophet has whiplash and stiffens his or her neck all the more, thus allowing Leviathan to immobilize the prophet by ruining the prophet's reputation.

9. Burning bridges unprovoked. For whatever reason, many prophets find it difficult to host more than one relationship on the same plane. Let me make it make sense. I have a mentorship program. Whenever a prophet joins the program, they are incredibly excited, loyal, and ready for what they believe is about to happen. But again, prophets are emotional

junkies; they want to be entertained, excited, and stimulated at all times; that is, of course, until they heal and mature. While in the program, the inevitable happens: monotony. They wait for a change, a spark, or a foreign sound, but the silence is maddening. So, they start looking for other opportunities, and it doesn't take them long to find a few. This is great (sometimes), but here's the problem. They often believe that they have to slam the old doors to open new ones, and this is as asinine as it is untrue. For example, if they leave one church because they're bored, they feel like they have to badmouth the church that they left to fully embrace their newfound church homes when the churches that they left were actually good to them, or they'll create a problem at their local assemblies, and then use that problem to justify walking away. This often stems from their childhoods, wherein, some of their mothers, for example, made them feel like they were evil and disloyal for still loving and desiring to be around their estranged fathers. So, to prove their loyalty to their mothers, they would cut their fathers off, or to rid themselves of their mothers' narcissistic burdens, they would connect with their fathers silently and privately, but then loudly and publicly disconnect from their mothers. Over time, they come to believe that they have to sever old ties to create new ones, thus provoking them to burn bridges for no other reason than the fact that they got bored or felt unseen.

10. Loving comfort, not growth. While (some) prophets may have a rabid disdain for monotony, they often do love comfort, familiarity, and tight-knit circles. So, you will find a lot of monotonous behavior with a prophet, but with that behavior, you will also find a hatred for or a fear of new beginnings. For example, if you are close friends with a prophet and you try to invite a new face into your friendship circle with them, you will likely be met with resistance, and if they are immature, you may be met with rejection or retaliation. So, your best bet is to keep the friends you've made outside of your friendship with the prophet separate (unless they say otherwise). All the same, you will find that prophets love to move in prophetic companies; what I mean by this is—they will have their

circle of friends and trusted folks, and that circle is tight-knit, closed, and in many cases, shrinking. Most leaders come to understand that if they want their organizations to grow, they can't always call on the prophet when they raise their hands because prophets tend to like small circles. They are great at drawing crowds, but they will go out of their way to escape them. Furthermore, since they are super-sensitive, they typically fear (loathe even) the thought of new people coming into a four-walled space or a tight space. This is why prophets don't always do well in closed settings; they can't be treated like domestic animals. Sure, they can be house prophets of specific churches and organizations, but they can't peacefully limit themselves to four walls because familiarity stunts their growth and limits their gifting. This is why Jesus said in Mark 6:4, "A prophet is not without honor, but in his own country, and among his own kin, and in his own house." One of the traps of the enemy is to lock a prophet in a church using the strongman of religion, and to make that prophet feel that their gifting and their loyalty belongs to that house unless they are given permission by senior leadership to prophesy elsewhere. You'd be amazed at the number of true prophets who are locked in religious institutions who are still waiting on permission from their leaders to do and say what God instructed them to do and say. And all too often, they are instructed to remain silent when God told them to cry out and spare not.

11. Witchcraft. One of the works of the flesh, according to the Bible, is witchcraft. And because prophets are super-sensitive, they typically toy around with witchcraft in their youth, and if they don't stop, many prophets go on to become practicing witches. Witchcraft often involves, but is not limited to manipulation, seduction, twisting the truth, fornication (this falls under manipulation), practicing dark arts, using the vices of control and intimidation, reactive abuse, etc. And get this—Jezebel is attracted to witchcraft, so many prophets find themselves in the custody of Jezebel, not because they're anointed, but because they were playing in Jezebel's yard and Jezebel liked what she saw.

12. Trusting the wrong people until they feel they can't trust anyone. This

pattern leads many prophets into captivity, where they will happily and repeatedly befriend people, join churches and religious organizations, and jump into romantic relationships with souls that they have yet to pray about and test. These rookie mistakes almost always end with them being soul-tied to a narcissist. This is when they enter another season of trauma, trials, and tribulations. Once they are delivered from those seasons, many prophets continue to chase after Jezebel until they either settle down with that demon or become so fearful of that spirit that they isolate themselves in an attempt to escape Jezebel. They may create a few friendships and relationships here and there, but their fear of Jezebel and all that comes with her often leads them to be super cautious, sometimes to the point of distrust. This can be great and beneficial when they come in contact with the wrong people, but it can also be a hindrance to their assignments when their destiny helpers show up.

The aforementioned list is a short list of patterns I've witnessed with many prophets, and please note:

1. This list isn't for everyone! This is not a "12 signs to tell if you're a prophet" type list. These are just some of the patterns I've noticed.
2. Not all prophets fall into these patterns. Most do, from what I can see, but I haven't seen everything nor have I met everyone. This is just my own observation.
3. This list deals with prophets in varying degrees of maturity, but many of the issues I mentioned are crimes often committed by immature prophets.

What stage are you in? Did you recognize some of your patterns and proclivities in this chapter? How do you break these demonic and flesh-driven patterns?

1. Seek God above all else (see Matthew 6:33).
2. Study the Word of God daily.
3. Don't forsake wise counsel; be accountable in every stage.
4. Fast and pray often.
5. Journaling helps.

6. Therapy is key.
7. Be careful who you partner or associate yourself with.
8. Forgive like your life depends on it because it does.
9. Learn to test the spirits by the Spirit. You do this by examining their fruits, after all, God said that you will know them by their fruits. What fruits? The fruits of the Holy Spirit, of course. Grow and examine the fruits of the Spirit in your life so that you can see clearly and be content enough to examine the fruits in someone else's life. Look to see what's in their gardens, whether it be the works of the flesh or the fruits of the Spirit, and respond accordingly.
10. Break free from Jezebel's control by repeatedly identifying, renouncing, and breaking your idols. Be sure to repent for idolatry, and give God back His rightful seat in every place in your heart.

Works of the Flesh	Fruits of the Spirit
Adultery	Love
Fornication	Joy
Uncleanness	Peace
Lasciviousness	Long-suffering
Idolatry	Gentleness
Witchcraft	Goodness
Hatred	Faith
Variance	Meekness
Emulations	Temperance
Wrath	
Strife	
Sedition	
Heresies	
Envying	
Murders	

Works of the Flesh	Fruits of the Spirit
Drunkenness	
Revelings	

The Beginning

We all know the story. God created Adam. Not long after this, He took one of Adam's ribs and created Eve. He placed the couple in a garden east of Eden, and this garden would come to be referred to as the Garden of Eden. He then told the couple that they could eat from any of the trees in the garden except for the Tree of the Knowledge of Good and Evil. One day, Satan entered the body of a serpent, and he walked into the garden. He went and had a conversation with Eve that would change the trajectory of the human race. Genesis 3:1-7 reads, "Now the serpent was more subtil than any beast of the field which the Lord God had made. And he said unto the woman, Yea, hath God said, Ye shall not eat of every tree of the garden? And the woman said unto the serpent, We may eat of the fruit of the trees of the garden: But of the fruit of the tree which is in the midst of the garden, God hath said, Ye shall not eat of it, neither shall ye touch it, lest ye die. And the serpent said unto the woman, Ye shall not surely die: For God doth know that in the day ye eat thereof, then your eyes shall be opened, and ye shall be as gods, knowing good and evil. And when the woman saw that the tree was good for food, and that it was pleasant to the eyes, and a tree to be desired to make one wise, she took of the fruit thereof, and did eat, and gave also unto her husband with her; and he did eat. And the eyes of them both were opened, and they knew that they were naked; and they sewed fig leaves together, and made themselves aprons." And thus came the fall of man. The couple was evicted from God's presence (the Garden of Eden) and their judgment was detailed in Genesis 3:16-19 reads, "Unto the woman He said, I will greatly multiply thy sorrow and thy conception; in sorrow thou shalt bring forth children; and thy desire shall be to thy husband, and he shall rule over thee. And unto Adam he said, Because thou hast hearkened unto the voice of thy wife, and hast eaten of the tree, of which I commanded thee, saying, Thou shalt not eat of it: cursed is the ground for thy sake; in sorrow shalt thou eat of it all the days of thy life; thorns also and thistles shall it bring forth to thee; and thou shalt eat the herb of the field; In the sweat of thy face shalt thou eat bread, till thou return unto the ground; for out of it wast thou taken: for dust thou art, and unto dust shalt thou return." Therein, the judgment is:

1. Pain and discomfort during pregnancy.
2. Labor pangs for the woman during delivery.
3. The woman's desire would be to her husband. Notice here that the husband's desire would not be for his wife; at least, not as a judgment. God would eventually tell wives how to unlock their husband's desire in Ephesian's 5:22-23, which states, "Wives, submit yourselves unto your own husbands, as unto the Lord. For the husband is the head of the wife, even as Christ is the head of the church: and he is the savior of the body. Therefore as the church is subject unto Christ, so let the wives be to their own husbands in everything." All the same, to unlock the respect of his wife, the husband, according to Ephesian 5:25, had to love his wife like Christ loves the church.
4. The woman would be ruled by her husband. In other words, the husband, an imperfect creature, would be given the charge to lead his household, and the wife had to respect him enough to follow his lead.
5. The man, on the other hand, would no longer be given any Heavenly handouts. Instead, he would be required to work both hard and diligently to provide for his family.
6. While working the ground (the makeup of the flesh), man would see thorns and thistles; this wasn't just a natural judgment, it was a spiritual one. Thorns and thistles represent the issues of the flesh; thorns represent demons, while thistles represent the works of the flesh. Apostle Paul said in 2 Corinthians 12:7, "And lest I should be exalted above measure through the abundance of the revelations, there was given to me a thorn in the flesh, the messenger of Satan to buffet me, lest I should be exalted above measure." Therefore, to pull out his potential, a man would have to repeatedly crucify his flesh.
7. And the final judgment was death.

After Adam and Eve were evicted from the garden, Eve went on to conceive Cain, and then, Abel. Cain was the very first human narcissist to be born. Adam and Eve displayed signs of narcissism after they'd sinned. How so? Neither of them had taken accountability for their actions. Instead, Adam blamed Eve for his sin, Eve blamed the devil, and the devil had no one to blame. One thing you'll come to learn about God while reading this book is, He loves a repentant heart, but pride provokes His judgment. We would see this pattern repeated by Cain. Genesis 4:2-16 details the story of Cain and his brother, Abel. It reads, "And she again bare his brother Abel. And Abel was a keeper of sheep, but Cain was a tiller of the ground. And in process of time it came to pass, that Cain brought of the fruit of the ground an offering unto the Lord. And Abel, he also brought of the firstlings of his flock and of the fat thereof. And the Lord had respect unto Abel and to his offering: But unto Cain and to his offering he had not respect. And Cain was very wroth, and his countenance fell. And the Lord said unto Cain, Why art thou wroth? And why is thy countenance fallen? If thou doest well, shalt thou not be accepted? And if thou doest not well, sin lieth at the door. And unto thee shall be his desire, and thou shalt rule over him. And Cain talked with Abel his brother: and it came to pass, when they were in the field, that Cain rose up against Abel his brother, and slew him. And the Lord said unto Cain, Where is Abel thy brother? And he said, I know not: Am I my brother's keeper? And he said, What hast thou done? The voice of thy brother's blood crieth unto me from the ground. And now art thou cursed from the earth, which hath opened her mouth to receive thy brother's blood from thy hand; when thou tillest the ground, it shall not henceforth yield unto thee her strength; a fugitive and a vagabond shalt thou be in the earth. And Cain said unto the Lord, My punishment is greater than I can bear. Behold, thou hast driven me out this day from the face of the earth; and from thy face shall I be hid; and I shall be a fugitive and a vagabond in the earth; and it shall come to pass, that every one that findeth me shall slay me. And the Lord said unto him, Therefore whosoever slayeth Cain, vengeance shall be taken on him seven-fold. And the Lord set a mark upon Cain, lest any finding him should kill him. And Cain went out from the presence of the Lord, and dwelt in the land of Nod, on the east of Eden." Notice here that Cain did not apologize for his behavior, nor had he repented or shown pity for his brother. Instead, his response was incredibly narcissistic. He was more concerned about how people would view him and what they would do to him than he was about his brother's untimely death or how his brother's death would affect his parents. This is to say that while Adam and Eve had become relatively narcissistic, Cain, on the other hand, was a full-blown narcissist. Nevertheless, even in the midst of it all, God still extended mercy to Cain.

What had been Cain's initial crime? Why had God rejected his offering? Simply put, Abel gave God the first-fruits of his increase, whereas, Cain had given the Lord something that was accursed. Remember, the ground had been cursed, and while Cain was a farmer, there was an acceptable offering to give to the Lord. What was it? Matthew 5:23-24 says, "Therefore if thou bring thy gift to the altar, and there rememberest that thy brother hath ought against thee; leave there thy gift before the altar, and go thy way; first be reconciled to thy brother, and then come and offer thy gift." After God rejected Cain's offering, Cain became indignant towards his brother, but believe it or not, this issue wasn't just sibling rivalry. The issue was how Cain saw God and how he saw himself; this would ultimately lead to how he saw his brother. Let me explain. Cain's offering was rejected because it revealed his disdain towards or dishonor of the Most High God. One thing you'll come to know about narcissists is this—regardless of whether they claim to be Christians or not, they all have a deep-seated hatred towards God, and this shows up in their disdain for God's children, especially prophets and prophetic people. You see, it takes a measure of prophetic sensitivity to understand what offerings are good to God versus the unacceptable ones. A good offering is one given in reverence and in love; an unacceptable offering is one given in fear, religion (repetition) or transactionalism (a desire to get something in return). So, before Cain approached the Lord with his offering, he needed to be reconciled not just with God, but with his prophetic brother, Abel. Instead, he chose to slaughter his brother in cold blood. This is to say that a lot of our issues with our brothers and sisters in Christ are underlying issues that we have with God, and by reconciling ourselves to them, we will better understand our need to be reconciled with God. This is also to say that Cain was undoubtedly the first full-fledged human narcissist to ever walk the Earth. This is also to say that Cain was bound by the Jezebel spirit. This was the first time we got to witness this particular devil in operation. Throughout the rest of this book, we will witness the many movements of Jezebel against the will and the Word of God. Understand this—you are *a* word of God, just as Jesus is *the* Word of God. This means that, while your body was formed, your spirit was created. In other words, God spoke you into existence. To understand this, consider Genesis 1:26-27, which reads, "And God said, Let us make man in our image, after our likeness: and let them have dominion over the fish of the sea, and over the fowl of the air, and over the cattle, and over all the earth, and over every creeping thing that creepeth upon the earth. So God created man in his own image, in the image of God created he him; male and female created he them." In this, we witness God creating the spirit of what would later be referred to as mankind. In Genesis 2, we will witness Him transferring this spirit into the body of a man (Adam). Genesis 2:7 reads, "And the Lord God formed man of the dust of the ground, and breathed into his nostrils the breath of life; and man became a living soul." Please note that the Greek word for breath is *pneuma*, which means *breath* or *spirit*. God inhaled what He'd created and exhaled man's spirit into one body, but remember, He'd created them male and female. This means that what we now identify as the X chromosome and what we refer to as the Y chromosome were both placed in the male, thus giving men the ability to produce both boys and girls. God would go on to pull a rib from Adam, and use that rib to create Eve (XX chromosome). This would ensure that the man would need a woman to reproduce, and women would need men to reproduce.

Lucifer: The Very First Narcissist

The name "Lucifer" itself comes from the Latin word "lucifer," which means "light-bringer" or "morning star." In ancient times, the morning star, Venus, was seen as a symbol of hope and new beginnings, but over time, the name became associated with the fallen angel who'd rebelled against God and was cast out of Heaven.

Ezekiel 28:11-19 reads, "Moreover the word of the Lord came unto me, saying, Son of man, take up a lamentation upon the king of Tyrus, and say unto him,

Thus saith the Lord God; Thou sealest up the sum, full of wisdom, and perfect in beauty. Thou hast been in Eden the garden of God; every precious stone was thy covering, the sardius, topaz, and the diamond, the beryl, the onyx, and the jasper, the sapphire, the emerald, and the carbuncle, and gold: the workmanship of thy tabrets and of thy pipes was prepared in thee in the day that thou wast created. Thou art the anointed cherub that covereth; and I have set thee so: thou wast upon the holy mountain of God; thou hast walked up and down in the midst of the stones of fire. Thou wast perfect in thy ways from the day that thou wast created, till iniquity was found in thee. By the multitude of thy merchandise they have filled the midst of thee with violence, and thou hast sinned: therefore I will cast thee as profane out of the mountain of God: and I will destroy thee, O covering cherub, from the midst of the stones of fire. Thine heart was lifted up because of thy beauty, thou hast corrupted thy wisdom by reason of thy brightness: I will cast thee to the ground, I will lay thee before kings, that they may behold thee. Thou hast defiled thy sanctuaries by the multitude of thine iniquities, by the iniquity of thy traffick; therefore will I bring forth a fire from the midst of thee, it shall devour thee, and I will bring thee to ashes upon the earth in the sight of all them that behold thee. All they that know thee among the people shall be astonished at thee: thou shalt be a terror, and never shalt thou be any more." What is significant about this particular verse of scripture is the fact that God went from speaking to the King of Tyre to speaking to the spirit behind the matter. He began to address Lucifer. Now, if you don't know, Lucifer was once one of God's angels. The Bible tells us that his body was made of jewels (sardius, topaz, diamonds, beryl, onyx, jasper, sapphire, emeralds, carbuncles, gold) and instruments (tabrets; also known as tambourines, and of pipes; these are fluted instruments or instruments that require breath). Additionally, Lucifer was a covering cherub, which meant that he was a high-ranking angel of God. Before we go any further, let's get an understanding of the word rank.

Everything God creates, He places in order. As a matter of fact, order is a Godly concept, whereas, disorder is ungodly. In other words, every system is hierarchical. God gave Lucifer a high place; this meant that he had:

1. More power than the angels that didn't rank as high as him.

2. More access to God.
3. More responsibility.
4. A greater degree of accountability.
5. More information.

Think of the military. Every officer has access to a measure of information. Officers who rank high have access to more sensitive or intimate information than petty officers. With this access and information comes more trust and more responsibility which, in turn, could lead to more accountability. This is to say that Lucifer knew God more than many of God's angels. He had more intimate access to God and more insight into the mysteries of God. His body was covered in jewels. The purpose of these jewels was to absorb and reflect the light of God to God's angels. This meant that Lucifer had to go into the presence of God in the same manner that Moses ascended Mt. Sinai to meet with God. Exodus 34:29-35 reads, "And it came to pass, when Moses came down from Mount Sinai with the two tables of testimony in Moses' hand, when he came down from the mount, that Moses wist not that the skin of his face shone while he talked with him. And when Aaron and all the children of Israel saw Moses, behold, the skin of his face shone; and they were afraid to come nigh him. And Moses called unto them; and Aaron and all the rulers of the congregation returned unto him: and Moses talked with them. And afterward all the children of Israel came nigh: and he gave them in commandment all that the LORD had spoken with him in Mount Sinai. And till Moses had done speaking with them, he put a veil on his face. But when Moses went in before the LORD to speak with him, he took the veil off, until he came out. And he came out, and spake unto the children of Israel that which he was commanded. And the children of Israel saw the face of Moses, that the skin of Moses' face shone: and Moses put the veil upon his face again, until he went in to speak with him." Notice that anytime Moses left the presence of God, he returned with something (glory and instructions). The same was true for Lucifer. He would go into the presence of God, and he'd return to the angels filled with light; he would be wrapped in the glory of God. This would cause the angels to worship the Most High all the more. Their worship would penetrate Lucifer's body, causing the tabrets and timbrels to play, and this would continue until the presence of God would swell and radiate through him. Lucifer's body also served as an instrument through which God would speak. The angels would absorb the light that radiated from Lucifer's body, and this cycle would repeat itself. Nevertheless, Lucifer began to covet the glory of God for himself. He saw the angels bowing before him, and at some point, he did not give God the glory that belonged to Him. Instead, he decided to keep it for himself. This is how pride entered his heart. Eventually, Lucifer's narcissism overtook him. He decided to create a language that would allow him to speak to the angels of God; this language is what we call lies. A lie is nothing but a rearrangement of words or, in many cases, the adding on or removal of words. For example, God said that He will never leave us. Satan takes this statement and removes the word "never." This is what formulates a lie. And this is how spells are created. They are nothing but the rearrangement or perverting of words. And remember, Lucifer ranked pretty high in the Kingdom, so when he went before God's angels to teach them his new language, he'd told them the very same lie he'd told Eve. He caused them to believe that God was not being completely honest with them. He also introduced them to the concept of independent spirituality; he did this by convincing them that they could become their own gods, knowing all things. You see, the crime that Satan committed in the Garden of Eden wasn't new; it was the same crime he'd committed in Heaven. And once he had a third of God's angels on board with his wicked plan, he finally felt confident enough to make his move. Revelation 12:7-9 states, "And there was war in heaven: Michael and his angels fought against the dragon; and the dragon fought and his angels, and prevailed not; neither was their place found any more in heaven. And the great dragon was cast out, that old serpent, called the Devil, and Satan, which deceiveth the whole world: he was cast out into the earth, and his angels were cast out with him." Did Satan repent? No. Instead, he used the knowledge he'd acquired while serving as one of God's angels to rebel against God's plans. Revelation 12:17 reads, "And the dragon was wroth with the woman, and went to make war with the remnant of her seed, which keep the commandments of God, and have the testimony of Jesus Christ."

What you'll come to know about rank is this:

1. The higher God promotes you, the lower you'll have to go; this means that you have to intentionally and consistently humble yourself.
2. The more man praises you, the more you have to glorify God.
3. The more man fears you, the more you have to increase your love and reverence of God.

If you are not consistent with this, pride will be waiting at the threshold of your door. This is what happens to so many well-meaning men and women of the cloth. They were bombarded with praise until it consumed them with vanity. This is especially true in the Americas, where people actually get offended if you give God the glory they just gave you. For example:

> **Karen:** Pastor Jenkins, you just preached a fiery message! Oh my goodness! I have never heard anyone preach so eloquently! You truly are anointed!
>
> **Pastor Jenkins:** Thank you so much, but all the glory goes to God. I always pray before I preach, and He has never let me down.
>
> **Karen:** (*Grows agitated and sighs*). Of course, all the glory goes to God, pastor, but there's nothing wrong with me honoring you for being an obedient vessel. I mean, you don't have to be so deep. God doesn't mind me bestowing honor upon one of His servants.
>
> **Pastor Jenkins:** You're right. Thank you for the compliment.
>
> **Karen:** (*Smiles sheepishly*). You're welcome. Keep tearing down the kingdom of darkness, man of God! There is truly no pastor like you on Earth!
>
> **Pastor Jenkins:** Yes ma'am. Thank you. To God be the glory.
>
> **Karen:** (*Sighs, walks away offended, and then looks at her husband*). Some people are so heavenly minded that they are no earthly good!

Believe it or not, this particular dialogue is incredibly common in North America. In this, Pastor Jenkins will eventually get tired of offending the people who are dead-set on praising him, and he'll begin to absorb the praise. In the beginning, he will silently return the praise to God, but after some time, he'll start forgetting to give God what belongs to Him. Before long, you'll find him praising himself and competing with other leaders. This is how pride spreads.

Of course, God referred to Lucifer as Satan. The word "Satan" isn't necessarily a name; it literally means "adversary." To understand the word *adversary*, think of the word *adverse*. According to Oxford Languages, the word *adverse* is defined as "preventing success or development; harmful; unfavorable." Merriam Webster defines adverse as "acting against or in a contrary direction." Think of it this way. God is Spirit. Again, the Greek word for spirit is pneuma, which means breath or wind. Let's say that God's will moves to the right; this would mean that anything adverse to God's will would move towards the left. This is what we refer to as opposition. Opposition is the opposing of a position. All the same, the name "Lucifer" means "shining one" or "light-bearer," but when he went in the opposite direction, he would become the opposite of what he was initially created to be. In this, he became the Prince of the Power of Darkness. He would go on to encourage anything or anyone who would listen to him to move independently of God, thus landing them under his jurisdiction.

Adam and Eve

The story of Adam and Eve is one of the most well-known and fascinating tales in history. According to the Bible, Adam and Eve were the first humans to be created by God. They lived in the Garden of Eden or, better yet, the garden east of Eden, which was a beautiful paradise filled with everything they could ever need, including a multitude of trees, fruits, and animals. All the same, the love of God engulfed and filled them; they had no want or need. As the story goes, God gave Adam and Eve one simple rule: they were not to eat from the Tree of Knowledge of Good and Evil. However, they were tempted by a serpent to defy this commandment and eat the forbidden fruit. As soon as they ate the fruit, they became filled with knowledge and became aware of their nakedness. This means they became independent of God. Look at the word independent. It means in-dependent or inwardly dependent. This can also be translated as prideful, self-reliant, self-absorbed, self-serving, self-seeking, and self-critical. Consequently, they became individuals. The word individual means to inwardly divide, and it doesn't just mean for a person to be double-minded; it also means to be divided from within and to divide from within. A good example is—a husband is one with his wife, and a wife is one with her husband, however, it is possible and common for one of the spouses in a marriage to suddenly want more independence from the other spouse or the spouse may decide that he or she wants to separate some of their marital assets such as money, certain items in the home, responsibilities, and the list goes on. In such a case, that particular spouse is dividing the house from within, and according to the scriptures, a house divided *cannot* stand. Adam and Eve were divided, albeit briefly, when Eve took a bite of the forbidden fruit. They were essentially divorced in that moment, but Adam reconciled with his wife in sin, since they were no longer one in righteousness.

God, being just, punished Adam and Eve for their disobedience. He expelled them from the Garden of Eden and cursed them with a life of hardship and toil. Eve was also punished with pain during childbirth, and Adam was condemned to work for his food. Let's look at this story in the scriptures. Below is Genesis 3:1-22 (ESV).

> "Now the serpent was more crafty than any other beast of the field that the LORD God had made. He said to the woman, 'Did God actually say, 'You shall not eat of any tree in the garden'?' And the woman said to the serpent, 'We may eat of the fruit of the trees in the garden, but God said, 'You shall not eat of the fruit of the tree that is in the midst of the garden, neither shall you touch it, lest you die.' But the serpent said to the woman, 'You will not surely die. For God knows that when you eat of it your eyes will be opened, and you will be like God, knowing good and evil.' So when the woman saw that the tree was good for food, and that it was a delight to the eyes, and that the tree was to be desired to make one wise, she took of its fruit and ate, and she also gave some to her husband who was with her, and he ate. Then the eyes of both were opened, and they knew that they were naked. And they sewed fig leaves together and made themselves loincloths. And they heard the sound of the LORD God walking in the garden in the cool of the day, and the man

and his wife hid themselves from the presence of the LORD God among the trees of the garden. But the LORD God called to the man and said to him, 'Where are you?' And he said, 'I heard the sound of you in the garden, and I was afraid, because I was naked, and I hid myself.' He said, 'Who told you that you were naked? Have you eaten of the tree of which I commanded you not to eat?' The man said, 'The woman whom you gave to be with me, she gave me fruit of the tree, and I ate.' Then the LORD God said to the woman, 'What is this that you have done?' The woman said, 'The serpent deceived me, and I ate.' The LORD God said to the serpent, 'Because you have done this, cursed are you above all livestock and above all beasts of the field; on your belly you shall go, and dust you shall eat all the days of your life. I will put enmity between you and the woman, and between your offspring and her offspring; he shall bruise your head, and you shall bruise his heel.' To the woman he said, 'I will surely multiply your pain in childbearing; in pain you shall bring forth children. Your desire shall be contrary to your husband, but he shall rule over you.' And to Adam he said, 'Because you have listened to the voice of your wife and have eaten of the tree of which I commanded you, 'You shall not eat of it,' cursed is the ground because of you; in pain you shall eat of it all the days of your life; thorns and thistles it shall bring forth for you; and you shall eat the plants of the field. By the sweat of your face you shall eat bread, till you return to the ground, for out of it you were taken; for you are dust, and to dust you shall return.' The man called his wife's name Eve, because she was the mother of all living. And the LORD God made for Adam and for his wife garments of skins and clothed them. Then the LORD God said, 'Behold, the man has become like one of us in knowing good and evil. Now, lest he reach out his hand and take also of the tree of life and eat, and live forever—' therefore the LORD God sent him out from the garden of Eden to work the ground from which he was taken. He drove out the man, and at the east of the Garden of Eden he placed the cherubim and a flaming sword that turned every way to guard the way to the tree of life."

Even though this story is packed with revelation, I want to highlight a few facts that stand out.

1. Satan destabilized Eve by convincing her that the God who cannot tell a lie had breached His own character and lied to her. This was an attack against God's name and His character.

2. After creating a problem, Satan then offered Eve an incredible solution. She could become like God by eating from the forbidden fruit or, better yet, she'd become her own god. After all, who would want to be affiliated with a God who couldn't be trusted? Of course, we know that YAHWEH is trustworthy and it is impossible for Him to lie, howbeit, Satan managed to convince Eve otherwise. Note: Eve's desire to be "like God" was truly her desire to be in control, which is one of the most prominent and defining symptoms of the Jezebel spirit.

3. After Eve had fallen into sin, she then tempted her husband into sin. This is the nature of sinful and rebellious people altogether. Whatever sins they partake in, they will offer to others.

4. After the couple bit into the forbidden fruit, their eyes were opened, and they immediately experienced, for the first time in their lives: guilt, shame, and condemnation. This is because they were now filled with iniquity.

5. After being confronted by God, Adam shifted the blame to God, and then to his wife. He said, "This woman that YOU gave me," before posting her sin up for the Lord to see. Eve then blamed the devil. Satan, on the other hand, did not have anyone to blame. In short, no one took accountability!

6. God confronted Adam first because he was the one who God had spoken face-to-face with.

7. The Lord then covered the couple with the skin of an animal (likely a lamb) before sending them out of the garden.

Despite the tragic story, there are many lessons to be learned from the tale of Adam and Eve. Their story emphasizes the importance of obeying God's commandments and avoiding temptation. It also highlights the consequences of disobedience, which can lead to a life of hardship and suffering. However, there are also many interpretations and analyses of this story. Some critics argue that the story of Adam and Eve is a metaphor for the fall of humanity and the loss of innocence. Others suggest that it is a moral tale meant to demonstrate the dangers of impulsive decision-making. Regardless of the many interpretations out there, the story of Adam and Eve has played a significant role in shaping human culture and beliefs. Many religions include it as a fundamental part of their teachings, and it has inspired countless works of art and literature. This is because the tale of Adam and Eve remains a powerful allegory that continues to intrigue and inspire people around the world. It serves as a reminder of the importance of obedience, the consequences of our actions, and the power of temptation. Whether it is interpreted literally or metaphorically, it remains a thought-provoking story that has managed to stand the test of time.

Another lesson to take away from the couple's story is this—what Adam and Eve did when they bit into the forbidden fruit is what we regard today as a witchcraft ritual. How was this a ritual? Because they didn't consume the food for pleasure, they consumed it for power. They consumed the forbidden fruit so that they could become like God or, better yet, independent of God. Imagine them closing their eyes as they bit into the fruit, and then opening them hoping to see the world from God's point of view. Instead, they saw their own naked bodies from a fallen perspective. And it was in this moment that they realized that they'd been duped. It was also in this moment that fear entered their souls. This is similar to a married woman being seduced by a married man who is not her husband. That man promises to leave his wife for his married mistress. He also promises that he will marry her after he divorces his wife, and his seemingly never-ending wealth would be at his new bride's disposal. Elated and filled with ambition, the wife rushes home, tells her husband that she wants a divorce, moves out of the house, leaving her three children behind. She then moves into a hotel room that her lover has promised to pay for. "Once I file for divorce and get my attorney to divide our assets, I'll let you move into my beachfront property in Maine, and I'll move in with you once the divorce is finalized," Mr. Hawkins says to his mistress. Elaine, the mistress, sits on the bed at the hotel, excitedly thinking about what the next chapter of her life is going to look like. And true to his word, Mr.

Hawkins (also known as Hunter) pays for the hotel room every week. He does this for three months straight, and in that time, Elaine's husband has filed for divorce, demanded full-custody of the children (to which, Elaine happily obliged), and has taken full possession of their property. Again, Elaine doesn't put up much of a fight because she's unequivocally convinced that she's about to become a wealthy woman. "How crazy would I be to waste resources and time fighting over a three-hundred thousand dollar home?" she once joked with her niece. After all the papers were signed and filed with the courts, Hunter began to become more and more distant. He downgraded Elaine to a cheaper hotel room, before sending her to a low-end hotel altogether. Feeling the soul-tie straining and breaking, Elaine reached out to her married beau time and time again to get an explanation as to why he'd had a sudden change of heart. However, Hunter doesn't answer her calls as frequently as he once did, and he rarely returns her calls. Realizing that she's being duped and dumped, Elaine starts to reminisce about what she once had with her soon-to-be ex-husband, but he's already divorced the idea of them being together. "I want my family back," Elaine said to Timothy, her husband, as she cried hysterically into the phone's receiver. "I completely understand, Elaine," Timothy said gently, "But I don't want you back. I don't want another episode of 'us.' The kids and I are just fine without you. Please heal." All of a sudden, fear and panic enters Elaine's soul. Where will she live?! Who's going to take care of her?! What about her children?! This is similar to, but not as intense as the fear, shame, and regret that Adam and Eve felt when they realized that they'd divorced the one and true living God for a lying devil.

The point is—narcissism entered into mankind the moment Eve pondered on the lies the devil told her. In that moment, she became self-absorbed, self-seeking, self-serving, and just plain selfish. In other words, even though Adam and Eve were created in the image of God, they were now operating under a different spirit. This spirit would ultimately show up in their son, Cain.

A Narcissist Named Cain

According to the Bible, Cain and Abel were the sons of Adam and Eve. The story tells us that Abel was a shepherd while Cain was a farmer. The two were instructed to bring offerings to God, and while Abel brought the firstborn of his flock, Cain brought some of the fruits of the soil. Keep in mind that after the fall of mankind, God cursed the soil. God was pleased with Abel's offering, but not with Cain's. This caused Cain to become bitter and jealous, and in his anger, he lured Abel out to a field where he proceeded to take his life. When God asked Cain where Abel was, he replied: "Am I my brother's keeper?" This answer didn't impress God, and as a punishment, Cain was condemned to a life of wandering. Cain's answer showed:

1. His true disdain for God.
2. His inability to take accountability for his actions.
3. His incredibly thick pride.
4. His narcissistic view on life.
5. His inability to love anyone other than himself.

Let's take a look at their story. Genesis 4:1-16 reads:

"And Adam knew Eve his wife; and she conceived, and bare Cain, and said, I have gotten a man from the LORD. And she again bare his brother Abel. And Abel was a keeper of sheep, but Cain was a tiller of the ground. And in process of time it came to pass, that Cain brought of the fruit of the ground an offering unto the LORD.

And Abel, he also brought of the firstlings of his flock and of the fat thereof. And the LORD had respect unto Abel and to his offering: But unto Cain and to his offering he had not respect. And Cain was very wroth, and his countenance fell. And the LORD said unto Cain, Why art thou wroth? And why is thy countenance fallen? If thou doest well, shalt thou not be accepted? And if thou doest not well, sin lieth at the door. And unto thee shall be his desire, and thou shalt rule over him. And Cain talked with Abel his brother: and it came to pass, when they were in the field, that Cain rose up against Abel his brother, and slew him. And the LORD said unto Cain, Where is Abel thy brother? And he said, I know not: Am I my brother's keeper? And he said, What hast thou done? The voice of thy brother's blood crieth unto me from the ground. And now art thou cursed from the earth, which hath opened her mouth to receive thy brother's blood from thy hand; when thou tillest the ground, it shall not henceforth yield unto thee her strength; a fugitive and a vagabond shalt thou be in the earth. And Cain said unto the LORD, My punishment is greater than I can bear. Behold, thou hast driven me out this day from the face of the earth; and from thy face shall I be hid; and I shall be a fugitive and a vagabond in the earth; and it shall come to pass, that every one that findeth me shall slay me. And the LORD said unto him, Therefore whosoever slayeth Cain, vengeance shall be taken on him seven-fold. And the LORD set a mark upon Cain, lest any finding him should kill him. And Cain went out from the presence of the LORD, and dwelt in the land of Nod, on the east of Eden."

As you can see from the aforementioned story, Cain and Abel are famously known in the Bible for their tragic story of sibling rivalry and murder. Their story is a powerful one that has been told and interpreted in different ways throughout history. In this chapter, we will discuss the biblical account of Cain and Abel, analyze their mindset, and examine the lessons that can be learned from their story, but before we go any further, let's take a few nuggets from the aforementioned scriptures.

1. Cain was the firstborn son of Adam and Eve, while Abel was their second born son. Why is this important? When a father died, the firstborn son would inherit all that belonged to his father. Sure enough, this particular tradition came about after Cain and Abel were born, but the principle had always been present. This is to say that Cain likely had favor with his natural father, Adam, whereas Abel had favor with God. Another way of saying this is—it is possible that Cain was the golden child of his family. This is significant because the golden child in the toxic family dynamic typically goes into a narcissistic rage if any of his or her siblings get more attention than he or she gets.

2. Abel gave God the firstlings or, better yet, the first-fruits of his animals, whereas, Cain gave God whatever he saw fit to give Him. In other words, there was no love, honor, reverence, or gratitude in his offering.
3. Cain's response to his brother being favored caused what was in his heart to surface. Jealousy didn't provoke Cain to kill his brother, the spirit of murder provoked Cain to jealousy! Jealousy was just the instigator.
4. After being confronted by God, Cain showed no remorse, nor did he take accountability for his wrongdoings.
5. When God handed Cain his punishment, he only expressed concern for himself. He worried about what people would do to him whenever they came across him.

This is to say that Cain was the classic narcissist. He was riddled with jealousy, accountability was not even in his vocabulary, and he only showed concern for himself whenever he was addressed. One thing you'll come to see is that whenever you confront a narcissist and you hold that person accountable for his or her wrongdoings, the narcissist will typically explode into a narcissistic rage. What is a narcissistic rage? The following information was taken from Very Well Mind:

> "Narcissistic rage is a term that was first coined by author Heinz Kohut in 1972 to refer to the tendency for people with narcissistic personality disorder (NPD) to fly into a rage with what might seem like the slightest provocation or no obvious provocation at all.
> People with NPD require that others give them consistent admiration and positive feedback. When this doesn't happen, it can elicit underlying feelings of shame that trigger an instant angry response and cause them to lash out without considering how it impacts the recipient.
> It is the narcissist's thin skin and sensitivity that leads to this rage because of a deep-seated fear of being 'found out' for not being the person they portray themselves to be" (Source: VeryWellMind.com/What is Narcissistic Rage/Arlin Cuncic, MA).

What are the signs and symptoms that someone you know is having an episode of narcissistic rage?

Incredible Anger	Sarcasm
Screaming/Raising Voice	Physical Assault/Abuse
Passive Aggressive Behaviors	Twisting Words/Confusion
Abuse	Damaging Property
Bitterness/Resentment	Narcissistic Discard

Narcissistic rage is oftentimes provoked by what the world of psychology refers to as a narcissistic wound, also known as narcissistic injury. What is narcissistic injury? The following information was taken from Choosing Therapy's website.

"Narcissistic injury–sometimes known as a narcissistic wound, wounded ego, or ego deflation–happens when those with **narcissistic personality disorder** (NPD) face criticism, betrayal, or perceived abandonment. Narcissists often respond to perceived slights with hostility disproportionate to the event.

Narcissists typically don't feel remorse or empathy for others, so they may readily resort to anger or rage when confronted. Moreover, narcissists possess grandiose self-images and 'higher than thou' attitudes connected to beliefs of superiority and greatness. However, when their behavior is questioned, the deep-rooted insecurities hidden behind this facade are called to attention. Emotional wounds of this caliber are challenging for narcissists to move past, as being vulnerable or held accountable is unbearable. Therefore, they will seek revenge against the inflictor when their self-esteemed is threatened or injured" (Source: ChoosingTherapy.com/Narcissistic Injury: Definition, Signs, & Examples/Kaytee Gillis, LCSW-BACS

This is what happened to Cain. His fragile ego was wounded, and he therefore went into a narcissistic rage where he murdered his brother, Abel. Was this a crime of passion? No, because Cain felt no remorse for his crime. It was more of a crime of opportunity. He was the firstborn son. In his mind, he was entitled to God's favor, but when God applauded Abel for his offering instead, Cain decided, without a conscience, to take his brother's life.

In short, Cain was definitely a bound man whose outlook on life revealed an incredibly wicked and self-serving heart. One of the many life lessons that we can all extract from their story is this—sometimes, the most dangerous person in our lives is someone we grew up with or someone we trust enough to bring close to us. This includes our parents, siblings, extended family, close friends, etc. All the same, Cain and Abel's story provides an excellent example of how even close siblings can fall out and take drastic measures if they allow jealousy and envy to overcome them. Cain's jealousy towards Abel was driven by his desire to be similarly favored by God. It also shone a light on the importance of bringing sincerity and goodwill when offering to God. It's easy to offer things and compliments to God without genuinely meaning it or doing it out of a sense of obligation. In other words, Cain's offering was the equivalent of works, while Abel's offering revealed his love and pursuit of God. It showed that he was truly in tune with the Spirit of God and not operating out of a sense of pride, arrogance, and transactionalism. Abel wasn't in it for what he could get out of God. He truly loved the Lord and took pleasure in pleasing Him, whereas Cain's service to God was nothing but a religious routine.

In addition to the lesson about the dangers of jealousy and the significance of sincerity, Cain and Abel's story brings to light the importance of accepting responsibility and accountability. Cain's "Am I my brother's keeper?" statement was an attempt to evade responsibility for what he had done. Unfortunately, Cain's action could not be reversed, and so he would have to live with the consequences of his actions forever.

The story of Cain and Abel is not just a religious account but also one of humanity's earliest literary works that reflect timeless elements of the fallen nature of humans. The brothers were symbols of contrasting themes in human psycology. Abel represents the pure and innocent, while Cain is the embodiment of human wickedness and pettiness. Their story showcases how people are capable of both good and evil. This is to say that Cain and Abel's story has been interpreted and analyzed throughout human history and continues to be a source of inspiration for many people today. Their tale warns of the dangers of jealousy, promotes the need for sincerity, and underscores the importance of accepting accountability. Cain and Abel teach us that success carries with it a certain amount of responsibility, and that we need to be careful of negative emotions that can lead us astray. Cain and Abel's powerful story reminds us to be vigilant, sincere, and accountable in our actions.

Your Very First Narcissist

At some point in your life, you came in contact with your very first narcissist or narcissistic person. This person may have been a classmate, a cousin, a coworker, an ex; then again, it may have been a parent. The truth of the matter is—many prophets and prophetic individuals were raised by Jezebel. They weren't just raised by Jezebel, but they were bullied in their own homes by the very parent or parents who were supposed to love, nurture, and shield them. This is why many prophets are called by God, but only a small percentage are chosen to do the work of a prophet. This is to say that many don't survive Jezebel's narcissism, and by survive, I'm not talking about a natural death. I'm talking about a spiritual death. Consider what happened to Jezebel, the woman who was on the surface of this Earth reigning as queen over North Israel. What happened to the prophets of God during her reign?

1. Many turned away from God and became prophets of Baal.
2. One hundred prophets were hidden in caves by Obadiah.
3. The ones who did not and would not bow their knees to Baal were slaughtered by Jezebel's henchmen.

I think that we can safely assume that many prophets turned to other destructive behaviors, and some of them may have even taken their lives in that era. Can you imagine the terror that struck the land during that time? Can you imagine being forced to choose between YAHWEH and another deity, and being told that your decision would be a life and death decision? Can you imagine witnessing the mass slaughtering of other prophets, and then hearing your name called by the council, knowing that you were about to make one of the most important decisions of your life? Beautifully enough, some prophets held true to their faith in God, while others bent their knees and declared Baal as their god. Did you know that the prophets of today will face the same decision? They will choose between YAHWEH and Baal, but not in the same context as their primitive brethren. No, every time you're being seduced, tempted, manipulated, and charmed by the world, you are in the process of being bewitched by Baal. Who was Baal? Check out the following article from Bible Study Tools:

"Baal was, to some extent, a rather generic name that various cultures applied to various deities in and around the land of Canaan. It could be used as a generic term for 'lord' or 'master'. It was applied to specific deities that influenced the Israelites at key points in its history.

The Baal mentioned in the Bible was a universal fertility god and a storm god associated with bringing rain and dew in the Canaan area. The Phoenicians called him the Lord of the Heavens. Based on archaeological discoveries in Syria, there appears to have been a mythos around Baal, as the fertility god, in combat with the god of sterility, Mot, in a seven year cycle. Whoever won determined the state of the crops for the next seven years. Baal got credit for a good harvest cycle, and Mot disdain for famine. In the myths of the region, he became the dominant deity by defeating all other gods, including the creator god El" (Source: Bible Study Tools/Who Was Baal?/Bethany Verrett).

Crops and livestock were the currencies of that day and time. This is to say that Baal, in modern-day terms, was considered a god of blessings, wealth, prosperity, and sexuality. What's even crazier is the fact that Baal worshipers would engage in orgies, all the while, slaughtering children to Baal. Many of the women would find themselves pregnant as a result of these orgies, and they'd turn and sacrifice most of those children as well. This is to say that while Baal was considered a god of fertility, the people of that day and time didn't see children as a way to carry out their legacies; they saw infants as sacrifices. Is this still happening today? Yes, absolutely! Many people worship the god of Hollywood; they are worshipers of fame, money, and the power that comes with it. They no longer burn their children in a fire as an offering to Baal; instead, they offer their children to this deity through:

1. Abortion.
2. Abuse (Physical and Sexual).
3. Abandonment.
4. Neglect.
5. Exposure to the evils of this world.

Log into any major social media network and you will find children behaving like adults. You may even find videos of mothers recording their young daughters while those girls dance seductively. There is a new trend where parents are permitting their children to use profanity for a minute or less. The parent (oftentimes the mother) will walk out of the bathroom leaving her children (many of which are toddlers) in front of a mirror. Behind the child is the parent's camera. The child is instructed to curse while the parent is away. This means that the souls of children are being perverted and sold for likes. This is a form of trafficking. People are even reporting that stores like Sephora and Ulta are the new hubs for ten and eleven year old girls whose parents happily support them buying makeup and behaving like adults. Then again, it's not uncommon these days for parents to allow their children to disrespect them. In this, the children are being offered to demons, albeit, indirectly. This is to say that while many of these parents are not in their living rooms surrounded by candles, an Ouija board, an altar, and a bunch of incense, they are still Baal practitioners, and their children are but sacrifices to their many gods. This is also to say that many people, nonbelievers and believers, are polytheistic, meaning they serve many gods. And the interesting thing about Baal worship is—this particular practice allowed the followers of Baal to have and worship many other deities, only Baal had to be considered the supreme god. In other words, they had to exalt Baal over every other deity that they served. This is what Jezebel offered God's prophets in her heyday. They could continue to worship and serve YAHWEH, but they had to exalt Baal over Him. Remember what God said in Exodus 20:3: "Thou shalt have no other gods before me."

What I'm trying to say is that your very first narcissist was someone who, more than likely, was a worshiper of self. In other words, they were selfish, self-centered, self-absorbed, and self-serving. You were nothing but a sacrifice to that person's many gods. But don't feel like a victim just yet! After all, some of the most effective, powerful, and secure prophets and prophetic people were raised by Jezebel, and this is where they got their training! They have sound minds, pure hearts, and an unyielding fervor for the Most High God. You can't offer them affirmation, success, fame, or power. They are not interested in any of these things, even though many of them are blessed by God to enjoy the trappings of success without the demons that typically come with it. This is because they've learned how to reach into Heaven without partnering with hell to get there.

Take a moment to reflect. Who was the first narcissist or narcissistic person you came in contact with, and how old were you at the time? As you read this book, you will get a better understanding of who you are, why you went through whatever it is that you went through, and how you can get in position to be used by the only true and living God: YAHWEH.

Prophetically Wired and Narcissistically Challenged

The five-fold offices include:
1. The Office of the Pastor.
2. The Office of the Teacher.
3. The Office of the Evangelist.
4. The Office of the Prophet.
5. The Office of the Apostle.

You may be called to one of these offices; then again, you may be an ordinary Kingdom citizen, and get this—being ordinary is the same as being extraordinary because you have access through the Holy Spirit, to the gifts of the Spirit. All the same, many people are not pastors, but they are pastoral; many people are not called to the office of the teacher, but they are anointed to teach. Many people are not called to the office of the evangelist, but they are evangelistic. Many people are not Apostles by calling, but they are apostolic. All the same, there are some people who are called to the office of the prophet; then again, there are some people who are prophetic. This means that they are wired like prophets, even though they are not prophets by calling. The same is true for narcissists. There are people who are full-blown narcissists; all the same, there are people who are narcissist-like or, better yet, narcissistic.

How do you know if you are a prophet or a prophetic person?

1. God will tell you when you're mature enough to hear the truth. This typically happens after you've given the Lord an unconditional yes.

2. God will use others to confirm your calling. In most cases, the people to confirm this will be your pastors, mentors, and the people called to walk alongside you.

How do you know if the person you're entertaining or the person you once entertained is a narcissist or a narcissistic person?

1. Demons move in rank, so the level or rank of the unclean spirit sent after you is typically associated with your rank in the spirit. Please note that your rank is not identified by the office you're called to. Your rank is given to you by God, and in most cases, your rank increases every time you overcome an issue and you download the revelation regarding that season.

2. This isn't something you need to figure out. You simply need to know Christ and who you are in Him. Everything else is irrelevant, however, I will go out on a limb and say that mature prophets tend to attract narcissists, whereas, prophetic people tend to attract narcissistic people. Now, this hasn't been proven; it's just a theory and an observation of mine.

Isaiah 59:19 reads, "So shall they fear the name of the LORD from the west, and his glory from the rising of the sun. When the enemy shall come in like a flood, the Spirit of the LORD shall lift up a standard against him." According to the

National Weather Service, "Flooding typically occurs when prolonged rain falls over several days, when intense rain falls over a short period of time, or when an ice or debris jam causes a river or stream to overflow onto the surrounding area. Flooding can also result from the failure of a water control structure, such as a levee or dam" (Source: National Weather Service/Flood Related Hazards). So, the enemy coming in like a flood means:

1. The enemy consistently attacks you over a period of time.
2. The enemy's attack is intense and almost unbearable.
3. When an issue arises and creates a domino effect of Satanic attacks.
4. When your defenses are so low or weak that it becomes nearly impossible for you to defend yourself.

It is also important to note that the word "standard" here comes from the Hebrew word "nō·sə·sāh," and according to the Englishman's Concordance, it means "the wind of the LORD drives." In this, we find the Lord saying that whenever the enemy comes in intensely, consistently, and overwhelmingly, the Spirit of the Lord will drive him back. In other words, JEHOVAH NISSI, our Banner, fights for us. This is also to say that whatever battles you've fought with the enemy, you were equipped enough to overcome them, and if you were not, God got in the fight with you. All the same, whenever you invite or allow a narcissist to have space in your life, especially for a considerable amount of time, your crime is more than likely idolatry. This is important because, legally speaking, that spirit in the narcissist has a right to you until you renounce idolatry and put on the full armor of God (see Ephesians 6:8-10).

In Jeremiah 1:5, we find the Lord talking to the Prophet Jeremiah about the call on his life. He said, "Before I formed thee in the belly I knew thee; and before thou camest forth out of the womb I sanctified thee, and I ordained thee a prophet unto the nations." Of course, we know that the word "sanctify" means to set apart; to purify, but let's look at the word "ordain." The Greek word for "ordain" is "tassō," and according to Thayers Greek Lexicon, it means:

1) to put in order, to station

1a) to place in a certain order, to arrange, to assign a place, to appoint

1a1) to assign (appoint) a thing to one

1b) to appoint, ordain, order

1b1) to appoint on one's own responsibility or authority

1b2) to appoint mutually, i.e. agree upon

Again, it means to place in a specific order. Why is this important? The order of a thing determines its strength, its function, and most of all, its purpose. This is to say that prophets are wired a certain way; the same is true for every office in the five-fold. Prophets and prophetic people tend to be sensitive, with some being more sensitive than others. This is why many of them who don't know who they are in Christ identify themselves as empaths. According to Very Well Mind, "An empath is a person highly attuned to the feelings and emotions of those around them." This has everything to do with sensitivity, but the truth of the matter is—many, if not most prophets and prophetic people can sense the emotions of others, and this can be overwhelming to the untrained prophet. Consequently, many prophets or highly prophetic people tend to be introverted to one degree or another, and many of them tend to self-isolate in an attempt to avoid experiencing this phenomenon. Of course, there are prophets and prophetic people who are extroverted or ambiverted, but in many cases, these prophets aren't as sensitive as their introverted brethren. This doesn't mean that they aren't as anointed; the calling on their lives may require them to be exposed to crowded spaces, so they are wired a little differently. And because prophets and prophetic people are wired to be sensitive, they typically love to be love-bombed; they love anything that positively heightens their emotions. And this is how the narcissist or the narcissistic party comes in. Satan understands the wiring of a prophet, so he uses the prophet's makeup against him or her. He does this through the use of trauma, media, relationships, etc. Think about the realm of music. A man drives down the street with his music playing loudly. His windows are down, and he's driving slowly through a residential area. He passes by a group of women, but none of them budge; they don't turn their heads to look at him, nor do they appear to notice his loud music, so he keeps driving. A few blocks down, he passes by another group of women, but this time, one of the women in the group turns her head. She then begins to dance. The man slows his car down until he comes to a complete stop. "What's your name?" he asks the beautiful young lady. She smiles confidently and says, "Why do you need my name?" Let's end this story here. What's happening here? It's spiritual! Every song has what's called a hook, and it's called a hook for a reason. Every human being is an instrument; whether we yield ourselves to God or not, we are still instruments, and we will all be used by a force that we cannot see. In this scenario, the man is likely a fisherman for the enemy. He's not out and about looking for a wife; like Satan, he's looking for someone to devour. When the woman began to wriggle and dance around, her sensitivity went on display; it pretty much told the enemy that she is an instrument, and what's even more delightful to Satan is this—she clearly does not know who she is! To the man driving the car, she is an object; she is simply someone to boast about, show off, engage with sexually, potentially live with, and someone who can help him attain a few of his goals. When she danced, to Satan, she mirrored a fish on a hook. This is why the guy pulled his vehicle over. However, if she's a small fish, he'll toss her back by either driving away or by ghosting her whenever he gets bored with her. This is to say that the same way God told us to test the spirits, Satan has a way of determining what office you are called to (if any). After getting access to the woman, that spirit in the man in question will start to see what rank she is in the realm of the spirit or, better yet, what rank she's called to. This is how the enemy will determine if she's a small fish or a great catch. If she's not worth the effort, the man will break her all the more, and then rid himself of her. If she is called to do great things for the Kingdom of God, the enemy may cause the man to become obsessed with her. If she's a high-level prophet, for example, and she's called to ascend the heights of the Kingdom, Satan may use the narcissistic male to prepare her for the narcissist he wants to send her way. To do this, he would ensure that the guy stayed around long enough for the Jezebel spirit in him to become a familiar spirit to her. In other words, he will go out of his way to help her become comfortable with Jezebel. What this does is, it helps to accelerate any future relationships she may have with men who have that same spirit. Because the man in question has a low-ranking Jezebel, Satan will often send a tow truck after him in the form of the infamous other woman. This woman will often have a Jezebel spirit that's stronger than his own. Once he's out of the picture, Satan may send men her way who have no ambition, no power, and no long-term goals. He's not sending them for her to marry; he sends these men so that she will feel that the narcissist who comes her way is one in a million. In other words, she will come to believe that most men are like the low-ranking guys who'd attempted to romantically link themselves to her, so whenever she meets the high-ranking Jezebel (narcissist), she will breathe a sigh of relief. And she will be more likely to accelerate or allow her new lover to accelerate the relationship because she will feel as if she already knows her new lover. Because prophets and prophetic people are oftentimes addicted to serotonin, dopamine, adrenaline, and oxytocin, she won't mind the relationship moving too fast because she too will be in a rush to get to her drug of choice. This is to say that once a prophet or a prophetic person becomes acquainted with a certain spirit, they will often turn to that spirit to have their emotions tantalized and pacified. This is why they have to break up with the spirit of Jezebel, rather than constantly breaking up with the person of Jezebel. Breaking up with a narcissist or a narcissistic person can be difficult, but breaking up with an unclean spirit requires a stronger relationship with God, a deeper sense of self, and a greater love for God and self. All the same, accepting your call in Christ requires a greater love for God's people.

With such sensitive wiring comes a great deal of issues, one of those issues being perversion. Don't mistake what I'm saying. A prophet or a prophetic person is not automatically perverted. Everything that the prophetic individual gets addicted to is something they've discovered while toying around with the wrong thoughts or the wrong people. This is why a bored prophet or a comfortable prophet can become his or her own enemy. How so? Prophetic types love to play around with their own wiring, especially when they are immature, undeveloped, and broken. They like to experiment with relationships and in relationships. For example, a prophet can easily exchange numbers with or potentially date someone he or she is not attracted to just out of curiosity. They will ask questions, pretend to be in love with their new lovers in the making, and even dare themselves to do things with the person they wouldn't ordinarily do. Yes, this includes having sex! It is during this stage or phase of their development that their soul ties with Jezebel are formed or strengthened. This is because, believe it or not, they are narcissistically challenged. What does this mean? Simply put, prophets and prophetic types, in their infancy, are incredibly self-centered and relatively narcissistic. Does this mean that they have the Jezebel spirit? No, not at all. Can a prophet pick up the Jezebel spirit? Absolutely! Many of the narcissists and narcissistic people you have come in contact with are prophets who have gone rogue; these are prophetic souls who stopped developing because:

1. They fell in love with the world and all it has to offer.
2. They fell in love with their wiring, and became addicted to playing with themselves, spiritually speaking.
3. They wandered into the dark arts looking for another high or a way to take control of a situation, a person, or the future at large.
4. They became angry with God, and decided to withdraw and withhold themselves from Him in an act of revenge.
5. They have idols that are preoccupying their minds and their time.

This is to say that prophets and prophetic people are more narcissistically challenged than most people because of their wiring, and the majority of them repeatedly run from their assignments, constantly telling themselves and God that once they reach a certain space, age, or event in their lives, that they will finally surrender themselves to Him. This does not happen because we don't get to choose when and how God uses us; the only choice we have is to yield or not. Because of this, you will find most prophets and prophetic people hiding in the following spaces (see chart below).

Common Hiding Places for Prophets and Prophetic Types

Career/Job	Congregation	False Religion	Marriage
Trauma	Family	Parenthood	Victimhood
Friendships	Music	Film	Media (at Large)
Sex Industry	Wrong Region	Fear	Perversion
Co-Dependency	Poverty	Offense	Food

Note: these are not the only hiding places for prophets and prophetic people, but they are some of the most common ones. What does it mean to hide yourself behind these things?

1. People hiding behind their careers or jobs tend to busy themselves, and they use their lack of available time as an excuse.

2. People hiding in the congregation tend to refuse to acknowledge the call on their lives; they won't serve at church or do anything that would get them identified. And many of them, if prophesied to, will leave the churches they are in after they've been found out.

3. People hiding in false or useless religions will often use their church or religion's policies or beliefs to justify hiding from their assignments.

4. People hiding in marriages use their not-so-better halves as a justification for their rebellion against God. This is why many prophets and prophetic people who cry "narcissists" are not victims. They are manipulators who toss themselves into the lion's den, and then use their wounds to get out of doing their assignments.

5. People hiding behind trauma refuse to get therapy, they quit every program that could possibly help them, and they repeatedly use their traumas as an excuse as to why they can't be used at the time.

6. People hiding behind family often blame their families' dysfunctional ways for their decisions to not serve in ministry or not allow God to use them; they almost always promise to be used by Him later on in life.

7. People hiding behind parenthood tend to use their children as an excuse to not do ministry.

8. People hiding on the wrong side of the music or movie industry, or anywhere in the media find pleasure and joy in using their gifts, all the while, giving God a shout out every now and again, hoping this will pacify His wrath.

9. People hiding in victimhood are individuals who repeatedly use their traumatic pasts and the situations that they are presently in as their hiding places.

10. People hiding behind poverty typically won't do anything to change their situations, but they will use those situations to justify rejecting or

repeatedly putting God on the back-burner.

These are just some of the examples so you can get a better idea of what hiding looks like.

Narcissism at its Core

Let's start here. What are the symptoms of Narcissistic Personality Disorder? They include:

Grandiose feelings of self-worth.
Lack of empathy.
Inability to assume responsibility for one's own actions.
Entitlement.
The objectification of others.
A need for excessive admiration.
Hypersensitivity to criticism.
A need to be in control.
Vanity or a fixation on one's own appearance.
Preoccupation with power, success, or fame.
Manipulative tendencies.
Envy.
Jealousy.
Verbal, emotional, physical, and spiritual abuse.
Desire to be seen as important or powerful without doing the work to earn this privilege.
Attempting to connect with people who are powerful, influential, and/or successful.
High sense of self-importance.
Mean girl syndrome (tendency to look down on people who appear to be of little or no importance).

Discarding people after using them.
Tendency to belittle others in an attempt to appear and/or feel superior.
Fear of rejection.
Fear of abandonment.
Lack of boundaries or inability to respect the boundaries set by others.
Obsession with perfection.
Fragility.
Chronic depression.
Extreme impatience.
Punishes or persecutes anyone who says no.
Lack of emotional control (rage, anger, impulsivity).
A tendency to hold grudges or use the faults of others to gain control of the individuals in question.
Excessive talks about themselves.
Self-worship.
A tendency to give backhanded compliments.
Chronic feelings of emptiness or boredom.

It goes without saying that these are not the only signs, symptoms, and characteristics of Narcissistic Personality Disorder, but the aforementioned list is a compilation of the most common characteristics of this disorder/demon. Additionally, people with NPD won't always have every characteristic on the list.

Narcissism, at its core, has everything to do with self-worship, conceit, and vanity. It is a widely recognized personality disorder that has been found to cause a considerable negative impact on the lives of those who suffer from it as well as those with whom they interact. Characterized by excessive self-admiration, lack of empathy, and an inflated sense of entitlement, narcissism can have debilitating consequences on all aspects of an individual's life, including their relationships, career, and overall well-being. Narcissists often manipulate those around them to maintain their inflated sense of self, which can lead to toxic behaviors, damaged relationships, and mental deprivation. One of the defining features of narcissistic behavior is their unyielding obsession with achieving and maintaining a certain image of themselves in the eyes of others. Narcissists prioritize their own needs and desires above those of others because they believe that they are somehow more special or important than those around them. They may become highly controlling, demanding, or even abusive, treating others as if they are objects to serve and gratify their needs or desires. The result of this behavior is that the narcissist may eventually alienate those closest to them. Those who are close to a narcissist may struggle with feelings of inadequacy, as the narcissist's behavior often belittles or even mocks the accomplishments of others, which can cause the victim to feel like they are no longer valued and are simply a means to an end. This can result in damaged emotional connections and ultimately lead to a breakdown in the relationship. Furthermore, people with narcissistic tendencies may find it difficult to form authentic, deep connections with others. Narcissists are often so preoccupied with their own needs and desires that they are unable to relate to the experiences of others, leading to a profound lack of empathy and understanding for others. This can make it tough for them to develop a meaningful emotional connection with anyone and may lead to a life lived in isolation.

Ultimately, narcissism can be a dangerous personality disorder with far-reaching consequences. Narcissists' behaviors are often driven by a deep-seated need to feel superior to those around them, which can lead to a range of negative outcomes, including toxic relationships, conflicts with peers, and ultimately, profound feelings of unhappiness and disillusionment as they fail to achieve their goals and desires despite their best efforts. For individuals with narcissistic tendencies, addressing their behavior and working to develop deeper connections with others can be a crucial step towards reclaiming their sense of self-worth and cultivating meaningful relationships with those around them.

Narcissus: Short Version

During the late 1800's, the term "narcissism" began to find its way into English literature. However, the concept of narcissism was not a new one. It derived from Greek mythology after the story of a Greek deity had been created and shared in Ovid's Metamorphoses, a Latin narrative poem that was written around 8 AD. What is the story of Narcissus?

Narcissus is a name that came to be associated with the concept of self-love and vanity. In ancient Greek mythology, Narcissus was a beautiful young hunter who fell in love with his own reflection, ultimately leading to his tragic demise. The story of Narcissus has been retold in various forms across literature, art, and popular culture. According to the myth, Narcissus was the son of a river god and a nymph. He was known for his exceptional beauty, which attracted the attention of many suitors, both male and female. But, despite receiving numerous offers of love and admiration, Narcissus remained indifferent and cold towards his admirers. One day, while out on a hunt, he stumbled upon a pool of water. As he bent down to drink from it, he caught sight of his own reflection in the water and was immediately captivated by its beauty. Consequently, Narcissus became so infatuated with his own reflection that he could not bear to leave the pool. He spent his days gazing at himself, becoming increasingly deluded by his own beauty. His obsession with his reflection drove him to the brink of insanity, and he eventually perished beside the pool, consumed by his own self-love.

The story of Narcissus has captured the imagination of artists and writers throughout history, inspiring countless works of art, literature, and music. In literature, the concept of narcissism has become a widely recognized trait, used to describe those who are obsessed with themselves and their own image. For example, in the world of psychology, the term narcissism is used to describe a personality disorder characterized by an excessive sense of self-importance and a lack of empathy for others. While narcissism can manifest in a variety of ways, it bears many similarities to the myth of Narcissus in its focus on self-love and self-obsession.

Narcissus and Echo: Long Version

In Greek mythology, the tales of Narcissus and Echo are regarded as some of the most intriguing and timeless tales to ever be told. These two characters are intertwined in a story that has both tragic and cautionary elements. According to the story, Narcissus was a beautiful and proud young man who was known for his exceptional good looks and charm. Many believed him to be the most attractive man in the world, and he was fully aware of the effect he had on people. Narcissus was so enamored with his own image that he often stared at himself in a pool of water, often becoming lost in his own reflection.

Echo, on the other hand, was said to be a nymph who could only repeat the last few words spoken by anyone around her. She was known for her beauty as well, but she often felt lonely and isolated due to her inability to communicate properly. When she met Narcissus by chance, she instantly fell in love with him, but he was too self-absorbed to notice her. However, Echo longed to express her love and feelings for Narcissus, but she could only repeat the words spoken by him. Narcissus, however, was more interested in his own reflection in the water than in Echo's words, and therefore ignored her.

The tragic end to this tale came when another nymph watched Narcissus admiring himself in the water and prayed to the gods that he would only feel the same unrequited love that Echo felt for him. The gods granted her wish and made Narcissus fall in love with his own reflection in the water, causing him to waste away and eventually die from unrequited love, meaning one-sided love. In the end, only a flower bloomed where Narcissus had perished, giving birth to the eponymous plant known as the narcissus flower.

The moral of the story is—Narcissus's relentless admiration of his own beauty blinded him to the world around him, ultimately leading to his destruction. Similarly, Echo's blind adoration of Narcissus led to her loneliness and isolation. This story was written to serve as a warning to individuals who are consumed by ego and pride, as it reminds us that obsession with ourselves is futile, and can only lead to our own downfall. In short, the tale of Narcissus and Echo is a powerful myth that holds significant meaning for modern-day society. It reminds us of the dangers of arrogance and vanity, and how they can ultimately lead to our demise.

The Truth

Narcissus did not exist; Lucifer did. Echo did not exist; Jezebel did. Greek myths, while untrue, often bear some semblance of the truth. For example, Lucifer was fixated with himself. Remember in Ezekiel 28:17, God rebuked Lucifer with these words, "Thine heart was lifted up because of thy beauty, thou hast corrupted thy wisdom by reason of thy brightness..." Jezebel, on the other hand, bears an odd resemblance to the nymph, Echo, only she wasn't obsessed with a person. She was obsessed with her deity, Baal, which (of course) was and is a demon. She'd echoed the words spoken by her father, Ethbaal, thus continuing the spread of Baal worship. All the same, she'd loved a deity that could not love her back.

The truth is that at the very core of narcissism, you will find self-worship, which is another form of idolatry. Another word for self-worship is sin. The word "sin" is translated as "hamataria" in Greek, and it means "to miss the mark." And contrary to popular belief, sin isn't just the physical act of rebelling against God. Spiritually speaking, sin starts in the heart. It comes when we don't believe or trust God, or whenever we have a belief that opposes God's Word. So, if God told you to go right, but you instead chose to go left, believe it or not, the root of the sin has everything to do with the thought or belief that seduced or ushered you into making a left turn. The thought could be anything from:

- "I don't think it's as bad as God says it is. I'll go and see for myself."
- "Does God truly exist in the first place?"
- "I think the voice from within is just me answering myself."
- "God wants me to turn right, but there are a lot of delays, storms and frustration on that path. The other route looks more like a shortcut. I'll take it and repent later."

When you execute the act, you are in rebellion; this means that the thought that was just in the spirit realm is no longer a thought. It is a seed sown in the natural realm. This seed is called rebellion, and the hard outer shell around it is called pride. This means that you are now moving adversely against God. This is to say that narcissism stems from us choosing ourselves over God; it's when we don't follow the Lord's command to seek Him first. Instead, we become self-seeking, proud, haughty, and independent of God, and we, in turn, teach others to do the same.

The truth is, the enemy tells his story in Greek mythology using a host of fictional characters; he does this so that he can control the narrative. All the same, most mythological beliefs are rooted in false religions. Satan did this because religion tends to root itself in our unconscious mind; in other words, most people will throw away everything including their families, their careers, their friends, and everything of value before they allow anyone to challenge their religious beliefs. Satan knows this! It is for this reason that he creates the doctrines of demons, and then he feeds these lies to any person or group of people that he comes across. He does this using the pipelines of culture and tradition. Note: the following definitions were taken from Oxford Languages:

◆ **Culture:** the customs, arts, social institutions, and achievements of a particular nation, people, or other social group.

◆ **Tradition:** the transmission of customs or beliefs from generation to generation, or the fact of being passed on in this way.

Once a custom or practice is taught to, believed by, and executed by the next generation, it becomes a tradition. All the same, it is important to note that wherever you find people disregarding the Most High God and worshiping other gods, you will also find a host of demonic spirits being worshiped as gods. These demons will pretend to be whatever the people believe them to be, and they will use their trust against them. For example, let's say a nation rejects YAHWEH and embraces familiar spirits. These demons will disguise themselves as gods and angels of light, all the while, accusing that nation before God. They will then use the people's trust against them by stealing their resources and telling some of the more demonized people in that family or nation that the gods are not pleased; this is why there is, for example, a drought, famine, corruption, and the list goes on. This leads the people further into witchcraft and idolatry, thus giving the enemy a legal right to them. The people make sacrifices to demons unknowingly, and this only worsens the problem because it allows more demons to enter that nation, and it allows the demons in that nation to grow in rank and in strength.

The Core of Narcissism

"Then shall they deliver you up to be afflicted, and shall kill you: and ye shall be hated of all nations for my name's sake. And then shall many be offended, and shall betray one another, and shall hate one another. And many false prophets shall rise, and shall deceive many. <u>And because iniquity shall abound, the love of many shall wax cold</u>. But he that shall endure unto the end, the same shall be saved. And this gospel of the kingdom shall be preached in all the world for a witness unto all nations; and then shall the end come" (Matthew 24:9-14).

Who is love?
5. God is love (1 John 4:8).

How is love? 1 Corinthians 13:4-8 answers this question; it says:
1. Love is patient.
2. Love is kind.
3. It does not envy.
4. It does not boast.
5. It is not proud.
6. It is not rude.
7. It is not self-seeking.
8. It is not easily angered.
9. It keeps no account of wrongs.
10. Love takes no pleasure in evil, but rejoices in the truth.
11. It bears all things, believes all things, hopes all things, and endures all things.
12. Love never fails.

What is love?

1. It is one of the fruits of the Spirit (see Galatians 5:22).

Why do we love?

1. We love because He first loved us (see 1 John 4:19/ESV).

How long is love?

1. Love never fails (see 1 Corinthians 13:8).

When is love?

1. In due season (see Ecclesiastes 3:7-8).

Where is love?

1. Everywhere, since God is omnipresent (see Psalm 139:7-10).

There are many more scriptures in the Bible that we can read about what love is, who love is, how love is, and why love came to exist in the first place. However, it can all be simplified in the fact that God is love and He first loved us. This is to say that, contrary to popular belief, love is not a feeling; it is not an emotion. There is an emotional aspect to love, don't get me wrong, but love cannot be locked in the prison of human interpretation, nor can it be limited to what we feel or how we feel. As humans, we have taken the concept of love and humanized it. It is difficult for us to see or understand the spirit of love because the media has captivated us with the nature of love. The nature of love, by the way, is the natural benefits and expressions of love. This has everything to do with what we can or cannot see. And because most people do not understand love as a spirit, they have reduced it to an emotion. Emotions are unstable, but love is stable. This is why it cannot fail. 1 John 4:20 reads, "If a man say, I love God, and hateth his brother, he is a liar: for he that loveth not his brother whom he hath seen, how can he love God whom he hath not seen?" Why did God say that a man who says that he loves God, all the while, hating his brother is a liar? The answer is simple—God is love. It's not just how He is, it's who He is. So, when someone says that they love you, they are simply saying they have God's heart for you. However, if they do not have God's heart, it is impossible for that person to have God's heart for you. In other words, if God isn't first and foremost in that person's life, that individual will not and cannot have the spirit of love, even though he or she may demonstrate some of the many natures of love. The nature of love includes the following:

Showing Care	Showing Concern	A Sense of Oneness
A Sense of Responsibility	A Need to Protect	A Need to Provide
High Prioritization	A Sense of Safety	Empathy
Acceptance	Meaningful Conversation	Listens Intently
Trust	Support	Quality Time
Thoughtfulness	A Sense of Longing	Planning Future with You
Affection	Initiates You Into Circle	Correction
Commitment/Loyalty	Adoration	Like-Mindedness

These are some of the many natures or, better yet, symptoms of love, but get this—you can cough, sneeze, and have chest congestion, but this does not mean that you have a common cold. You may have the influenza virus (also known as the flu), COVID 19, a respiratory infection, seasonal allergies, and so on. This is to say that the symptoms of love aren't always the evidence of love. The evidence of love is found in 1 Corinthians 13:4-8 (see 'How is love' above). But notice that the Apostle John prophesied that love would wax cold in the last days. What he was saying was this—in the last days, the Earth will be overcome by individualistic, self-centered, egotistical, and self-absorbed narcissists and narcissistic people. This will result in an increase in:

1. Crime.
2. Divorces.
3. Me-Minded People.

Love is not self-seeking; this is what the scripture tells us. However, what we see today is an explosion of what we've come to know as narcissism rapidly spreading across the Western world and abroad. In truth, narcissism has become a pandemic. What we are seeing now is the modern-day version of the living dead. This is to say that narcissism isn't limited to a person. Besides individual narcissism, there is familial narcissism, regional narcissism, tribal narcissism, corporate narcissism, etc. Once narcissism spreads, for example, from a mother to her daughter, it becomes generational narcissism, and if it is an issue within the family, it then becomes familial narcissism. This is why you can come across an entire family of narcissists or incredibly narcissistic people. All the same, you can come across an individual prophet in the same manner you can come across an entire family of prophets and prophetic people. Furthermore, within the context of familial narcissism, it is possible to come across two narcissistic people who happen to be married to one another (more on this later). It is also possible that one of the parties involved in the marriage didn't come into the marriage as an incredibly narcissistic person. Instead, after being married to a narcissist or a narcissistic person, a lot of people tend to become more self-centered or, better yet, narcissistic. Many of them feel they have to be this way. This is because narcissists are like vampires; they will suck the life (virtue) out of a person non-stop until that human ceases to exist or function, and to maintain any semblance or measure of sanity, lovers of narcissists (who still have some fight left in them) typically become more individualistic or self-centered as the relationship eats away at their souls. They do this in an attempt to stay above the surface of what we call sanity; they do this so that they can maintain some measure of humanity, dignity, and identity. This is what we call "survivor's mode." However, the more they lose themselves in the narcissist's demented world, the more "ahabish" or Ahab-like they become. In other words, many of them begin to center their entire lives around making the narcissist happy or pacifying the narcissist's wrath, and believe it or not, this is a full-time job.

Before we go any further, let's get a practical understanding of what narcissism is, and as we delve deeper into this book, we will get a more in-depth understanding of narcissism. In simplistic terms, narcissism is a religion within itself. While it does not have a physical assembly or logo, narcissism, simply put, is one man or woman's desire and demand to be worshiped. The narcissistic individual will center himself or herself as a deity of sorts in the lives of others, whereas he or she will demand the support, praise, and loyalty of others. In this, the narcissist becomes the first member in his or her own congregation, and everyone who enters the narcissist's life has to join his or her cult. The word "religion," as defined by Oxford Languages is, "A pursuit or interest to which someone ascribes supreme importance." This is what it means to be self-centered. Another word for self-centered is sinful, and another word for sin is self-worship. Of course, we also know it as selfishness, self-seeking, self-absorption, self-obsession, and egotism. Sin centers itself around selfish desires; it robs you of the love you were supposed to share with others and causes you to overwhelm yourself with your own version of love. This creates an addiction of sorts, and this addiction is what we refer to as narcissism. Narcissism is false self-love. It's the spirit behind today's trending self-love movement. How so? The doctrine of self-love always seeks to remove God from the picture or make Him equal to or less than the practitioner of the doctrine, all the while giving the practitioner spiritual principles to live by. Spiritual practices are illegal without the Spirit of God. Without Him, the practitioner finds himself or herself dabbling in rebellion or witchcraft. Remember, according to the Bible, rebellion is as the sin of witchcraft. According to Galatians 5, witchcraft is one of the works of the flesh, after all, there is a natural side of witchcraft, and then there is a spiritual side of it, both of which are ungodly. The natural side of witchcraft is called rebellion. The spiritual side of witchcraft involves the practices of sorcery, black magic, white magic, hoodoo, astrology, etc. Rebellion is wicked, but witchcraft is both wicked and evil. What's the difference between evil and wicked? Evil deals with morality, whereas to be wicked means to intentionally harm others or break the rules. The evil level of witchcraft is when the practitioner uses it to harm, manipulate, seduce, or control others. And, of course, to be evil is to be far more sinister than to be wicked. Nevertheless, regardless of how it is used, witchcraft is still illegal and ungodly in the realm of the spirit. How does this tie in to narcissistic abuse? A narcissistic person is typically wicked, but a narcissist is pure evil. This doesn't just deal with morality; it should help you to understand the depths of darkness that narcissists and narcissistic individuals reside in. And with narcissism, there is a spectrum. Think about it this way. The Bible refers to some spirits being more wicked than others. This deals with rank. This is to say that not every Jezebel spirit ranks the same. If Todd, Jessica, and Bradley all had the Jezebel spirit, they wouldn't be sharing a demon; instead, they'd have their own demons. The Jezebel spirit in Jessica might outrank the one in Todd, and the Jezebel spirit in Bradley might outrank the one in Jessica. If all of these characters were in a room together, they'd likely challenge each other for control over the space that they're in. The highest ranking devil would likely rise above the rest by causing its host to behave in a more sinister way. For example, Bradley would potentially go "too far" by Todd and Jessica's standards, meaning, he's willing to risk the most to get what he wants. After this, you would witness both Todd and Jessica suddenly being super nice to Brad; they may even become close friends. Then again, Jessica may get close to Brad, and the two of them would pair up against Todd. While the kingdom of darkness is not divided, like animals, demons are territorial. Think of a human king. He may get along with the king who runs the kingdom next door to him; he may even loan his troops to that king in battles and wars. All the same, both kings may allow the people in their kingdoms to intermarry. However, neither king is going to want to run or rule the same kingdom together. The same is true for demons. They have what they consider to be their own domain, which we know, of course, is the human soul. Two high-ranking devils do not care to share souls; that is unless one is evicted and it comes back with seven more spirits more wicked than itself (see Matthew 12:45). This is to say that the core of narcissism is a lack of love, and not just a lack of love for others, a lack of love for God and self, and wherever there is a lack of love, you will find unclean spirits.

The cure to narcissism is found in Matthew 22:37-40, which reads, "Jesus said unto him, Thou shalt love the Lord thy God with all thy heart, and with all thy soul, and with all thy mind. This is the first and great commandment. And the second is like unto it, Thou shalt love thy neighbor as thyself. On these two commandments hang all the law and the prophets." Narcissism creeps or slithers in when Matthew 6:33 is not honored; this scripture denotes chronology or, better yet, chronological order. It reads, "But seek ye first the kingdom of God, and his righteousness; and all these things shall be added unto you." What happens with many believers is—they seek God, but they don't seek Him first. 1 Corinthians 11:3 reads, "But I want you to realize that the head of every man is Christ, and the head of the woman is man, and the head of Christ is God. When God is not first, another head has to be erected; this head then serves as a god or, better yet, an idol. This head, for most people, is their plans, their emotions, and their preferences. This is to say that the average Christian in the Western Hemisphere is unknowingly polytheistic, meaning, they have more than one god. What's amazing about this is the fact that Jezebel was polytheistic, and contrary to popular belief, Jezebel, the woman, wasn't against the worship of YAHWEH. Polytheistic people don't mind you adding your God to the lineup, but in Baal worship, Baal had to be worshiped as the supreme god, whereas YAHWEH warned us this way, "Thou shalt have no other gods before me" (Exodus 20:3). Notice the word "before" in the aforementioned scripture. The word "before," according to Oxford Languages means, "In front of someone or something." Does this mean that you can have another god as long as you put that god second to the Most High God? No, because Matthew 6:24 reads, "No man can serve two masters: for either he will hate the one, and love the other; or else he will hold to the one, and despise the other. Ye cannot serve God and mammon." The Lord used the word "before" because He understands the nature of false gods. They are but demons masquerading as deities and they will always seek to take His place and demote Him in the eyes and lives of His people. They will always seek to be your top priority. Consequently, when God is not first in your life, by default, you will have an idol, and that idol will demand more of your time, attention, energy, and resources; this way, you'll find yourself giving the Lord what's left instead of what's best or what's first. Now, you can understand why God requires our first-fruits. The objective of this was to help us to put and keep Him first. However, most believers serve God, but He's just not their top priority. And this is how the Jezebel spirit manages to ensnare them because the moment they entered polytheism, they entered into Jezebel's domain. You are a ruler over the world God entrusted you with; this world is what you refer to as your reality. When you enter Jezebel's domain as a ruler, she will partner with you and allow you and your household to intermarry with the devils in her kingdom. This is why you can't effectively break up with a narcissist without first breaking up with:

1. Idolatry.
2. The spirit of Jezebel.
3. The spirit of Ahab.
4. Witchcraft and control.
5. Self-worship.

And you can't break up with idolatry without putting God first. He's not asking you to worship Him harder or louder; He's not asking you to be more demonstrative in your worship. He's simply asking you to put and keep Him first. This is how you address the core of your soul and uproot Jezebel and her cohorts from your life once and for all.

The Spectrum of Narcissism

According to Oxford Languages, a "spectrum" is "used to classify something, or suggest that it can be classified, in terms of its position on a scale between two extreme or opposite points." To better understand the concept of a spectrum, please note that every adjective or word used to describe something or someone is on a spectrum, and on the other end of that spectrum is its antonym. For example, check out the chart below.

Light	Dark
Blessed	Cursed
Good	Bad
Heavy	Light
White	Black
Hot	Cold
Tall	Short
Wide	Narrow

Every spectrum is a gradient, meaning, there are other descriptors that lead you from one extreme to the other. For example, check out the chart below.

Hot	Lukewarm	Cold
Large	Medium	Small
Up	Middle	Down

The same is true for the spectrum of narcissism, but first, let's establish a few facts and truths.

1. Every human being on the face of this planet is narcissistic. Narcissism, at its core, means self-centered, self-worship, and sinful.

2. When a child is young, that child is incredibly narcissistic, and the child's narcissistic ways will continue for years; that is until the child reaches a certain age or stage of maturity.

3. We've been unknowingly testing our children's development by, for example, handing them a huge bag of chips when they were toddlers. We would then ask for some of their chips, and we have watched them cry at the thought of us eating what they consider to be theirs. In this, we find them lacking in gratitude; this doesn't mean that they are bad. It simply reflects the stage of development they are in. As a toddler progresses in maturity, we will typically notice the child putting random chips up to our mouths, and at first, we will pretend to eat the chips, all the while, leaving them intact. To this, the child normally laughs. One day, we actually bite the chip, and we witness the child having yet another emotional tantrum. This signals that the child is still in a particular stage of development. However, most parents will continue to eat the food until their toddlers smile at them while they do so. This tells us that the child is developing.

4. If a nine-year old boy thinks and behaves like a three-year old, we will typically take him to a mental health specialist to have him tested, as this signals that he may be suffering from some form of arrested development.

5. Arrested development is mostly caused by trauma, grief, or neglect.

6. Narcissism is the result of arrested development; it is typically the product of an emotional freeze, whereas, children tend to get stuck mentally and developmentally at the point of extreme trauma.

Flynn Effect
Three facets of emotional intelligence declined over time: well-being, self-control, and emotionality. Access to technology was associated with decreased well-being and self-control.

Source: Psychology Today/Why Emotional Intelligence Is in Decline/Madeleine A. Fugère Ph.D.

Here's the deception. The human race is getting smarter and dumber at the same time. According to the Flynn Effect, our IQ (intelligence quota) has grown, but according to science, our emotional intelligence is rapidly declining and will continue to do so if we keep going the route we're going. So, we're left with a bunch of people who know a lot, but are sabotaged by their lack of emotional maturity. All the same, we have a generation of people who have a surplus of knowledge, but a deficient of understanding. The Bible tells us that (1) knowledge puffs us up or, better yet, it makes people prideful, and (2), above all our getting, we must get understanding. In this, we come to understand that knowledge, while good and pivotal to our development, is only one side of the coin. The other side of that same coin is understanding, and to get to understanding, we need to (1) study and show ourselves approved, (2) get wise counsel, and (3) grow the fruits of patience because understanding comes over time. Understanding often shows up when what we've come to understand is confronted by experience; this is when, for example, we may find ourselves saying things like, "Now, I know why my parents were so overprotective" or "I was mad at my coworker, Hannah, at first, but now that I've worked with the new girl, I fully understand Hannah's stance." And once understanding enters the equation, we can take our knowledge to a new level; this level, when executed, is called wisdom, and according to the Bible, wisdom is the principle or, better yet, the most important thing. However, we are living in a time where people study to be right, not righteous. They don't want revelation; they just want to argue their points. This is to say that narcissism is on the rise. This is why we find a lot of young people quitting their jobs; they call it a revolution, but for those of us who've been around for a long time, we see it for what it is. A lot of people today lack the intrapersonal and interpersonal skills needed to manage workplace conflict. All the same, a lot of young people lack discipline; they find it difficult, if not nearly impossible, to sustain jobs, relationships, and wealth altogether. This leads to us having a generation of people chasing wealth, but they don't have the discipline needed to access, garner, or sustain the very thing that they are idolizing. This also leads to them growing in narcissism because, once again, narcissism is nothing but selfishness on display. Simply put, it is often the result of a person being knowledgeable, but lacking emotional intelligence, interpersonal skills, and love altogether. What you'll come to discover is that every generation is more narcissistic than its generational predecessor, but we don't necessarily recognize this fact because we have a tendency to fix our eyes and our attention on the areas in which we've elevated above our parents, grandparents, and ancestors. This is to say that what our society renders to be normal or standard today would have been considered abnormal in the 1960's. What we laugh at today could have earned us a straitjacket in our parents' time. And believe it or not, this is not because our parents were lacking in intelligence; this has everything to do with the people of our nation, much like the people of Israel, demanding that our government and our society normalize the evils they've come to love. So, what we're witnessing is narcissism becoming a standard, whereas having a sound mind, a Godly moral compass, and a true fear of God is becoming not only abnormal, but it's considered to be hateful and outdated. Speaking up about God is considered to be hate speech. Jesus warned us of this in Matthew 24:10-12; He said, "And then shall many be offended, and shall betray one another, and shall hate one another. And many false prophets shall rise, and shall deceive many. And because iniquity shall abound, the love of many shall wax cold."

Again, every human being is narcissistic or, better yet, we display narcissistic traits from time to time. This is why there is normal or standard narcissism; then again, as a person moves from one side of the spectrum towards the other, that person grows more and more narcissistic. By the time the individual in question reaches the center or middle of the spectrum, the individual will be considered by most people to be toxic or relatively narcissistic. Once he or she moves past the middle of the spectrum, the individual is considered to be narcissistic, but as he or she progresses, the person slowly is considered to be incredibly narcissistic. Once the individual reaches the far left of the spectrum, the individual is said to have Narcissistic Personality Disorder, meaning, they don't just have moments of narcissism; they are narcissistic pretty much around the clock.

Why is it important that we know about narcissism being on a spectrum? Simply put, being able to measure narcissism helps us to understand where we stand on that spectrum versus where others stand. This helps us to not only measure ourselves, but to create a standard for ourselves, and to establish and enforce boundaries around ourselves, understanding that the boundaries we set for one person may not be the boundaries we've set for another person. This is because one person may be mentally healthy and emotionally stable, whereas a more narcissistic relative or friend may be emotionally unstable and incredibly narcissistic. But before we go further into this book, let's talk about what this looks like spiritually.

Jezebel, the Reprobate

Let's start here. What the world of psychology refers to as the narcissist, the church knows and understands to be someone who is bound by the Jezebel spirit. Sure, our entire nation is narcissistic, and this does not mean that we all have the Jezebel spirit. Think back to the spectrum. As we move across that spectrum from normal narcissism to incredible narcissism, we become more and more prone to the Jezebel spirit. Once that particular spirit enters a person, it accelerates the individual's move from one side of the spectrum to another; it does this through suggestive thoughts. So, someone bound by the Jezebel spirit may have thoughts like, "They think they're better than you. That's why they didn't invite you to their party." They may think, "They're jealous of you. You should provoke them by (insert narcissistic suggestion here)" or "They are intimidated by your anointing!" Every demonic suggestion causes the individual to feel victimized, rejected, and misunderstood. In the beginning, this often leads to the person trying to prove himself or herself, but over time, the person graduates from disappointment to hurt, and finally from hurt to vengeance. Now, the people that the narcissistic person is angry with may be completely innocent; they are just going about their days, doing their jobs, or serving at their local churches, however, the person being groomed by the Jezebel spirit doesn't see it this way. They believe they are being intentionally targeted, rejected, and mismanaged. Slowly but surely, they become more self-centered and self-reliant. This is where the spirits of control and witchcraft enter the equation. As the bound individual deals with the highs and lows of his or her own emotions, the individual will find himself or herself having more and more episodes of narcissistic injury and rage. Lacking the maturity needed to control himself or herself, narcissists start trying to control the people around them. And get this, power is an addictive drug! Check out the following articles:

"The pursuit of power may also have a neurochemical component. Having power over others has an intoxicating effect. It boosts testosterone, which in turn increases the supply of dopamine (a feel-good neurotransmitter) in the brain's reward system. This dopamine rush explains the addictive quality of power and why it's so hard to let it go" (Source: https://knowledge.insead.edu/Are You Addicted to Power?/Manfred F. R. Kets de Vries , INSEAD Distinguished Clinical Professor of Leadership Development & Organisational Change).

"The primary neurochemical involved in the reward of power that is known *today* is dopamine, the same chemical transmitter responsible for producing a sense of pleasure. Power activates the very same reward circuitry in the brain and creates an addictive 'high' in much the same way as drug addiction. Like addicts, most people in positions of power will seek to maintain the high they get from power, sometimes at all costs. When withheld, power – like any highly addictive agent – produces cravings at the cellular level that generate strong behavioural opposition to giving it up. In accountable societies, checks and balances exist to avoid the inevitable consequences of power. Yet, in cases where leaders possess absolute and unchecked power, changes in leadership and transitions to more consensus-based rule are unlikely to be smooth. Gradual withdrawal of absolute power is the only way to ensure that someone will be able to accept relinquishing it" (Source: The Oxford University Politics Blog/The Neurochemistry Of Power: Implications For Political Change/Nayef Al-Rodhan).

This is all to say that as the narcissistic person slowly becomes thirsty for more and more power, the individual will become more controlling, seductive, and manipulative. Spiritually speaking, it is illegal to control another human being, after all, God gave us the freedom of will. He allows us to make whatever decisions we want to make, but of course, every decision has rewards, perks, penalties, or punishments associated with it. In truth, it is the demon in that person that craves power. Why is this? To make it simple, consider these factors.

- God is Abba, and Abba means Source. He is our Source of everything, including power.
- Because God is our Source, like cell phones, we must remain plugged into Him.
- When Satan and his angels rebelled against God, the Lord unplugged them. Because of this, they now have no source of power, and like a cellphone powering down, they have to use whatever energy they have left to find something or someone to plug into.
- God divorced the devil and his angels, but He separated Himself from mankind. This means that we are still plugged into God, and when we get saved, we can once again access the power of God.
- Being in the darkness, we look radiant to demons. The more God we have, the more radiant we are. This light is what some witches refer to as auras. Do auras exist? Not really. What they are seeing is the measure of God that we have.
- Demons seek to possess or, at minimum, oppress us; this way, they can plug into us and steal God's glory from us.
- The more power a demon has, the more it ascends in rank and authority. Just like humans, demons too want to be promoted. This is why, according to the Bible, there are some spirits "more wicked" than others. This isn't just dealing with morality, it's talking about rank.

So now, you have a woman who's bound by the Jezebel spirit, and she's learned to manipulate others so that she can rob them of their authority. That spirit in her is not going to want to go out and about constantly looking for people to charm; instead, it will look for a primary source of power. This is when Jezebel goes out and finds herself an Ahab. Ahab is typically someone who is called by God, but because of their ambitious ways, lack of faith (fear), self-centered attitude, and idolatrous patterns, they have ignored the call of God to pursue what they believe will make them happy and safe. Ahabs are typically fearful, and most of them are relatively or incredibly lazy. They want the trappings of success and power without the responsibilities that come with it. They have a good amount of God in them because they are called by God. Many of them are called to the office of the prophet, the apostle, the pastor, the teacher, or the evangelist, but because they have exalted their preferences over God's plans, they are often resisted by God. This leads to them looking for an external source to get whatever it is that they are seeking, whether it's a spouse, wealth, or a word from God. This is what happened to King Saul. 1 Samuel 28:3-7 (ESV) reads, "Now Samuel had died, and all Israel had mourned for him and buried him in Ramah, his own city. And Saul had put the mediums and the necromancers out of the land. The Philistines assembled and came and encamped at Shunem. And Saul gathered all Israel, and they encamped at Gilboa. When Saul saw the army of the Philistines, he was afraid, and his heart trembled greatly. And when Saul inquired of the LORD, the LORD did not answer him, either by dreams, or by Urim, or by prophets. Then Saul said to his servants, 'Seek out for me a woman who is a medium, that I may go to her and inquire of her." And his servants said to him, "Behold, there is a medium at En-dor.' Once Saul noticed that God had left him, he didn't do like most believers; he didn't repent. Instead, Saul chose to look for another source. And this wasn't a strange thing given the fact that the king had rebelled against God before, and even then, he hadn't repented, signaling that Saul had the Jezebel spirit. Keep in mind in Revelation 2:21, God gave us one of the traits or characteristics of the Jezebel spirit, and that is—they cannot and will not repent. The scripture reads, "And I gave her space to repent of her fornication; and she repented not." The world of psychology echoes this truth as it states that narcissists will not change; they will not take accountability. Check out the scriptural story below to get a better understanding of Saul's previous crime against God.

- **1 Samuel 15:1-23:** Samuel also said unto Saul, The LORD sent me to anoint thee to be king over his people, over Israel: now therefore hearken thou unto the voice of the words of the LORD. Thus saith the LORD of hosts, I remember that which Amalek did to Israel, how he laid wait for him in the way, when he came up from Egypt. Now go and smite Amalek, and utterly destroy all that they have, and spare them not; but slay both man and woman, infant and suckling, ox and sheep, camel and ass. And Saul gathered the people together, and numbered them in Telaim, two hundred thousand footmen, and ten thousand men of Judah. And Saul came to a city of Amalek, and laid wait in the valley. And Saul said unto the Kenites, Go, depart, get you down from among the Amalekites, lest I destroy you with them: for ye shewed kindness to all the children of Israel, when they came up out of Egypt. So the Kenites departed from among the Amalekites. And Saul smote the Amalekites from Havilah until thou comest to Shur, that is over against Egypt. And he took Agag the king of the Amalekites alive, and utterly destroyed all the people with the edge of the sword. But Saul and the people spared Agag, and the best of the sheep, and of the oxen, and of the fatlings, and the lambs, and all that was good, and would not utterly destroy them: but everything that was vile and refuse, that they destroyed utterly. Then came the word of the LORD unto Samuel, saying, It repenteth me that I have set up Saul to be king: for he is turned back from following me, and hath not performed my commandments. And it grieved Samuel; and he cried unto the LORD all night. And when Samuel rose early to meet Saul in the morning, it was told Samuel, saying, Saul came to Carmel, and, behold, he set him up a place, and is gone about, and passed on, and gone down to Gilgal. And Samuel came to Saul: and Saul said unto him, Blessed be thou of the LORD: I have performed the commandment of the LORD. And Samuel said, What meaneth then this bleating of the sheep in mine ears, and the lowing of the oxen which I hear? And Saul said, They have brought them from the Amalekites: for the people spared the best of the sheep and of the oxen, to sacrifice unto the LORD thy God; and the rest we have utterly destroyed. Then Samuel said unto Saul, Stay, and I will tell thee what the LORD hath said to me this night. And he said unto him, Say on. And Samuel said, When thou wast little in thine own sight, wast thou not made the head of the tribes of Israel, and the LORD anointed thee king over Israel? And the LORD sent thee on a journey, and said, Go and utterly destroy the sinners the Amalekites, and fight against them until they be consumed.

Wherefore then didst thou not obey the voice of the LORD, but didst fly upon the spoil, and didst evil in the sight of the LORD? And Saul said unto Samuel, Yea, I have obeyed the voice of the LORD, and have gone the way which the LORD sent me, and have brought Agag the king of Amalek, and have utterly destroyed the Amalekites. But the people took of the spoil, sheep and oxen, the chief of the things which should have been utterly destroyed, to sacrifice unto the LORD thy God in Gilgal. And Samuel said, Hath the LORD as great delight in burnt offerings and sacrifices, as in obeying the voice of the LORD? Behold, to obey is better than sacrifice, and to hearken than the fat of rams. For rebellion is as the sin of witchcraft, and stubbornness is as iniquity and idolatry. Because thou hast rejected the word of the LORD, he hath also rejected thee from being king.

Now that we understand Saul's sin, let's check out his response to having been dethroned by God as king.

- **1 Samuel 15:24-30:** And Saul said unto Samuel, I have sinned: for I have transgressed the commandment of the LORD, and thy words: because I feared the people, and obeyed their voice. Now therefore, I pray thee, pardon my sin, and turn again with me, that I may worship the LORD. And Samuel said unto Saul, I will not return with thee: for thou hast rejected the word of the LORD, and the LORD hath rejected thee from being king over Israel. And as Samuel turned about to go away, he laid hold upon the skirt of his mantle, and it rent. And Samuel said unto him, The LORD hath rent the kingdom of Israel from thee this day, and hath given it to a neighbor of thine, that is better than thou. And also the Strength of Israel will not lie nor repent: for he is not a man, that he should repent. Then he said, I have sinned: yet honor me now, I pray thee, before the elders of my people, and before Israel, and turn again with me, that I may worship the LORD thy God.

Check out Saul's response! He wasn't appalled that he'd disappointed God, he was more concerned about his self-image. He made excuses for his behavior, and when the prophet began to walk away from him, he grabbed Samuel's skirt and ripped it. He said, in so many words, that if you come and honor me before the people, I will then be able to worship the Lord. This is to say that his obedience and his worship were conditional. Like many Jezebels before and after him, Saul saw God as *a* source and not *the* Source. And hear me, when the Lord left Saul, this was the equivalent of Him turning the king over to a reprobate mind. What exactly does it mean to have a reprobate mind?

The Greek word for "reprobate" is "adokimos," and it means unaccepted, rejected, or unapproved; it means to be condemned. To simplify this, demons have reprobate minds. Saul ended up with a reprobate mind because he refused to obey God. He then refused to repent after he'd been confronted by Samuel. Absalom had a reprobate mind, as he'd been given space and time to repent so that he could reconcile with his father, but his ambition, unforgiving nature, and bitterness blinded him to the opportunities that were before him. The Philistines were an entire nation of people who had reprobate minds in the Bible, as they seemed to be infatuated with taking the Hebrews down; the same was true for the Canaanites. You see, God gives us access to His Word, but many of us blindly read the Bible, not understanding most of what we've read. God treats our minds like they are our legs. Just like we can wonder with our minds, we can wander with our feet. In this, God ushers us forward or, better yet, into a greater measure of truth by illuminating what we've read in His Word. This is why you can read a scripture over a hundred times, and it won't make any sense to you; that is until one day, you open the Bible and read that scripture. All of a sudden, the scripture seems to jump off the page at you. Not only does it make sense, but it produces a tree called Revelation, whereas, everywhere you apply your newfound knowledge, you will find yourself gaining more knowledge and understanding. These are our proverbial Gardens of Eden; this is where we are able to access different types, heights, and depths of revelation, depending on how much God has illuminated or, better yet, revealed to us. This is the progression and ascension of the mind, not in thought as the pagans do, but in revelation. Revelation is a God-revealed truth. And get this—even the unsaved have a measure of access to these truths. This is what allows God to draw their hearts. However, to have a reprobate mind means that God has cut the cord between Himself and the person in question. It means that He has turned that individual over to (1) the lusts of the person's flesh or (2) a demon or Satan himself. Check out the following chart.

Crime	Scripture
Unforgiving nature	This charge I commit unto thee, son Timothy, according to the prophecies which went before on thee, that thou by them mightest war a good warfare; holding faith, and a good conscience; which some having put away concerning faith have made shipwreck: Of whom is Hymenaeus and Alexander; whom I have delivered unto Satan, that they may learn not to blaspheme. 1 Timothy 1:18-20
Dishonor	It is reported commonly that there is fornication among you, and such fornication as is not so much as named among the Gentiles, that one should have his father's wife. And ye are puffed up, and have not rather mourned, that he that hath done this deed might be taken away from among you. For I verily, as absent in body, but present in spirit, have judged already, as though I were present, concerning him that hath so done this deed, In the name of our Lord Jesus Christ, when ye are gathered together, and my spirit, with the power of our Lord Jesus Christ, to deliver such an one unto Satan for the destruction of the flesh, that the spirit may be saved in the day of the Lord Jesus. 1 Corinthians 5:1-5
Tolerating Jezebel	I know thy works, and charity, and service, and faith, and thy patience, and thy works; and the last to be more than the first. Notwithstanding I have a few things against thee, because thou sufferest that woman Jezebel, which calleth herself a prophetess, to teach and to seduce my servants to commit fornication, and to eat things sacrificed unto idols. And I gave her space to repent of her fornication; and she repented not. Behold, I will cast her into a bed, and them that commit adultery with her into great tribulation, except they repent of their deeds. And I will kill her children with

		death; and all the churches shall know that I am he which searcheth the reins and hearts: and I will give unto every one of you according to your works. Revelation 2:19-23
	Blasphemy	This charge I commit unto thee, son Timothy, according to the prophecies which went before on thee, that thou by them mightest war a good warfare; holding faith, and a good conscience; which some having put away concerning faith have made shipwreck: Of whom is Hymenaeus and Alexander; whom I have delivered unto Satan, that they may learn not to blaspheme. 1 Timothy 1:18-20

What we discover through the text is that a reprobate mind was God's way of not only casting someone out of His presence, in biblical times, many Israelites were cast out from among the people as well. Think of the curse of leprosy. Believe it or not, having leprosy during that stage and age was a death sentence; it also served as a divorce between the stricken person and the camp of Israel. Yes, this included their families; this is because, like sin, leprosy was highly contagious. Of course, there were several occasions when a leper had been miraculously healed by God, but other than that, leprosy was an incurable disease. Those instances included:

1. Moses' hand is suddenly leprous and is healed instantly (see Exodus 4:6-7).
2. The curing of Miriam (see Numbers 12:15).
3. The healing of Naaman (see 2 Kings 5:13-14).
4. Jesus cures a single leper (see Mark 1:40-45).
5. The curing of the ten leprous men by Jesus (see Luke 17:12-24).

Notice that outside of Moses' incident, every leper needed an intercessor to be restored. This brings some light to the question, "Can someone with a reprobate mind be restored?" The answer is this—a person who has been turned over to a debased or reprobate mind has no desire to be restored. That person, quite frankly, is not only narcissistic, but that individual is a full-blown narcissist. He or she may even be a sociopath or a psychopath. But notice that the people who were guilty of lying with and tolerating Jezebel could repent and be delivered from the woes of Jezebel. This is what Jonah did. He repented from within the flesh-covered grave he found himself in; he'd repented while inside of the great fish (likely Leviathan), and because of this, God delivered him. But Jonah didn't just repent, Jonah said yes to his assignment. This is to say that the key to breakthrough from Jezebel is locked behind your yes to God. Going back to the topic at hand. Can someone with a reprobate mind be restored? Potentially, but I wouldn't count on it. An intercessor can potentially get that person back into the fold; that is if the person desires God once God opens the way of escape for him or her, but the likelihood of a narcissist becoming a productive, loving, or sane member of a family, a society, or an organization is slim to none. I don't share this to discourage you; I share this to enlighten you. You see, a lot of people tolerate Jezebel because they can clearly see the potential of the narcissistic person. As a matter of fact, one of Satan's favorite games is to:

1. Let you meet the person who your friend, lover, or family member was supposed to be; this is the human, the gifted individual, and the masterpiece of God. This is what draws you in; this is what charms you.

2. Draw you into the person's potential. After you meet the individual in question, you may find yourself, for example, falling in love with the person.

3. Get you to sign a contract with your tongue. The narcissistic individual may say things like, "Everyone leaves me. I know you're going to leave me at some point" or "Promise me that you won't ever walk away from me? I love you." From there, you begin to make a ton of oaths, promises, and declarations; in this, you sign an agreement with Jezebel promising not to walk away. Satan continues to get you to initial and sign your name on different pages of the contract when, for example, you are engaging in sex with the narcissist, and while in the middle of the act, you will likely find yourself proclaiming that your body, your genitals, or your soul altogether belongs to the person you're sleeping with. Once again, this is a verbal contract, and it is the reason that so many people find it nearly impossible to walk away from Jezebel.

4. Get you to start mixing your stuff with Jezebel's stuff. For example, your new boyfriend may start letting you drive his car, or your new girlfriend may encourage you to leave some of your possessions at her house. All of these are offerings to Jezebel.

5. Peel back the mask one conversation, one argument, and one incident at a time. Now that you are soul-tied to Jezebel, that devil in Jezebel needs to become a familiar spirit in your life; it needs to create an addiction of sorts so that even if you leave your narcissistic lover, you will constantly run into the arms of another narcissist. This is because per your contract, you are now Jezebel's property.

This is to say that while not all narcissistic people have been turned over to reprobate minds, many of them have; this is especially true for the ones who have been diagnosed or could be diagnosed with Narcissistic Personality Disorder if they were to be tested. Is there hope for the incredibly narcissistic ones? Yes, but again, you'd have a better chance at winning the lottery one-hundred times over than witnessing an incredibly narcissistic person truly repent. Howbeit, with God, all things are possible.

Also note that while children are naturally narcissistic, this does not mean that they have the Jezebel spirit. Some of them do, but you won't know which child is bound versus which ones are not until a child reaches a certain age. In the field of psychology, a child cannot be diagnosed with Narcissistic Personality Disorder until that child is an adult (at least 18-years of age).

Covert Narcissism

Narcissism is a personality disorder characterized by grandiosity, a sense of entitlement, and a lack of empathy. A narcissist, in general, is someone who is excessively self-centered, self-absorbed, and has an inflated sense of self-importance. While most people have a reasonable degree of self-love and self-esteem, narcissists take it to the extreme. However, not all narcissists are the same, and some have a covert form of the disorder, flying under the radar, and remaining hidden in the shadows. In this lesson, we'll discuss covert narcissism—what it is, how it works, and why it's essential to recognize and understand it.

The concept of covert narcissism appears to be a somewhat new development in the field of psychology. Whereas in the past, the focus was on identifying the more traditional, grandiose narcissist, researchers and clinicians have now identified a sub-type of narcissism that is not as obvious or easily identifiable. These individuals are referred to as covert narcissists, and they tend to be introverted, hypersensitive, and present themselves as victims. Since they don't display the typical features of a narcissist, they can be challenging to recognize, but their effects are no less damaging. One of the reasons that covert narcissism is difficult to identify is because the narcissistic behavior is suppressed, repressed, or hidden beneath a veneer of self-sacrifice and humility. Covertness is exemplified in the individual's unwillingness to share their feelings and thoughts, or to reveal their true intentions or desires to others. They may seem genuine and open, but in reality, they are only sharing the parts of themselves that they want others to see. They are capable of living an apparently selfless lifestyle, appearing to put others first and regularly working behind the scenes to maintain their sense of superiority and control.

Another characteristic feature of covert narcissism is a pervasive hypersensitivity to criticism or perceived slights of any kind. They are highly reactive to perceived rejection, and seek constant validation and approval from others. Along with this comes a need to control others and their environment, which can manifest in two ways: either aggressively, through manipulation and coercion, or passively, by presenting themselves as helpless or ineffectual. Whichever way it shows up, the goal is always to maintain power and control over others. For example, covert narcissists always maintain an imaginary sense of vulnerability and victimization, despite the fact that, in reality, they are manipulating and controlling others to maintain a fragile ego. They may appear sympathetic, charming or cooperative, but it is all a means to an end, demonstrating the mastery of their social performance. These individuals possess an unshakable sense of entitlement, which fuels their demands for admiration and loyalty. They feel that they deserve to be treated special at all times, and when they are not—the perceived slight usually leads to them showing their true colors eventually.

This is to say that covert narcissism is a challenging and complex aspect of narcissistic personality disorder. Its covert nature and the deceptive strategies make it difficult to identify and often enable it to go unrecognized, both by the narcissists themselves and by those around them. Their ability to hide behind a façade of humility, pretentiousness, and personable charm presents a notable contrast to the grandiose, overtly narcissist counterpart, making diagnosing it a complex and often frustrating task. Regardless of this, however, it is crucial that we recognize and understand covert narcissism since it can be equally, if not more, damaging to those who are in its proximity. These individuals can cause intense emotional damage to those who dare to question their self-image, and it can escalate to a point of severe emotional control and manipulation. As such, knowledge and awareness of covert narcissism may cease the harm it causes in its tracks, which is undoubtedly a good thing.

This particular narcissist is incredibly intelligent, and may demonstrate a level of mastery over his or her emotions that the overt narcissist does not possess. If you have ever had the displeasure of emotionally engaging a covert narcissist, one thing you've likely come to realize is that these particular types of Jezebels love to surround themselves with people who are more assertive and confident than they are. The reason for this is—most people tend to see the assertive, more outspoken person as the villain when issues arise between that individual and the covert narcissist who appears to be more soft-spoken, shy, and peaceable. All the same, covert narcissists specialize in reactive abuse. What is reactive abuse? Choosing Therapy published the following info:

> "In a situation where one person abuses another, the other person may react. When this happens, the person who caused harm may be on the receiving end of an attack. They may then claim that the abused individual (who is acting in self-defense) is the abuser. This is a type of gaslighting called reactive abuse. It gives the one causing harm something

to hold over the abused person's head" (Source: Choosing Therapy/Reactive Abuse: Signs, Effects, & How to Get Help/Silvi Saxena, MBA, MSW, LSW, CCTP, OSW-C)

A great example of reactive abuse is—let's say that Tony is a narcissist, and his wife, Trudy, has been on the receiving end of his narcissism for four years. And Tony isn't your ordinary narcissist. He's a covert narcissist.

It's Thanksgiving Day, and the couple have left the house of Trudy's parents to go and eat dinner with a few of their friends. The couple has been arguing all day about Tony's ex-girlfriend, Sonya. Trudy had just found out that her husband is still in contact with his ex, and the two have been in contact for well over three years, nearly the length of their marriage. Trudy is incredibly upset, and rightfully so! Tony, on the other hand, claims that it's no big deal, the two are just friends, and that their contact has been strictly over the phone, but Trudy knows better. After all, Tony has been behaving oddly for the last few months, including his insistence on getting a new wardrobe, his sudden fascination with silk boxers, and his newfound interest in veneers. To make matters worse, Tony received a text message from Sonya earlier that day, and his wife saw the message. In the message, Sonya thanked Tony for showing her such a good time at the park. Of course, Tony told his wife that she was talking about a park visit they'd had some five years prior. "I don't know why she's thanking me about something that happened five years ago," Tony says nervously. After this, Tony changes the password to his phone, and the two begin to argue all the more. An hour later, they arrive at Brenda's, a popular restaurant in their city. After they arrive, Tony attempts to hold his wife's hand, but Trudy snatches her hand away and marches ahead of her husband. Not wanting their friends to know that they've been fighting, the couple fight back their anger as they open the door to the restaurant. Twenty minutes later, Trudy looks over at her husband, who happens to be sitting across from her, and notices that he keeps looking at his phone and chuckling. It's clear that he's been receiving text messages from someone, but it's also clear that he doesn't want her to know who he's texting. This is because every time Tony responds to a message, he places his phone face-down on the table. "Crazy," Tony says, giggling as he prepares to respond to another message, but before he can finish typing, he sees his wife stand to her feet. As he looks up at her, he's suddenly doused with the sweet tea she'd been drinking. Trudy then throws her glass at Tony's chest before storming out of the restaurant. This is an example of reactive abuse; it's when an abuser silently triggers his victim, thus provoking the victim to react loudly and violently. This causes the abused party to appear to be mentally unstable, hotheaded, and violent, thus allowing the victimizer to play the role of the victim. Covert narcissists are often masters of this particular game, as they often appear to be innocent, shy, and incredibly kind. And with these particular types of narcissists, the more assertive and confident party often appears (to others) to be the Jezebel or the toxic individual, whereas the manipulator is able to cast himself or herself as the pushover.

Overt Narcissism

Again, narcissism is a term that has been utilized to describe individuals who exhibit excessive admiration and love for themselves. Overt narcissism specifically pertains to the manifestation of narcissistic behavior through grandiose and attention-seeking actions. This type of narcissism is often characterized by a lack of empathy, arrogance, and a sense of entitlement that can significantly impact the individual's relationships and overall quality of life. While some may argue that a certain level of narcissism is necessary to foster self-confidence and success, overt narcissism can have detrimental effects on both the individual and those around them. Why is this? Individuals with overt narcissism often exhibit an inflated sense of self-worth and importance. They may engage in grandiose behaviors, such as boasting about their talents and achievements without considering the opinions of others. These individuals crave attention and admiration and may go to great lengths to obtain them. They may seek out praise and admiration from others, even going as far as to manipulate situations to gain attention. Overtly narcissistic individuals may also disregard the needs and feelings of others, believing that they are the only ones who matter. However, behind this seemingly confident exterior, overt narcissists may be deeply insecure. They often use their grandiose and attention-seeking behaviors as a mask to hide their true feelings of inadequacy, inferiority, and self-doubt. While this may explain some of the reasons why an individual may engage in overtly narcissistic behaviors, it does not excuse their actions. An individual's insecurity does not give them the right to treat others poorly or engage in behaviors that negatively impact those around them.

Overt narcissism can have significant effects on relationships. Individuals with overt narcissism may be difficult to be around, and their inability to empathize with others can make them harsh and judgmental. Their sense of entitlement can cause them to disregard the feelings of others and view others as simply objects or tools to be used for their own benefit. These attitudes can lead to difficulties in both personal and professional relationships, making it challenging for overtly narcissistic individuals to form and maintain healthy connections with others. Additionally, the presence of overt narcissism can also impact the individual's overall well-being. It can lead to a great deal of stress, anxiety, and depression, as the individual struggles with the realization that their grandiose beliefs may not match up with reality. These individuals may also struggle with feelings of loneliness, as their behaviors and attitudes often push others away. While overt narcissists may initially appear to be confident and self-assured, their true inner turmoil can often go unrecognized, leading to a further deterioration of their mental health.

This is simply to say that overt narcissism is a dangerous manifestation of narcissistic behavior that can have significant impacts on both the individual and those around them. These individuals often exhibit grandiose behaviors and a sense of entitlement that can make it difficult to form and maintain healthy relationships. However, it is important to recognize that overt narcissism may stem from feelings of inadequacy and insecurity that should not be ignored. Rather than enabling or validating these behaviors, the individual should seek professional help, along with deliverance, and work towards improving their overall well-being.

Adaptive Narcissism

Adaptive narcissism is characterized by a grandiose sense of self-importance and a constant need for admiration, while yet possessing the ability to use these traits in a functional and even beneficial manner. While narcissism is often portrayed in a negative light, adaptive narcissism has unique characteristics that make it distinct from pathological narcissism.

One of the key features of adaptive narcissism is the ability to use one's self-confidence and high self-esteem to achieve success in various areas of life. People with adaptive narcissism tend to be ambitious, driven, and highly motivated individuals who are not afraid to take risks and pursue their goals with determination. They are often seen as charismatic and influential leaders, utilizing their self-assuredness to inspire and motivate others.

Another aspect of adaptive narcissism is the ability to effectively manage relationships. Unlike pathological narcissists who often struggle with maintaining meaningful connections with others, those with adaptive narcissism are adept at forming and sustaining positive and mutually beneficial relationships. They are often seen as charming and sociable, using their charisma and confidence to gain the admiration and support of others. Furthermore, adaptive narcissism is associated with a strong sense of resilience and the ability to bounce back from setbacks. While narcissists are often seen as fragile and easily wounded, individuals with adaptive narcissism possess a robust sense of self and are able to weather criticism and adversity with grace and composure. They do not let rejection or failure derail their ambition and drive, but instead, use it as fuel to further propel themselves towards their goals.

In addition, individuals with adaptive narcissism also have a keen sense of self-awareness. They are able to recognize their own strengths and weaknesses, and are open to feedback and self-improvement. They do not perceive themselves as infallible and are willing to learn and grow from their experiences. This self-awareness allows them to navigate their own narcissistic traits in a way that benefits both themselves and those around them. However, it is important to note that while adaptive narcissism possesses many positive attributes, there is a fine line between adaptive and maladaptive narcissism. It is essential for individuals with adaptive narcissistic traits to remain mindful of their behavior and its impact on others. Without proper self-awareness and self-regulation, adaptive narcissism can easily evolve into a more harmful form of narcissism that is detrimental to both the individual and those around them. In other words, in adaptive narcissism, the spirit of Jezebel may be in its infancy stage, thus allowing the human to retain a great deal of his or her humanity. However, over time, that demon can and often does grow in rank, and when it does, it reappears as maladaptive narcissism.

Antagonistic Narcissism

Antagonistic narcissism is a personality disorder characterized by a grandiose sense of self-importance, a lack of empathy for others, and a tendency to manipulate and exploit others for personal gain. Individuals with antagonistic narcissism often display a hostile and aggressive attitude towards others, seeking to undermine and belittle them in order to elevate their own sense of superiority. These individuals may exhibit traits such as arrogance, a sense of entitlement, and a need for constant admiration and attention. They may also engage in behaviors such as lying, manipulation, and exploitation in order to achieve their goals and maintain their self-image.

Antagonistic narcissism can have a detrimental impact on interpersonal relationships, as the individual's lack of empathy and regard for others can lead to harm and exploitation of those around them. Their tendency to manipulate and exploit others will often result in negative outcomes for those who come into contact with them.

Antagonistic narcissism differs from other types of narcissistic behavior in that it is characterized by a more hostile, aggressive, and confrontational approach to interpersonal relationships and interactions. This type of narcissism is often marked by a need to dominate and control others, as well as a tendency to be overly critical, judgmental, and vindictive towards others. Antagonistic narcissists may also exhibit a lack of empathy and a tendency to exploit or manipulate others for their own gain. Overall, their behavior is marked by a more overt and aggressive expression of narcissistic traits, as compared to other types of narcissistic behavior which may be more subtle or covert.

Cerebral Narcissism

Cerebral narcissism is a psychological condition characterized by an individual's excessive focus on their intellectual abilities and achievements. This often includes feelings of superiority. People with cerebral narcissism often display a sense of grandiosity, lack of empathy, and a strong need for admiration and validation from others.

Individuals with cerebral narcissism tend to constantly seek out opportunities to showcase their intellectual prowess and knowledge, often belittling others in the process. They may also engage in conversations or debates solely to prove their superiority and display their intellectual dominance. Additionally, they may have a limited capacity for genuine emotional connections and empathy, as they are primarily focused on their own intellectual achievements and status.

Cerebral narcissism can have a significant impact on an individual's relationships and social interactions. Their need for constant admiration and validation can lead to difficulties in maintaining healthy and meaningful connections with others. Furthermore, their lack of empathy can result in a lack of understanding and consideration for the feelings and perspectives of those around them.

Communal Narcissism

Communal narcissism refers to the shared sense of grandiosity, entitlement, and self-importance within a group or community. This phenomenon can manifest in various social, religious, or national groups, where collective identity is emphasized and celebrated above individual accomplishments. Communal narcissism can lead to an exaggerated sense of superiority and a belief in the group's inherent sovereignty, often leading to the exclusion or devaluation of outsiders. All the same, communal narcissism can have both seemingly positive and overtly negative implications for the group. On one hand, it can foster a strong sense of unity and cohesion, creating a sense of unity and togetherness for its members. On the other hand, it can fuel hatred, prejudice, and hostility towards those who are perceived as different or inferior.

Moreover, communal narcissism can lead to a group's resistance to change or criticism, which can hinder growth, progress, and collaboration with others. It is important for communities to recognize and address any tendencies towards communal narcissism in order to promote God's love, acceptance, and empathy.

Exhibitionist Narcissism

Exhibitionist narcissists are individuals who derive their self-worth and validation from seeking attention and admiration from others. These individuals display a grandiose sense of self-importance, a constant need for admiration, and a lack of empathy for others. They often engage in exaggerated self-promotion and seek to be the center of attention in social and professional settings.

Exhibitionist narcissists often engage in attention-seeking behaviors such as constant bragging, excessive self-admiration, and a tendency to exaggerate their achievements and talents. They may also seek out opportunities to be in the spotlight, whether it be through public speaking, performing, or displaying their physical appearance. This need for constant attention and validation causes exhibitionist narcissists to become highly competitive, demanding, and intolerant of criticism.

While exhibitionist narcissists may appear confident and charismatic on the surface, their constant need for admiration and attention can often mask a deep-seated insecurity and fear of rejection. This can lead to volatile and unstable relationships, as well as feelings of emptiness and low self-worth. They exhibit a pattern of behavior that is characterized by an excessive need for attention, a lack of empathy, and an inflated sense of self-importance.

Maladaptive Narcissism

Maladaptive narcissism refers to a maladaptive personality trait; characterized by an excessive need for admiration, a lack of empathy, and a sense of entitlement. It is a personality disorder that can have a significant impact on an individual's personal and professional relationships, as well as their overall well-being.

Maladaptive narcissism is a complex personality trait that can manifest in various ways. Individuals with maladaptive narcissism often display grandiosity, a sense of superiority, and a need for constant validation from others. They may believe that they are special and unique, and may expect special treatment from others. Additionally, they may lack empathy for others and have difficulty understanding or relating to the emotions of others. This can lead to difficulties in forming and maintaining close relationships, as well as conflicts in interpersonal interactions. Furthermore, individuals with maladaptive narcissism may struggle with a fragile sense of self-esteem, and may be highly sensitive to criticism or perceived slights. They may become defensive or angry when their self-image is challenged, and they may resort to manipulation, humiliation, or aggression in order to maintain their sense of superiority. This can lead to conflict and tension in relationships, as well as difficulties in the workplace or other social settings.

The causes of maladaptive narcissism are complex and multifaceted. Research suggests that genetic and environmental factors play a role in the development of maladaptive narcissism. Individuals who have experienced early childhood trauma, neglect, or abuse may be more likely to develop maladaptive narcissism as a way of coping with their emotional pain. Additionally, a lack of appropriate parental role models or family dynamics that emphasize achievement and superiority can contribute to the development of maladaptive narcissism. In addition to these environmental factors, there is evidence to suggest that genetic factors may also play a role in the development of maladaptive narcissism.

Studies have shown that individuals with a family history of narcissistic personality traits may be more likely to develop maladaptive narcissism themselves. Furthermore, certain personality traits, such as low self-esteem or a fragile sense of self, may also contribute to the development of maladaptive narcissism.

Malignant Narcissism

Malignant narcissism is a clinical term used to describe individuals who exhibit extreme narcissistic behaviors coupled with a marked lack of empathy and a propensity for exploiting others for their own gain. This condition is characterized by a pervasive pattern of grandiosity, a need for admiration, and a lack of empathy for others. In addition to these core features, individuals with malignant narcissism may also demonstrate a high level of aggression, manipulation, and a willingness to exploit others without remorse.

One of the most concerning aspects of malignant narcissism is the potential for individuals with this condition to engage in harmful and abusive behaviors towards others. This may include emotional, psychological, and even physical abuse. Individuals with this condition may view others as mere objects to be manipulated and used for their own benefit without any consideration for the well-being of others.

It is important to recognize the signs of malignant narcissism in order to protect oneself and others from potential harm. If you suspect that someone in your life may exhibit malignant narcissistic traits, it is important to seek support and take steps to protect yourself from potential harm. It is also important to seek professional help in order to better understand and address this condition.

Somatic Narcissism

Somatic narcissists are individuals who primarily focus on their physical appearance and attractiveness as a means of seeking validation and admiration from others. These individuals often prioritize their looks, fitness, and sexual prowess above all else, and are overly preoccupied with their physical appearance, often engaging in excessive self-care routines while seeking out attention and praise for their physical attributes.

Somatic narcissists use their physical appearance as a tool to gain attention and admiration from others, often using their looks to manipulate and control those around them. They may become enraged if they feel that they are not receiving enough attention or admiration for their physical attributes, and may go to great lengths to seek out validation from others.

While somatic narcissists may present themselves as confident and self-assured, their obsession with their physical appearance often masks deep-seated insecurities and a fragile sense of self-worth. Their constant need for validation and admiration can lead to shallow and superficial relationships, as they are unable to form deep, meaningful connections with others beyond the physical realm.

Ultimately, the somatic narcissist's focus on their physical appearance serves as a means of masking their deep-seated insecurities and lack of emotional depth, making it difficult for them to form genuine and meaningful connections with others.

Jezebel

Jezebel - the name itself has become synonymous with manipulation, deceit, and seduction. She's the ultimate femme fatale whose name has echoed throughout history as a blood-thirsty, ravenous, and deceitful woman.

Jezebel was the queen of Israel during the reign of King Ahab, her husband. She was a powerful and influential woman who was known for her ruthlessness. Jezebel was the daughter of the King of Tyre, a wealthy and powerful city-state in ancient times. Her marriage to King Ahab was a strategic alliance, designed to strengthen the relationship between Israel and Tyre. This is why the name Ahab is synonymous with fear, betrayal of the faith, and ungodly ambition. You see, back in that time, it was not uncommon for smaller or weaker nations to partner with other nations that were deemed to be larger, stronger, richer, and more influential. However, God had already warned Israel not to partner or yoke themselves with the surrounding pagan nations. This is to say that Ahab's decision to create a pact with Ethbaal, Jezebel's father, was in direct defiance of God. This signaled that:

1. He did not trust God to protect Israel.
2. He had been led astray by the spirit of fear.
3. He was ambitious; he put his desires and demands before God's will.
4. Because of his selfishness and idolatrous ways, he did not have God's heart for God's people.
5. He wrestled with the spirit of rebellion.

Amazingly enough, all of the aforementioned traits perfectly describe the spirit of Ahab that many people are bound by today. All the same, believers who wrestle with rebellion also wrestle with pride, ego, jealousy, envy, and entitlement.

Jezebel was a woman of extraordinary ambition, and she did not hesitate to use her position and power to further her demonic agenda. This truth became evident when her husband, Ahab, started lusting after the vineyard of a citizen named Naboth. The story is found in 1 Kings 21:1-16, which reads, "And it came to pass after these things, that Naboth the Jezreelite had a vineyard, which was in Jezreel, hard by the palace of Ahab king of Samaria. And Ahab spake unto Naboth, saying, Give me thy vineyard, that I may have it for a garden of herbs, because it is near unto my house: and I will give thee for it a better vineyard than it; or, if it seem good to thee, I will give thee the worth of it in money. And Naboth said to Ahab, The LORD forbid it me, that I should give the inheritance of my fathers unto thee. And Ahab came into his house heavy and displeased because of the word which Naboth the Jezreelite had spoken to him: for he had said, I will not give thee the inheritance of my fathers. And he laid him down upon his bed, and turned away his face, and would eat no bread. But Jezebel his wife came to him, and said unto him, Why is thy spirit so sad, that thou eatest no bread? And he said unto her, Because I spake unto Naboth the Jezreelite, and said unto him, Give me thy vineyard for money; or else, if it please thee, I will give thee another vineyard for it: and he answered, I will not give thee my vineyard. And Jezebel his wife said unto him, Dost thou now govern the kingdom of Israel? Arise, and eat bread, and let thine heart be merry: I will give thee the vineyard of Naboth the Jezreelite. So she wrote letters in Ahab's name, and sealed them with his seal, and sent the letters unto the elders and to the nobles that were in his city, dwelling with Naboth. And she wrote in the letters, saying, Proclaim a fast, and set Naboth on high among the people: And set two men, sons of Belial, before him, to bear witness against him, saying, Thou didst blaspheme God and the king. And then carry him out, and stone him, that he may die. And the men of his city, even the elders and the nobles who were the inhabitants in his city, did as Jezebel had sent unto them, and as it was written in the letters which she had sent unto them. They proclaimed a fast, and set Naboth on high among the people. And there came in two men, children of Belial, and sat before him: and the men of Belial witnessed against him, even against Naboth, in the presence of the people, saying, Naboth did blaspheme God and the king. Then they carried him forth out of the city, and stoned him with stones, that he died. Then they sent to Jezebel, saying, Naboth is stoned, and is dead. And it came to pass, when Jezebel heard that Naboth was stoned, and was dead, that Jezebel said to Ahab, Arise, take possession of the vineyard of Naboth the Jezreelite, which he refused to give thee for money: for Naboth is not alive, but dead. And it came to pass, when Ahab heard that Naboth was dead, that Ahab rose up to go down to the vineyard of Naboth the Jezreelite, to take possession of it."

Jezebel was a fierce advocate for the worship of Baal, a demon disguising itself as the god of fertility and prosperity; this devil was widely worshiped in the Eastern world. She built temples to Baal and encouraged the Israelites to abandon their traditional worship of YAHWEH, the God of Israel who, of course, is the one and only true and living God." As you can see, anything or anyone who got in Jezebel's way would be demolished, as one of the tell-tale traits of the Jezebel spirit is its inability to control itself when someone denies it access to whatever it is that Jezebel wants. This is why people who have this vile spirit can be incredibly malicious whenever someone tells them no.

Jezebel was idolatrous; she was a polytheistic woman. Polytheism is the worship of multiple deities. Jezebel's zeal for Baal worship made her enemies among the Israelites, particularly among the prophets of YAHWEH. They saw her for what she was—a dangerous influence, leading the people of Israel astray from the true faith. Of course, Jezebel was not one to take criticism lightly, and she responded to this opposition with brutal force. She ordered the execution of many of God's prophets and she pursued those who opposed her with a fierce determination. This is why Obadiah hid 100 of God's prophets in caves. "For it was so, when Jezebel cut off the prophets of the Lord, that Obadiah took an hundred prophets, and hid them by fifty in a cave, and fed them with bread and water" (1 Kings 18:4). This is also why I often tell people that Satan destroys more prophets than God gets to use. A prophet in a cave is, in most cases, impotent. While the prophet can be delivered, many prophets who go into the cave season never escape that particular season because they often become slaves of:
1. The spirit of fear.

2. The stronghold of comfort.

Yes, this is to say that comfort is the enemy of progression, and the large majority of God's prophets are called, but only a few are chosen; this is because most prophets and prophetic people idolize comfort. This anchors the prophetic individual, thus making the prophet or prophetic person a sitting duck for Jezebel (the narcissist).

Of course, Jezebel's power, privilege, and influence did not go unchallenged. The prophet Elijah, one of the most revered figures in the Old Testament, rose up to challenge her. He called down fire from Heaven to defeat the prophets of Baal in the oh-so-famous showdown on Mount Carmel. Jezebel did not take this defeat lightly, however. She swore vengeance against Elijah, thus striking fear in the heart of the prophet. In 1 Kings 18, we witness Elijah walking in the fullness of his God-given authority when he confronted the prophets of Baal. He challenged Baal's prophets to a showdown, where God showed up and showed out by raining fire on Elijah's altar. You would think that would be enough to turn the hearts of the people for good, but understand this—any kingdom, family, or organization that is ruled by someone who has the Jezebel spirit will be filled with both men and women who are bound by that wicked entity. In other words, wherever Ahab serves as a ruling spirit, you will find a lot of men and women bound by the Ahab spirit. One thing you'll come to learn about people who are bound by the Ahab spirit is that they are addicted to Jezebel's abuse and control; they may complain about their narcissistic spouses, lovers, or parents, and every time you think they are finally ready to leave Jezebel, they will go back into her custody for another round of mistreatment. This is what many of the Israelites did after Elijah demonstrated that YAHWEH is the only true and living God. A day later, they were unsure again. How do we know this? Because Jezebel was still in authority. Jezebel cannot remain in power unless she has an Ahab to steal authority from and rule over. Ahab cannot remain in authority unless he has people under his rule that he can rob of their authority. This is why many men and women bound by the Ahab spirit are often thought to be bound by the Jezebel spirit, and this is not entirely wrong. After all, Ahab and Jezebel are married in the realm of the spirit, and what belongs to Ahab belongs to Jezebel, but what belongs to Jezebel is given as an offering to Baal.

Going back to the statement, "A prophet in a cave is, in most cases, impotent," let's look at 1 Kings 19 to see how this looks to God. 1 Kings 19:1-16 reads, "And Ahab told Jezebel all that Elijah had done, and withal how he had slain all the prophets with the sword. Then Jezebel sent a messenger unto Elijah, saying, So let the gods do to me, and more also, if I make not thy life as the life of one of them by tomorrow about this time. And when he saw that, he arose, and went for his life, and came to Beersheba, which belongeth to Judah, and left his servant there. But he himself went a day's journey into the wilderness, and came and sat down under a juniper tree: and he requested for himself that he might die; and said, It is enough; now, O Lord, take away my life; for I am not better than my fathers. And as he lay and slept under a juniper tree, behold, then an angel touched him, and said unto him, Arise and eat. And he looked, and, behold, there was a cake baken on the coals, and a cruse of water at his head. And he did eat and drink, and laid him down again. And the angel of the Lord came again the second time, and touched him, and said, Arise and eat; because the journey is too great for thee. And he arose, and did eat and drink, and went in the strength of that meat forty days and forty nights unto Horeb the mount of God. And he came thither unto a cave, and lodged there; and, behold, the word of the Lord came to him, and he said unto him, What doest thou here, Elijah? And he said, I have been very jealous for the Lord God of hosts: for the children of Israel have forsaken thy covenant, thrown down thine altars, and slain thy prophets with the sword; and I, even I only, am left; and they seek my life, to take it away. And he said, Go forth, and stand upon the mount before the Lord. And, behold, the Lord passed by, and a great and strong wind rent the mountains, and brake in pieces the rocks before the Lord; but the Lord was not in the wind: and after the wind an earthquake; but the Lord was not in the earthquake: And after the earthquake a fire; but the Lord was not in the fire: and after the fire a still small voice. And it was so, when Elijah heard it, that he wrapped his face in his mantle, and went out, and stood in the entering in of the cave. And, behold, there came a voice unto him, and said, What doest thou here, Elijah? And he said, I have been very jealous for the Lord God of hosts: because the children of Israel have forsaken thy covenant, thrown down thine altars, and slain thy prophets with the sword; and I, even I only, am left; and they seek my life, to take it away. And the Lord said unto him, Go, return on thy way to the wilderness of Damascus: and when thou comest, anoint Hazael to be king over Syria: And Jehu the son of Nimshi shalt thou anoint to be king over Israel: and Elisha the son of Shaphat of Abelmeholah shalt thou anoint to be prophet in thy room." What can we take from this story?

1. Even though Elijah had just witnessed the miraculous power of God, he became fearful when Jezebel sent a threat promising to have him slaughtered in 24 hours or less.

2. Elijah forgot about his mantle and his assignment, and went on the run for his life. Read this carefully—fear enters the prophet/prophetic person whenever the enemy can usher that individual into self-preservation, also known as selfishness, survivor's mode, self-worship, and self-righteousness.

3. When Elijah ran, not just from Jezebel, but from God's will, he was stricken with depression, and thus became suicidal. This was the proverbial "great fish" that swallowed him for a season.

4. Even though Elijah was now in rebellion, God sent an angel to comfort, feed, and minister to him.

5. For 40 days and 40 nights, God strengthened Elijah until he went into a cave. This is when the Word of the Lord came to him. In other words, Elijah had an encounter with God.

6. God confronted Elijah because the strength of the prophet is found in the will of God, and Elijah had been given time to heal, repent, and return to God's will, but instead of doing any of these, his mental health continued to decline. Again, this has everything to do with selfishness and comfort. You see, you can become comfortable with being a victim.

7. When God questioned Elijah, the prophet began to exalt himself, all the while, putting God's people down. He said, "I have been very jealous for the Lord God of hosts: for the children of Israel have forsaken thy covenant, thrown down thine altars, and slain thy prophets with the

sword; and I, even I only, am left; and they seek my life, to take it away." This is INCREDIBLY common for prophets and prophetic people, especially after they have been in a great deal of warfare. They begin to think that they are the only prophets left or that there are only a handful of true prophets left. They see every other believer who claims to be a prophet as a defector. These days, you will find that these types of prophetic voices are often bound by the spirit of religion, they center their ministries around messages of doom and gloom, they tend to self-isolate, and they often come against other men and women of God because they are absolutely convinced that they are alone in their endeavors to serve the Most High God. This is almost always the evidence that the prophetic individual has been wounded, and this particular wound can and does lead to depression, isolation, social anxiety, suspicion, schizophrenia, and demonic bondage.

8. God called Elijah out of the cave before He began to destroy it. This is because a cave, for a prophet, can and does become a coffin of sorts.

9. Once Elijah came out of the cave, God questioned him again, and once again, Elijah blamed his decision to go on the run on the state of God's people. This is never the correct answer! Accountability and humility moves God, but finger-pointing and self-exaltation both signal to God that the burden or the assignment is too heavy for the prophet/prophetic individual.

10. After God ministered to Elijah, he had Elijah to pass on his mantle to the prophet, Elisha.

Needless to say, Jezebel's story ends in tragedy (for her) but deliverance (for Israel). She was ultimately thrown out of a window by her own servants, at the command of Jehu, a rival king who had come to power in Israel. Her body was eaten by dogs, and her story serves as a cautionary tale of the dangers of ambition and power. Remember, Jezebel was the daughter of Ethbaal, the king of Sidon, and married King Ahab of Israel, who reigned in the ninth century BCE. Ahab was notorious for allowing the worship of other gods, in contrast to the Jewish monotheistic belief, and Jezebel, who was a priestess of the cult of Baal, reportedly encouraged him to do so. She also persecuted the prophets and followers of YAHWEH and had them killed. This led to her being known as the evil and manipulative woman who corrupted the king of Israel and brought down God's wrath upon the nation. Jezebel's endorsement of Baal worship and her hostility towards the prophets of God made her an enemy of the Jewish people, whose religion, faith, and culture were threatened by Ahab's alliance with her.

In popular culture, Jezebel's name often symbolizes promiscuity, control, and wickedness in women. This perception can be traced back to the medieval church, which associated Jezebel with the whore of Babylon from the Book of Revelation. In modern times, Jezebel's name is sometimes used to describe assertive or opinionated women who challenge male authority and the status quo, however, as you'll soon come to learn, the Jezebel spirit can inhabit both men and women. As a matter of fact, Narcissistic Personality Disorder is more prevalent in men than it is in women. According to Promises Behavioral Health, "While approximately 7.7% of men have diagnosable NPD, just 4.8% of women have diagnosable symptoms of the disorder" (Source: Promises.com/Narcissistic Personality Disorder in Women/Family Resources, Mental Health, Recovery, Women's Mental Health). This is to say that Jezebel's favorite hiding place is in men. We will discuss the reason for this later. This is in stark contrast to what we once knew about Jezebel. Now, this isn't to say that Jezebel has always found men to be her favorite hosts; it may have been different in the 1800's. This is to say, however, that the spirit of Jezebel prefers to inhabit men over women because men were given authority over their wives, and demons know that if you bind or cut off the head of the house, you can rob the whole house. "Or how can someone enter a strong man's house and plunder his goods, unless he first binds the strong man? Then indeed he may plunder his house" (Matthew 12:29). While this may be a scripture denoting one of the principles of deliverance, it is a principle nonetheless, meaning, it is applicable in every world.

Hurricane Jezebel

Have you ever wondered why we refer to the demonic cluster associated with witchcraft, domination, and control as the Jezebel spirit? Was it named after Jezebel, or is it the spirit of Jezebel herself? In this lesson, we will explore the origins of Jezebel's name and more.

The following information was taken from the Jewish Library.

JEZEBEL
JEZEBEL (Heb. אִיזֶבֶל, perhaps from זבל, "the exalted one" with the prefix [*i*;] meaning "Where is the Exalted One / Prince?" (cf. Ichabod, "Where is the Divine Presence?). Another possibility is "The Prince Lives," by assimilation from *'š zbl > yzbl > 'yzbl* and the addition of prothetic *aleph*; see Cogan, 420). "Prince" should be connected to an attested epithet of Baal. Jezebel's father's name, Ethbaal, would indicate devotion to Baal going back at least two generations, and presage her own Baalistic enthusiasm. Jezebel was the daughter of Ethbaal king of the Sidonians, wife of *Ahab king of Israel, and mother of *Ahaziah and *Jehoram (Joram), sons and successors of Ahab (note their Yahwistic names).

Source: The Jewish Virtual Library/A Project of AICE/Sourced from Encyclopaedia Judica/Jezebel

The name Jezebel is Hebrew, and it originates from a Phoenician name containing the Semitic root "zbl" which means "to exalt, to dwell." Jezebel, like her father, had been named after Baal, a Phoenician-Canaanite deity that the Syrians worshiped. The name Baal means "owner" or "lord." This is to say that Jezebel was named after a principality (principle demon/ruler). By naming their children after Baal, many Phoenicians demonstrated their loyalty to this Phoenician deity. Worshipers of Baal would often sacrifice their firstborn male children as an offering to their god.

But how did the Jezebel spirit come to be known as the Jezebel spirit? For example, in the book of Revelation, God spoke about the false prophetess, Jezebel. In Revelation 2:20, the Lord rebuked the Church at Thyatira about their tolerance of Jezebel. He said, "But I have this against you: You allow that woman

113

Jezebel, the one who calls herself a prophetess, to deceive my servants and to teach them to commit sexual immorality and eat things offered to idols." However, by this time, Jezebel, the woman, had been dead for well over two-thousand years, so how is it that God was still referencing someone who was no longer amongst the living? The answer is simple—the Lord was addressing a spirit named Jezebel, and not the spirit of the woman, Jezebel. This is to say that a demon is named after the former Phoenician princess, but why is this? Consider how our nation names hurricanes. The names for the hurricanes that hit the United States were given by the World Meteorological Organization, and they are named alphabetically. There is a list of names that start with A, a list of names that start with B, and the list goes on. For example, if a hurricane comes in January, it may be given a name that starts with the letter A. The next hurricane would be given a name that starts with the letter B, and then, the C hurricane would be next. These names are often reused every six years. CBS News reported, "The names given to hurricanes are pretty much already set. There are six alphabetical lists of names for Atlantic hurricanes, maintained by the World Meteorological Organization, and they are rotated every six years. Therefore, the 2023 list that starts with Arlene and ends with Whitney will be used again in 2029."

But, did you know that the name of a hurricane can be retired? They can and they often are! This happens whenever a storm touches down and does a substantial amount of damage. For example, there have been a total of three hurricanes named Katrina, but the infamous Hurricane Katrina that struck New Orleans and many parts of the American Southeast led to the name Katrina being retired. Hurricane Katrina resulted in the deaths of 1,390 (or more) people, cost our country $125 billion in damage, and led to one of the largest internal displacements in U.S. history. It is for this reason that Katrina went on the retired hurricanes list. Four other storm names were retired that year as well; they are hurricanes Dennis, Rita, Stan, and Wilma, but the news behind Katrina's devastation caused the media to not report on the other hurricanes as much.

Why are we talking about hurricanes? The truth of the matter is—we use this same principle when naming demons. You see, the Jezebel spirit wasn't a new demon when the woman, Jezebel, was walking the Earth. It's a fallen angel; it was cast out of Heaven along with Lucifer and the rest of the fallen angels. It is the same spirit that provoked Cain to murder his brother, Abel. It is the same spirit that instigated the hatred in King Saul's heart towards David. It was the same spirit that used Delilah to seduce Samson. It is the same demon that was in Herodias when she demanded to have John, the Baptist, beheaded, and his head placed on a platter. It was the same demon that was in King Ramses II (the Pharaoh over Egypt) who'd bound and enslaved God's people in Egypt. It was the same devil that tormented Miriam, provoking her to want to overthrow her brother so that she and Aaron could reign in his stead. It was the same demon that caused Judas Iscariot to betray Jesus. And get this, it was the same spirit behind the Holocaust; it instigated the massive slaughter of more than six million Jews. The Jezebel spirit has always been after God's people; this particular spirit is always trying to stop a move of God by hindering the progression of His people, and what better way to do this than to go after His prophets? However, this spirit was named after Jezebel because, like Hurricane Katrina, the woman, Jezebel, caused a great deal of devastation in the land of Israel, so much so that her name would go down in history as one of the most wicked women to ever live. Nowadays, the name Jezebel is used to describe a wicked and immoral woman, however, as we discussed earlier, the Jezebel spirit can and does inhabit men as well.

The Name of the Game is Control

We can go throughout this entire book talking about the symptoms, characteristics, mindsets, and deficiencies of someone who has the Jezebel spirit, but if we don't understand the objective, everything we learn is for nothing. Why do people belittle, mismanage, abuse, harm, slaughter, sexually assault, or antagonize other people? A simple answer is—it is oftentimes a display of dominance; it is a way of one person sending a message to another human being that he or she owns or has a great measure of authority over the person that's being harassed. These animalistic tendencies are rooted in evil; after all, when God created man, He called us good. Therefore, if our behavior is not good, our misbehavior is rooted in something evil and dark, whether that is an evil heart or an evil spirit. Either way, whenever you are dealing with a narcissist or a narcissistic individual, the reason that person behaves the way that he or she behaves has everything to do with control. You see, whenever we don't grow the fruit of self-control, we will often engage in people-control. This has everything to do with the inflated sense of self that we tend to pick up whenever we've been traumatized in one way or another, or whenever we've been exposed or prematurely exposed to a world, an event, or a reality that we weren't equipped to handle. This is to say that every person who has ever repeatedly abused or mismanaged you likely had an issue with control; that is, of course, if you aren't the villain in their story. The reason I mention this is—I used to host one-on-one life coaching sessions, and I can remember several times when I found myself on the phone with individuals who'd told me that their mothers were narcissists. They would talk about her abusive ways, how she starts an argument every time they leave their rooms, and the many abusive behaviors she would exhibit whenever she did not get her way. They wanted to know what they could do about their mothers. My first question to them would be, "How old are you?" In the large majority of these situations, the individuals were over 25-years of age. In a few of these scenarios, the individuals were no younger than 22-years old. Nevertheless, regardless of what their ages were, I would always tell them to move out of their mothers' homes. The silence on the line after this statement would be deafening. This isn't what they wanted to hear. They wanted to figure out how to control the controller, and this told me that many of them were hosting the same spirit that their mothers hosted; they were also bound by the Jezebel spirit. However, they'd convinced themselves that they were the victims, and their mothers were the villains because, get this—the Jezebel spirits they had did not have the same rank as the Jezebel spirits their mothers were hosting. I'd break the silence, and start offering them solutions, all of which they would immediately challenge. "I can't do that because ...." or "Yeah, I wish I could, but my financial situation won't allow me to move." They weren't willing to do anything; they simply wanted to know what they could do about their mothers. I suspect that many of them were looking for some type of apostolic prayer that would force their mothers' demons to go away; then again, some of them wanted to learn a few tactics and wiles that they could use on Jezebel to get that spirit to fear them. I would often answer with something along the lines of, "Your mother has a right to be as toxic and as narcissistic as she wants in the home that she's paying for. She has to want to change in order for her process of healing to begin, but in the meantime, there is nothing I can legally do, both practically and spiritually, to force her to behave in her own home. I can pray for her, but God won't force her to behave. He will simply address her heart, but in all truth, her issue is with Him, not you, so chances are, she's not going to listen to Him either. Your best option is to move out of her home and deal with the inconveniences that come with taking full responsibility for yourself." After this, I would anticipate the silence because the individual on the other end had not paid for a coaching call only to be told that he or she has to take responsibility for himself or herself. The silence would often be interrupted by a sigh, a cough, or the sound of the individuals clearing their throats. Not knowing what else to say, they would start to briefly consider the words I'd just spoken, but in the large majority of these cases, they would not adhere to the advice. You see, Jezebelic mothers specialize in destabilizing their children; this way, whenever those children become adults, they are too weak, too fearful, or too entitled to live outside of Jezebel's means. Consequently, they find themselves wanting to extract the benefits of living with Jezebel without having to endure Jezebel's complaints, tantrums, and abusive ways. In other words, the spirit of control that is in their mothers is also in them, but they can't see it yet because, once again, they've convinced themselves that they are the victims and their narcissistic mothers are the villains who have been making their lives much harder than it has to be. However, the name of the game is control. Everything that a narcissist does is centered around controlling others, and the more beneficial you are to a narcissistic person, the more that individual will seek to control you. For example, a Jezebelic, narcissistic woman who pays all of the bills in her house, keeps the refrigerator stocked with food, and absorbs most of the negative events that tend to plague her home would be an invaluable asset to her children. The problem is, however, she will complain almost nonstop, she'd be abusive with her words, and she may even use financial control to get a handle on her adult children. Her children would clearly see how narcissistic, toxic, and broken their mother is, and in many cases, they would reason with themselves that she is a needed and necessary force in their lives, but they no longer want her to complain about:

1. Paying all of the bills by herself.
2. Cleaning up the messes they've made.
3. The people they choose to bring to her house, and what they decide to do with those people.
4. Having to cook their meals.
5. Their choices to sleep in, play video games, refuse to get a job, etc.

In this, you see that both of the parties involved are villains to one another, and because of this, they tend to victimize one another. This is the toxic cycle of a Jezebelic or narcissistic relationship. Think about all of the toxic people you've had in your life. If you were to closely examine the things they once said or did to you, you'd soon discover that everything they did was centered around them controlling you, controlling a certain narrative, controlling a situation, or controlling others.

In this particular chapter, we are going to look at a few personality disorders that border narcissism or Narcissistic Personality Disorder. This is not a complete list of these disorders, but the main disorders are mentioned in this list. Also, please note that I am not licensed to give any medical advice. Most of what I say is not and probably will never be supported by the world of psychology, and this is because science looks at psychology from a biological point of view. However, as a minister of deliverance and a demonologist, I tend to look at things first spiritually, and then biologically. This is to say that I support the scientific views of personality disorders (most of them anyway), but through experience, I have witnessed the spiritual side of them as well. With that said, the following disorders are typically the signs and symptoms of an individual who has the Jezebel spirit. And before we delve into this list, please note that not everyone who has been diagnosed with any of these disorders is bound by the Jezebel spirit. Many of them are bound by other unclean spirits such as Beelzebub,

Leviathan, Control, Witchcraft, etc. Then again, it is possible, but not likely, that some of these individuals are not in need of deliverance; instead, they need psychiatric help. Realistically speaking, every person bound by an unclean spirit should seek therapy because, get this, that spirit didn't come in and cause the issues. It came as a result of the individual having those issues or repeatedly engaging in ungodly behavior, even after they'd been warned.

- **Proverbs 16:18:** Pride goeth before destruction, and an haughty spirit before a fall.
- **Proverbs 18:12:** Before destruction the heart of man is haughty, and before honor is humility.
- **Revelation 2:20-23:** Notwithstanding I have a few things against thee, because thou sufferest that woman Jezebel, which calleth herself a prophetess, to teach and to seduce my servants to commit fornication, and to eat things sacrificed unto idols. And I gave her space to repent of her fornication; and she repented not. Behold, I will cast her into a bed, and them that commit adultery with her into great tribulation, except they repent of their deeds. And I will kill her children with death; and all the churches shall know that I am he which searcheth the reins and hearts: and I will give unto every one of you according to your works.

The Many Faces of Jezebel

The following conditions are often the symptoms of either the Jezebel spirit, the Leviathan spirit, the Beelzebub spirit, or a list of other unclean spirits. Once again, please seek medical advice; do not stop taking your medication unless advised by a health professional. I do advise that you also seek deliverance, therapy, and surround yourself with wise counsel.

Disorder	Breakdown
Psychopathy	Psychopathy is a personality disorder characterized by persistent antisocial behavior, diminished empathy and remorse, and bold, uninhibited, and egotistical traits. Psychopaths tend to lack genuine emotions and can be

Disorder	Breakdown
	manipulative and deceitful, often exhibiting a grandiose sense of self-worth and a lack of regard for the rights and feelings of others.
	One of the most prominent characteristics of psychopathy is the inability to form genuine emotional connections with others. This lack of empathy allows psychopaths to engage in callous and manipulative behavior without experiencing guilt or remorse. Additionally, psychopaths tend to have a superficial charm and charisma that allows them to easily manipulate and charm others to achieve their own goals.
	Psychopaths also exhibit high levels of impulsivity and a tendency to engage in risky and thrill-seeking behavior. They often have a lack of realistic long-term goals and can be impulsive in their decision-making, leading to a disregard for potential consequences.
	Furthermore, psychopaths commonly exhibit a parasitic lifestyle, taking advantage of others for their own gain without feeling guilty or remorseful. This can lead to a pattern of exploiting and manipulating others for personal benefit.
	In conclusion, the hallmark traits of a psychopath include a lack of empathy, manipulative behavior, impulsivity, and a tendency to exploit and manipulate others. Understanding these characteristics is crucial for identifying and addressing the presence of psychopathy in individuals.

Disorder	Breakdown
Machiavellianism	Machiavellianism is a concept derived from the works of Niccolò Machiavelli, an Italian diplomat, and philosopher, best known for his treatise, "The Prince." Machiavellianism is characterized by cunning, manipulative, and opportunistic behavior aimed at achieving one's goals, regardless of the moral implications. Individuals who exhibit Machiavellian traits are often skilled at manipulating others to serve their own interests. They are shrewd, strategic, and willing to resort to deceit and manipulation to gain and maintain power. These individuals are often driven by a strong desire for influence and control. Machiavellianism has been studied extensively in psychology and is considered one of the "dark triad" traits, along with narcissism and psychopathy. It is associated with a lack of empathy, a cynical view of human nature, and a willingness to exploit others for personal gain. While Machiavellianism can be advantageous in certain contexts, such as politics and business, it can also have detrimental effects on interpersonal relationships and ethical decision-making. Individuals high in Machiavellianism may engage in deceitful and exploitative behaviors that can harm others and undermine trust within social and organizational settings.
Antisocial Personality Disorder	Sociopathy is a personality disorder characterized by a lack of empathy and a disregard for societal norms and rules. Individuals with sociopathic tendencies often exhibit manipulative and charming behavior, allowing them to

Disorder	Breakdown
	superficially blend in with those around them. However, they also display a lack of remorse or guilt for their actions, and tend to be aggressive and impulsive. One of the key characteristics of a sociopath is their inability to form genuine emotional connections with others. They may feign emotions in order to manipulate those around them, but underneath the facade lies a lack of genuine empathy. This allows them to exploit and take advantage of others without feeling any remorse. Sociopaths also display a disregard for rules and social norms, often engaging in criminal or unethical behavior without feeling any guilt. They have a tendency to be highly impulsive, making decisions without considering the potential consequences. Their charm and ability to manipulate others allow them to manipulate situations to their advantage. Sociopathy is characterized by a lack of empathy, disregard for societal norms, and manipulative behavior. These individuals may appear charming on the surface, but their inability to form genuine emotional connections and their propensity for aggressive and impulsive behavior set them apart from the general population.
Borderline Personality Disorder	Borderline personality disorder (BPD) is a mental health condition characterized by intense mood swings, impulsive behavior, unstable relationships, and a distorted self-image. Individuals with BPD often struggle to regulate their emotions, leading to feelings of emptiness, anxiety, and depression. This can result in a heightened sensitivity

Disorder	Breakdown
	to perceived rejection or abandonment, which can trigger episodes of anger, anxiety, or depression.

People with BPD may engage in self-destructive behaviors such as substance abuse, binge eating, or self-harm in an attempt to cope with their emotional turmoil. Additionally, they may have difficulty maintaining stable relationships and may engage in intense, chaotic relationships with others.

The exact cause of BPD is not fully understood, but it is believed to be a combination of genetic, environmental, and neurological factors. It is often diagnosed in adolescents or young adults, and tends to improve with age and treatment.

Effective treatment for BPD typically includes a combination of therapy, medication, and support groups. Dialectical behavior therapy (DBT) is a type of therapy that has been found to be particularly effective for individuals with BPD, as it helps them learn coping skills to manage their intense emotions. |
| **Histrionic Personality Disorder** | Histrionic personality disorder (HPD) is a mental health condition characterized by a pattern of excessive and attention-seeking behaviors. Individuals with HPD often display dramatic and exaggerated emotions in order to garner the attention and approval of others. They may engage in seductive or provocative behavior, and have difficulty maintaining relationships due to their shallow emotions and constant need for validation.

Symptoms of HPD include constant seeking of reassurance |

Disorder	Breakdown
	or approval, rapidly shifting emotions, and an excessive concern for one's physical appearance. Individuals with HPD may also be prone to outbursts of anger and tantrums when they feel they are not receiving enough attention.

Cluster B Personality Disorders

You'll notice that every one of these personalities, in the world of psychology, falls under what is referred to as Cluster B personalities. It is also important to note that any personality that is not good is not your personality. It is often the result of:

1. Who you became or who you're becoming.
2. Who you've learned to be.
3. Who you're pretending to be.
4. Who you think you are.
5. Who you're practicing to become.

All of which represent you having an identity crisis. Who are you? The truth of the matter is, the answer to this question is found in the mouth of God. You are a child of the Most High God, but everything you need to know about yourself will be revealed to you as you seek Him and advance in your journey in Him. "But seek ye first the kingdom of God, and his righteousness; and all these things shall be added unto you" (Matthew 6:33).

Cluster B personality disorders are a group of mental health conditions characterized by erratic, dramatic, and overly emotional behavior. Once again, this cluster includes four types of personality disorders: antisocial, borderline, histrionic, and narcissistic personality disorders.

Individuals with antisocial personality disorder often display a lack of regard for the rights and feelings of others, as well as a tendency to engage in impulsive and irresponsible behavior. Borderline personality disorder is marked by intense and unstable relationships, self-image, and emotions, often resulting in self-harm and suicidal behaviors. Histrionic personality disorder is characterized by attention-seeking and overly dramatic behavior, particularly in social settings. Narcissistic personality disorder involves an inflated sense of self-importance, a constant need for admiration, and a lack of empathy for others.

Soul Recovery

While each type of cluster B personality disorders present a unique set of symptoms, they all share a common thread of unstable and extreme emotional and behavioral patterns. These disorders can significantly impact an individual's ability to maintain healthy relationships, hold down a job, and function in society. All the same, these disorders signal the presence of an unclean spirit. Will casting the spirit out make the disorder go away? No, it won't. To recover your soul (mind, will, and emotions), you need to also address the strongholds that have formed in your life. Furthermore, you need to:

1. Create new, healthy, and Godly habits to replace the unhealthy and ungodly habits you once embraced.
2. Change your circle. The people around you can help you sustain your deliverance or they can be the reason you find yourself being recaptured by the enemy time and time again.
3. Study your Bible daily and meditate on God's Word daily.
4. Pray without ceasing; this means to pray daily on schedule and outside of a schedule.
5. Get into a good church home so that you can build a Godly community around yourself. Be sure to avoid the narcissistic personalities at your local church, but do engage and embrace the Godly people that you meet.
6. Get therapy. Deliverance without therapy is often short-lived.
7. Surround yourself with wise counsel, and submit to their leadership. Proverbs 11:14 (ESV) reads, "Where no wise guidance is, the people falleth: but in the multitude of counselors there is safety."

8. Heal, forgive, and take accountability for your actions—repeatedly! A season doesn't end until you find your role in the center of your pain. This is when a season becomes a full circle or cycle, and this is when you will likely receive your next set of instructions from God.
9. Stay away from the sin and the sinners that cost you your freedom in the first place.
10. Journal. Journaling is a great way to dump the trash out of your soul so that you can look at it from an objective point of view.

The soul of the human is comprised of the mind, will, and emotions. The mind is what the Bible refers to as the heart. In Proverbs 4:23, God told us to guard our hearts; the scripture reads, "Keep thy heart with all diligence; for out of it are the issues of life." How do you guard your heart? The answer is simple. You establish guardrails or, better yet, boundaries, understanding that bound people hate boundaries. All the same, you have to establish standards for yourself. What is the difference between a standard and a boundary? I like to describe it this way—imagine that you are at a carnival and you want to ride a specific ride. Each ride has a height requirement; this is what's referred to as a standard of rule. This means that you have to be a certain height to get on the ride. Each ride has rules. For example, you have to wear your seat belt or whatever gadget they use to secure you in your seat. This is called a boundary. The standard is what's required to get on the ride, but the boundary is what's required to stay on the ride. A better and more practical way to explain this is to think about dating. As a single Christian, a woman may say that in order for a man to take her on a date or establish a courtship with her, he must be saved, sanctified, filled with the Holy Spirit, employed, have no more than two children, have a church home, be accountable to someone, etc. That's her standard; it is the way in which she measures a man to determine whether or not he's equipped enough to walk with her. However, her boundaries dictate the limitations or perimeters she's set around herself in order to keep the relationship Godly. So, she may say, for example, that her love interest cannot come to her house, she will not go to his house, the two must remain in a public space when together, there will be no sex outside of marriage, the two cannot talk past eleven o'clock post meridian, etc.

These are boundaries, and boundaries come with penalties. These penalties can include taking a temporary break or a permanent break from the relationship if certain boundaries are not honored, changing or tightening up on the rules to ensure that certain boundaries are no longer breached, etc. This is how the heart is properly guarded. There has to be standards of rule and boundaries, and both have to be consistently enforced, solidified, and evaluated to adjust to the growing relationship or whatever it is that you want to guard.

Satan comes to steal, kill, and destroy (see John 10:10), and the only way that he can rob you of something that belongs to you is through a door (legal access) or a window (illegal access). This is to say that Satan can and does steal pieces of the human soul; he uses trauma, ungodly soul ties, and fear to accomplish this agenda. Consider this—you have two jars of clay; one jar has blue clay in it and the other jar has red clay in it. You remove the clay from the jars, and you begin to mix them together. Eventually, you decide to take them apart again so that you can put them back in their jars, but you realize it's extremely difficult to separate the red clay from the blue clay after they've been mixed. You are relatively successful in your attempts, however, you can see the residue from the blue clay on the mound of red clay that you've created, just as you can see the residue of red clay on the mound of blue clay you've formed. This is what a soul tie looks like. It is literally impossible for you to disconnect your soul from the soul of another human being; in short, only God can fully deliver you from a soul tie. And because we go about meeting and mixing ourselves with others through association, ungodly practices and the like, we have scattered pieces of ourselves, and it is through this scattering that the enemy is able to come in. Consider the story of the ten lepers. Luke 17:11-19 reads, "And it came to pass, as he went to Jerusalem, that he passed through the midst of Samaria and Galilee. And as he entered into a certain village, there met him ten men that were lepers, which stood afar off: And they lifted up their voices, and said, Jesus, Master, have mercy on us. And when he saw them, he said unto them, Go shew yourselves unto the priests. And it came to pass, that, as they went, they were cleansed. And one of them, when he saw that he was healed, turned back, and with a loud voice glorified God, And fell down on his face at his feet, giving him thanks: and he was a Samaritan. And Jesus answering said, Were there not ten cleansed? But where are the nine? There are not found that returned to give glory to God, save this stranger. And he said unto him, Arise, go thy way: thy faith hath made thee whole." Notice here that the nine men who did not return were all healed, but the one leper who returned to give God glory was not only healed, he was made whole. To be made whole means that God restores everything that the enemy took from you, even the parts of you that were scattered through sin, trauma, soul ties, and ignorance.

To be made whole means to be made complete, whereas there is nothing missing, nothing broken. Instead, you will enjoy the perfect peace of the Lord; this is the peace that surpasses all understanding.

Jezebel, the Narcissist or Psychopath

Narcissists and psychopaths are both characterized by their lack of empathy and manipulative behavior, but their underlying motivations and behaviors differ in significant ways. What are the differences between the two, you ask? Narcissists are primarily driven by an inflated sense of their own importance and a constant need for admiration. They often seek validation through attention and praise, and can become envious or dismissive of others who they perceive as a threat to their own self-image or agenda. While narcissists can be deceptive and lack a true understanding of empathy, their behaviors are often driven by a deep-seated insecurity and fear of not being seen as superior. On the other hand, psychopaths are characterized by a complete disregard for the rights and feelings of others. They lack a moral compass and are often impulsive and prone to engaging in criminal behavior. Psychopaths are skilled at manipulating and exploiting others for their own gain, and do not feel guilt or remorse for their actions. Unlike narcissists, who may maintain a facade of charm and likability, psychopaths are often more overtly aggressive and display a lack of remorse or empathy for their actions.

This is to say that while both narcissists and psychopaths share some common traits, such as manipulation and lack of empathy, their underlying motivations and behaviors set them apart.

Jezebel, the Psychopath or Sociopath

The terms "psychopath" and "sociopath" are often used interchangeably to describe individuals who display antisocial and manipulative behavior. However, there are distinct differences between these two personality types. For example, a psychopath is characterized by a lack of empathy and remorse, as well as an inability to form genuine emotional connections with others. They are often charming and manipulative, able to mimic emotions to blend into society. Psychopaths are also known for their impulsivity and tendency to engage in risky and harmful behaviors without considering the consequences. On the other hand, a sociopath also lacks empathy and remorse, but they may form shallow, parasitic relationships in order to satisfy their own needs. Sociopaths are often the products of their environments, having experienced childhood trauma or abuse, which can lead to their antisocial behaviors. They may also be more prone to outbursts of anger and violence, compared to the more calculated and controlled nature of psychopaths.

While both psychopaths and sociopaths display similar characteristics, the underlying causes and behaviors of each differ. Psychopathy is believed to have a stronger genetic basis, while sociopathy is more influenced by environmental factors.

Jezebel, the Drama Queen/King or Narcissist

Histrionic personality disorder (HPD) and narcissistic personality disorder (NPD) are two distinct mental health conditions, each with its own set of symptoms and characteristics. While both disorders fall under the category of Cluster B personality disorders in the Diagnostic and Statistical Manual of Mental Disorders (DSM-5), they exhibit unique patterns of behavior and thought.

Individuals with HPD tend to seek attention and validation from others, often exhibiting dramatic and exaggerated emotions and behaviors. They may also be overly flirtatious or seductive, and have difficulties maintaining long-term relationships due to their impulsive and attention-seeking tendencies. On the other hand, individuals with NPD display an excessive sense of self-importance and a lack of empathy for others. They often seek admiration and validation from others. They may also exploit or manipulate those around them to maintain their grandiose self-image.

While both disorders involve a need for attention and validation, individuals with HPD may seek it through excessive emotional displays, whereas individuals with NPD may seek it by emphasizing their own greatness. Additionally, individuals with HPD may be more likely to engage in attention-seeking behaviors in response to perceived rejection, while individuals with NPD may exhibit a general lack of empathy and concern for others. Simply put, while both HPD and NPD share some similarities in their desire for attention and validation, their specific patterns of behavior and thought distinguish them as separate mental health conditions but the same demon. It is important for individuals with these disorders to seek professional help, along with deliverance to address their unique challenges and facilitate their journey toward healing and recovery.

The Vampiric Effect

The following information was taken from Encyclopedia Britannica:

"Creatures with vampiric characteristics have appeared at least as far back as ancient Greece, where stories were told of creatures that attacked people in their sleep and drained their bodily fluids. Tales of walking corpses that drank the blood of the living and spread plague flourished in medieval Europe in times of disease, and people lacking a modern understanding of infectious disease came to believe that those who became vampires preyed first upon their own families. Research from the 20th and 21st centuries has posited that characteristics associated with vampires can be traced back to certain diseases such as porphyria, which makes one sensitive to sunlight; tuberculosis, which causes wasting; pellagra, a disease that thins the skin; and rabies, which causes biting and general sensitivities that could lead to repulsion by light or garlic.

Vampire myths were especially popular in Eastern Europe, and the word vampire most likely originates from that region. Digging up the bodies of suspected vampires was practiced in many cultures throughout Europe, and it is thought that the natural characteristics of decomposition—such as receding gums and the appearance of growing hair and fingernails—reinforced the belief that corpses were in fact continuing some manner of life after death. Also possibly contributing to this belief was the pronouncement of death for people who were not dead. Because of the constraints of medical diagnosis at the time, people who were very ill, or sometimes even very drunk, and in a coma or in shock were thought dead and later "miraculously" recovered—sometimes too late to prevent their burial. Belief in vampires led to such rituals as staking corpses through the heart before they were buried. In some cultures the dead were buried face-down to prevent them from finding their way out of their graves.

The modern incarnation of vampire myth seems to have stemmed largely from Gothic European literature of the 18th and 19th centuries, about the time vampire hysteria was peaking in Europe. Vampiric figures appeared in 18th-century poetry, such as Heinrich August Ossenfelder's "Der Vampyr" (1748), about a seemingly vampiric narrator who seduces an innocent maiden. Vampire poems began appearing in English about the turn of the 19th century, such as John Stagg's "The Vampyre" (1810) and Lord Byron's The Giaour (1813). The first prose vampire story published in English is believed to be John Polidori's "The Vampyre" (1819), about a mysterious aristocrat named Lord Ruthven who seduces young women only to drain their blood and disappear. Those works and others inspired subsequent material for the stage. Later important vampire stories include the serial Varney, the Vampire; or, The Feast of Blood (1845–47) and "The Mysterious Stranger" (1853), which are cited as possible early influences for Bram Stoker's Dracula (1897), and

Théophile Gautier's "La Morte amoureuse" (1836; "The Dead Lover") and Sheridan Le Fanu's Carmilla (1871–72), which established the vampire femme fatale.

While the concept of vampirism traces its roots back to Europe, make no mistake about it, every evil fictional character that's popularized in Hollywood is a true depiction of an actual demon. Every person who has ever written a movie script, a play, or developed any type of media/imagery was inspired by something or someone, and every thought that has ever been developed into something tangible was first established in the realm of the spirit. This is to say that the devil tells on himself! This is also to demonstrate that vampirism is theft; it is a form of piracy. Piracy, according to Oxford Languages, is: "the practice of attacking and robbing ships at sea." The human body is made up of 60% water. All the same, you are a bearer of Heaven's treasures because Heaven is locked up within you. This is to say that you are a ship at sea and Satan is a pirate; his objective is to steal, kill, and destroy. Vampires were believed to steal the lives and/or identities of their victims, whereas one of two things would happen to someone who had been bitten by a vampire:

1. The person would die.
2. The person would become a vampire.

Amazingly enough, according to most horror stories about vampires, whether the person lived or died was the decision of the vampire who bit the individual. Some people were deemed not attractive or relevant enough to live, while others were spared by the vampire's obsession with them. What stands out the most is that, in the world of narcissism, the fates of Jezebel's victims were:

1. They would become narcissistic.
2. They would die of their wounds in isolation or by living a life that God hasn't called them to.

However, the truth of the matter is—you will essentially become the very thing that hurt you. That is if you don't heal, take accountability, and deal with that thing in the realm of the spirit. Like the mythological vampire, Jezebel cannot be killed with modern weapons. As a matter of fact, demons don't die. This is because they are spirits, and anything that God speaks into existence can never cease to exist. His Word can never return unto Him void. Whatever He speaks will remain for all of eternity, but whatever He forms is destructible. This is why He created the spirit of mankind in Genesis 1, but He formed the body of mankind in Genesis 3. This is how we, as humans, became living souls. This is also why God created hell. Hell is the trash bin or, better yet, the landfill of the spirit realm. It's where God sends those who spent their lives rejecting and/or opposing Him.

Consider the story of Elijah. After being threatened by Jezebel, Elijah ran and hid himself. In short, he went into isolation. What was happening in this scenario? Elijah was well on his way to:

1. Embracing the Jezebel spirit because of his fear.
2. Embracing the Ahab spirit because of his fear.
3. Taking his own life.

Elijah had just been verbally attacked by a vicious and ruthless queen, but more than that, the spirit of Jezebel was after him. This is to say that, while Jezebel was a narcissist, Elijah was well on his way to becoming narcissistic. We witness the evidence of this once he'd been confronted by God regarding his decision to hide himself in a cave. He began to tell the Lord that he was the only true prophet left on the planet. The same is true for Ahab. Ahab is the traditional, soft-spoken, seemingly harmless fellow that most people would trust around their purses, but underneath the mask, he is both fearful and covertly narcissistic. This is because he was likely intimidated by Jezebel's father, Ethbaal, and he was fearful of breaking whatever pact he'd made with the Sidonian king. All the same, Ahab, like most people who find themselves becoming one of Jezebel's collectibles, was highly ambitious. His treaty or pact with Jezebel's father afforded him some of the wealth and pleasures of Ethbaal's thriving kingdom, along with the protection of a very powerful military. Before you build a thing, count the cost. This is something both Elijah and Ahab neglected to do. Ahab didn't fully understand how expensive his decision to rebel against the God of Israel would be. Elijah hadn't fully realized how tormenting it could be and would be to live a life surrendered to God. The difference between the two men is obvious. Elijah's assignment, while incredibly frustrating, would yield him an everlasting reward, while Ahab's rebellion would cause him to spend eternity in a place that was created for Satan and his angels.

I can't tell you how many times I've ministered to people who yelled and cried about their narcissistic lovers or spouses. After being cut off several times and listening to what I call narcissistic reasoning, I would think to myself, "Is your spouse the narcissist or is it you? Because your reasoning is narcissistic." Of course, I would silently remind myself that a person who has been in a smoke-filled room will undoubtedly smell like smoke. In other words, people who've spent considerable amounts of time with a narcissist often become narcissistic in their attempts to navigate through their narcissistic lover or parents' abuse. So, they may:

1. Dominate the conversation.
2. Use love-bombing and flattery to establish a connection.
3. Have trouble taking accountability.
4. See constructive criticism as abuse.
5. Be easily offended.
6. Show no regard for others.
7. Run away when confronted.
8. Attack the very person or people who offers them assistance.

And the list goes on. Nevertheless, I have been exposed to Jezebel, narcissistic abuse, and demonology long enough to understand that I need to listen, pray, watch, and more than anything, test the spirit by the Spirit. What I've come to discover is the fact that people who've been exposed to narcissists for lengthy amounts of time often need deliverance from either the Jezebel spirit or the Ahab spirit. Yes, it is possible for Jezebel to date or to marry Jezebel, however, whenever this happens, you will find that one individual will act as the dominant Jezebel (typically the overt narcissist), while the other will serve as the lesser Jezebel or, better yet, the Ahab (typically the covert narcissist). *Of course, this can be reversed! The covert narcissist can be the ruling spirit over a home, whereas the overt narcissist can be the Ahab'ed one.* And whenever this happens, most of us sympathize with the lesser Jezebel, not realizing that we are literally watching a snake fight. This has everything to do with the fact that we tend to follow the villain on victim story-line model, whereas a victim (the good guy) is being abused, controlled, bullied, or taken advantage of by a villain (the bad guy), and in the genesis or beginning of this war of morals, the good guy loses. Over time, however, a hero is introduced into the story-line. The hero could be an external player; then again, the hero could turn out to be the good guy himself. Needless to say, in the end, the good guy takes home the win, and the villain is terminated, exiled, or incarcerated. When we embrace this Western way of viewing things, we find it hard to conceptualize that it is possible for two villains to form a relationship with one another, just as it is possible for two victims to meet, marry, and start a family. All the same, contrary to popular belief, the good guy, in real life, doesn't always remain the good guy. Instead, the good guy often becomes bad after enduring years of mistreatment and abuse. And get this—whenever this happens, Jezebel (the narcissist) will oftentimes discard his or her partner, and then blame the failed relationship on the good guy gone bad. The narcissist will point out, for example, the other party's recent behavior, never stopping to explain why the individual is behaving that way in the first place. For example, let's create two fictional characters: Bell and Bob. Bob is a pretty decent guy. He's God-fearing, faithful, and a man of integrity. He's a hard-worker who prides himself on spoiling his family. Bell, on the other hand, is a narcissist. The two have been married for 17 years, but four years into their marriage, Bell had an affair, and ever since then, she hasn't been the same. She became verbally abusive, manipulative, independent, suspicious, and controlling. After Bob found out about her affair, he chose to forgive his wife. This was after they'd gone through a few months of counseling. Bell never truly took accountability for her actions, blaming the affair on Bob being a workaholic, leaving Bob to feel as if he was responsible for her decision to cheat. After Bell cut ties with her lover, she spent a little over a year trying to be a better wife, but over time, she found herself feeling bored in her relationship with Bob. Bob was too mundane; he was too predictable for the self-proclaimed firecracker. So, Bell started going to the gym more, and it was at the gym that she met Fred. Fred was tall, handsome, and assertive. Furthermore, Fred loved to have a good time. Bell repeatedly flirted with Fred until one day, she found herself at a hotel with her new lover. Things were steamy between the two. As a matter of fact, Bell would later tell her best friend, Tammy, that Fred was the best lover she'd ever had. And this time, Bell was more than unwilling to let her husband come between her and her lover. So to keep him from questioning her repeated runs to the gym, her decision to get a new wardrobe, her dwindling libido, and her sudden need to hang out with her friends a little more, Bell became super aggressive, controlling, demeaning, and hateful towards her husband.

- Her first order of business was to point out Bob's many flaws.
- Her second order of business was to remind Bob of some of the offensive and hurtful things he's said and done over the course of their marriage.
- Her next order of business was to make Bob feel that she is superior to him, and that he is "lucky" to have pulled a woman like herself.
- After this, Bell went on to make Bob feel that she had been robbed of the life she could have lived had Bob not come into her life. For example, she once told Bob, "I had rich men lined up to be with me, and I settled for your broke self!"
- Her final order of business was to instill fear in Bob as it related to him questioning her decisions, her whereabouts, or anything that he would witness.

This worked. To keep peace in his home and to avoid breaking up his family, Bob chose to allow his wife to have the freedoms she wanted. This included her decision to rarely, if ever, have sex with him. After two years of this abuse, Bob had grown weary of his wife's late night runs, her disrespectful ways, her verbal abuse, and her many attempts to make him feel small and insignificant, so he didn't resist the woman he'd met at the supermarket while out getting snacks for his wife. Donna was beautiful, petite, and incredibly soft-spoken, unlike his wife, Bell. Over time, Bob started staying overnight with his new lover; he'd even started taking better care of himself, both mentally and physically. Realizing that her husband no longer cared for their marriage, Bell cut ties with her lover and began to fight for her marriage, but it was too late. Bob continued to ignore his wife while spoiling his mistress. Bell turned to therapy for help, she insisted that the couple get marriage counseling, and she even turned to the church for spiritual guidance, but to no avail. She did, however, manage to convince everyone she met that her husband was a narcissistic cheater who had been mentally torturing her with his silence and his overnight stays away from home. However, Bell had been the vampire that Satan used to turn Bob into the narcissistic individual he had become. This exemplifies the full vampiric effect! Then again, I've seen cases where a Jezebelic man will mistreat, mismanage, and mishandle his wife until their marriage finally gave up its ghost. The wife would go on to remarry, and this time, she'd marry a pretty decent man, however, she'd be the narcissist in this particular relationship. Did she pick up her narcissistic ways from her husband? Possibly. However, the truth is she may have been narcissistic the whole time she was married to her husband, but again, she was the lesser of two evils. Howbeit, now that she's married to a good guy, she can let her hair down and let her fangs hang low. In this case, I've noticed that the women or men in question would start to do to their new lovers what their former lovers had done to them. Why is this? It's what I called the unsettled Jezebel. Think of it this way. Charlie is pretty much homeless, but he tends to go from house-to-house. He lived with his brother, Jason, for a year before Jason's wife demanded that he leave. After this, he moved in with Jason's adult son, Jason, Jr., but he only lived there for three months before getting evicted by his son. After moving out of his son's house, Jason moved in with his ex-girlfriend, Hannah. Hannah allowed Jason to sleep in her basement, but a month later, Hannah asked Jason to leave her house after Jason kept questioning her about their failed relationship. After moving out of Hannah's house, Jason moved in with one of his colleagues named Christopher. He lived with Christopher for six months, but after Christopher's wife had a baby, Jason had to move out to make room for the new infant. After moving out of Christopher's house, Jason started living in his car. Four months later, Jason married his short-term girlfriend, Wynter. Wynter owned her own home, so Jason moved in with her. As the months went by, Wynter began to notice and complain about Jason's unpacked bags. "Why are you living out of a suitcase?" she repeatedly asked her husband. Jason shrugged his shoulders and said, "It doesn't bother me." What's happening here? Jason is used to being homeless; he's used to living out of his suitcase, so even when he finds himself in a place of his own, he will find it incredibly difficult to unpack, relax, and focus-forward. Instead, he has grown so accustomed to being evicted that he refuses to unpack his clothes and put them away in his new home. But one day, Jason finally decided to listen to his wife. He decided to unpack his bag after she agreed to put his name on the house's lease. While unpacking the bag, Wynter noticed a foul odor emitting from the suitcase, and every time Jason pulled a garment or an item out of his suitcase, that putrid smell would get stronger as it followed him to the closet or the dresser. Before long, the room smelled like death. Furthermore, Jason's suitcase had pictures of his exes, a machete, and what appeared to be a decomposed animal. This is to say that every person has baggage, and you don't know what they're bringing with them until they settle down.

Going back to the concept of the unsettled Jezebel, a woman could have been the lesser of two evils in a relationship, and when that particular relationship ended, she could have found herself in a relationship with a decent guy. And while she was angelic and committed to the narcissist that she was first married to, you would find her mistreating and abusing her current husband. Again, this is a man who has been good to her. Why is she mishandling him? Because in her previous relationship, she wasn't truly settled enough to show her husband who she really was. After all, she was too busy being introduced to his many faces. Consequently, she couldn't be herself. She was too busy trying to defend herself, save her marriage, and endure the many traumas that her ex-husband put her through. But now that she's got a good guy, she can unpack what's really in her soul, after all, out of the abundance of the heart, the mouth speaks. Does this mean that her new husband should have been a two-timing, double-minded, abusive, arrogant, and condescending narcissist in order to garner her respect? No. Anytime you have to come out of character to host a relationship with someone, you are with the wrong person. It means that her new husband should have discerned that spirit in her before he proposed to her. He should have run for his life when God gave him the way of escape. And anyone who knew her while she was with her narcissistic first husband would assume that her new husband is the villain because they'd only seen her in a weakened state. But now that she is the villain, she would transfer her demons to her new husband or, at minimum, introduce them to him. Before long, Jezebel would become a familiar spirit to her new husband, and after the couple's divorce is finalized, Jason may find himself mirroring the behaviors of his ex-wife. This is because the spirit of Jezebel would whisper sweet nothings in his ear that sound like:

1. You have to start treating women the way they treated you.
2. Women don't respect good guys. You have to become ruthless if you want to be respected.
3. All women are trash! They're only good for one thing!

These thoughts, if not cast down, will begin to seep into Jason's soul as he comes into agreement with them, thus opening him up for the Jezebel spirit. You may come across Jason and say, "I remember him. He's always been a really decent guy! He has one of the most beautiful hearts I've ever come across! If he's single, I want to introduce him to my friend, Shayla. She's a really sweet girl, and I think the two of them would make a great match." In this, you are approaching someone other than the man you remember, and if you introduce him to Shayla, you've just introduced him to your friend to her next season of warfare.

The goal of the vampiric effect is real estate. Demons need bodies to live in, so Jason's demons know that Jason may become too weak to be used by them, after all, they are usurpers of power and authority. They also know that it is possible for Jason to die prematurely. He could become disabled. Then again, what if he truly surrendered himself to the Lord and underwent several rounds of deliverance? Where would they go? So, they will use Jason to create as many soul ties as possible; this way, Jason will serve as their primary resident, while all of his friends and former lovers serve as hotels (short-term and extended-stay).

In summary, understand that whenever a narcissist attempts to enter your life, Satan's goal is to:

1. Use that narcissist to destroy you.
2. Use that narcissist to attack your character.
3. Turn you into a narcissist or a narcissistic individual.

Jezebel, a Master of Sensuality

Sense is the ability to observe and understand the world around us through our five basic senses, which are:

Sight	Sound	Touch	Taste	Smell

Sight

The first sense we will consider is sight, the sense of vision. Sight is one of the primary senses humans rely on to navigate their surroundings. Without it, people would have a harder time reading, driving, walking, or any activity which depends on detecting and navigating the environment. This sense of vision has helped humans to identify color, shape, distance, and size – all of which are essential in daily life. Proper hygiene and careful lifestyles contribute significantly to the maintenance of this sense.

The sense of sight is perhaps the most important of all our senses. It allows us to see the world in all its natural splendor, from the vastness of the ocean to the intricate details of a texture. Sight also allows us to recognize facial expressions and to interpret body language, which is essential in communication. Sight not only helps us to navigate through our day-to-day lives but also influences how we perceive ourselves and others.

Sound

Another sense we rely on is the sense of hearing, or auditory sense. This sense enables humans to perceive sound waves and interpret them as music, speech, or noises. The ear is the primary sensory organ for this sense – shaped like a funnel, the ear collects sound waves, directing them into the auditory nerve, which sends the interpreted waves to the brain, allowing us to perceive the audible world. It is important to maintain the health of our ears to ensure that cognition of sounds is optimal.

Hearing is often considered the second most important sense, as it enables us to communicate with others through spoken language, music, and sound. Our sense of hearing plays a significant role in social interactions and learning, allowing us to comprehend complex ideas, follow instructions, and understand the world around us. Furthermore, hearing enables us to experience the joys of music, a form of art that has the power to evoke strong emotions and change our mood.

Touch

The sense of touch is also fundamental to the human experience. It enables us to detect physical pressure and temperature changes, and it plays an essential role in physical interaction with our surroundings and other people. Without this sense, human beings would have a hard time navigating the ever-changing sensation of the environment as well as miss out on the tactile pleasures that make life rich and worthwhile.

The sense of touch provides us with information about the texture and temperature of objects and allows us to communicate our intentions and emotions physically. Touch is crucial for bonding and intimacy, such as holding hands with our loved ones. Our sense of touch also plays a significant role in our physical health, as touch therapy has been shown to reduce stress and lower blood pressure.

Taste

Taste is another important sense, which is closely connected with our sense of smell. The taste buds on our tongues interpret the flavor of food, while the sense of smell is responsible for the aroma. The sense of taste and smell work together to allow us to enjoy complex flavor combinations and distinguish between savory, salty, sweet, and sour tastes. The value of this sense of taste cannot be overstated, as it creates a pleasurable experience during eating.

Taste not only helps us to understand what we are eating, but it also plays a crucial role in our overall health and nutrition. Our sense of taste can also evoke strong emotions, such as the pleasure of enjoying a favorite meal or the disgust of eating something distasteful.

Smell

Finally, the last sense is the sense of smell or olfactory sense. Humans use their sense of smell to detect odors and determine if things are safe and pleasant. This sense is responsible for triggering memories, which can evoke strong emotional responses, both positive and negative. It is important to protect this sense by avoiding direct or extreme exposure to harsh chemicals and pollutants.

The sense of smell is often an overlooked sense, but again, it plays a vital role in our memories and emotions. Smell has the power to transport us to a different time and place, triggering memories and emotions associated with a particular scent. Our sense of smell also helps to identify potential dangers, such as gas leaks and fires.

How is this relevant to the topic at hand? Simply put, Jezebel is a sensualist. This particular spirit has mastered the five senses. Many people who are bound by this incredibly vicious spirit are incredibly sensual. This is how the narcissist ensnares you.

- They appeal to your eyesight by spending extra time in front of a mirror to ensure that they are as irresistible as possible. This is what Jezebel did when Jehu came to kill her. According to the Bible, she painted her eyes. In other words, she put on makeup in an attempt to sway Jehu's decision. Some historians believe that she painted her face in preparation for her own burial, but this likely isn't true.

- They appeal to your sense of hearing by flattering you repeatedly; this flattery is what is commonly known as love-bombing. Not only do they flatter you, they will play music in their attempts to get you to lower your guard. For example, let's say that Ronnie just started talking to Brenda. Brenda is guarded because she doesn't know Ronnie just yet. However, Ronnie wants to speed past all of the phases and stages that make up the beginning of a relationship so that he can potentially sleep with Brenda. To help speed up this process, Ronnie will likely employ the use of slow jams. Brenda will begin to notice that whenever Ronnie calls her, he's always playing music in the background, plus, there are certain times during the song when Ronnie becomes incredibly quiet. This is because he wants her to hear the lyrics of the song. In this, he is appealing to her ability to hear.

- They appeal to your sense of touch by caressing you, hugging you, or sexing you (if you let them). They are masters of all-things-touch related! Touch creates some of the most powerful memories. For example, when your new boyfriend/girlfriend touched your hand for the first time, a memory was created. When they touched your lips with their lips for the first time, a memory was created and stored. When they adjusted your clothing, ran their fingers through your hair, popped a pimple on your face, pulled food out of your beard or hair, or when they touched your face with their hand, a memory was formed.

- They appeal to your sense of taste by cooking you some amazing meals! Narcissists oftentimes know their way around the kitchen, and the ones who don't are often familiar with some of the tastiest restaurants in town.

- And finally, they appeal to your sense of smell by lathering themselves in cologne or perfume. I remember the first narcissistic individual I dated. He had a specific cologne that he would put on before making his way to my house. After we broke up, I kept smelling that cologne everywhere and it was one of the many things that made breaking the soul tie a lot harder than it should have been.

Understand this—music and smells make it incredibly difficult to break ungodly soul ties; this is because whenever you break up with a person, for example, someone else will pass by you wearing the same perfume or cologne that your ex wore. All the same, the songs you like to listen to are powerful enough to make you cough up a long-forgotten memory, and then use that memory to return to the moments in time when those particular songs were played.

As humans, our senses play a vital role in our overall perception of the world and how we interact with it. Our senses allow us to experience the beauty of nature, appreciate art, and communicate with others effectively. Understanding our senses is essential in enabling us to make meaningful connections with our surroundings, thus enriching our lives. Simply put, our senses are the windows through which we perceive and interact with the world around us. Each sense plays a critical role in our ability to understand, connect, and communicate effectively. Appreciation and understanding our senses are both essential in helping us to lead fulfilling lives and fostering meaningful relationships. Therefore, we should strive to cultivate and nurture our senses to enhance our experiences and better understand the world around us. Each sense plays a vital role in our daily lives, from allowing us to recognize a loved one's voice to experiencing the texture of our favorite foods. However, if we are not careful, unclean spirits can use those same senses to ensnare and/or delay us. Jezebel is a master of sensuality because that wicked spirit falls under the principality called Baal. Considered a fertility god, Baal was also synonymous with pleasure. If Baal had a slogan, it would be, "Do as you will."

Jezebel's Household

Growing up under Jezebel's care is, quite frankly, the same as being raised by demons because, in truth, the children being raised by Jezebel are consistently exposed to his or her narcissistic rage fits, gaslighting, manipulation, physical abuse, and the tactics that Jezebel uses to get his or her way. What's far worse is when children are raised by two narcissistic parents or one parent who is incredibly narcissistic, while the other parent goes out of his or her way to avoid triggering Jezebel.

In the narcissistic family, the following roles are common:

Enabler	Mascot	Hero
Lost Child	Scapegoat	Golden Child

In this chapter, we will examine some of the roles found in the narcissistic family structure, and again, we won't just look at this psychologically, we will look at each role spiritually or biblically so that we can get a better understanding.

The Enabler (Psychological)	The Enabler (Spiritual)
The enabler is often the member who takes on the role of maintaining the status quo and the peace, even at the expense of their own well-being and those who are affected by the narcissist's toxic behavior. This individual may constantly make excuses for the dysfunctional behavior of other family members, deny that there is a problem, or enable destructive patterns to continue by their lack of action or confrontation. The enabler may believe that they are doing the right thing by avoiding conflict and keeping the family together, but in reality, they are contributing to the dysfunction by allowing it to persist and by protecting the narcissistic individual from facing the consequences of his or her actions.	In the book of Revelation, the Church at Thyatira was rebuked by the Lord for "tolerating" Jezebel. This means that they could clearly see that the woman in question was toxic, narcissistic, and evil, and yet, there was some benefit that they were extracting from Jezebel. It is for this reason that they allowed a false prophetess to lead God's people astray. This is to say that the Church at Thyatira turned a blind eye to Jezebel's evil ways, thus, making them serve in the role of the enabler. Of course, this is still a common scenarop today in churches, organizations, institutions, and families. The person often bound by the spirit of Jezebel is oftentimes useful or beneficial to the structure that tolerates him or her.
Oftentimes, the martyr of the narcissistic or toxic family, the enabler frequently sacrifices their own happiness and health in order to appease and accommodate the dysfunctional behavior of the narcissist or narcissistic individual. They may constantly put the needs of others before their own, neglect their own well-being, and endure emotional or even physical abuse in order to	In the narcissistic family dynamic, this is the person bound by the Ahab spirit. For example, if the mother is a narcissist who repeatedly abuses her daughters, the Ahabish father will try to calm the mother down, redirect her anger to himself, or attempt to lessen the fury behind Jezebel's rage. And while this may sound heroic, where Jezebel's abuse ends, his starts. This is because he will defend Jezebel and her wicked ways, chastise his daughters for

The Enabler (Psychological)	The Enabler (Spiritual)
maintain the illusion of family harmony. This dysfunctional family martyr often feels a sense of obligation or guilt to continue enabling the dysfunctional patterns, as if they are responsible for keeping the family together.	questioning the narcissist, and may even punish them in an attempt to keep the family together. Believe it or not, while Jezebel is evil, that spirit usurps its authority from the Ahab'ed individual.

The Mascot (Psychological)	The Mascot (Spiritual)
In a dysfunctional family, the mascot often plays a significant role in maintaining a sense of normalcy within the family dynamic. The mascot is typically the one family member who uses humor and lightheartedness to deflect attention away from the family's problems and dysfunction. They may use comedy, silliness, or attention-seeking behaviors as a means of coping with the difficulties within the family. In this, the mascot often presents a cheerful and optimistic facade to the external world, but underneath the humor lies a deep sense of insecurity and pain. They may feel compelled to keep the peace within the family by using their humor as a tool to diffuse tension and conflict. However, this can lead to their emotional needs being overlooked, as	Where does the mascot fit in Jezebel's world? In truth, the mascot is the equivalent of what we've come to know as a monitoring spirit or any spirit sent to spy on, entertain, distract, or redirect a person, an organization, an institution, or a movement. These low-level Jezebels are secured or anchored in their ranks by fear, insecurity, laziness, unforgiveness, and a strong need for affirmation. Brought into captivity by their own tongues, people with this spirit spend an incredible amount of time focusing their attention on others, and then gossiping about everything to see, believe, or have heard from others. These entertainers of Jezebel are very skilled at flattery or making you feel comfortable enough to share your thoughts, concerns,

The Mascot (Psychological)	The Mascot (Spiritual)
they may not feel comfortable expressing their own struggles amidst the chaos of the dysfunctional family. Furthermore, the role of the mascot can hinder the family from addressing and resolving their underlying issues, as their humor can serve as a distraction from the seriousness of the problems at hand. As a result, the mascot may struggle with their own emotional well-being and may find it challenging to develop healthy coping mechanisms outside of humor and comedy. All the same, the mascot, like the enabler, will often stop at nothing to keep the family together. While their heroic ways don't go unnoticed, they often serve as flying monkeys for the narcissist whenever one of the victims of the narcissist's abuse chooses to confront, expose, or go no contact with the narcissist.	fears, complaints, insecurities, or whatever you have in your heart with them, as they tend to come off as incredibly sincere and caring. But make no mistake about it. Their allegiance is to Jezebel, even though they can, do, and will gossip about her as well. People with this particular spirit do not typically fare well in life. They spend their lives being incredibly "family-oriented," often known to show up at every family gathering, have the "inside scoop" on most family members, and they will stop at nothing to be praised by Jezebel. Also note that the mascot is not loyal to a specific Jezebel; they will easily betray one Jezebel for another one if it is beneficial for them to do so. However, they will often return to their original Jezebels as time progresses forward.

The Hero (Psychological)	The Hero (Spiritual)
The hero is often the overachiever, the responsible and successful one who strives to uphold the family's image and maintain a sense of normalcy. They take on the role of the "good child" and may feel an intense pressure to live up	The hero is also another child who is set to receive the Jezebel spirit, but they often receive a lower-ranking spirit than that of their narcissistic parent(s). They go on to become overachievers, perfectionists, and

to the expectations placed upon them by their narcissistic parent or parents.

The hero is often highly sensitive to the needs and emotions of others, and may be driven by a desire to seek validation and approval from their narcissistic parent. This can lead to perfectionism and a fear of failure, as well as an excessive need to be in control.

While the hero may receive praise and admiration from their family for their achievements, they often struggle with feelings of inadequacy and low self-worth. They may feel trapped in the role of the hero, unable to express their own needs and desires for fear of disappointing or angering their narcissistic parent.

incredibly driven people. You will find them in just about every industry serving in the role of a supervisor, a manager, or the CEO himself or herself. Because they are hard on themselves, they are oftentimes harder on the people around them. Nothing, for this Jezebel, is ever good enough, as the hero will continue to see the validation and affirmation of others. They do, however, tend to be favored in the workplace by their higher-ups; that is in exception to the higher-ups who tend to be a little more relaxed and forgiving of the employees as it relates to performance and attendance. However, the hero is oftentimes despised by the people that he or she rules over, as the hero tends to rule with an iron fist. Note: these souls are often covert narcissists who will stop at nothing to win themselves a seat at Jezebel's table.

The Lost Child (Psychological)	The Lost Child (Spiritual)
In many families, there exists the archetype of the "lost child." This role is often associated with a child who is quiet, withdrawn, and sometimes overlooked within the family dynamic. The lost child may be overshadowed by	While the world of psychology refers to this particular individual as the "lost child," the truth is that this is the "hidden child." This is often the individual who has been called or chosen by God to confront Jezebel;

The Lost Child (Psychological)	The Lost Child (Spiritual)
more outgoing siblings or may deliberately seek to avoid conflict and attention by retreating into their own world. The lost child role can have a significant impact on family dynamics. In some cases, the lost child may be perceived as the "easy" child, causing parents to focus their attention and energy on their more demanding children. For example, children who were born with mental or physical restrictions can oftentimes require more time, attention, and assistance. This can lead to feelings of neglect, rejection, and loneliness for the lost child, as well as feelings of guilt and inadequacy for the parents. Additionally, the lost child may struggle with developing a strong sense of self and may have difficulty asserting their needs and desires within the family. This can lead to challenges in forming healthy relationships and navigating social interactions outside of the family unit.	that is if he or she heals. You see, the lost child often deals with a whiplash of sorts, whereas, they don't typically feel the full effects of Jezebel's fangs until they have gotten out of Jezebel's house and out on their own. One of the protective coatings that God has equipped them with is the ability to not see Jezebel's rejection, neglect of them, and her terroristic threats for what they are—a bunch of adult-sized tantrums. In other words, many lost children learn not to take Jezebel's ugly deeds personal. However, this does not mean that they do not crave Jezebel's love, affirmation, and acceptance. And again, people who serve in this role often go in one of two directions. They either go from relationship to relationship, oftentimes with narcissists or narcissistic people, hoping to get the love that they couldn't get from their narcissistic parents, or they may go no contact with Jezebel, and go on to become incredibly successful.

The Scapegoat (Psychological)	The Scapegoat (Spiritual)
In a dysfunctional family, the scapegoat is the individual who is blamed for the	This is the eunuch of the family; this is the one who is repeatedly castrated,

The Scapegoat (Psychological)	The Scapegoat (Spiritual)
family's problems and is often the target of criticism, ridicule, and scapegoating behavior. This role is typically assumed by one family member, and they become the focal point for all the family's issues, allowing the other members to avoid taking responsibility for their own actions. They may be chosen for various reasons. They may be the most sensitive or vulnerable member of the family, making them an easy target for the other family members to project their own issues onto. Additionally, the scapegoat may be seen as a threat to the dysfunctional family system, as they may be the only ones willing to address or challenge the underlying problems within the family. The scapegoat is often labeled as the "troublemaker" or "problem child" of the family, and they are frequently subjected to emotional, verbal, and sometimes even physical abuse. This can have detrimental effects on the individual's self-esteem, mental health, and overall well-being. They may also develop maladaptive coping mechanisms, such as substance abuse, self-harm, or other destructive behaviors.	humiliated, and mismanaged by Jezebel. This particular individual receives the brunt of Jezebel's rage, criticism, and abuse. Spiritually speaking, Jezebel attempts to and sometimes successfully robs the scapegoat of his or her vitality; she usurps some of this power for herself, and then transfers the rest to the Golden Child, thus teaching the Golden Child that the Scapegoat is at his or her disposal. The Golden Child comes to believe that the Scapegoat is his or her punching bag, ATM machine, or supplier of whatever the Golden Child needs. This creates a wedge between the Scapegoat and the Golden Child, especially if the Scapegoat fights off the Golden Child's growing narcissism. Scapegoats, in most cases, were rejected not just by their Jezebelic parent(s), they were rejected by the Jezebel spirit. For example, in a movie about vampires, one of two things would happen whenever a person was bit by a vampire: that person would either become a vampire or they'd be killed. The scapegoat would be the ladder. The scapegoat is a sacrifice. The good news is, the ones who go no contact with the Jezebels in their lives and seek healing often fare well,

The Scapegoat (Psychological)	The Scapegoat (Spiritual)
The impact of being a scapegoat in a dysfunctional family can be profound, leading to feelings of shame, worthlessness, and low self-esteem. The scapegoat may also suffer from mental health issues such as anxiety and depression as a result of their role within the family.	especially in business affairs. The not-so-good news is, many of them turn to a life of crime, oftentimes turning their rage towards, for example, women who remind them of their abusers. In other words, they can sometimes pick up a higher ranking Jezebel spirit, thus causing them to become antisocial, psychopathic, and/or highly suicidal.

The Golden Child (Psychological)	The Golden Child (Spiritual)
In many families, there is a child who is often perceived as the favorite, receiving preferential treatment and attention from parents and other family members. This child is often held to high standards and praised for their achievements, often becoming the center of attention in the family. This child, of course, is the Golden Child. The Golden Child role can have various effects on family dynamics. On one hand, the Golden Child may feel pressured to live up to the high expectations placed upon them, leading to feelings of stress and insecurity. They may also experience resentment from their siblings who feel	The Golden Child, practically speaking, is the narcissist in training, but spiritually speaking, the Golden Child is the child who's been appointed by the Jezebel spirit as its next home. Keep this in mind—demons are not omnipresent. The Jezebel spirit that's in Aunt Rosie, for example, cannot inhabit Aunt Rosie and you at the same time. Therefore, if you are its next planned place of residency, that spirit would begin to prepare a place for itself in your heart, and it would do this by grooming you. This may look like Aunt Rosie favoring you, pitting you against your cousins, and always insisting on having you around her. In this, that spirit would be getting you to open your heart to Aunt Rosie in an

The Golden Child (Psychological)	The Golden Child (Spiritual)
overshadowed by their success. On the other hand, the Golden Child may feel a sense of entitlement and superiority, leading to a strain in their relationships with other family members. All the same, the Golden Child role can also perpetuate a pattern of favoritism and unequal treatment in the family, leading to jealousy and resentment among siblings. This can create a toxic environment in which family members compete for attention and validation.	event called trust. From there, it would create an ungodly soul tie between you and your aunt. The same is true for the Golden Child. If Pamela had the Jezebel spirit, and it chose her daughter, Six, to be its next place of residency, it would cause Pamela to favor Six. All the same, Pamela would set the stage for entitlement in her daughter by making her feel like the rest of her siblings are jealous of her when, in truth, Jezebel is grooming Six to be its next home.

Narcissistic Reasoning

Reasoning or leveling with a narcissist can be pretty challenging, and sometimes, impossible. This is often driven by the fact that narcissists and highly narcissistic people tend to have what I call narcissistic reasoning. What is narcissistic reasoning, you ask? In simplistic terms, what most people consider to be "common sense" tends to evade a narcissistic individual. For example, let's say that there is a narcissistic man named Jerry, and Jerry has a wife. One day, Jerry's wife, Lola, discovers a receipt lying on the floor of Jerry's car. While Jerry is driving, Lola leans over and picks up the receipt. As she holds the paper in her hand, she notices that Jerry used his debit card to purchase a bouquet of roses, a box of chocolates, and a promise ring. She looks at the date on the receipt, and it says that the purchase was made a little over two weeks ago. Of course, she questions her husband about the charges and, at first, he lies. However, Lola dismantles all of his lies, so Jerry decides to say what is on his mind. "Okay, I bought the roses, the candy, and the promise ring for Rhonda! Is that what you want to hear?!" Who is Rhonda, you ask? It's Jerry's ex-girlfriend; this is the woman he has claimed to hate with all of his soul. This is the woman he speaks reproachfully about every chance he gets (which is a red flag within itself). This is the woman who has filed countless restraining orders against Jerry, but they always manage to rekindle their toxic relationship. Rhonda sits silently for a while. Annoyed by the silence, Jerry continues to elevate his voice. "You women are so stupid! You look for problems, and then when you find one, you have the nerve to sit and look stupid! Yes, I bought my ex-girlfriend a few gifts because I wanted to! Are you happy now, Lola … I mean, Rhonda?!" Rhonda still doesn't answer her husband. She allows herself to feel the intensity of every emotion that surfaces, but she'd promised herself a month ago that she would no longer argue with Jerry because those arguments always ended in him subjecting her to some type of punishment, whether that punishment included:

1. Leaving the house for a few days.
2. Staying out overnight, and then coming home at the break of dawn.
3. Giving her the silent treatment for a week or two.
4. Making the atmosphere in the home incredibly uncomfortable by slamming doors, blasting the television set, snatching the covers off Rhonda, or calling people and talking loudly about his plans to leave Rhonda. He may say something along the lines of, "Hello, Jacob. Hey man, do you know anyone who has a house or an apartment for rent? I need to move ASAP."
5. Cooking for himself or bringing home food for himself without preparing, purchasing, or offering any food to his wife.
6. Requesting demeaning sexual favors in an attempt to make his wife feel lower than low. This may look like him refusing to have sexual intercourse with his wife; instead, he may ask for oral sex and, more than likely, he will use derogatory language when making this request. I'm talking about language that men typically use on women who they view as sex workers or promiscuous.
7. Turning the thermostat in their shared home up or down in an attempt to make Rhonda uncomfortable.
8. Being physically, mentally, emotionally, verbally, morally, or spiritually abusive.
9. Destroying Rhonda's property, whether virtual or realistic.

10. Blocking his wife on social media because Rhonda is a private person; she likes to work out her conflicts face to face.

Three days after finding the receipt, Rhonda decides to confront her husband and this time, he appears to be more humble. What's worse is that even outside of anger, he still can't seem to understand what he's done wrong. He grabs his wife by the hands, looks her in her eyes and says, "She simply fell on my mind and I wanted to do something nice for her. Don't read into it. If it will make you feel better, I bought you some roses and chocolates today; they are sitting in the car. Wait right here while I go and retrieve them." What's happening here? Rhonda is dealing with a narcissistic male who can't seem to grasp common sense, and what you will find with narcissists and narcissistic people is that they will often get angry with you for not "understanding" their out-of-this-world reasoning. Another example of narcissistic reasoning starts at a restaurant in the center of town. Out of the restaurant storms a very angry Chloe. As she exits the restaurant, she turns around and begins to swear at someone. A few minutes later, she makes her way over to her best friend's car. "Thank you for picking me up on such short notice, girl!" she shouts. She then goes on to explain that she'd been terminated from her job because her manager didn't like her. After the two speak for a little over an hour, Chloe's friend, Sharon, discovers that Chloe doesn't seem to possess the basic principles needed to even function in the workplace. She learns that Chloe has been late a total of six times, even though she's been working for the restaurant for only three weeks! She also learns that Chloe tends to challenge her supervisor's authority; she even routinely leaves her job post to engage in gossip or conversation. However, she genuinely cannot understand why she was never considered an asset to the company or why she was easily dismissed by the company. She rants on and on about how she has been on time most of the time. She whines, "They knew that I didn't have a car when they hired me! They knew my situation!" Her narcissistic rant ends with her accusing the boss of sleeping with one of the supervisors, and then shouting, "Plus, my boyfriend wanted to spend some extra time with me today! That's why I was late! He kept complaining about how often I have to go to work, so I decided to stay home for the day, but he talked me into going to work! So while I was late, they should be happy that I came to work in the first place!" These are examples of narcissistic reasoning; this is when sound wisdom and logic seems to be out of reach for a person.

Lucifer had narcissistic reasoning and, of course, he was the first narcissist to ever exist. According to Isaiah 14:13-14, he'd said in his heart, "I will ascend into heaven, I will exalt my throne above the stars of God: I will sit also upon the mount of the congregation, in the sides of the north: I will ascend above the heights of the clouds; I will be like the most High." He eventually shared his narcissistic reasoning with Eve when he said (after tempting her to eat from the Tree of the Knowledge of Good and Evil, and hearing her rebuttal), "Ye shall not surely die: For God doth know that in the day ye eat thereof, then your eyes shall be opened, and ye shall be as gods, knowing good and evil." Did he know that he was lying to Eve? Yes, he did. Did he know that he was lying to himself when he thought that he could make himself equal to God? Probably not; this is because narcissists rarely, if ever, correct themselves. They tell themselves what they want to hear, all the while, tuning out the voices of sound logic and reasoning. They are haughty souls whose hearts are guarded by the Leviathan spirit.

This is to say that before you befriend or date someone, follow the steps below:
1. Pray about the individual, and do not give them a role, responsibility, or a title until you hear back from God.
2. Make sure you get wise counsel regarding your potential relationship before you establish it and announce it.
3. Listen more than you speak! For the ladies, we have a BAD habit of telling our potential love interests and friends EVERYTHING that we want them to know and EVERYTHING that they want to know. In order to discern some spirits, you have to listen! Let the person who is auditioning for a role in your soul say what's in and on his or her heart. If the person doesn't seem to grasp the basic fundamentals of sound judgment and native intelligence, you're probably dealing with a narcissist or an incredibly narcissistic individual. One conversation that tends to cause narcissists to expose their demonic, immature, or manipulative reasoning

is the discussion of one of their exes. They may say something along the lines of, "He had the audacity to get mad at me because he caught me kissing my ex! Like I told him, Craig was teaching me how to perform CPR! I invited him over to our house because I wanted to learn how to do CPR, and yes, Craig kissed me, but I can't control what another person does! How is this my fault?!"

4. Take them outside of their element. Every narcissist and/or narcissistic person has a habitat; this is an environment, an attitude, a climate, and a group of people that the narcissistic individual thrives in or around. They will want to cut you off from your family and surround you with their friends and not-so-loved ones. They will attempt to control the information that you take in by determining whose voice plays or echoes in your life. This is why one of the ways to test and see the kind of person you're dating or building a friendship with is to take that individual outside of what he or she deems to be "comfortable."

5. Pay attention to their friends and the people they surround themselves with. If they are the smartest people in their circles, they are likely narcissistic. Narcissists love to surround themselves with people who have low intelligence quotients and/or low self-esteem; this allows them to control the people by controlling the conversations.

Don't allow your imaginations to run ahead of the moment you're in! Matthew 6:34 says it this way, "Take therefore no thought for the morrow: for the morrow shall take thought for the things of itself. Sufficient unto the day is the evil thereof." Don't allow fantasy to introduce you to a character who simply doesn't exist in the person you're entertaining. And last but not least, pray against the idols in your heart! Tear them down piece by piece, day by day, and moment by moment! It's a process, but it's worth it because whatever you don't tear down will ultimately tear you down.

Visual Acuity

When I was 17 years old, I got my first job. A few months later, I went to an eye doctor for the first time in my life. I'd always known that my eyesight was poor, but I didn't know how poor it was because I'd grown accustomed to squinting my eyes to see objects and people that were afar off. I'd grown comfortable greeting people before I could make out their faces. This is to say that my visual acuity was low. Visual acuity is one of the most important aspects of our eyesight. It refers to the sharpness or clarity of our vision or, better yet, the ability to see objects clearly and distinguish their details. Visual acuity is essential for reading, driving, and any other activity that requires precise visual discrimination. I remember how amazed the doctor was upon hearing that I'd never had an eye exam or worn corrective lenses. His amazement was heightened when he saw just how poor my eyesight was. "How do you see the blackboard at school?" he asked. "I can't," I responded. "I just ask the teacher if I can approach the board so I can see it clearer." When the exam was over, he handed me a pair of corrective lenses, and he jokingly said, "Here's my business card. Call that number on the card to let me know when you're on the highway so I can make sure I'm not on it." We both had a good chuckle, and I left the exam room amazed at how clear my world had just become. It was weird seeing people's faces from where I was, instead of seeing shapes.

The measurement of visual acuity is based on the Snellen chart, which consists of letters or symbols arranged in decreasing size. The chart is placed at a distance of twenty feet from the person being tested, and the person is asked to read the smallest line of letters that they can see. The results are recorded in terms of a ratio, such as 20/20, which indicates that the person being tested can see the same level of detail at 20 feet that a person with normal vision can see at 20 feet.

Visual acuity can be affected by various factors, including genetics, age, disease, and injury. My issue wasn't genetic, as both my parents had 20/20 vision, but they often blamed it on the fact that I loved sitting close to the television when watching it. Refractive errors such as myopia (nearsightedness), hyperopia (farsightedness), and astigmatism can also affect visual acuity. According to Oxford Languages, astigmatism is "a defect in the eye or in a lens caused by a deviation from spherical curvature, which results in distorted images, as light rays are prevented from meeting at a common focus." These conditions occur when the shape of the eye or curvature of the cornea does not allow light to focus properly on the retina, resulting in blurred vision. Presbyopia is another common condition that affects visual acuity, particularly in people over the age of 40. It occurs when the lens of the eye loses its flexibility, making it difficult to focus on close objects. The symptoms of presbyopia can be corrected with reading glasses or contact lenses. Similarly, cataracts can also affect visual acuity. A cataract is a clouding of the eye's natural lens, which can cause blurred vision and difficulty seeing at night. Cataracts can be treated through surgery to remove the cloudy lens and replace it with an artificial one.

Visual acuity can also be affected by eye diseases such as glaucoma and macular degeneration. Glaucoma is a condition in which the optic nerve that connects the eye to the brain is damaged, leading to gradual vision loss. Macular degeneration is a condition that affects the central portion of the retina, leading to blurred or distorted vision. All of this is to say that visual acuity is crucial for daily activities and is affected by various factors such as age, genetics, diseases, and injuries. Refractive errors, presbyopia, cataracts, and eye diseases can all affect visual acuity and require medical attention. Therefore, regular eye exams are essential to maintain good visual acuity and detect any potential visual problems that may need treatment. It is important to prioritize our eyesight and take steps to maintain our visual acuity for optimal vision and quality of life.

Why are we talking about visual acuity? Simply put, you need to understand the science behind vision; this will undoubtedly help you to better understand the prophet's ability to see in the realm of the spirit. For example, some prophets and prophetic people have sharp vision, spiritually speaking. What dims the prophet's ability to see in the realm of the spirit or hear from the Most High is sin, rebellion, witchcraft, lack of faith, fear, unforgiveness, ungodly soul ties, unresolved trauma, and bad associations. Don't get me wrong. God can speak to and through whomever He chooses to speak to and through regardless of where that person stands in relation to Him. However, a man's ability to hear from God or see visions is largely determined by the health of his heart. For example, think of a wind instrument (by the way, a wind instrument, according to Wikipedia, is "a musical instrument that contains some type of resonator in which a column of air is set into vibration by the player blowing into a mouthpiece set at or near the end of the resonator." Examples of wind instruments include, but are not limited to saxophones, clarinets, flutes, trumpets, harmonicas, and the list goes on. These instruments require the musician to blow into them in order for them to release a sound. Now, imagine that you have a flute, but it's been dented up pretty badly, especially the embouchure hole. Do you think it would sound the same as it would have sounded had it been in mint condition? Not at all. The shape of the instrument largely affects its sound. Also consider the body of Lucifer. Ezekiel 28:13-18 records YAHWEH's response to Lucifer's rebellion. It reads, "Thou hast been in Eden the garden of God; every precious stone was thy covering, the sardius, topaz, and the diamond, the beryl, the onyx, and the jasper, the sapphire, the emerald, and the carbuncle, and gold: the workmanship of thy tabrets and of thy pipes was prepared in thee in the day that thou wast created. Thou art the anointed cherub that covereth; and I have set thee so: thou wast upon the holy mountain of God; thou hast walked up and down in the midst of the stones of fire. Thou wast perfect in thy ways from the day that thou wast created, till iniquity was found in thee. By the multitude of thy merchandise they have filled the midst of thee with violence, and thou hast sinned: therefore I will cast thee as profane out of the mountain of God: and I will destroy thee, O covering cherub, from the midst of the stones of fire. Thine heart was lifted up because of thy beauty, thou hast corrupted thy wisdom by reason of thy brightness: I will cast thee to the ground, I will lay thee before kings, that they may behold thee. Thou hast defiled thy sanctuaries by the multitude of thine iniquities, by the iniquity of thy traffick; therefore will I bring forth a fire from the midst of thee, it shall devour thee, and I will bring thee to ashes upon the earth in the sight of all them that behold thee."

As you can see, Lucifer's body was a work of art! It was also an instrument. God is a Spirit, therefore, all who worship Him must worship Him in Spirit and in Truth. By the way, the Greek word for "spirit" is "pneuma," and it means breath or wind. Think about it. God is Spirit; Lucifer's body was made of instruments. To make it as practical as it is spiritual, before Lucifer's great rebellion, the wind of God would pass through his body. According to the scripture, Lucifer was perfect in all his ways. This is to say that Lucifer would release a beautiful sound whenever He was in the presence of God. However, once Lucifer started having ungodly thoughts, he likely didn't give God all the glory anymore, meaning, he didn't release the worship that belonged to God. You see, Lucifer was the worship leader in Heaven, and as the worship leader, he would go into the presence of God, and not only was he filled by God, every instrument on his body was illuminated by God, causing the light to refract and reflect. Whenever he went before the angels to lead them in worship, he would be illuminated by the light, much like Moses' face lit up after having been in the presence of God for 40 days. And the sounds that would pour out of Lucifer's body would cause the angels to worship the Lord all the more. Their worship would go through Lucifer's body, and his job was to return the worship to God, but it is likely that Lucifer decided to keep some of God's worship for himself. Get this—a lot of what we see taking place in the scriptures are often natural events that once reflected events that took place in the realm of the spirit. For example, take into account the story of Ananias and Sapphira. Acts 5:1-11 reads, "But a certain man named Ananias, with Sapphira his wife, sold a possession, and kept back part of the price, his wife also being privy to it, and brought a certain part, and laid it at the apostles' feet. But Peter said, Ananias, why hath Satan filled thine heart to lie to the Holy Ghost, and to keep back part of the price of the land? Whiles it remained, was it not thine own? And after it was sold, was it not in thine own power? Why hast thou conceived this thing in thine heart? Thou hast not lied unto men, but unto God. And Ananias hearing these words fell down, and gave up the ghost: and great fear came on all them that heard these things. And the young men arose, wound him up, and carried him out, and buried him. And it was about the space of three hours after, when his wife, not knowing what was done, came in. And Peter answered unto her, Tell me whether ye sold the land for so much? And she said, Yea, for so much. Then Peter said unto her, How is it that ye have agreed together to tempt the Spirit of the Lord? Behold, the feet of them which have buried thy husband are at the door, and shall carry thee out. Then fell she down straightway at his feet, and yielded up the ghost: and the young men came in, and found her dead, and, carrying her forth, buried her by her husband. And great fear came upon all the church, and upon as many as heard these things." For context, Acts 4:32-35 tells us why this duo ended up paying for their deceptive ways with their lives. It reads, "And the multitude of them that believed were of one heart and of one soul: neither said any of them that ought of the things which he possessed was his own; but they had all things common. And with great power gave the apostles witness of the resurrection of the Lord Jesus: and great grace was upon them all. Neither was there any among them that lacked: for as many as were possessors of lands or houses sold them, and brought the prices of the things that were sold, and laid them down at the apostles' feet: and distribution was made unto every man according as he had need." The nation of Israel had made a covenant to sell their houses and their properties and bring back the money from those sales. They would then lay that money at the apostles' feet. The apostles would then distribute the money, ensuring that the needs of every Israelite were met. Ananias and Sapphira went along with this agreement, but they conspired with one another to hold back a portion of the money they'd acquired from selling their land. They also conspired to lie to the apostles. This angered Peter because his ability to hear God was nearly unmatched.

An Ananias or Sapphira type of prophet would likely have trouble hearing from God. They'd likely complain about the fact that they haven't been dreaming, seeing visions, or getting any prophetic instructions from God for a certain amount of time. This has everything to do with their minds being twisted instruments that the winds of God cannot flow through freely. Every believer is an instrument of God, and not all instruments, as we know, make the same sounds. This is to say that:

1. God doesn't use all prophets or prophetic people in the same measure.

2. A prophet or prophetic individual who repeatedly goes between light (God's presence) and darkness (sin) will likely not have the same measure of clarity as a prophet or prophetic individual who lives a life fully surrendered to Christ.

3. Prophets and prophetic individuals who repeatedly turn their heads when help is needed will often find themselves locked out of revelation.

4. Jonah type prophets who run from God's instructions cannot be trusted until they surrender to God, and these types of prophets often have to endure the hardships of being swallowed whole by Leviathan (the principality behind pride) for a season before they will fully surrender to God. Many of them never surrender. Consequently, they live their lives in the custody of a narcissist.

5. Rebellious prophets often experience the phenomenon of hearing many voices, and many times, they cannot differentiate these voices from the voice of God. This causes them to lose the health of their minds.

In truth, our mental institutions are filled with prophets and highly prophetic people who do not understand that they are instruments of God, and as such, they don't have the luxury of being normal. Their abilities to hear in the realm of the spirit, as well as see dreams and open-eyed visions make them a magnet for demons who desire to use, sift, humiliate, and destroy them. This is especially true for Jezebel. This particular spirit has been after God's mouthpieces since the dawn of its waking. This is why it is important for the prophet or prophetic individual to not only have visual acuity, but also take the proper steps to correct any issues that may be affecting the prophetic individual's sight and insight, prophetically speaking. Please keep in mind that, in the natural, some conditions occur when the shape of the eye or curvature of the cornea does not allow light to focus properly on the retina, resulting in blurred vision. The same is true for the shape of your soul. The shape of your soul is largely determined by what you put in it and the people you've allowed to help shape the way you see yourself. For example, if you're a prophetic individual who's been married to Jezebel for the last eight years, you're likely out of shape, spiritually speaking. This is because Jezebel has repeatedly placed you in a proverbial box of sorts, and that spirit has not only abused you over the years, but it has also used your spouse to pervert how you see the man or woman in the mirror. The good news is—your prophetic lens can be adjusted and cleansed, but in order for you to submit to this process, you must first recognize when they're dirty. You may be comfortable squinting prophetically, waiting for the picture to become clearer over time; then again, you may be comfortable using your emotions to feel around in the spirit, hoping to get a good grasp on what the Lord is saying. But don't let your comfort become your cave. It is always wise to get a spiritual exam from your leaders, mentors, or whoever God has led you to be accountable to. All the same, accountability is only effective if you allow your leaders to correct you. This is important because there are a lot of people out there who have pastors and leaders from whom they refuse to receive correction. This means that their leaders are nothing but props. If you want to grow your visual acuity, you have to be accountable for what you see, what you hear, and a lot of the activity that goes on in your mind.

Spiritual Acuity

In contemporary society, having 20/20 vision is perceived as the standard for good eyesight. But what exactly does it mean to have 20/20 vision? Plainly put, the term 20/20 vision refers to a person's ability to see a certain size of letter at a distance of 20 feet. The term "visual acuity" is used to describe this ability, with 20/20 vision being considered "normal" or "standard acuity." A person with 20/20 vision can see what a person with "normal" vision should be able to see at a distance of 20 feet, but how is our visual acuity determined? The answer is—to measure visual acuity, an eye chart is used. As we discussed earlier, the most well-known eye chart is the Snellen Chart, which consists of letters of varying sizes arranged in rows. The top row contains one large letter, with subsequent rows containing smaller letters. A person with 20/20 vision should be able to read all the letters on the chart from a distance of 20 feet. If a person cannot read the smallest letters, the distance between the person and the chart is reduced until the individual can read them. The distance is then recorded as the person's visual acuity. If the individual in question can read the smallest letters on the chart from a distance of 20 feet, that person is said to have "20/20 vision." Keep in mind that the concept of 20/20 vision is highly valued in contemporary society, as it is seen as an indicator of good health and optimal eyesight. People with 20/20 vision are often thought to have an edge over those who do not have this level of visual acuity. They may be able to perform certain tasks better, such as driving or reading, and they are less likely to experience eye strain or other visual problems.

However, it is important to note that the concept of 20/20 vision is not the be-all-and-end-all of visual acuity. A person can have better than 20/20 vision, such as 20/15 or 20/10, which means they can see letters at 20 feet that the average person would need to be at 15 or 10 feet respectively to read. On the other hand, a person can have worse than 20/20 vision, such as 20/30 or 20/40, which means they need to be closer to the chart to read the same sized letters as someone with 20/20 vision. Furthermore, visual acuity is not the only factor that contributes to good eyesight. Other factors include depth perception, peripheral vision, color vision, and eye coordination. A person can have 20/20 vision but still experience other visual problems, such as poor depth perception or color blindness. In short, this is to say that 20/20 vision refers to a person's ability to see a certain size of letter at a distance of 20 feet. It is measured using an eye chart, with the Snellen Chart being the most well-known. Although highly valued in contemporary society, 20/20 vision is not the only indicator of good eyesight, and a person can have better or worse than 20/20 vision. Overall, while 20/20 vision is an important benchmark for visual acuity, it should not be viewed as the only measure of good eyesight.

Now that we have a grasp on the natural world of sight, let's talk about spiritual sight and insight. As we've already discussed, not all prophets and prophetic people have the same spiritual acuity. In 1 Corinthians 13:9, the Apostle Paul went on record with these words, "For we know in part, and we prophesy in part." This is to say that God often shows us parts and pieces of a vision. The reason for this is to encourage unity in the body of Christ, plus, we all have a capacity. In other words, we can only bear so much. Think about it this way. Let's say a 13-year old boy was helping you move your possessions out of one house into a moving truck. You've already handed him a box filled with clothes, but he asks you to stack another box on top of the box he's holding. However, you notice that his posture is off. His knees are severely bent, he's leaning back at a very uncomfortable angle, and his voice sounds strained. Chances are, you will not place another box on top of the one he is holding. All the same, you may even lighten his load. The measure in which he can bear is largely determined by how much he can manage without bending his posture or putting strain on his heart. This is how God measures our acuity. God will give you a burden, for example, and He will watch and see how you manage what He's already given you. If the burden provokes you to sin against God, you are simultaneously revealing to God the measure of weight that you can bear. The following signs show that what you are carrying is too heavy for you:

1. You complain about the burden.
2. You keep putting the burden down to go back into sin or comfort.
3. You isolate yourself because you don't want to carry the burden.
4. You refuse to lift the burden; instead, you keep it around, promising to lift it later once, for example, "you've gotten yourself together."
5. The burden provokes you to sin against God.
6. You keep trying to give the burden and the blame to someone other than yourself.
7. You keep falling into the trap of self-preservation every time the burden gets heavier.

Please note that the burden is not designed to remain the same weight. God wants to uplift you by increasing what you can bear. This is because He wants to increase Himself in you, but to do this, He has to put you within certain feet of someone who's carrying the same or a similar mantle that you are set to carry. This is the prophet or the prophetic person's version of a Snellen Chart. For example, God will give you leaders after His own heart (see Jeremiah 3:15), and your job is to honor them, submit to them, and glean from them. If the concept of submission bothers you, you have to get a true definition of what submission is. All the same, you may have to heal from whatever abuse you've suffered at the hands of an authority figure. Then again, you may have to overcome generational pride, whereas you've managed to convince yourself that everyone who walks with you must walk alongside you or behind you, but no one can walk ahead of you. In order for a cup to be poured into, there has to be another container above that cup pouring into it; this has everything to do with position and posture. The container must be in position to pour, and you must have the right posture to be poured into. Going back to the example of the 13-year old helper, in order for him to grab one of the boxes, he has to come into the house; that is if the boxes are not outside, and we all know that when we're moving, we don't typically take the boxes outside. So, he'd have to come in the house, go into the room where the boxes are that he intends to carry, and then he must bend himself (this represents humility) in order to pick up the box. If the box is too heavy for him, he has a few choices.

1. He can leave the box where it is so that someone stronger than himself can carry it.
2. He can push the box to the car, instead of carrying it.
3. He can use a trolley to transport the box from the house to the moving truck.
4. He can have someone else who is in the house to help him carry the box to the moving truck.
5. He can carry the box another way. For example, if it's too heavy for him to carry the standard way, he may be able to carry it on his back, on his shoulders, or on his head.

Again, we all have a capacity in the natural just as we do in the realm of the spirit. God might trust one prophetic person with a burden that would absolutely crush another prophetic person. Now, if the individual with the lightest load becomes envious of the person who has the heavier load, he may find himself attempting to sabotage the one who God trusts. Simply put, he may try to increase that prophet's load by giving the individual more responsibilities. Then again, he may decide to become the burden. In this, the prophet or prophetic person in question has volunteered his prophetic services to the kingdom of darkness, thus making him a part-time sorcerer, and if he is in a position of authority over the other prophet, he will serve as a pharaoh of sorts. Consider the story of Joseph. God entrusted him with a prophetic gift, and this gift seemed to be more dominant (at first) whenever he went to sleep. In his immaturity, he told his brothers about his dreams, not realizing that they despised him. In truth, I suspect that he knew that they were no fans of his, and being a young man, he likely chopped it up to being nothing more than a little sibling rivalry, but as we all know, it was much more than that. The greater lesson in this is—prophets who have strong spiritual or prophetic acuity are oftentimes hated by their not-so-gifted brethren. This is because, like Cain, many of them see their brethren as a threat to their agendas. This is especially true for some of the prophetic individuals who grew up in the church or who've been in church for an extensive amount of time. Not all of them, of course, but many of these individuals tend to see their newly converted brethren as threats to their positions, their names, and their agendas. They often reason this way, "I've been saved for the last 18 years. I've served my pastor faithfully for the last 12 and a half years! Who does she think she is that she can walk in here after only being saved for four years, and mess up how we do things in this church?!" Many of the church-hurt stories that plague our airways today come from prophets and prophetic people who walked into a new church, only to be met with competition, sabotage, prophetic resistance, and warfare from some of the people who'd been entrusted to grow that particular church. This has everything to do with the fact that new converts are not yet slaves of church politics. Don't get me wrong. Not all church politics are bad, but a large number of them are restrictive, constrictive, outdated, and in some cases, demonic. All the same, not every prophet or prophetic person who ran out of a church screaming "church hurt" was actually hurt by a church. Many of them go into churches with unrealistic expectations and dreams of grandeur, and when things don't pan out the way they thought they would, they leave their prospective churches. After this, they launch a smear campaign hoping to bring that church to its knees.

Your spiritual acuity doesn't have as much to do with how clearly you can see a vision versus how much revelation God can trust you with. It also involves how much warfare God can trust you with. How much can you endure before your character is bent out of shape? How much can you bear before you break? Believe it or not, when God says that He can trust you, He's simply saying that He can trust you with warfare. He's saying that you can carry heavy burdens without compromising His Word or your relationship with Him. To understand this more, think about this fact—in the Old Testament times, there were many prophets roaming around, but only a select few were trusted to prophesy to kings. There were many prophets around when the Prophet Elijah was out and about, but God saw fit to trust the Prophet Elisha to carry the mantle and the burden He'd entrusted Elijah with. This is to say that not all prophets or prophetic people are equal in rank, relevancy, or accuracy. There are people out there who don't trust prophets because they came in contact with one of the following:

1. A false prophet.
2. An immature prophet.
3. A double-minded prophet.
4. A broken prophet.
5. A prophet whose visual acuity wasn't up to par.
6. A prophet who didn't test the spirits behind his or her visions.
7. An unforgiving prophet.

Your prophetic acuity, on the other hand, deals with your accuracy or your ability to see what God is showing you or hear what God is saying. Your spiritual acuity deals with your maturity. This is important because people often think that the ability to accurately prophesy means that the prophet is mature, healed, and trusted by God, but this isn't necessarily true. God may have entrusted the prophet with the information He shared with him or her, but this does not mean that the prophet or prophetic person is trustworthy. Many churches and individuals have discovered this truth the hard way. For example, consider the unnamed prophet who was devoured by a lion simply because another prophet gave him instructions that were antithetical to what God told him to do. Let's look at that story. 1 Kings 13:1-26 reads:

> "And behold, a man of God came out of Judah by the word of the LORD to Bethel. Jeroboam was standing by the altar to make offerings. And the man cried against the altar by the word of the LORD and said, 'O altar,

altar, thus says the LORD: 'Behold, a son shall be born to the house of David, Josiah by name, and he shall sacrifice on you the priests of the high places who make offerings on you, and human bones shall be burned on you.' And he gave a sign the same day, saying, 'This is the sign that the LORD has spoken: 'Behold, the altar shall be torn down, and the ashes that are on it shall be poured out.' And when the king heard the saying of the man of God, which he cried against the altar at Bethel, Jeroboam stretched out his hand from the altar, saying, 'Seize him.' And his hand, which he stretched out against him, dried up, so that he could not draw it back to himself. The altar also was torn down, and the ashes poured out from the altar, according to the sign that the man of God had given by the word of the LORD. And the king said to the man of God, Entreat now the favor of the LORD your God, and pray for me, that my hand may be restored to me.' And the man of God entreated the LORD, and the king's hand was restored to him and became as it was before. And the king said to the man of God, 'Come home with me, and refresh yourself, and I will give you a reward.' And the man of God said to the king, 'If you give me half your house, I will not go in with you. And I will not eat bread or drink water in this place, for so was it commanded me by the word of the LORD, saying, 'You shall neither eat bread nor drink water nor return by the way that you came.' So he went another way and did not return by the way that he came to Bethel. Now an old prophet lived in Bethel. And his sons came and told him all that the man of God had done that day in Bethel. They also told to their father the words that he had spoken to the king. And their father said to them, 'Which way did he go?' And his sons showed him the way that the man of God who came from Judah had gone. And he said to his sons, 'Saddle the donkey for me.' So they saddled the donkey for him and he mounted it. And he went after the man of God and found him sitting under an oak. And he said to him, 'Are you the man of God who came from Judah?' And he said, 'I am.' Then he said to him, 'Come home with me and eat bread.' And he said, 'I may not return with you, or go in with you, neither will I eat bread nor drink water with you in this place, for it was said to me by the word of the LORD, 'You shall neither eat bread nor drink water there, nor return by the way that you came.' And he said to him, 'I also am a prophet as you are, and an angel spoke to me by the word of the LORD, saying, 'Bring him back with you into your house that he may eat bread and drink water.' But he lied to him. So he went back with him and ate bread in his house and drank water. And as they sat at the table, the word of the LORD came to the prophet who had brought him back. And he cried to the man of God who came from Judah, 'Thus says the LORD, 'Because you have disobeyed the word of the LORD and have not kept the command that the LORD your God commanded you, but have come back and have eaten bread and drunk water in the place of which he said to you, 'Eat no bread and drink no water,' your body shall not come to the tomb of your fathers.' And after he had eaten bread and drunk, he saddled the donkey for the prophet whom he had brought back. And as he went away a lion met him on the road and killed him. And his body was thrown in the road, and the donkey stood beside it; the lion also stood beside the body. And behold, men passed by and saw the body thrown in the road and the lion standing by the body. And they came and told it in the city where the old prophet lived. And when the prophet who had brought him back from the way heard of it, he said, 'It is the man of God who disobeyed the word of the LORD; therefore the LORD has given him to the lion, which has torn him and killed him, according to the word that the LORD spoke to him.'"

Isn't it crazy that the same prophet who lied to the prophet who was on an assignment is the very prophet that God used to prophesy to him about his disobedience and the punishment that would ensue? Some people would argue that the old guy was a false prophet when, in truth, the Bible does not refer to him as a false prophet. He was likely a demonized prophet. He was in a region that was filled with idolatry and witchcraft, so we can safely assume that he had been impacted and infected by the demonic altars that had been erected in that region. The older prophet had a greater measure of spiritual acuity, whereas the unnamed prophet had a pretty sharp measure of prophetic acuity. In other words, the unnamed prophet was not that mature. He likely allowed himself to be manipulated by this prophet because the older man was more seasoned, plus, he may have allowed his hunger to overtake him, given the fact that he was fasting. Notice that the older prophet tempted him with food. Remember, Jezebel is sensual; that spirit will always go out of its way to appeal to your sensual needs. The point of this is, as a prophet or a prophetic person, it is absolutely imperative for you to have a pastor or someone who is set in place to pour into you and hold you accountable. This is why the Bible says in Proverbs 11:14, "Where no counsel is, the people fall: but in the multitude of counselors there is safety." Another way of saying this is, "There is danger in the lack of wise counsel." This is largely because there are prophets out there, both false and true, who will lead you astray if you don't guard your heart. Some people will argue with you, saying things like, "I've been saved ever since I was in diapers, and I have served in my church for the last 18 years." In many if not most cases, these people are using their tenure to exalt themselves and their words above whatever it is that God is showing you. Yes, you should have someone who outranks you in place to help you with whatever you believe God is showing you, but you should not receive counsel from everyone who calls himself a prophet or a highly prophetic individual because, while they may be accurate, they could also be bound. Then again, they may have prophetic acuity, but it's not balanced with spiritual maturity. Get this—old doesn't mean wise, and a man or woman's church tenure isn't a revelation of their spiritual acuity. Their pastors' ability to trust them is not the same as God's ability to trust them.

Prophetic Acuity

As we discussed in the previous lesson, your prophetic acuity has everything to do with clarity or, better yet, your ability to hear what God is saying or understand what God is showing you. Just like an optometrist or ophthalmologist, God will often test your prophetic acuity to see just where you stand in Him. We see the evidence of this in the following scriptures:

- **Genesis 2:19 (ESV):** Now out of the ground the LORD God had formed every beast of the field and every bird of the heavens and brought them to the man to see what he would call them. And whatever the man called every living creature, that was its name.

- **Jeremiah 1:11:** Moreover the word of the LORD came unto me, saying, Jeremiah, what seest thou? And I said, I see a rod of an almond tree. Then said the LORD unto me, Thou hast well seen: for I will hasten my word to perform it.
- **Jeremiah 1:13:** And the word of the LORD came unto me the second time, saying, What seest thou? And I said, I see a seething pot; and the face thereof *is* toward the north.
- **Jeremiah 24:3:** Then said the LORD unto me, What seest thou, Jeremiah? And I said, Figs; the good figs, very good; and the evil, very evil, that cannot be eaten, they are so evil.
- **Amos 8:2:** And he said, Amos, what seest thou? And I said, A basket of summer fruit. Then said the LORD unto me, The end is come upon my people of Israel; I will not again pass by them any more.

Take into consideration the moment Jesus opened a blind man's eyes. Mark 8:22-26 tells this story; it reads, "And he cometh to Bethsaida; and they bring a blind man unto him, and besought him to touch him. And he took the blind man by the hand, and led him out of the town; and when he had spit on his eyes, and put his hands upon him, he asked him if he saw ought. And he looked up, and said, I see men as trees, walking. After that he put his hands again upon his eyes, and made him look up: and he was restored, and saw every man clearly. And he sent him away to his house, saying, Neither go into the town, nor tell it to any in the town." In this, we find the Lord first taking the man out of the town he lived in. Why did He do this? Because He had to take him outside the place of familiarity, because familiarity interrupts and disrupts the moves of God. Next, we see the Lord doing something unconventional. He spat on the man's eyes. After this, He put His hands on the man and asked him what he saw. The man replied, "I see men like walking trees." After this, the Lord laid His hands upon the man's eyes for a second time, and this time, his sight was fully restored. In this, the man's vision had been restored with the first touch, but his visual acuity was less than perfect. Instead, mildly put, the man's eyesight was poor. You see, some people

172

would have stopped right in this moment, rejoicing in the fact that a man who was once blind could now see, albeit, poorly. But Jesus shows us how to respond to unfinished miracles. He laid His hands upon the man's eyes again, and this time, the man's eyesight was restored. It's amazing how the natural realm gives us insight into the spiritual realm. In this, we learn that all miracles aren't instantaneous (on Earth, that is); this has everything to do with our faith or, better yet, whether we believe in God or not. The same is true for the prophetic. Some prophetic individuals don't have great prophetic acuity because their faith is shortsighted. In other words, it's hard for them to see past their own selfish needs and desires. Consequently, while they have the gift, they don't necessarily have the clarity.

Today, we have too many prophets and prophetic people who are overly obsessed with being accurate when they should be focused on being holy. Accuracy has everything to do with our posture and maturity; it is a revelation of how much we trust God, as well as how much He trusts us. Understand that God can give a foolish man a prophetic word or a vision, and that man may be able to see that vision very clearly. How he communicates what he's seen is a different story altogether. This is because whatever truths God reveals to that man has to go through the filters of:

1. His faith.
2. His fear.
3. His experiences in life.
4. His experiences with God.
5. What he consumes daily (conversations, media, etc.).
6. His understanding.
7. His ability to communicate (language/language barriers).

This is why Satan uses a demon called Leviathan who the Bible refers to as the "king of the proud" to bind and blind prophets and prophetic people. The objective of Leviathan is to feed the prophetic individual a diet of falsehoods and misinterpretations; this way, the prophet will usher in the spirit of pride. God resists the proud and gives grace to the humble (see 1 Peter 5:5). The Greek word for "resist" is "antitassetai," and according to the Englishman's Accordance, it means:

- God is opposed to the proud.
- God sets Himself against the proud.

What is the significance of God setting Himself against the proud? Simply put, it means that God is an adversary of the proud at heart. In layman's terms, God will not partner with a proud prophet. Satan knows this, so he goes out of his way to wound prophets and prophetic individuals; this way, he can offer them relief and false healing in exchange for their voices. How does a proud prophetic person sound or how do they behave?

- They talk excessively about their "haters."
- Most of their messages and social media posts are about them rising above their enemies.
- They do things like randomly and drastically change their appearances, delete their social media profiles, delete a mass number of people from their social media pages, and then post about it.
- They brag about cutting people off easily.
- They talk excessively about what you'll have to do to walk in their circles or what could get you kicked out of their lives.
- They post a lot of pictures of themselves, for example, in the gym, at an outing, or eating at a high-end restaurant. (Note: this is normal behavior for many people, but for the wounded prophetic individual, these posts are usually preceded by statements like, "They wish they could be like you, but they can't because God made you different."
- They randomly or sometimes frequently attack other leaders because they see ministry as a competitive sport.
- Most of their messages reek of bitterness. For example, they may say, "It's stupid to date a prophet and then try to cheat. God shows us everything! Surprise, we can see you!" That post may be followed by, "Most of these men out here who claim to be Christians cheat so much that they cheated themselves out of an opportunity to be with great women, and then they have the nerves to complain when they find themselves in Jezebel's lair!" This isn't to say that everyone who posts a

negative relationship message is bitter; it is to say that wounded and prideful prophets tend to post excessively about their broken love lives.

- They speak and post more about themselves than they do about Christ.

Of course, this is just a short list of symptoms showing that a prophetic person has been wounded. And get this—anytime a prophetic person experiences an inordinate amount of pain OR that person keeps dealing with the same issue on a different day, most prophetic people fall into the trap of creating covenants with their lips. They may say things like, "I will never let someone get that close to me again," or "I don't think I'll ever look at marriage the same again." From there, an agreement is formed, after all, two people can walk together when they are in agreement (see Amos 3:3). Once the prophetic individual unwittingly starts ensnaring himself or herself by the words of his or her mouth, the enemy then strengthens his campaign against them. He always sends demonized people or demonic opportunities to wounded prophets, because a wounded soul will stop at nothing to get relief. If Satan can get the individual in question to repeatedly rebel against the Word and ordinances of God, he can successfully blur the vision of the prophet. In other words, he can take a prophetic individual who has stellar prophetic acuity and make them see men as trees. Simply put, they will see people as nothing but mere objects or a means to an end.

Prophetic Range

In this section, we will talk about the three types of prophetic ranges; they are:

Nearsightedness	Farsightedness	Astigmatic

You will see me referring to the prophets and prophetic people with these ranges as:

- The Nearsighted Prophet.
- The Farsighted Prophet.
- The Astigmatic Prophet.

Please note that this is referring to the prophet's range, and not necessarily his or her wiring. God uses us all in different ways, so if you find that you fit, for example, under the Farsighted Prophet's category, please don't limit yourself by thinking that's the fullness of your range. God can (and oftentimes does) increase the range of the people He uses as they mature and heal. The point, however, of this lesson is to help you to mentally map just where you are prophetically. This is not to label or limit a prophet or a prophetic voice that God is using or intends to use. Labels are great when you don't adopt them as your personal identity.

Every prophet has a range, and your range is determined by how much God can trust you. Again, we all have filters, and anytime God speaks to and through an individual, what God says has to go through that person's filters. Think of it this way—you can invite 25 women to a birthday party, and you can say to them all, "You guys look great! You are some absolutely beautiful women! I thank God for you!" This is a compliment, and most people with a healthy heart would take it as such. However, every one of those women has filters, and their filters are coated with:

1. Their experiences in life.
2. How they've interpreted those experiences.
3. Their relationships with God.
4. Their knowledge or lack thereof.
5. Their understanding or lack thereof.
6. Whatever they've filled their hearts with.
7. Their preferences, plans, and opinions.

Out of those 25 women, let's say that 15 of them said, "Thank you," before proceeding back to what they were doing before they were interrupted. Five of them gave you an odd look, signaling that they were confused and a tad bit offended, but they too went back to doing what they had been doing before you complimented them. However, the other five decided to address the matter.

- One woman said, "What do you mean by 'you guys'? We're women, of course."
- Another woman chimed in with, "Why are you commenting on our appearances?"

- A third lady said, "So, you thought it was a good idea to stop everyone from doing what they were doing just to hear what you had to say? How rude!"
- The woman next to her yells, "Who told you that we were women?! I'm tired of all of misgendering!"
- And finally, the fifth woman replies, "For God's sake, it's your birthday! Take a day off from your religion, why don't you!"

As you can see, these five women took a standard compliment completely out of context. This has everything to do with the health of their hearts' filters. You see, trauma bends the filters, and the Leviathan spirit, whenever it surfaces, will twist the words of the people speaking to you. This is because, according to the scriptures, Leviathan is a covenant-breaking spirit. It works closely with the spirit of offense to keep the truth from entering a person's heart. This is to say that whenever God speaks to us, what He says has to go through our filters. If your filters are severely bent, you will often take what God says to you out of context. For example, have you ever heard someone try to misinterpret their own dream or someone else's dream? Was God communicating with that person through the dream? He probably was! But the individual in question would need to ask someone who is more mature, more healed, and more in tune with the Most High God to help the individual get the interpretation of the dream in question. In other words, it would be wise for the person to seek someone who has greater prophetic range.

With that said, when you're reading about the nearsighted prophet, the farsighted prophet, and the astigmatic prophet, don't pick a category and claim it. Just see this as a marker on a map, instead of seeing it as your identity.

The Nearsighted Prophet

Nearsightedness, also known as myopia, is a common refractive error of the eye that affects millions of people worldwide. It is a condition where distant objects appear blurry, while close objects remain clear. Myopia occurs when the eyeball is too long, or the cornea, the clear front cover of the eye, is too curved. This causes light to focus in front of the retina, rather than directly on it, resulting in a blurred image. Myopia can also be caused by a genetic predisposition, where a person's family history increases the likelihood of developing the condition.

The most common symptom of myopia is difficulty seeing distant objects, such as street signs or the board in a classroom. People with myopia may squint or strain their eyes to see clearly, and may also experience headaches or eye fatigue. If left untreated, myopia can lead to further complications such as retinal detachment or glaucoma.

How does any of this relate to the prophet or the prophetic person? There are prophets who are nearsighted, just as there are prophets who are farsighted. In this particular lesson, we will focus on the nearsighted prophet. As you have just learned, nearsightedness is the ability to see things clearly that are close, but items that are far off are not that clear. To make it plain, nearsighted prophets are not that discerning whenever they come in contact with people they don't know. Consequently, they oftentimes let people get close to them who are toxic, demonized, and needy. But here's the kicker: once a broken and ungodly soul manages to get close to the nearsighted prophet, the prophetic individual can often see everything they need to see about that person. There's a problem with this, however. By the time they see the issues at hand, they are already soul-tied to the broken individuals or they may have yoked themselves with these people in marriage, in business, or by forming some sort of alliance. Consequently, the nearsighted prophet spends more time healing than he or she does prophesying.

A good biblical example of a nearsighted prophet was Samson. He was so focused on Delilah's beauty that by the time he saw her heart and her demons, he was too infatuated with her to walk away. This is to say that Samson was soul-tied to the weapon that had been formed against him, and he was willing to risk it all to prove himself to her. This is also to say that Samson, while strong and mighty, was likely bound by the Ahab spirit. Understand this—a person who is bound by the Ahab spirit can be strong physically, strong in the marketplace, and strong in any or every arena you can think of. However, with Jezebel, they are but puppets. This is because they have repeatedly surrendered their authority to Jezebel, so much so that they now rely on Jezebel for their self-worth, their identities, and their peace. Jezebel has now become a source of security for them, despite how insecure, controlling, and manipulative their Jezebelic counterparts are. Get this—Samson likely suspected that Delilah was going to cost him his life, but the problem with nearsighted prophets is—once people get close to them, they find it hard to let those people go. All the same, they will often ignore all of the red flags waving around them, and they will gaslight themselves into believing that their enemies are truly just misunderstood friends. In many cases, they'll simply convince themselves that they have trust issues, thus encouraging themselves to tolerate Jezebel. That is until Jezebel does significant damage to them and their ministries. Nearsighted prophets tend to treat others better than they treat themselves, oftentimes to their own detriment.

Many nearsighted prophets and prophetic people tend to prophesy about events that are just around the corner, but these events have been brewing for years. This is not to discredit the prophets; after all, we prophesy in part. If anything, the failure to report or pray against these issues falls upon the farsighted prophet.

The Farsighted Prophet

Farsightedness, also known as hyperopia, is a condition that affects millions of people worldwide. It is a refractive error, which means that the eye does not bend light properly, leading to a distorted or blurred image. This condition often causes difficulty in focusing on objects that are close, resulting in eyestrain, headaches, and other visual disturbances. Farsightedness can occur at any age, but it is most commonly diagnosed in children and becomes more prominent in adults over 40 years old. What is the cause, you ask? Farsightedness is caused by a mismatch in the shape and length of the eyeball. In a normal eye, the cornea and the lens focus light directly onto the retina, allowing us to see clearly.

However, in a farsighted eye, the eyeball is too short, or the lens is too weak, causing light to focus behind rather than on the retina. This causes images of close-up objects to appear blurry, and the eyes must strain to focus on them.

What about the farsighted prophet? Unlike the nearsighted prophet, the farsighted prophet is incredibly discerning. They can see Jezebel from a mile away or a smile away. When these types of prophets are in a church, for example, they will oftentimes notice people with demonic agendas before most of the leaders in that building discerns them. They may even warn leadership about certain people and express their concerns, but to no avail. This is how and where the farsighted prophet is wounded (if he or she is not yet mature). Over time, farsighted prophets will typically shrug their shoulders whenever they see demonized people moving up the ranks. This is a sign that, like the retina of an eye, the prophetic individual has detached himself or herself from the emotional aspect of doing ministry.

Another issue of the farsighted prophet is the closer people get to them, the harder it becomes for them to see their issues and demons. For example, a lot of farsighted prophets are still closely attached to their demonic, narcissistic family members. This is because their family got close to them before their gifting matured. All the same, whenever the narcissistic Jezebel goes after this type of prophet or prophetic individual, that spirit typically migrates into the prophet's life through a third-party; this is often someone the farsighted prophet trusts. A great example of this is—Tonya is very careful about who she allows in her life. As a farsighted prophet, she can often see danger from afar. However, Tonya's best friend, Donna is a nearsighted prophet. Donna loves and trusts just about anyone who utters the name of Jesus. She also extends herself to anyone who appears to want help. Because of this, it is not uncommon for Donna to form friendships with some of the people she was supposed to be ministering to. Donna occasionally meets new people who she passionately wants to introduce to her best friend, Tonya, but Tonya is too reserved. However, because Tonya trusts Donna, she has allowed her to introduce her to three women, two men, and a life coach. Donna reassured her friend each and every time that, while she could clearly see a few issues here and there with the people in question, these people were as harmless as a truckload of fireflies. In most of these cases, Tonya managed to escape these people before she got emotionally involved with them, but she did not cut ties with Patrick fast enough to prevent a soul-tie from forming. Because of this, Tonya would spend the next two years being delayed and damaged by her narcissistic lover. She would then spend the next four years healing from the damage that was brought on by Patrick.

Another trait of the farsighted prophet is this—they tend to prophesy about events that are years away from happening. Sometimes, they may prophesy about events that are scheduled to take place hundreds of years from the moments they are in. Then again, they often ignore what God shows them because they keep questioning the dreams and visions that God gives them. This is why the nearsighted prophet is needed. They typically warn the body of Christ about events that the farsighted prophet failed to share with God's people.

A good biblical example of a farsighted prophetic person is St. Luke. While Luke was an evangelist, he was highly prophetic. In Acts 2:17-21, he prophesied, "And it shall come to pass in the last days, saith God, I will pour out of my Spirit upon all flesh: and your sons and your daughters shall prophesy, and your young men shall see visions, and your old men shall dream dreams: And on my servants and on my handmaidens I will pour out in those days of my Spirit; and they shall prophesy: And I will shew wonders in heaven above, and signs in the earth beneath; blood, and fire, and vapour of smoke: The sun shall be turned into darkness, and the moon into blood, before that great and notable day of the Lord come: And it shall come to pass, that whosoever shall call on the name of the Lord shall be saved." In this, we find Luke talking about events that were afar off (depending on what branch of theology you subscribe to). Another example of a farsighted prophet is John, the Baptist. He'd repeatedly prophesied about Jesus, and when he saw Jesus in the flesh for the first time, he immediately knew that Jesus was the one he'd been prophesying about. But the closer he got to Jesus, the more his prophetic vision began to blur. Check out the following scriptures.

- **John 1:14-18:** And the Word was made flesh, and dwelt among us, (and we beheld his glory, the glory as of the only begotten of the Father,) full of grace and truth. John bare witness of him, and cried, saying, This was he of whom I spake, He that cometh after me is preferred before me: for he was before me. And of his fullness have all we received, and grace for grace. For the law was given by Moses, but grace and truth came by Jesus Christ. No man hath seen God at any time; the only begotten Son, which is in the bosom of the Father, he hath declared him.
- **John 1:29-34:** The next day John seeth Jesus coming unto him, and saith, Behold the Lamb of God, which taketh away the sin of the world. This is he of whom I said, After me cometh a man which is preferred before me: for he was before me. And I knew him not: but that he should be made manifest to Israel, therefore am I come baptizing with water. And John bare record, saying, I saw the Spirit descending from heaven like a dove, and it abode upon him. And I knew him not: but he that sent me to baptize with water, the same said unto me, Upon whom thou shalt see the Spirit descending, and remaining on him, the same is he which baptizeth with the Holy Ghost. And I saw, and bare record that this is the Son of God.
- **John 1:35-37:** Again the next day after John stood, and two of his disciples; and looking upon Jesus as he walked, he saith, Behold the Lamb of God! And the two disciples heard him speak, and they followed Jesus.
- **Matthew 11:2-3:** Now when John had heard in the prison the works of Christ, he sent two of his disciples, And said unto him, Art thou he that should come, or do we look for another?

Notice that John initially declared who Jesus is before the Lord said anything to him, but after John had been arrested, he began to question Jesus' deity. Believe it or not, he did what a lot of farsighted prophets do; they are confident with the words they speak. That is until they see those words coming to pass. The reason for this is—prophecy imagined is not always prophecy realized. What this means is, what you see play out before you doesn't always look the way you thought it would look when the Lord gave you a vision of what was to come. It is for this reason that many farsighted prophets tend to sabotage their blessings whenever those blessings begin to materialize themselves.

The Astigmatic Prophet

Astigmatism is a common vision condition that causes blurred or distorted vision at all distances. It occurs when the cornea or lens of the eye has an irregular shape, leading to light rays not focusing properly on the retina. This results in a blurry image and difficulty seeing fine details. Other symptoms of astigmatism can include headaches, eye strain, squinting, and trouble seeing clearly at both near and far distances. Many people are born with astigmatism, while others can develop it over time due to eye injuries, scarring, or changes in the shape of the cornea.

Of course, there are believers out there who have the gift and the grace of prophecy, but they are prophetically astigmatic. Simply put, it means that they have no discernment, both near and far. These types of prophetic individuals are dealing with anything from trauma to generational curses, both of which tend to dull their vision. This means that their issues are deeply rooted, and while they are treatable, one of the greatest enemies of the prophet is pride. Many prophets and prophetic types are too prideful to admit that they need help. And because they typically have trouble seeing whatever it is that God wants to show them, these types of prophetic individuals may hear what the Lord is saying, but they don't have dreams or visions very often, if at all. And don't get me wrong—if God isn't showing you anything, it doesn't mean that there's something wrong with you. It may very well be the way that He uses you, after all, as believers, we are all members of the body of Christ. You may be a single eye, while someone else may be the equivalent of a set of eyes. However, whenever a prophetic person is wounded, while their gift is still functional, that prophetic individual may operate in a way that does not align with how God designed them to operate, or it can lead to the person having trouble hearing the voice of God. Then again, the individual may struggle with differentiating the voice of God from their own voice or the voice of the enemy.

It's worth mentioning too that the opposite of the astigmatic prophet is the prophet who has better than standard prophetic acuity, along with spiritual acuity. This is to say that whenever a prophetic individual is designed, wired, and commissioned by God to be, for example, a seer or a prophet to the nations, the enemy will stop at nothing to break that prophet; this way, the prophetic person can and often will operate contrary to his or her own design.

Prophetic Sensitivity

Prophetic sensitivity refers to an individual's capacity to sense, discern, and interpret divine messages or revelations from Heaven. Sensitivity to the prophetic is a spiritual gift that allows one to hear, see, feel, or sense God's guidance. It is the ability to be sensitive to the voice of God and to have a deep understanding of His ways, along with His heart for His people.

In biblical times, prophets played a significant role in the spiritual life of the Jewish community. They were chosen by God to bring messages of judgment, redemption, and hope. The message of the prophets was intended to prepare the people for the coming of the Messiah and to help them live in accordance with God's Word and His will. In many instances, those who did not heed the warnings of the prophets faced severe consequences, such as exile or destruction. This is why prophetic sensitivity was and is still needed. Prophetic sensitivity is a crucial gift for those who seek to follow the path of God. It enables us to hear His voice and to recognize when He is leading us. In short, we know that God communicates with His people, and these messages can come through dreams, visions, or through the ministry of the Holy Spirit. Prophetic sensitivity is thus a key factor in spiritual growth, as it fosters a deeper sense of intimacy with God and encourages a greater understanding of his will, and this is crucial for the prophet or the prophetic person. The importance of prophetic sensitivity can be seen in the examples of biblical figures who exhibited this gift. One such example is Samuel, who was chosen by God to be a prophet while still a young boy. Samuel was sensitive to God's voice and could recognize His call when he heard it. He followed God's instructions when he anointed Saul as king over Israel and later when he anointed David as king in Saul's place. Samuel's prophetic sensitivity allowed him to play an essential role in the history of Israel. Another example is Elijah, who was a powerful prophet who'd demonstrated remarkable prophetic sensitivity when he listened to God's voice and boldly confronted King Ahab and Queen Jezebel for their wickedness. Elijah's sensitivity enabled him to hear the still, small voice of God when he was hiding in a cave, and God directed him to perform various tasks to fulfill his prophetic calling.

Prophetic sensitivity also helps people to discern false prophets and deception. In the New Testament, Jesus warned His followers to beware of false prophets who would come in His name and deceive many. Jesus taught that false prophets could be known by their fruits, and that it was essential to test all messages against God's Word. A person with prophetic sensitivity is better equipped to detect false teachings and messages that are not from God.

Prophetic sensitivity can be developed by cultivating a deeper relationship with God. It requires spending time in prayer, studying the Bible, and being open to the leading of the Holy Spirit. A person with prophetic sensitivity must also be willing to submit to God's will and to be used by Him and Him alone. It is essential to avoid pride and to seek humility, as pride can hinder the flow of prophetic revelation. All the same, it is important to cast down imaginations and any thoughts that could potentially lead you astray, after all, one of the prophet's greatest enemies is his or her imagination. This is because thoughts produce feelings, and these feelings can become relatively addictive. This is why a prophet's drugs of choice are oftentimes adrenaline, dopamine, oxytocin, and serotonin. This is why it is common to find prophets and highly prophetic individuals in theaters, gyms, trap houses, drug stores, and in relationships with Jezebel. It shouldn't be a secret by now that prophets and prophetic people tend to be thrill-seekers, with the more introverted ones seeking excitement from the comforts of their own home. This way, they can get the laughs, the fuzzy feelings, and the feelings of fear, trepidation, and anger without the soul ties that typically come with these emotions. One of the reasons for this is—highly prophetic people can sense and feel the emotions of others, and this can be overwhelming and maybe even traumatic to a prophet who has no wise counsel or no one to help him or her better understand what the prophet is experiencing.

This is to say that prophetic sensitivity is a gift within itself that is vital for spiritual growth and discernment. It allows people to hear the voice of God, to discern His will, and to be used by Him. It requires a deep relationship with God, a willingness to submit to His will, and openness to the leading of the Holy Spirit. Developing this gift is crucial for leading a life that is pleasing to God and that fulfills one's own God-established purpose.

The Well-Rounded Prophet

Moses was a well-rounded prophet. Not only did God use him to lead the Israelites out of Egypt, through the Red Sea, and into the wilderness, God spoke face-to-face with Moses. The Lord met with Moses on Mount Sinai on two separate occasions. Let's look at those scriptures.

- **Exodus 24:12-18:** And the LORD said unto Moses, Come up to me into the mount, and be there: and I will give thee tables of stone, and a law, and commandments which I have written; that thou mayest teach them. And Moses rose up, and his minister Joshua: and Moses went up into the mount of God. And he said unto the elders, Tarry ye here for us, until we come again unto you: and, behold, Aaron and Hur are with you: if any man have any matters to do, let him come unto them. And Moses went up into the mount, and a cloud covered the mount. And the glory of the LORD abode upon Mount Sinai, and the cloud covered it six days: and the seventh day he called unto Moses out of the midst of the cloud. And the sight of the glory of the LORD was like devouring fire on the top of the mount in the eyes of the children of Israel. And Moses went into the midst of the cloud, and gat him up into the mount: and Moses was in the mount forty days and forty nights.
- **Exodus 34:27-28:** And the LORD said unto Moses, Write thou these words: for after the tenor of these words I have made a covenant with thee and with Israel. And he was there with the LORD forty days and forty

nights; he did neither eat bread, nor drink water. And he wrote upon the tables the words of the covenant, the Ten Commandments.

What made Moses a well-rounded prophet? The truth is, he hadn't been subjected to the abuse or the realities that the other Jews had been subjected to. In other words, he could see their world from the outside in. He knew what was wrong with the Egyptians, but after a few brushes with the Israelites, he understood what needed to be changed within their camps and within their hearts. What you will soon come to discover is that God doesn't always use people from the worlds you've been exposed to; He oftentimes uses outsiders because outsiders can see what you may be blind to.

What are some of the characteristics of well-rounded prophets?
1. They spend notable time with God.
2. They read their Bibles daily.
3. They do not forsake the congregating of the saints.
4. They are in no rush to deliver a prophetic message to an individual. Instead, they test the spirit, pray about when, how and where to release the Word, and deliver the message when they feel a release from God to do so.
5. They are in no rush to post a dream or a vision online just to prove their prophetic prowess. Instead, they sit back, pray, and watch the other prophetic individuals rush to report on what they believe they are hearing or seeing. They post when they feel a release to do so.
6. They will not gossip about what God has shown them.
7. They are intentional about healing; they are never just sitting in the process of healing, but they take the necessary steps to ensure that they heal properly.
8. They are mindful of their associations.
9. They are avid intercessors.
10. They don't boast and brag about a gloomy dream, and then wait for it to come to pass just to prove that they are prophetically inclined. Instead,

when they are warned in dreams about disasters, they intercede and ask God to prevent the attacks; they ask God for mercy.

11. They are always cleaning out their prophetic filters with wise counsel, deliverance, and studying to get understanding.
12. They are not easily offended.
13. They don't mind prophesying to people who've hurt them.
14. They do not church-hop; they pray and ask the Lord where He wants them to be, and they stay there until He tells them to move. All the same, they make sure that they get wise counsel to ensure they are truly hearing from God before making a decision.
15. They practice sexual abstinence if they are unmarried. If they are married, they honor their spouses, both privately and publicly.
16. They don't steal prophetic words and repackage them as their own. In short, they don't operate in prophetic plagiarism. Instead, they give credit to whomever it is due.
17. They will not echo what they hear other prophets and prophetic people saying just because everyone seems to be prophesying the same thing. Instead, they say what they hear God saying to them.
18. They will not allow people to pressure them into prophesying when they haven't heard anything from God.
19. They are not afraid of demons, but are apt to, instead, cast them out.
20. They put God's plans before their own.
21. They will not tolerate Jezebel.
22. They are always seeking to grow spiritually.
23. They don't chase platforms, mics, and opportunities; they chase God.
24. They will prophesy the truth at any cost!
25. They understand the art of pain, and they will separate themselves from anyone who attempts to poison their destinies!

This is a short list of the traits that you will find in a well-rounded prophet or prophetic individual. If you can't relate to this list, don't fret. We are all growing. Just seek to grow your relationship with God all the more, and you will begin to see the many fruits of the Spirit, and all that comes with them over time. The objective isn't to be used by God faster; your assignment is just to follow His pace and His lead, and to endure all that challenges your walk with Him as you journey with Him in purpose on purpose.

- **Ecclesiastes 9:11:** I returned, and saw under the sun, that the race is not to the swift, nor the battle to the strong, neither yet bread to the wise, nor yet riches to men of understanding, nor yet favor to men of skill; but time and chance happeneth to them all.
- **Matthew 6:34:** Take therefore no thought for the morrow: for the morrow shall take thought for the things of itself. Sufficient unto the day is the evil thereof.

Blinders and Muzzles

As we all know, there are certain diseases and issues that can potentially affect our eyes, and most of these conditions are preventable and treatable. The problem is that, for whatever reason, many Americans don't have routine health checkups. PBS News Weekend reported the following:

> "Nearly a third of Americans lack access to primary care services, including routine checkups, while 40 percent of U.S. adults say they're delaying care or going without because of the financial costs" (Source: pbs.org/Why More Americans Are Putting Off Going To The Doctor).

Let's look at a few common issues that affect the eyes.

Glaucoma

Glaucoma is a group of eye conditions that cause damage to the optic nerve, leading to vision loss and blindness <u>if left untreated</u>. It is one of the leading causes of blindness worldwide, affecting more than 80 million people. The disease is often referred to as "the silent thief of sight" because it can develop gradually without any noticeable warning signs until it is too late.

There are two main types of glaucoma, open-angle glaucoma and angle-closure glaucoma.

- **<u>Open-angle glaucoma</u>** is the most common form of the disease, accounting for about 90% of cases. It occurs when the drainage canals in the eye become clogged over time, leading to an increase in intraocular pressure. This pressure damages the optic nerve, causing vision loss. There are usually no noticeable symptoms until the late stages of the disease, when significant vision loss has already occurred.
- **<u>Angle-closure glaucoma</u>**, on the other hand, is a less common form of the disease. It occurs when the iris blocks the drainage canals, causing a

sudden increase in intraocular pressure. This type of glaucoma can cause vision loss and eye damage rapidly, and can be associated with symptoms such as severe headache, eye pain, nausea, and vomiting.

In the realm of the spirit, there is something that robs the prophet or the prophetic person of their ability to see or hear what God is saying, and this disease is just as progressive as natural glaucoma. It is sin. Sin blinds the eyes of the prophets by deforming the prophet's heart. For example, it is never wise to trust a fornicating prophet because that prophet has yielded his or her members to the enemy. Consequently, the prophet's wires are oftentimes crossed, whereas the prophet (in many if not most cases) cannot distinguish the voice of God from the many voices of the enemy. Because of this, relying on such a prophet could open you up to unclean spirits and a lot of unnecessary warfare. Like all civilians, prophets are tempted by the enemy, and it is for this reason that they need healed hearts, wise counsel, and a heart of obedience to God. If they are not fully submitted to the Lord but are, instead, bound by the spirit of this world, they are not trustworthy. Sure, the gifts and the callings are without repentance, but when a prophet or prophetic person is blinded by what this world has to offer, that prophet's prophecies will oftentimes be as contaminated as the prophet himself or herself. This is why and how so many of God's prophets have become witches.

Cataracts

Cataract is a common eye condition that affects people of all ages. It is marked by a clouding of the eye's natural lens that leads to vision impairment and, if left untreated, blindness. The condition can be caused by a variety of factors, including aging, genetics, injury, and disease. In this essay, we will discuss the causes, symptoms, diagnosis, and treatment of cataract in detail.

Cataract can have many underlying causes, but the most common cause is age-related changes to the lens of the eye. As the lens ages, its proteins break down and clump together, forming a cloudy area that obstructs vision. Other causes of cataract include long-term exposure to UV rays, genetic mutations, injury to the eye or head, diabetes, smoking, and prolonged use of corticosteroids. The main symptom of cataract is blurred or hazy vision, which gets progressively worse over time. Other symptoms include sensitivity to glare, double vision in one eye, halos around lights, reduced night vision, and a yellow tinge to objects. These symptoms may start off mild, but as the cataract grows, they become more pronounced and can affect daily activities such as reading, driving, or watching television.

For the prophet or prophetic person, the issue that can be compared to cataracts is comfort. Yes, you read that correctly. Comfort is the enemy of the prophetic. How so? Consider the story of Jonah. God told Jonah to go to Ninevah and prophesy to His people. Jonah was so comfortable in the lifestyle that he'd been living that he fled, thinking he could outrun God. Jonah 1:3 reads, "Now the word of the LORD came to Jonah the son of Amittai, saying, 'Arise, go to Nineveh, that great city, and call out against it, for their evil has come up before me.' But Jonah rose to flee to Tarshish from the presence of the LORD. He went down to Joppa and found a ship going to Tarshish. So he paid the fare and went down into it, to go with them to Tarshish, away from the presence of the LORD." Instead of obeying God, Jonah was more willing to go on the run from God so that he could find comfort elsewhere. The same is true for many, if not most of God's prophets and prophetic people today. Many of them have heard God telling them to move to other cities, states, and countries. Many of them are slowly losing the health of their minds because God gave them the same instructions that He'd given Abram, and that is to leave their countries or communities and get away from their kinfolks, and to follow God wherever He should take them. Now, get this—for some of these prophets, God is saying to simply move to another city, put space, distance, and time between themselves and their narcissistic families, and trust Him to provide for them. Their sin is that they are comfortable trusting Jezebel and not God. Many prophets live with their narcissistic mothers; these are women who went out of their way to ensure that their children would forever rely on them. This way, the children, even after they'd become adults, would continue to be supply for their mothers, fathers, or the Golden Child in that household. These prophets and prophetic people will complain about

Jezebel, but they are still sucklings of Jezebel, meaning they have not been weaned from Jezebel's system. Consequently, they adapt to becoming Ahabs, Eunuchs, or Jezebels themselves. Prophets have addictive personalities, and many of them turn to the government to pay their bills, feed their children, and to sustain their lifestyles. This would be okay if they were simply transitioning, but most are not. They've found comfort in codependency, not realizing that the American system itself is the system of Jezebel. This is why comfort is so dangerous. Comfortable prophets almost always find themselves in the lap or custody of Jezebel because Jezebel provides them free rent, free childcare, and whatever else they feel they need at the expense of their destinies. Please keep in mind that comfort isn't just associated with where you stay or how you live, it is also associated with the company you keep.

Macular Degeneration

Macular degeneration is a common eye condition that affects the macula, the part of the retina responsible for central vision. This condition is a leading cause of vision impairment and blindness in older adults, with over 11 million people in the United States alone affected by the disease.

There are two types of macular degeneration: dry and wet. Dry macular degeneration is characterized by the presence of dry, yellow deposits under the retina. This form typically progresses slowly and can cause gradual central vision loss. Wet macular degeneration, on the other hand, is marked by the growth of abnormal blood vessels under the retina. These vessels can leak fluid and blood, leading to sudden and severe vision loss.

Risk factors for macular degeneration include age, family history, smoking, and obesity. While there is currently no cure for the disease, there are treatment options available to help manage its progression and symptoms. These treatments may include nutritional supplements, injections, and laser therapy.

Spiritually speaking, there are two prophetic conditions that are common in prophets and similar to macular degeneration, and they are rebellion and witchcraft. As a matter of fact, the Bible tells us that rebellion is as the sin of witchcraft (see 1 Samuel 13:23). In Jonah's case, we find several issues; the first being that he'd tried to run away from God, and the second being, his attempt to run from God was also his way of saying "no" to God regarding the assignment God had given him. This is what rebellion looks like. It's not just resisting a direct or indirect order from God, rebellion is doing what God said not to do. Rebellion involves knowledge, meaning the person in rebellion is aware of the fact that he or she is out of order with God, and rebellion involves action. This is the seed sown into another system with the intent to get something out of that system. For example, most believers are aware of the fact that fornication is a sin. However, despite knowing this, many believers (including prophets and prophetic people) still sow into this system hoping to get a spouse. Prophets and prophetic people are also known for taking people who are a part of those ungodly systems and attempting to build romantic relationships with them, all the while, attempting to win their hearts for the Lord or, better yet, they tend to fall into the evangelistic dating trap. This is why so many prophets and prophetic people are having an identity crisis right now. They refer to themselves as empaths because the only thing they seem to know in this moment is that they tend to attract narcissistic people, not realizing that the coin flips to the other side. In other words, they not only attract narcissists and narcissistic people, they are often attracted to narcissists and narcissistic people.

The second crime is witchcraft. The amount of prophets and prophetic people who have willfully handed their souls over to Satan is astronomical, to say the least. It is a trend these days for people to get involved in New Age, not realizing how New Age practices work. In short, the enemy loves to use the gift of the prophet and prophetic person. He then tempts them to put their trust in sage, crystals, nature, the universe, or something tangible; this way, they will never know how powerful they are in Christ. This isn't just a form of idolatry, it is pure idolatry! Romans 1:24-25 reads, "**Therefore God gave them up in the lusts of their hearts to impurity, to the dishonoring of their bodies among themselves,** because they exchanged the truth about God for a lie and worshiped and served the creature rather than the Creator, who is blessed forever! Amen." What is the creature mentioned here? Is it Satan? Yes, but not just Satan directly. Satan will steal your worship by disguising himself as an angel of light. He loves to seduce us, the creatures or created things to serve and worship other creatures or things that have been created by our hands or by God. And the problem with most prophets or prophetic people is that they are so addicted to dopamine, serotonin, adrenaline, and oxytocin that they aren't willing to go through the prophetic processes needed to help develop their gifting. This is because they have not developed the fruits of the Holy Spirit, with one of those fruits being long-suffering (patience). It is for this reason that prophets are prone to witchcraft, and this is what causes many of them to decline mentally, morally, and spiritually.

Shortsighted Prophets

When we start talking about prophets and prophetic people falling away from God or not being able to be used by God to their full capacity, everyone in the room looks for someone to blame, including the blind prophet himself or herself. As prophetic people, we tend to blame our parents, our grandparents, our spouses, our exes, our friends, our churches, and when all else fails, we blame the devil. Prophets who take accountability for themselves are prophets who can see past themselves. In other words, their prophetic prowess is sharper than most prophetic people because they have not limited themselves to the accuser of the brethren's worldview (think about it). Instead, they look for themselves in every equation, understanding that they themselves are the common denominators in all of their pain. God can trust these prophetic vessels with information and increase because He knows that they will steward their assignments well. However, prophets and prophetic individuals who repeatedly, incessantly, and excessively place the blame on others for their sins, their harvests, and their failures in life can only be trusted with little because of their shortsightedness.

Luke 12:48 (NIV) states, "But the one who does not know and does things deserving punishment will be beaten with few blows. From everyone who has been given much, much will be demanded; and from the one who has been entrusted with much, much more will be asked." Pay attention to the highlighted sentence. When we read this particular scripture, we often think of money and material possessions, but this scripture is not limited to what we can see. It is also referencing gifts, talents, and opportunities. This is to say that God can and often does give people a measure of sight, but the first order of prophetic intelligence is to use that sight for insight. And by insight, I'm not talking about looking at another person intuitively, I'm talking about examining one's self from within; I'm talking about introspection. Oxford Languages defines the word "introspection" as "the examination or observation of one's own mental and emotional processes." This sounds simple enough until you start getting to know and walking with many of God's prophetic vessels, and what you'll come to see is that introspection isn't that popular because it requires a degree of humility that a lot of believers do not possess. Why is this? Because hurt people can only see what hurt them, but in their shortsightedness, it is hard for them to see the role they played in their own pain. This is to say that many prophetic people were hurt by Jezebel a long time ago. It may have started with their narcissistic parents; then again, it may have started with a two-timing ex of theirs who pushed them to the edge of their sanity. Believe it or not, the way that Jezebel holds the modern-day prophet or prophetic person in a cave is by ensuring that:

- The prophetic individual is traumatized by someone.
- The prophetic individual refuses to forgive the person or the people who hurt him or her.
- The prophetic individual remains in the environment that he or she was hurt in, or the prophetic individual remains connected to the person/people who hurt him or her.
- The prophetic person refuses to take accountability.
- The prophetic person pitches a tent in a mentality called victimhood, and over time, that tent becomes the prophet's permanent residence.

This is the degeneration of a prophet; it is a modern-day cave of sorts. Remember, caves are dark. All the same, there isn't much that can grow inside of a cave.

Please note that another word for "shortsighted" is "petty." The lesson here is this—prophetic people who are called to greatness are oftentimes distracted and led astray by small-minded people. What you'll come to witness is that most prophets and prophetic people are not attacked as much by unbelievers as they are by self-professing believers. The prophet's greatest enemy is a religious narcissist who knows scripture but does not know God. Religion is just the practice of any given faith, and people who are bound by the spirit of religion are often works-minded and pharisaic. What this means is that they don't know, understand, or embrace the works of Jesus Christ. Sure, they may acknowledge Jesus as Lord; they may profess to anyone who will hear them that Jesus is the Son of God, He died for our sins, He was resurrected on the third day, and He now sits at the right hand of God, making intercession for us. But that's as far as their faith goes. They are slaves to the letter of the law, and not necessarily servants of Christ. They often reject anything from the era that they are in, and they place a greater emphasis on what we do than they place on the heart behind what we do. They are still trying to earn their way into Heaven. They live, not in the fear of God, but in the fear of hell. They don't understand that the people in Jesus' day wore certain attire, and it wasn't the garments that made them holy; it was their decision to embrace and follow Christ. And because they don't understand this, many of them either wear old and outdated clothing or they will make their own clothing. They esteem themselves as protectors of the faith, and because they exalt their religions and their beliefs over other Christians, they often take to social media to attack any believer who does not embrace their religion. They go out of their way to learn how to speak every major religious word in Hebrew and Greek, thinking that doing so will help them to get closer to God and to stand out from other faiths. And it is these people who absolutely hate the prophets of God, but get this—they often have people in their churches who claim to be prophets, but they are known by many to be doom and gloom prophets because most of their prophecies are centered around the destruction of this Earth, the second coming of Christ, and the Great Judgment. Their messages are filled with fear and laced with envy, as they tend to go after well-known leaders instead of focusing on the lost sheep. This particular group of believers is effective at taking out prophetic voices that are in the infancy of their ministerial assignments.

Another common enemy of the prophet is what we have come to know as "church-folks." Church-folks aren't just believers; they are people who practice Christianity, but have no love, discipline, or faith to boast of. The only thing they have is tenure in a certain church and an over-exaggerated opinion. If you are truly going to be used by God, you cannot be afraid of men and their faces, nor can you allow them to ensnare you with their tongues. This is to say that you cannot be shortsighted; you cannot stop and focus on every minor or petty issue that dares to get in your way. You have to push past the unpleasant if you want to be used by God to the greatest of your ability.

Not-So-Foresighted Prophets

What does it mean to be foresighted? Foresighted, as defined by Merriam Webster, is "having or showing awareness of and preparation for the future." Get this—the idea behind prophets being nothing more than glorified fortune-tellers keeps a lot of people from having encounters with God through His truly appointed prophetic vessels. The prophet isn't designed to tell the future; the prophet is designed to shift it. The prophet is literally created to say to God's people what the Lord has said to them. Sure, God does speak to and through the prophet about events that have yet to come, but all too often, God isn't trying to get His people to prepare for an event. Instead, God is trying to activate the intercessors and get His people to repent. There are some storms that we don't have to go through if the people of God are to repent from their wicked ways! There are some storms that we don't have to endure if the people of God would have enough faith to rebuke the storm!

- **2 Chronicles 7:14:** If my people, which are called by my name, shall humble themselves, and pray, and seek my face, and turn from their wicked ways; then will I hear from heaven, and will forgive their sin, and will heal their land.

- **Mark 4:39:** And he arose, and rebuked the wind, and said unto the sea, Peace, be still. And the wind ceased, and there was a great calm.

A foresighted prophet, of course, is a prophet who hears God, and then prepares for whatever God has shared through the prophet. An example of a foresighted prophet would be Noah. Noah heard God about the impending flood, and he prepared himself and his family for the flood by building the ark. Another example of a foresighted prophet is Joseph. God warned Pharaoh in a series of dreams about a famine that was about to impact Egypt. Genesis 41:1-8 reads, "After two whole years, Pharaoh dreamed that he was standing by the Nile, and behold, there came up out of the Nile seven cows, attractive and plump, and they fed in the reed grass. And behold, seven other cows, ugly and thin, came up out of the Nile after them, and stood by the other cows on the bank of the Nile. And the ugly, thin cows ate up the seven attractive, plump cows. And Pharaoh awoke. And he fell asleep and dreamed a second time. And behold, seven ears of grain, plump and good, were growing on one stalk. And behold, after them sprouted seven ears, thin and blighted by the east wind. And the thin ears swallowed up the seven plump, full ears. And Pharaoh awoke, and behold, it was a dream. So in the morning his spirit was troubled, and he sent and called for all the magicians of Egypt and all its wise men. Pharaoh told them his dreams, but there was none who could interpret them to Pharaoh." Of course, Joseph was brought out of prison to interpret the dreams, and when Pharaoh saw just how valuable Joseph was to his kingdom, he made him his right hand man. Joseph then went on to prepare the kingdom for the famine that was about to strike the land. Therefore, a foresighted prophet is a prophetic individual who:

1. Hears what God says.
2. Shares what God says to whomever God commissions the prophet to speak to.
3. Does what God says.

So, what then is a not-so-foresighted prophet? This man or woman of God is, in many cases, a true prophet of God, but the issue with this type of prophet is that he or she tends to rush ahead of God to prepare for events that, quite frankly, God didn't tell them to prepare for. Why then is the prophet on the move? Simply put, the following issues tend to cause prophets and prophetic people to become impulsive:

1. Fear.
2. Trauma.
3. Ungodly ambition.
4. False doctrine.
5. Demonic dreams.
6. Listening to other prophetic voices without testing the spirits behind them.
7. Confusion.
8. Lack of discipline.
9. Impatience.
10. A need for deliverance.
11. Competition.
12. The spirit of rejection has enslaved them.

Another example of this behavior in a prophet is when the prophet has a dream and doesn't wait for God to give him or her the interpretation of that dream. Instead, the prophet rushes to a conclusion, and in many cases, the individual in question will lead others astray by sharing a false interpretation. This also happens when prophets and prophetic people allow other believers to rush them into prophesying when the Lord hasn't spoken. Remember, I told you that Satan uses and takes out more prophets than God gets to use. One of the reasons for this is because prophets often experience the following when dealing with people:

1. **The faces of man.** People use their facial expressions to control other people, and many prophets and prophetic people are afraid of confrontation.

2. **The negativity of man.** Have you ever walked into a room, and you could feel the negativity in the room without anyone saying a word? For a prophet or a highly prophetic person, this negativity can be debilitating and incredibly draining.

3. **The pressures of man.** People tend to beg, cry, yell, or do whatever they can to force prophetic people to do or to say something. Get this—nowadays, people will even pay prophets to prophesy to them.

4. **The movements of man.** Witchcraft is a work of the flesh, but it can and does become a spiritual issue if the individual bound by it doesn't repent or if they actively practice it. I'm saying this to say that not all witchcraft looks the same. One form of witchcraft is silent control. For example, when people don't approve of how a prophet or a prophetic person has been moving, they will often punish the prophetic individual through non-support. They will stop engaging with the prophetic person on social media, unsubscribe to their channels, or take to social media to air out their disdain for the prophetic person in question. Prophets have to become immune to this type of behavior, especially in the Western world, because narcissistic abuse isn't just a girlfriend/boyfriend or husband/wife crime; it is cultural!

5. **The threats of demons.** Quite frankly, people will threaten you as a prophet or a prophetic person, but keep in mind that the war is not and has never been against flesh and blood, but against the powers, principalities, the rulers of this dark world, and spiritual wickedness in high places. This is to say that, while people may threaten you, if you were to peel back the masks, you'd find a group of scared devils trying to get you to back up or back down.

The point is—wait on God. If He gives you a dream, write it down somewhere, pray about it, and then do the hard part of waiting for God to give you the interpretation of that dream. Some interpretations come almost instantaneously, while others can take years to be revealed, and many of them may be revealed in layers. This means you may get a partial understanding every now and again until you get the full understanding. "For we know in part, and we prophesy in part" (1 Corinthians 13:9).

Another example of a not-so-foresighted prophet is a prophet who hears from God, but does not adhere to the voice, instructions, or commands of God. These types of prophetic people often have trouble discerning between their own thoughts, the voice of God, and demonic thoughts, so they opt to play it safe by ignoring every voice that they hear outside of the voices that tell them what they want to hear. These prophets are called by God, but they aren't chosen by Him to carry out whatever they were initially commissioned by God to do. Therefore, they have to settle for being prophetic, whereas, they will hear from God, have dreams, and still experience visions occasionally, but they have, in many ways, rejected the office of the prophet. This isn't to say that God changes their wiring; they are still hardwired as prophets, but you won't find them serving in the seats God once prepared for them.

Always remember that one of the greatest expressions and demonstrations of faith is preparation. Simply put, this simply means that you aren't just a hearer of the Word, but you are to also be a doer of God's Word.

The Enemies of the Jews

Throughout history, the Jewish people have been faced with a myriad of enemies. The Bible details numerous instances where the Jewish people were persecuted and oppressed by individuals and nations. These enemies, both historical and modern, serve as a constant reminder of the challenges that the Jewish people have faced and continue to face in their journey to practice their faith and preserve their traditions. Who were the enemies of the Jews?

- **Pharaoh:** One of the earliest enemies of the Jewish people was Pharaoh, the ruler of Egypt. In the book of Exodus, Pharaoh enslaved the Jews and forced them to work on his over-the-top building projects. He also ordered the killing of all male newborns in an attempt to prevent the proliferation of the Jewish people. However, through the leadership of Moses and Aaron and, most importantly, the intervention of God, the Jewish people were eventually liberated from the grasp of Pharaoh and were able to flee Egypt.

- **Babylon:** Another notable enemy of the Jews was the Babylonian Empire. In 586 BCE, the Babylonians destroyed the First Temple in Jerusalem and exiled the Jewish people to Babylon. During their exile, the Jews faced challenges to their faith and traditions from the Babylonian culture and religion. However, despite the challenges, the Jews persevered and eventually were able to return to their homeland and rebuild the Temple.

- **Rome:** Throughout history, the Romans emerged as a formidable enemy of the Jewish people. In 70 CE, the Romans destroyed the Second Temple in Jerusalem and exiled many Jews from their homeland. Despite the challenges and persecution faced by the Jewish people during Roman rule, their faith endured and continued to flourish.

- **Antisemitism:** In modern times, the Jewish people have faced numerous enemies, including anti-Semitic regimes such as Nazi Germany. The Holocaust, one of the darkest periods in Jewish history, saw the mass murder of six million Jews in an attempt to eradicate Judaism and Jewish culture from the world. Antisemitism, both overt and subtle, remains a pervasive problem around the world. Additionally, the State of Israel, home to many Jews, has faced conflict and hostility from neighboring nations and terrorist groups.

Of course, this is just a short glossary of the Jews' enemies.

The Amalekites

The first encounter between the Amalekites and the Jews is recorded in the book of Exodus, where the Amalekites attacked the Israelites as they were leaving Egypt. This unprovoked attack led to a long-standing enmity between the two peoples. In the book of Deuteronomy, the Israelites are commanded to remember what the Amalekites did to them and to utterly destroy them. This command is repeated in the book of 1 Samuel, where King Saul is commanded to annihilate the Amalekites and everything that belongs to them. The Amalekites were relentless enemies of the Jewish people, seeking to destroy them through violent means. Overall, the relationship between the Amalekites and the Jews in the Bible is one of enmity and conflict. The Amalekites served as a recurring threat to the Jewish people, and their actions served as a warning to future generations to remain steadfast in the face of opposition and to trust in God's protection.

The Ammonites

In the Bible, the term "ammonite" refers to the people from the kingdom of Ammon, a region located east of the Jordan River. The Ammonites are mentioned numerous times in the Old Testament as adversaries of the Israelites. The Ammonites are also mentioned in the context of forbidden marriages, as the Israelites were forbidden to marry Ammonite women according to the book of Deuteronomy. The account of the Ammonites in the Bible reflects the historical conflicts between the Ammonites and the Israelites.

The Amorites

The Amorites were a Semitic-speaking people who inhabited ancient Mesopotamia and Syria during the 3rd millennium BCE. They were a prominent group in the Near East, with a rich history and culture. The Amorites are historically linked to the Bible as well, where they are depicted as adversaries of the Israelites.

The Amorites are mentioned several times in the Hebrew Bible as being in conflict with the Jews. For example, in Deuteronomy 3:8-9, it is recorded that the Israelites defeated the Amorites and took possession of their land. Additionally, in Amos 2:9-10, the Israelites are reminded of how the Amorites were destroyed by God to make way for the Jews to inhabit the land.

The antagonism between the Amorites and the Jews in the Bible reflects the historical conflicts and tensions between the two peoples in ancient times. The struggle for land, resources, and power undoubtedly led to friction between these two ancient cultures.

The Gibeonites

The Gibeonites were a prominent group of people in ancient Israel, whose history is detailed in the Old Testament of the Bible. The Gibeonites were a Canaanite tribe who lived in the land promised to the Israelites by God. When the Israelites, under the leadership of Joshua, began their conquest of the Promised Land, the Gibeonites feared their fate and devised a plan to deceive the Israelites into making a peace treaty with them. They dressed in worn-out clothes, took dry, moldy bread and cracked wine skins, and presented themselves to the Israelites as travelers from a distant land, seeking a treaty of peace. The Israelites, not consulting God about this matter, made a peace treaty with the Gibeonites, not realizing that they were actually their neighbors. When they discovered the truth, they honored their treaty with the Gibeonites, despite the deception.

The Gibeonites became servants to the Israelites and were integrated into their society, performing menial tasks and becoming part of the workforce in the tabernacle and temple. Their story serves as a lesson about the importance of seeking God's guidance in all matters and the need to honor commitments, even when made under false pretenses. The Gibeonites' legacy is a reminder of the complexity of human relationships and the importance of honesty and integrity in all dealings.

The Hittites

The Hittites are mentioned numerous times in the Old Testament, particularly in reference to their interactions with the Israelites. The Hittites were an ancient Anatolian people who inhabited the region of modern-day Turkey and were considered a powerful and influential civilization during the second millennium BCE. The Bible describes the Hittites as a significant force that the Israelites encountered during their conquest of the Promised Land. The Hittites are also mentioned in relation to intermarriage with the Israelites, as seen in the example of Esau's marriage to Hittite women, which caused grief to his parents, Isaac and Rebekah. Additionally, the Hittites are referenced in the context of diplomacy and trade, as they were known for their skills in these areas. For example, King Solomon is said to have formed an alliance with the Hittite ruler, which allowed for the import of valuable resources and materials for the construction of the temple in Jerusalem.

The Hivites

The Hivites are mentioned in the Bible as one of the peoples living in the land of Canaan at the time of the Israelite conquest. They are often grouped together with other Canaanite tribes as enemies of the Israelites. In the Book of Joshua, the Hivites are listed as one of the seven nations that the Israelites were commanded to drive out of the land. The Hivites are also mentioned in the context of the covenant between God and the Israelites, in which they were warned against making treaties or intermarrying with the Hivites, as their practices and beliefs were seen as contrary to the will of God. This was largely because the Canaanite tribes were idolatrous and morally corrupt.

The Ishmaelites

There was a long-standing conflict between the Ishmaelites and the Jews, which stems from the early history of the two peoples. According to the Book of Genesis, Ishmael was the son of Abraham and Hagar, while Isaac was the son of Abraham and Sarah. This familial relationship created a deep-seated rivalry between the descendants of Ishmael and the descendants of Isaac, which has continued through the ages.

The Bible describes the Ishmaelites as an aggressive people who were often into conflict with the Israelites. For example, in the story of Joseph, the Ishmaelites are described as trading in spices, balm, and myrrh—the products of their desert homeland. Throughout the Bible, there are instances of conflict between the Ishmaelites and the Jews, reflecting the historical animosity between the two peoples.

The Midianites

The Midianites were a people who inhabited the northern regions of the Arabian Peninsula, spanning from the eastern side of the Gulf of Aqaba to the ancient city of Midian. They are believed to be a Semitic people who are descended from the son of Abraham and his wife Keturah; their name derives from the Hebrew word "Midyan" which translates to strife. The Midianites are mentioned numerous times within the Old Testament as well as other ancient texts, but it is their interactions with the Israelites that have garnered the most attention. The conflict between the Midianites and Israelites is longstanding, as it can be traced back to the time of Moses. After killing an Egyptian, Moses eventually settled with the Midianites after encountering the priest Jethro. It was during his time with the Midianites that God called Moses from a burning bush and tasked him with leading the Israelites out of Egypt. Following the miraculous liberation of the

Israelites from slavery in Egypt, the Midianites once again became involved in their affairs. However, the Israelites, now wandering in the desert, encountered the Midianites and were seduced by their women to engage in idolatry and other sinful practices. The Israelites' leader, a man named Phinehas, took action by killing a fellow Israelite who had taken a Midianite woman into his tent to sin with her. This prompted a conflict between the two groups, which resulted in God commanding Moses to wage war against the Midianites. The Israelites emerged victorious and appropriated the Midianites' lands and wealth, but despite this victory, the tensions between the Israelites and Midianites continued. Gideon, a significant figure in Israelite history, led a campaign against the Midianites and defeated them with the help of God. Years later, during the time of the Judges, the Israelites once again fell into idolatry and were punished by God with a plague. A man named Phinehas, who was a descendant of the aforementioned Phinehas, took it upon himself to make amends with God by waging war against the Midianites once again. This time, the campaign resulted in the death of every Midianite man, the seizure of their livestock and wealth, and the take-over of their lands. Only the women and children were spared.

The Perrizites

Circumscribed within the Old Testament, the Perizzites are frequently referred to in both the Book of Genesis and the Book of Joshua, as one of the Canaanite groups whose land was promised by God to the Israelites. It is believed that they first settled in the central region of Canaan, in the hill country between Jerusalem and Shechem. Their influence in the political and social developments of their time was evident, as the Canaanite city of Beit Shean, classified as one of the oldest cities in the world, is thought to have been under their control. However, the Perizzites' relationship with the Israelites was not always peaceful. The Book of Joshua recounts a violent conflict between the two groups, with the Israelites ultimately defeating the Perizzites and taking control of their land. This struggle further highlights the Perizzites' prominence in the political and military spheres of their time.

The Philistines

The Philistines were a formidable enemy of the Israelites. Their interactions with the Israelites spanned centuries, and the narratives surrounding their relationship provide insight into the historical context of the region as well as the cultural and religious norms of the time.

The Philistines were an ancient people who first appeared in the historical record around 1200 BCE. They were seafaring people who migrated to the eastern Mediterranean from the Aegean region. The name "Philistine" is derived from the Hebrew term "pelishtim," which means "invaders" or "migrants." They settled on the coast of Canaan, in what is now modern-day Israel and Gaza, and established a number of city-states, including Gaza, Ashkelon, Ashdod, Ekron, and Gath.

The Philistines were a fierce enemy of the Israelites; they were a people who constantly threatened and attacked the Israelite tribes throughout their existence. The earliest mention of the Philistines in the Bible is found in the story of Abraham, who encountered the Philistine king Abimelech in the city of Gerar. Later, during the time of the judges, the Philistines consistently oppressed and battled against the Israelites, culminating in the famous story of Samson, who famously defeated the Philistines using his strength and cunning.

During the reign of Saul, the Philistines emerged as a major threat to Israelite sovereignty. In the battle of Michmash, the Philistines routed Saul's army and captured the Ark of the Covenant, a sacred relic of the Israelites. The Philistines took the Ark to their capital city of Ashdod, but suffered divine retribution in the form of plagues and calamities, which forced them to return the Ark to the Israelites. However, the most famous story featuring the Philistines is that of David and Goliath. In this tale, the Philistine champion Goliath challenges the Israelite army to send a warrior to engage in single combat with him. David, a young shepherd boy, accepts the challenge and defeats Goliath using a sling and a stone. This story has become a symbol of courage and faith in the face of overwhelming odds.

The Philistines were also known for their religious practices, which were focused on the worship of their deities, particularly the god Dagon. Dagon was a fertility god who was had the body of a fish and the head of a man. The Philistines believed that Dagon was responsible for their agricultural prosperity and military success, and many of their religious rituals and ceremonies were devoted to worshiping this false god (demon).

The Afterbirth of Rebellion

Many of Israel's greatest enemies, believe it or not, were created by their disobedience to God, and their rebellion as it relates to His instructions. Let's look at a few cases of Israel's custom-created enemies.

- **The Caananites (Genesis 9:20-25):** And Noah began to be an husbandman, and he planted a vineyard: And he drank of the wine, and was drunken; and he was uncovered within his tent. And Ham, the father of Canaan, saw the nakedness of his father, and told his two brethren without. And Shem and Japheth took a garment, and laid it upon both their shoulders, and went backward, and covered the nakedness of their father; and their faces were backward, and they saw not their father's nakedness. And Noah awoke from his wine, and knew what his younger son had done unto him. And he said, Cursed be Canaan; a servant of servants shall he be unto his brethren. (Note: It goes without saying that Ham's son, Canaan, would eventually become the father of the Canaanites, one of Israel's greatest and most formidable enemies).

- **The Moabites (Genesis 19:30-38):** Lot and his two daughters left Zoar and settled in the mountains, for he was afraid to stay in Zoar. He and his two daughters lived in a cave. One day the older daughter said to the younger, "Our father is old, and there is no man around here to give us children— as is the custom all over the earth. Let's get our father to drink wine and then sleep with him and preserve our family line through our father." That night they got their father to drink wine, and the older daughter went in and slept with him. He was not aware of it when she lay down or when she got up. The next day the older daughter said to the younger, "Last night I slept with my father. Let's get him to drink wine again tonight, and you go in and sleep with him so we can preserve our family line through our father." So they got their father to drink wine that night also, and the younger daughter went in and slept with him. Again he was not aware of it when she lay down or when she got up. So both of Lot's daughters became pregnant by their father. The older daughter had a son, and she named him Moab; he is the father of the Moabites of today. The younger daughter also had a son, and she named him Ben-Ammi; he is the father of the Ammonites of today. (Note: God told Abram to leave his country and his kin, but Abram decided to take Lot with him on his journey. Eventually, he'd parted ways with Lot after their herdsmen began to contend with one another. Abram would have to return and rescue Lot on two separate occasions, and it was after his last rescue from Sodom and Gomorrah that Lot's daughters devised a plan to sleep with their father in an attempt to preserve his name. This set the stage for the birth of the Moabites).

- **The Babylonians (Isaiah 39):** At that time Merodachbaladan, the son of Baladan, king of Babylon, sent letters and a present to Hezekiah: for he had heard that he had been sick, and was recovered. And Hezekiah was glad of them, and shewed them the house of his precious things, the silver, and the gold, and the spices, and the precious ointment, and all the house of his armor, and all that was found in his treasures: there was nothing in his house, nor in all his dominion, that Hezekiah shewed them not. Then came Isaiah the prophet unto king Hezekiah, and said unto him, What said these men? And from whence came they unto thee? And Hezekiah said, They are come from a far country unto me, *even* from Babylon. Then said he, What have they seen in thine house? And Hezekiah answered, All that *is* in mine house have they seen: there is nothing among my treasures that I have not shewed them. Then said Isaiah to Hezekiah, Hear the word of the LORD of hosts: Behold, the days come, that all that *is* in thine house, and *that* which thy fathers have laid up in store until this day, shall be carried to Babylon: nothing shall be left, saith the LORD. And of thy sons that shall issue from thee, which thou shalt beget, shall they take away; and they shall be eunuchs in the palace of the king of Babylon. Then said Hezekiah to Isaiah, Good *is* the word of the LORD which thou hast spoken. He said moreover, For there shall be peace and truth in my days

- **The Gibeonites (Joshua 9:3-27):** And when the inhabitants of Gibeon heard what Joshua had done unto Jericho and to Ai, They did work wilily, and went and made as if they had been ambassadors, and took old sacks upon their asses, and wine bottles, old, and rent, and bound up; and old shoes and clouted upon their feet, and old garments upon them; and all the bread of their provision was dry and moldy. And they went to Joshua unto the camp at Gilgal, and said unto him, and to the men of Israel, We be come from a far country: now therefore make ye a league with us. And the men of Israel said unto the Hivites, Peradventure ye dwell among us; and how shall we make a league with you? And they said unto Joshua, We are thy servants. And Joshua said unto them, Who are ye? and from whence come ye? And they said unto him, From a very far country thy servants are come because of the name of the LORD thy God: for we have heard the fame of him, and all that he did in Egypt, and all that he did to the two kings of the Amorites, that were beyond Jordan, to Sihon king of Heshbon, and to Og king of Bashan, which was at Ashtaroth. Wherefore our elders and all the inhabitants of our country spake to us, saying, Take victuals with you for the journey, and go to meet them, and say unto them, We are your servants: therefore now make ye a league with us. This our bread we took hot for our provision out of our houses on the day we came forth to go unto you; but now, behold, it is dry, and it is mouldy: And these bottles of wine, which we filled, were new; and, behold, they be rent: and these our garments and our shoes are become old by reason of the very long journey. And the men took of their victuals, and asked not counsel at the mouth of the LORD. And Joshua made peace with them, and made a league with them, to let them live: and the princes of the congregation sware unto them. And it came to pass at the end of three days after they had made a league with them, that they heard that they were their neighbours, and that they dwelt among them. And the children of Israel journeyed, and came unto their cities on the third day. Now their cities were Gibeon, and Chephirah, and Beeroth, and Kirjathjearim. And the children of Israel smote them not, because the princes of the congregation had sworn unto them by the LORD God of Israel. And all the congregation murmured against the princes. But all the princes said unto all the congregation, We have sworn unto them by the LORD God of Israel: now therefore we may not touch them. This we will do to them; we will even let them live, lest wrath be upon us, because of the oath which we sware unto them. And the princes said unto them, Let them live; but let them be hewers of wood and drawers of water unto all the congregation; as the princes had promised them. And Joshua called for them, and he spake unto them, saying, Wherefore have ye beguiled us, saying, We are very far from you; when ye dwell among us? Now therefore ye are cursed, and there shall none of you be freed from being bondmen, and hewers of wood and drawers of water for the house of my God. And they answered Joshua, and said, Because it was certainly told thy servants, how that the LORD thy God commanded his servant Moses to give you all the land, and to destroy all the inhabitants of the land from before you, therefore we were sore afraid of our lives because of you, and have done this thing. And now, behold, we are in thine hand: as it seemeth good and right unto thee to do unto us, do. And so did he unto them, and delivered them out of the hand of the children of Israel, that they slew them not. And Joshua made them that day hewers of wood and drawers of water for the congregation, and for the altar of the LORD, even unto this day, in the place which he should choose.

Of course, there are many more enemies of Israel in the Bible, and if you read the Bible from cover to cover, you'll soon discover a common theme. That is, a man's greatest enemies typically come out of his own household. The same is true for prophets and prophetic types, of course. Abel was betrayed by his brother, Cain. Joseph was betrayed by his brothers because they envied his relationship with their father. Saul betrayed David because of jealousy, fear, and entitlement. Absalom betrayed his father, David, because of unforgiveness, entitlement, envy, and ungodly ambition. Samson betrayed himself by engaging with Delilah, and ignoring the many red flags that she put out every single day. And then, there is the infamous betrayal of Judas Iscariot betraying Jesus Christ. The point is—many of a prophet's enemies are the people that the prophet trusts the most. This, in many cases, is the afterbirth of rebellion. This is when God gives us a way of escape, but we refuse to take it because we fear what's on the other side of change. One of a prophet's greatest enemies is comfort. This is to say that a comfort zone is nothing but a beautifully decorated prison.

The Prophet's Greatest Enemies

Now that you've read through the glossary of enemies that the Israelites had, you can better understand how Satan works. He will stop at nothing to get God's people to worship him. Everything that the devil does is centered around him controlling humanity at large. He wants power, authority, fame, glory, recognition, and most of all, he wants to be worshiped. However, God's prophets are the greatest enemies of the systems he's created in the Earth, and it is for this reason that he seeks to annihilate them. And of course, he uses the spirit and the system of Jezebel to destroy the prophets of God, but these aren't the only enemies of prophetic people. Some of the prophet's greatest enemies are:

Fear	Idolatry
Pride	Unforgiveness
Rejection	Worldliness
Rebellion	Ungodly Soul Ties
Ungodly Ambition	Comfort
Perversion	Toxic Loyalty
Comparison	Emotionalism

- **Fear:** Fear is the absence of faith, especially in the midst of a hardship, storm, or threat. It means to not know, understand, or trust God. Fear is the product of ignorance, and keep in mind that the word "ignorant" does not mean "stupid." It means that information is present and available, but the individual in question chooses to ignore it. It is a willful state of illiteracy and incompetence.

- **Pride:** Pride is often the result of voids, trauma, and rebellion. When prophets and prophetic people get wounded, they oftentimes try to self-heal, meaning they forsake wise counsel. Consequently, their hearts' wounds go untreated, thus setting the stage for the spirit of rebellion to enter them. With rebellion often comes more pride, since pride is one of the three guarding spirits found in most demonic networks. The Bible tells us that God resists the proud and gives grace to the humble (see 1 Peter 5:5). All the same, Proverbs 16:18 warns, "Pride goes before destruction, and a haughty spirit before a fall." By becoming prideful, the prophet lifts himself or herself against God in an attempt to lift themselves above God, and when this happens, the prophet or prophetic person can and often does pick up the Jezebel spirit (if it's not already binding them), along with a host of other unclean spirits.

- **Rejection:** Rejection is oftentimes a strategic attack from the enemy against the prophet, especially when the prophet or prophetic person is young and still unaware of his or her identity. As a matter of fact, this spirit loves to come into the prophet while the prophet is still in his or her mother's womb. Why is rejection so important to Satan? For one, Satan was and is perpetually forsaken and rejected by God, and two, rejection is a pretty deep wound that often leaves a hole in a person's identity. For example, if your father wasn't present in your life, the spirit of rejection would come and tell you that it's your fault, you're not good enough for your father, you're not manly enough for your father, or if you're a woman, you're not smart enough, pretty enough, or good enough for your father. Simply put, the enemy teaches you that you are not enough! When you believe this, you will often reject the unique traits that make you who you are in favor of what you think your father wants, what you think your mother wants, your current lover wants, your friends want, or the world at large wants. All the same, when you've experienced rejection for an extensive amount of time, you will often start rejecting people whenever you think they are about to reject you. This is what we refer to as a narcissistic discard.

- **Ungodly Ambition:** This is one of the biggest pit holes in the world of prophecy, and it is typically rooted in rejection. Many prophets and prophetic people were raised by the weapon that was formed against them, Jezebel herself or himself. In this, the prophetic person is repeatedly subjected to abuse, rejection, neglect, and a host of horrid things. This leads the individual in question into a realm of self-hatred, self-loathing, and selfishness, all of which ensure that the prophetic person will stay in the cycle of rejection for the rest of their lives. To counter this, many wounded prophets and prophetic types start seeking affirmation, validation, and success! They will chase money, careers, platforms, notoriety, and any opportunities that they feel will put them in the spotlight. This leads to them becoming manipulative, calculating, and an enemy of any person or people who hold the spots that they are coveting. This also leads to them becoming enemies of God's movements, especially when they feel overlooked or undervalued. With ambition, prophets and prophetic types will often step on the backs of others in their attempts to make their names known, accelerate their careers, or garner some measure of success. This often leads to a decline in the prophet's mental health because ambition will always overwork anyone who surrenders and submits themselves to it. There's nothing wrong with ambition, but anytime you are more focused on the means than you are on the ministry, you are operating as a narcissistic force against that movement.

- **Perversion:** Prophets were wired to be super sensitive, so I want you to imagine this. Imagine being hypersensitive to all-things-spiritual and all-things-natural. This is to say that hypersensitive people tend to be hyper-sexual. For prophets and prophetic types, this has everything to do with their incessant desire to be used by something or someone. This is why so many prophetic people fall into the many traps of perversion, including fornication, promiscuity, porn addiction, homosexuality, masturbation, and the list goes on. When an unyielding prophet is not being used by

God, that prophet will find himself or herself being used by something other than God. And because of the prophet's hypersensitivity, Jezebel often ensnares the prophet through the use of sensuality, whereas Jezebel appeals to the sight, smell, taste, touch, and hearing of the prophetic individual. Sadly enough, this tactic is super effective today because many prophets and prophetic types are isolating themselves; this has everything to do with the fact that they can feel the emotions of others whenever they are in crowded spaces, and no one has ever taught them how to navigate their gifting.

- **Comparison:** There are different types of prophets and prophetic people. Some people are like ears, while others serve as God's hands. Some prophets can be compared to the eyes of God, while others are super discerning, meaning they are like noses. Then again, there are prophets who are revelators; they are used by God like tongues; they teach people about the mysteries of God, all the while, coming against demonic doctrines. I said all of this to say—it is not wise to covet someone else's gift. It is not wise to forsake how God uses you because you adore how He uses others. This is what happened to Cain. He coveted the relationship Abel, his brother, had with God, not understanding that God was using them both differently, but the most important part was—He was using them, and that's what matters. Many prophets and prophetic people sabotage their assignments, their ministries, and their good names because they repeatedly compare themselves to other prophets and prophetic types. Consequently, they end up becoming another man or woman's warfare. While they are supposed to be ushering in a move of God, many prophets and prophetic people become relatively narcissistic, where they begin to challenge, block, and delay a move of God simply because God is using someone other than themselves.
- **Idolatry:** Idolatry is Jezebel's favorite cologne. Whenever Jezebel smells idolatry on a prophet or a prophetic person, that spirit then begins to stalk that prophet. As a matter of fact, most people who refer to themselves as "empaths" are guilty of this crime. This is what led them into the laps, arms, and beds of the narcissist. Looking for answers, many

of you found yourself reading New Age doctrines which, of course, are the doctrines of demons, and it was there that you received a false I.D. You were told that you were an empath when, in truth, you are a prophet or a prophetic person who simply does not know or understand the call that is on your life. And hear me, idolatry isn't just bowing to a golden cow or a statue; idolatry is putting your plans, your preferences, and your desires before God's plans. Many prophets of God are unknowingly polytheistic, whereas they worship many gods; these gods include themselves (self-worship), their feelings, their lovers, money, Heaven, their gifts, and their plans for themselves. And again, this is how Jezebel manages to find her way to the prophet because idolatry has a scent in the realm of the spirit, and Jezebel is attracted to that scent.

- **Unforgiveness:** This has taken out more prophetic people than cigarettes, alcohol, and drug use combined. Yes, we've all been hurt; we have all experienced pain, rejection, betrayal, persecution, and the like. As in all things, there is a wrong response and a correct response. The wrong response is to blame others when you are guilty as well. For example, Michael and Mia start dating. They both sin against God by engaging in premarital sex; they both decide to engage in gossip with a few messy people at their church, and they both choose to use profane language whenever they are upset or when they are around their more worldly friends. Eventually, harvest season makes its rounds, and Michael leaves Mia to be with another girl he'd met while on vacation. Mia is upset; she's hurt, angry, and confused, after all, she and Michael had a pretty decent relationship—or so she thought. So, for two years, Mia refuses to greet her ex whenever she saw him at church, plus, she'd tell anyone who'd listen how promiscuous, self-centered, and dishonest Michael was. Because of this, Mia repeatedly experiences depression, anger, bitterness, rejection, and a host of issues. She prays, but it would seem that her prayers have gone unheard. This has everything to do with the fact that she refuses to forgive her ex, and part of the reason that she can't forgive him is because she has yet to take responsibility for her role in her own pain. What Michael did to her mirrored what she'd done to God. She reaped what she'd sown, and the same would eventually happen to Michael. Many prophets and prophetic people get their hearts broken, and they'll preach more about their pain and the people who hurt them than they preach about Jesus. They can't teach or preach repentance because they themselves refuse to repent for their sins against God; instead, they focus on the crimes others have committed against them. Consequently, God has to quarantine them, meaning He has to lock them out of revelation and out of many of the blessings He's stored up for His children because they are repeatedly allowing the enemy to use them, instead of allowing God to use them.

- **Worldliness:** James 4:4 reads, "Ye adulterers and adulteresses, know ye not that the friendship of the world is enmity with God? Whosoever therefore will be a friend of the world is the enemy of God." John 15:20 states, "Remember the word that I said unto you, The servant is not greater than his lord. If they have persecuted me, they will also persecute you; if they have kept my saying, they will keep yours also." What is important about these two scriptures? How are they related? They are both referencing the people of the world. Yes, this includes believers who have submitted themselves to the spirit of this world. Remember, just a few paragraphs ago, we talked about rejection. Most prophetic people have experienced rejection, some more than others. One of the things that rejection does is, it makes you want to fit in because standing out can be lonely, embarrassing, and it can make you hyper-aware of the things you do, say, and wear. No one wants to repeatedly experience this awkwardness, so many prophetic types give their gifts to the world in an attempt to get some type of affirmation from the world and to finally fit into the spaces they were once laughed, chased, or locked out of. This is why many prophets today embrace the spirit of this world, and by doing so, they essentially reject their God-given assignments in favor of pleasing a bunch of broken, unsaved, or ungodly souls who love their gifts but hate their God.

- **Ungodly Soul Ties:** Satan uses soul ties as leashes. Because most prophets and prophetic types are super-sensitive, they tend to become addicted to oxytocin, dopamine, adrenaline, serotonin, and any hormone or neurotransmitter that tantalizes them emotionally. And it is for this reason that many of these individuals repeatedly find themselves in a web of ungodly soul ties, with the majority of those soul ties being with the spirit of Jezebel. Satan uses these soul ties to yank, pull, seduce, and drag God's prophets back into the limitations that their sins have enslaved them to. This is why it can sometimes be extremely difficult, for example, to lead a prophet out of perversion, unforgiveness, or rejection. Satan will allow them to go so far into ministry, building a family, writing a book, starting a business, or doing anything that God has commissioned them to do before he yanks their chains. And again, these chains are ungodly soul ties. It is not unusual for the prophet or the prophetic individual to experience a long-gone ex who suddenly reappears and wants to reenter the prophet's life. The problem with this is—in more than ninety percent of these cases, the individual is hosting a spirit that the prophet broke ties with, so to regain access to the prophetic person, that spirit will use a soul tie that the prophet hasn't yet severed. It is a wonder within itself to see a prophet return to a person that he or she has been warned about simply because the prophet is addicted to how that person made him or her feel. All the same, Jezebel uses the prophet's soul ties in the same manner in which a spider uses its web: to ensnare, to bind, and to limit the movements of its prey; this way, the spider can inject its venom into it.

- **Comfort:** We all love to be comfortable. When we are, for example, in the comfort of our own homes, we tend to feel more relaxed and secure. This feeling is addictive, and again, prophetic people tend to have addictive personalities, whereas they often commit to people, places, and things whenever they find comfort in those people, places, or things. It is for this reason that many prophets have to be peeled or plucked away from their comfort zones by God. Think of the story of Jonah. God told Jonah to go to Ninevah, but Jonah didn't want the assignment he'd been given. Maybe, like many modern-day prophets and prophetic people, he loved having the title of a prophet, but he wanted nothing to do with the responsibilities associated with being a prophet. So, Jonah went on the run; he went in the opposite direction of Ninevah, thinking that he could escape the plans of God. Of course, we all know the story, and if you don't, you can read it in the book of Jonah. After a huge storm came, Jonah had the men aboard the ship to throw him overboard into the sea, and it was there that he was swallowed whole by a great fish. He spent three days in the belly of that fish, and it was from within its belly that Jonah repented. Of course, it was his repentance that saved his life. Jonah had initially wanted to remain in his comfort zone, but his rebellion caused him to find himself in the most uncomfortable of places—inside the stomach of an enormous fish. Today, that great fish is Leviathan, and Leviathan is the castle that Jezebel lives in. Whenever prophets and prophetic people run from God, they typically run into the arms of Jezebel. This is why God doesn't accept their claims to be victims when, in truth, they are prophets and prophetic people on the run. Always remember that your anointing works best in your assigned place, just like a flashlight works best when it's in darkness. But if a flashlight preferred to sit in a well-lit room all day and all night, it would render itself ineffective, useless, and purposeless. If that flashlight surrounded itself with other flashlights, it would be common and relatively ineffective. This is to say that your anointing works best when you're uncomfortable.

- **Toxic Loyalty:** We get it. After experiencing so much pain and rejection, we all find solace, comfort, and security in the presence of people who love us back. And it is for this reason that many prophets and prophetic people ally themselves with seasons, people, places, things, and principles. One certain thing is—it is hard to win a prophet who is locked in a false religion. Satan loves to use the prophet's desire to fit in, to be a part of something bigger than himself or herself, and to be accepted by the world, the church, or a particular group/category of people. Consequently, many prophetic people find themselves in expired seasons and relationships even after God has moved on. Many of these saints feel the need to prove themselves and their loyalty to people, organizations, and systems. This has everything to do with their overwhelming sense of gratitude. Consequently, many prophetic types forfeit their assignments in their attempts to satisfy people, instead of pleasing and obeying God. As a prophetic person, your loyalty should be to God, and everyone who is a part of your life gets to tap into that loyalty, but if God moves, your assignment is to follow Him. It goes without saying that toxic loyalty has led so many prophets into idolatry, where they repeatedly cry out to God, but get this—He answers them in the places they should be, and not where they are. What this means is, they won't hear His response when they are outside His will. This is because His last set of instructions is still echoing in their souls, but they've learned to ignore those instructions, hoping to get a new set of instructions. This is why many of them can go years not hearing anything from God, and then suddenly, whenever they come outside of comfort, they get a Word from the Lord that convicts them and sets them free.

- **Emotionalism:** What is emotionalism, first and foremost? Merriam Webster's dictionary defines "emotionalism" as "undue indulgence in or display of emotion." I think we've already established that prophets and highly prophetic people are super-sensitive, which leads many of them to be incredibly emotional. This is why it is imperative for prophetic types to study and learn the Word of God, plus they need to grow in their emotional intelligence. Many prophets are wounded souls, and because of this, they are perpetually in the presence of God, after all, "the Lord is nigh unto them that are of a broken heart; and saveth such as be of a contrite spirit" (Proverbs 34:18). And because God is near them waiting on them to hand their burdens to Him and waiting on them to repent and take accountability for their roles in whatever they were wounded by, these prophets can go years being incredibly sensitive, emotional, and most of all, brokenhearted. Does God still use them? Yes, but whenever a prophet doesn't heal, Satan will use that prophet as well, especially if the prophet or prophetic person refuses to forgive the people who hurt him or her.

Of course, this is not a complete list of the prophet's enemies, but these are some of the major players. Simply put, prophets need the following to function properly and to be used by God to their full potential:

1. Faith in God.
2. Fear of God (reverence).
3. Consistent Prayer Life.
4. Consistent Bible Study.
5. Wise Counsel.
6. A Healed and Healthy Heart.
7. Emotional Intelligence.
8. Relational Intelligence.
9. Spiritual Intelligence.
10. Financial Intelligence.
11. A Prophetic Community.
12. Leaders After God's Own Heart.
13. Correction.
14. Obedience.
15. Therapy.
16. Deliverance (Regular Bouts).

The Devil's Toolkit

What exactly is the devil's toolkit? In simple words, it is a list of issues and principles that the kingdom of darkness employs to destabilize, delay, derail, or destroy someone's destiny. Your destiny has everything to do with your destination, and your destination, believe it or not, goes way further than your purpose in life. It is the principles/revelation that you extract while operating in your purpose. It is the conclusion that God wants you to come to. You see, whenever you come to the right conclusion, you set the stage for others to go further than yourself. For example, your finish line should be your children's starting point. The objective is for them to go further than you, go higher than you, to learn more than you, and to achieve more than you. This is why Jesus said in John 14:12 (ESV), "Truly, truly, I say to you, whoever believes in me will also do the works that I do; and greater works than these will he do, because I am going to the Father." In this, we see that Jesus, for one, is not competitive. This is because He understood and He understands His assignment. Ministry, for Him, wasn't about how many followers He had, or how much money He made. To Jesus, money is simply another tool by which He could help others, thus spreading the Word of the Kingdom. However, Satan wants to derail us; he wants us to reach a different conclusion, and he customizes his attacks against God's people in his attempts to get them to bow down to him and to embrace the doctrines of demons, and he uses certain tools to accomplish his agenda. In this chapter, we will explore some of the devices of the enemy.

Understanding Strongholds

Stronghold is a term that has been used throughout history to describe a fortified structure that serves as a defensive mechanism against attack. These structures were typically built in strategic locations such as high ground, near water sources, or along trade routes. The purpose of a stronghold was to protect the people and resources within its walls from raiders and invaders. Oxford Languages defines the word "stronghold" as "a place that has been fortified so as to protect it against attack." Another definition from Oxford Languages is, "a place where a particular cause or belief is strongly defended or upheld." The keyword here is "fortified." The word "fortify" is defined as "provide (a place) with defensive with defensive works as protection against attack." The Greek word for "fortify" is "batsar," and according to Strong's Hebrew, it means, "to cut off, make inaccessible, enclose."

Strongholds have been present throughout human history, dating back to ancient civilizations. In Mesopotamia, the earliest known civilization, strongholds were built to protect cities from would-be attackers. These structures were usually made from mud bricks and included walls, gates, and towers. The Babylonians built the Hanging Gardens, one of the seven wonders of the ancient world. This structure was also an elaborate palace fortress with walls and towers. In Europe, strongholds were built during the Middle Ages, a period known for its conflict and warring factions. Castles were constructed to defend against invaders and to maintain control over neighboring territories. These castles were typically built on high hills, cliffs, or along rivers and were often surrounded by a moat. According to Oxford Languages, the word "moat" means "a deep, wide ditch surrounding a castle, fort, or town, typically filled with water and intended as a defense against attack." Moats made the walls of a castle nearly inaccessible, especially for weapons typically used in a siege such as battering rams and catapults. The castle's walls were made from stone and were equipped with defensive measures such as battlements, murder holes and arrow slits. To better understand each of these, here are a few definitions:

- **Battering Ram (Oxford Languages):** a heavy beam, originally with an end in the form of a carved ram's head, formerly used in breaching fortifications.
- **Catapult (Merriam Webster):** an ancient military device for hurling missiles.
- **Battlement (Oxford Languages):** a parapet at the top of a wall, especially of a fort or castle, that has regularly spaced squared openings for

shooting through.

- **Murder Hole (Urban Dictionary):** A security function used in medieval castles where defenders can rain arrows or stones at invaders in hopes of thinning their numbers.
- **Arrow Slit (Oxford Languages):** a narrow vertical slit in a wall for shooting or looking through or to admit light and air.

The stronghold evolved over time and became more sophisticated as weapons and warfare evolved. During the Renaissance period, many castles were rebuilt or renovated to include artillery and fortifications that could withstand cannon fire. Some of the best examples of these structures can be seen in France where their architecture blends both defensive and elegant features. In the American West, however, strongholds were built during the late 19th century to protect settlers from Native American raids. These log cabins, known as 'forts', were constructed in strategic locations along the frontier and were used as a refuge for settlers during times of attack. These forts were equipped with defensive measures such as barricades and lookout towers.

Of course, in this particular lesson, we are focused on another type of stronghold, which is the stronghold of the mind. This stronghold strongly mirrors a military stronghold. The three words that we will focus on in this study are:

- Princes
- Principles
- Principalities

Of course, we know that a prince is the second in command in any kingdom; he is the son of a king. The oldest prince was and is oftentimes set to inherit the throne once his father abdicates it through death, denunciation, or defiance. Principles, on the other hand, are "a fundamental truth or proposition that serves as the foundation for a system of belief or behavior or for a chain of reasoning" (Oxford Languages). And finally, a principality is a state ruled by a prince. Why are these important? Simply put, we all build our lives upon a set of principles, and these principles dictate how we live, what we'll see and experience in this event called life, and how we'll respond to these experiences. And a principle isn't just a singular thought; it is a group of thoughts that have been formed over time, all of which merge to create what can best be described as a "state of mind." It's important to also know that principles center themselves around our core beliefs. These particular beliefs stand atop our foundational beliefs. Of course, most people think that core beliefs and foundational beliefs are one and the same, but they're not. A foundational belief is the foundation that you build every other belief upon. Most of our foundational beliefs are established in faith or religion. Furthermore, we don't always understand our foundational beliefs because they were often established when we were children. These are the most established beliefs that we have; these are the beliefs that we defend the most, even when we don't understand what it is that we are defending. Our core beliefs are the conclusions we've come to as a result of our foundational beliefs, life experiences, and the lessons from the many teachers we've encountered. These thoughts or principles are the filters that we use to sift through all of the information that we are bombarded with daily. When we talk about a principle, it is better described as a central belief by which all other beliefs are established. "For other foundation can no man lay than that is laid, which is Jesus Christ" (1 Corinthians 3:11).

Think of a solid foundation with an illuminated ball of words spinning around on it. The foundation represents our foundational beliefs, whereas the ball of information represents our core beliefs. Imagine that the ball in question has layers upon layers of words, with the words in the center being the most important, most established, and most guarded layers of information. Imagine that you can peel back each layer like a roll of paper towels. This is a picture of a stronghold. The words on the outskirt of the ball (first layer) are used to defend the words in the next level or layer. The second layer protects the third layer, the third layer protects the fourth layer, and this all continues until you get to the core. In this, we notice that all of the layers are set in place to protect and preserve the final layer, which is the core. Every word that protects the center is a stronghold. Here, you can see that a stronghold can be good, just as it can be bad. When we reference strongholds in the body of Christ, we are typically talking about the bad ones. We are discussing the strongholds of the mind that keep people in captivity to a thought, a principle, or an entire belief system. This is to say that some beliefs are easily eradicated, while others are not. It is incredibly difficult to challenge a person's religious beliefs because, again, religion often serves as a foundational belief for many, meaning if a person were to come out of agreement with his or her religious beliefs, every core belief that the individual has will be overthrown or the individual would have to go through the TSA of our minds once we establish a new foundational belief. This is why we often receive deliverance in layers. Demons typically attach themselves to certain beliefs and, of course, principalities (high-ranking spirits) typically seat themselves on principles. A principality or ruling spirit often monitors our lives, deploying other spirits to ensure that we don't come out of agreement with the principles that the principality is ruling from. The three spirits used to guard belief systems and principles are fear, pride (Leviathan), and offense. Fear causes people to fear change, fear the consequences of making adjustments to their beliefs, and to fear the faces of and responses from the people to whom our beliefs connect us. Leviathan, according to the Bible, is the king of the proud. It goes without saying that since Leviathan is a king, that spirit also has princes or, better yet, spirits that rule under its authority. These spirits include pride, ego, arrogance, haughtiness, vanity, and self-righteousness. The Bible describes Leviathan this way:

- **Job 41:15-25 (NLT):** The scales on its back are like rows of shields tightly sealed together. They are so close together that no air can get between them. Each scale sticks tight to the next. They interlock and cannot be penetrated. When it sneezes, it flashes light! Its eyes are like the red of dawn. Lightning leaps from its mouth; flames of fire flash out. Smoke streams from its nostrils like steam from a pot heated over burning rushes. Its breath would kindle coals, for flames shoot from its mouth. The tremendous strength in Leviathan's neck strikes terror wherever it goes. Its flesh is hard and firm and cannot be penetrated. Its heart is hard as rock, hard as a millstone. When it rises, the mighty are afraid, gripped by terror.

Each of the scales on Leviathan's back represents a core belief. Notice that the Bible says that no air can get between them, and each scale sticks to the next. This is how it works: one belief sets the stage for another belief. This means that you cannot challenge a single belief without causing a ripple in the other beliefs. This is why a group of ungodly, interconnected beliefs is so hard to free yourself from; this is also why it's called a stronghold. For example, Mandy repeatedly checks her pulse every day, and every time she does so, she finds herself in a panicked state. Her therapist questions her about this habit of hers, and Mandy tells her that her father suddenly dropped dead when she was 16-years old. She goes on to say that her father was a powerful man of God who the Lord wanted to use to perform signs and wonders, but he never got around to being used by God because, according to Mandy, a bunch of witches came together with the single agenda of annihilating what they deemed to be their greatest threat: Mandy's father. She tells her therapist that in her father's last year of living, he would repeatedly experience panic attacks, where he would tell anyone who'd listen that he'd lost his pulse for a few minutes. He believed that anytime the witches were chanting against him, he'd lose his pulse and this, in turn, would cause many of the panic attacks he experienced. The coroner ruled the cause of death as undetermined. This only heightened Mandy's fears and suspicions. In other words, some of the words or principles on that spinning ball of information that we just talked about shifted; they became more centralized, thus rearranging Mandy's priorities.

Every belief has a magnetic effect, whereby, it will attract other beliefs like itself. In Mandy's case, she genuinely believed that a group of witches had killed her father and were now after her. This belief is connected to her father's fears, insecurities, and ultimately, his death. These fears are also in alignment with Mandy's religious beliefs, where she passionately sees herself as a prophet called to the nations, and as such, she believes that she is a major threat to the kingdom of darkness. Romans 12:3 warns us, "For by the grace given to me I say to everyone among you not to think of himself more highly than he ought to think, but to think with sober judgment, each according to the measure of faith that God has assigned."

Idolatry

The Greek word for "idolatry" is "eidólolatria," and according to the Strong's Accordance, it means "image worship" or "worship of an image." The word "image" is where we get the word "imagination." Our imagination is filled with images, both good and bad. These images start off as external suggestions, but if we don't properly and consistently guard our hearts, they become internal thoughts. And get this—every image is auditioning for a role in your heart or, better yet, the enemy uses your imagination to lead you astray. His overall objective is to steal your worship from YAHWEH, but he knows that you would not worship him in his raw form as Satan, so he has to disguise himself as a pagan god or some nature deity in an attempt to get you to bow down and worship him. All the same, idolatry is one of those topics that people don't really talk about anymore. It's not a topic that comes up in everyday conversation, but it's still something that we should all be mindful of because, as humans, we are prone to it. We are always looking for a savior; this is why the marketplace continues to grow. We want help with our wrinkles, our hair, our money, our relationships, and the list goes on. We are looking for something or someone to provide us with a solution to the many problems that we're faced with on a daily basis. And whenever something or someone comes along and changes our lives altogether, we often fall into the trap of idolatry, but not idolatry in the sense where we are getting on our knees and saying, "Oh hail (insert idol's name here)." Instead, we worship things and people by:

1. Depending on them.
2. Giving them glory for the changes/improvements they've made to our lives.
3. Trusting more in them than we trust in God in certain areas of our lives.
4. Choosing them first, and then using YAHWEH as a backup or an alternative.
5. Building a stronger and better relationship with them than we've built with God.

So, what exactly is idolatry? Simply put, it's the worship or adoration of something other than God. It can be anything from money, power, fame, material possessions, or even relationships. Anything that we place above our relationship with God can be considered an idol. The word "idol," as defined by Oxford Languages, is "an image or representation of a god used as an object of worship." Now, I know what you're thinking—"I don't worship anything other than God, so this doesn't apply to me." But the truth is, idolatry can be subtle. We may not even realize that we're participating in it. For example, let's say that you're really invested in your career. You love your job and you work hard to advance in your field. There's nothing wrong with that, right? But what if you're so focused on your career that it consumes your thoughts and time? What if you're more interested in impressing your boss than serving God? That's when it becomes idolatry. The same goes for relationships. It's normal to desire close relationships with other people, but it becomes a problem when we rely on those relationships for our happiness and fulfillment. If we prioritize our relationships with people above our relationship with God, that's when we become guilty of idolatry.

So why is idolatry such a big deal? First and foremost, God Himself warns us against it in the Ten Commandments. He says, "You shall have no other gods before me" (Exodus 20:3). If we're truly committed to following God, we need to be mindful of what we idolize, after all, idolatry can have serious consequences. In the Bible, we see countless examples of God's wrath towards those who worshiped other gods. The Israelites, for example, often turned away from God to worship idols and, as a result, they faced punishment and exile. This doesn't mean that God is unloving or harsh; it just means that He takes our relationship with Him seriously and He wants us to prioritize our relationships with Him above everything else. After all, He is our Creator, and we were created to worship Him. When we give our worship to another created thing, we dishonor God and we reject Him at the same time. This leads to some pretty devastating consequences since idolatry provokes the wrath of God, but it's not all about punishment and fear. The truth is, idolatry can also harm us on a personal level. When we place our identity and worth in something other than God, we're setting ourselves up for disappointment, hurt, turmoil, and trauma. The things that we idolize are ultimately temporary and fleeting. They won't bring us true joy or fulfillment, but they can open the door for demons to enter our lives.

So what can we do to combat idolatry in our lives? First and foremost, we need to recognize what we're placing above God. This can be a difficult and painful process, but it's necessary for growth. Once we've identified our idols, we need to surrender them to God and ask for His help in overcoming them. This may involve giving up certain possessions, reevaluating our priorities, or even seeking counseling/accountability from others. Ultimately, it all comes down to our relationship with God. If we're truly committed to Him, we'll be willing to let go of anything that gets in the way of that relationship. It won't be easy, but it's worth it. As the Apostle Paul says, "I have been crucified with Christ and I no longer live, but Christ lives in me" (Galatians 2:20).

As a prophet or prophetic person, please know that you are prone to idolatry; this has everything to do with how you're wired. You were wired to be sensitive to God's presence, and the enemy often hijacks your sensitivity. The easiest and most efficient way to do this is through love-bombing. Oxford Languages defines "love-bombing" as "the action or practice of lavishing someone with attention or affection, especially in order to influence or manipulate them." If we're honest, prophetic people love to be love-bombed; this is because it often produces our drug of choice: dopamine. This is the reason why most prophets and prophetic souls find it difficult to cut ties with Jezebel. Jezebel is their supplier; this spirit dopes them up and helps them to temporarily escape their realities. These little miniature vacations away from the truth allow prophetic types to experience the comforts of normality, and get this—they can and oftentimes do become incredibly addictive. This leads the prophetic individual into the belly of the great fish (Leviathan) whenever the prophetic person decides to make his or her vacation permanent. Keep in mind that Leviathan is Jezebel's armor bearer.

Pride

Proverbs 16:18 reads, "Pride goeth before destruction, and a haughty spirit before a fall." But before we go any further, what exactly is pride? Merriam Webster's Online Dictionary defines "pride" as "too high an opinion of one's own ability or worth: a feeling of being better than others." Please note that the Greek word for "pride" is "huperéphania," and according to Strong's Dictionary, it means "haughtiness, disdain."

According to Job 41, Leviathan is the king of the proud; this means that Leviathan is a ruling spirit. Under Leviathan, you will find the following spirits:
1. Pride
2. Ego
3. Arrogance
4. Vanity
5. Offense
6. Haughtiness
7. Unforgiveness/Wrath
8. Stubbornness/Hardheartedness

These spirits/systems are responsible for:
1. Self-exaltation
2. Self-preservation
3. Self-worship
4. Self-loathing
5. False humility

Any and everything that places emphasis on self; this includes our self-esteem and/or self-image is rooted in pride. Consider the story of King Uzziah. His downfall is recorded in 2 Chronicles 26:16-21, which reads:

> But when he was strong, his heart was lifted up to his destruction: for he transgressed against the LORD his God, and went into the temple of the LORD to burn incense upon the altar of incense. And Azariah the priest

went in after him, and with him fourscore priests of the LORD, that were valiant men: And they withstood Uzziah the king, and said unto him, It appertaineth not unto thee, Uzziah, to burn incense unto the LORD, but to the priests the sons of Aaron, that are consecrated to burn incense: go out of the sanctuary; for thou hast trespassed; neither shall it be for thine honor from the LORD God. Then Uzziah was wroth, and had a censer in his hand to burn incense: and while he was wroth with the priests, the leprosy even rose up in his forehead before the priests in the house of the LORD, from beside the incense altar. And Azariah the chief priest, and all the priests, looked upon him, and, behold, he was leprous in his forehead, and they thrust him out from thence; yea, himself hasted also to go out, because the LORD had smitten him. And Uzziah the king was a leper unto the day of his death, and dwelt in a several house, being a leper; for he was cut off from the house of the LORD: and Jotham his son was over the king's house, judging the people of the land.

Notice that the priests rebuked Uzziah, but just like any narcissistic individual, he didn't like being corrected, so he got offended. This is why offense is one of the many expressions of pride; it is oftentimes pride's reaction to being confronted. All the same, only the Levitical priests were allowed to burn incense to the Lord, but for whatever reason, Uzziah had managed to convince himself that, as king, he could do whatever he wanted, whenever he wanted, and however he wanted to do it. He literally rebelled against a direct order from God, and consequently, he'd become leprous.

Understand this—Jezebel will go out of his or her way to get you to open the door for pride in your life. This is because, according to James 4:6, "God resisteth the proud, but giveth grace unto the humble." The American Dictionary of the English Language defines the word "resist" as:

> Literally, to stand against; to withstand; hence, to act in opposition, or to oppose. A dam or mound resists a current of water passively, by standing unmoved and interrupting its progress. An army resists the progress of an enemy actively, by encountering and defeating it. We resist measures by

argument or remonstrance.

(Source: American Dictionary of the English Language/ webstersdictionary1828.co)

The point is that pride is one of Satan's favorite ways to poison God's sheep, His shepherds, and most of all, His prophets because it is the one drug that is self-administered. And pride often comes in after a traumatic event; it usually starts when we:

1. Refuse to take accountability for our role in our own pain.
2. Refuse to forgive the people who hurt us.
3. Refuse to turn away from our wicked ways.

And pride often leads prophets and prophetic types into the custody of Jezebel because pride is an extension of idolatry. 1 Samuel 15:23 recants the Prophet Samuel's rebuke to King Saul. He said, "For rebellion is as the sin of witchcraft, and stubbornness is as iniquity and idolatry." Of course, stubbornness is one of the many forms or extensions of pride.

Witchcraft

What exactly is witchcraft? Oxford Languages defines "witchcraft" as "the practice of magic, especially for evil purposes; the use of spells." The Greek word for "witchcraft" is "pharmakeia," and, according to the Strong's Accordance, it means:

- the use of medicine, drugs or spells
- magic, sorcery, enchantment

Consider what Apostle Paul said to the Galatians. He said, "O foolish Galatians, who hath bewitched you, that ye should not obey the truth, before whose eyes Jesus Christ hath been evidently set forth, crucified among you?" (Galatians 3:1). Notice here that he used the word "bewitched," which means to bring under a spell; to deceive; to enchant or mesmerize. Simply put, it means to bring someone under the influence of words. This is why it's called a spell. The word "spell" is where we get the word "spelling." We spell words, right? For example, the word "cat" is spelled as c-a-t. The word "dog" is spelled as d-o-g. The word "monarch" is spelled as m-o-n-a-r-c-h. Oxford Languages defines the word "spell" as "write or name the letters that form (a word) in *correct* sequence." Who is Christ Jesus? John 1:1-5 sums this mystery up perfectly; it reads, "In the beginning was the Word, and the Word was with God, and the Word was God. The same was in the beginning with God. All things were made by him; and without him was not anything made that was made. In him was life; and the life was the light of men. And the light shineth in darkness; and the darkness comprehended it not."

When you read or hear the word "beginning," what do you think about? Chances are, you think about time or chronological order, and while the beginning is the start of something, it isn't necessarily locked in the realm of time. Who is God? God answers this question for us in Revelation 8:1: "I am Alpha and Omega, the beginning and the ending, saith the Lord, which is, and which was, and which is to come, the Almighty." We live in chronos; that is, we are trapped in the bubble of time; this represents a limitation. Going back to the word "spell," keep in mind that Jesus is the Word of God (capital case). Also note that we are words of God (lower case). This is to say that we were created in the mouth of God. Of course, someone would argue that man was created from dirt, and they would be partially correct. The body of mankind was formed from the dust of the ground, but the spirit of mankind was spoken into existence by the Most High God. How do we know this? Let's go back to the book of Genesis, where we will find God creating the spirits of Adam and Eve. Genesis 1:26-28 reads, " And God said, Let us make man in our image, after our likeness: and let them have dominion over the fish of the sea, and over the fowl of the air, and over the cattle, and over all the earth, and over every creeping thing that creepeth upon the earth. *So God created man in his own image, in the image of God created he him; male and female created he them.* And God blessed them, and God said unto them, Be fruitful, and multiply, and replenish the earth, and subdue it: and have dominion over the fish of the sea, and over the fowl of the air, and over every living thing that moveth upon the earth.'" God then went on to create or, better yet, form the body of the first man to ever live in Genesis 2:7, which reads, "And the Lord God formed man of the dust of the ground, and breathed into his nostrils the breath of life; and man became a living soul."

The Greek word for "spirit" is "pneuma," and it means "breath" or "spirit." Get this—we cannot speak without breathing. According to Wikipedia, "Speech production requires airflow from the lungs (respiration) to be phonated through the vocal folds of the larynx (phonation) and resonated in the vocal cavities shaped by the jaw, soft palate, lips, tongue and other articulators (articulation)" (Source: Wikipedia/Speech Science). What is the significance of all of this? Simply put, God is Truth. Everything He says is true; it is impossible for God to lie (see Hebrews 6:18). On the other hand, we are eternal beings trapped in a temporal body who were created in His image. In other words, He empowered us to do what He has done. Whatever our Father can do, we can also do. This is why John 5:19 said, "Then answered Jesus and said unto them, Verily, verily, I say unto you, The Son can do nothing of himself, but what he seeth the Father do: for what things soever he doeth, these also doeth the Son likewise." To bring it all full-circle, the Word creates words, and we were empowered to do the same. Check out the following scriptures for context:

- **Proverbs 18:21:** Death and life are in the power of the tongue: and they that love it shall eat the fruit thereof.
- **Matthew 16:19:** And I will give unto thee the keys of the kingdom of heaven: and whatsoever thou shalt bind on earth shall be bound in heaven: and whatsoever thou shalt loose on earth shall be loosed in heaven.
- **Mark 11:23:** For verily I say unto you, That whosoever shall say unto this mountain, Be thou removed, and be thou cast into the sea; and shall not doubt in his heart, but shall believe that those things which he saith shall come to pass; he shall have whatsoever he saith.

You and I both have the ability to decree a thing, and watch it come to pass. This isn't a rite of passage that's limited to believers; it's a spiritual law, which is why unbelievers can and often do take advantage of it. However, believers have keys to the Kingdom of Heaven; this allows us to legally pull down whatever it is that we desire to have. Unbelievers do not have keys; this is why the New Age concept of "manifestation" has proven to be effective for many non-believers. What they don't realize is that they are casting spells, meaning they are using their words or their God-given abilities to access and take things out of the spirit realm. However, without keys, they cannot access doors; therefore, they have to utilize windows. Windows, in the realm of the spirit, represent access points or opportunities. Jesus said in John 10:1, "Verily, verily, I say unto you, He that entereth not by the door into the sheepfold, but climbeth up some other way, the same is a thief and a robber." This is to say that practicing witchcraft means to illegally access the spirit realm, and anything that is illegal involves a legality. There are laws that dictate how we are to operate, and anytime those laws are violated, we can and will be bound. This is where demons come into the picture. While they are fallen angels who God has cast out of His presence, they can, will, and do collect the souls of bound people, and they bring those souls further into bondage by persuading, seducing, manipulating, or bullying those people to sin against God all the more. This allows them to take those souls further into captivity, and eventually devour the individuals in question.

I said all of this to say that as words of God (lowercase), we can and often do produce spells by not just putting letters together to form words, but by putting words together to form sentences. All the same, there are two types of sentences, both of which are relevant to this lesson. Let's look at their definitions (taken from Oxford Languages).

- A set of words that is complete in itself, typically containing a subject and predicate, conveying a statement, question, exclamation, or command, and consisting of a main clause and sometimes one or more subordinate clauses.
- The punishment assigned to a defendant found guilty by a court, or fixed by law for a particular offense.

This is to say that your sentence determines your sentence. Yes, this includes prophets and prophetic people. Because prophets are super-sensitive, it is not uncommon for them to fall into the trap of witchcraft, either knowingly or unknowingly. All too often, believers use their tongues to complain and express their disdain for an event, a person, an occurrence, an organization, etc. And whenever we complain, we are essentially giving praise to the devil because there is an alternate reality present that we are choosing to ignore. For example, let's say that Jason has abandoned his wife of four years, Trudy. Trudy can complain to the masses, talking about all of the evil things that Jason did to her; she can tell the whole world about his affairs, his abusive ways, his narcissism, and his meddling mother, and she wouldn't be lying. But there is an alternate reality that's present, and that is that God may have filled Trudy with so much of His light (love) that her presence tormented Jason until he left. In this, Trudy went through deliverance. So, the truth of the matter is that Trudy sinned to get Jason, she reaped what she'd sown, God's grace was sufficient for her, and she was eventually set free from a man who, quite frankly, was nothing more than a weapon that had been formed against her. However, pain makes it hard for us to praise God; instead, we often whine and complain until our realities match our words once again. This is to say that every word we stitch together creates a reality that we have to live in, but when we stitch together words that force others to live in realities that are contrary to the will of God, we have effectively (and foolishly) cast a spell on that person.

Lastly, to be under a spell means to be under the influence of a lie, an imagination, or a desire. As human beings or, better yet, humbled beings, it is not uncommon for us to look for solutions to the many problems that tend to formulate themselves in our lives. Job said it this way, "Man that is born of a woman is of few days, and full of trouble" (Job 14:1). In this, we discover that as long as we live on the face of this planet, we will be bombarded with problems, and while this may not be the most welcome news for most of us, the truth is that we were created to solve problems. Like God, we do this by:
1. Speaking to the situation at hand.
2. Forming solutions.
3. Being transformed by the renewing of our minds.

However, one of the most dangerous things a prophet or a prophetic person can do is to practice or submit himself or herself to witchcraft as this not only offends and provokes the wrath of God, it is an invitation for demons to enter the prophet's life. And, of course, one of those demons will be the Jezebel spirit.

Ambition

What exactly is ambition? According to Oxford Languages, the word "ambition" means "a strong desire to do or to achieve something, typically requiring determination and hard work." This sounds innocent enough, right? It can be, but understand this—everything has a season, and Satan knows this. For example, an apple out of season would be relatively bitter or it would be rotten. The same is true for prophets and prophetic people.

How does the enemy use ambition to lure, bind, pervert, and potentially destroy God's people? Consider the story of Ahab. God expressly warned the Israelites not to intermingle with their pagan neighbors, but Ahab did the opposite of what God commanded. Driven by fear, ambition, and a lust for power, Ahab partnered with Ithbaal, and it was through this partnership that Jezebel was erected as queen over Northern Israel. Of course, we all know the story. Once Jezebel became queen, she instituted the worship of Baal, killed off many of God's prophets, and sent shock waves of terror throughout the nation with her narcissistic ways. This is the ugly side of ambition; it is a lust that drives men and women, both saved and unsaved, into some incredibly dark places. Another great example of ungodly ambition can be found in Lucifer's story. Isaiah 14:12-15 reads, "How art thou fallen from heaven, O Lucifer, son of the morning! How art thou cut down to the ground, which didst weaken the nations! For thou hast said in thine heart, I will ascend into heaven, I will exalt my throne above the stars of God: I will sit also upon the mount of the congregation, in the sides of the north: I will ascend above the heights of the clouds; I will be like the most High. Yet thou shalt be brought down to hell, to the sides of the pit." Lucifer's greatest sin wasn't his decision to rebel against God; it was his desire to be like God, and it was this desire that led to his rebellion. Notice that Lucifer planned to exalt himself above the stars of God. Stars, in the Bible, represent God's angels. Lucifer already had rank. As a matter of fact, he was one of the highest-ranking angels, but he lusted for more rank and power. All the same, he wanted to be equal to God, and any person or spirit that desires to be equal to God has made himself or itself into an idol. What's worse is this same crime is replicated today by many men and women of God, some who are prophets, others who are pastors, teachers, evangelists, apostles, or just laymen. This is the crime that Satan tried to tempt Jesus with. Let's look at the three temptations of Jesus.

First Temptation	Second Temptation	Third Temptation
Matthew 4:1-4	Matthew 4:5- 7	Matthew 4:8-11
Then Jesus was led up by the Spirit into the wilderness to be tempted by the devil. And after He had fasted forty days and forty nights, He then became hungry. And the tempter came and said to Him, "If You are the Son of God, command that these stones become bread." But He answered and said, "It is written, 'MAN SHALL NOT LIVE ON BREAD ALONE, BUT ON EVERY WORD THAT PROCEEDS OUT OF THE MOUTH OF GOD.'"	Then the devil took Him into the holy city and had Him stand on the pinnacle of the temple, and said to Him, "If You are the Son of God, throw Yourself down; for it is written, 'HE WILL COMMAND HIS ANGELS CONCERNING YOU'; and 'ON their HANDS THEY WILL BEAR YOU UP, SO THAT YOU WILL NOT STRIKE YOUR FOOT AGAINST A STONE.'" Jesus said to him, "On the other hand, it is written, 'YOU SHALL NOT PUT THE LORD YOUR GOD TO THE TEST.'"	Again, the devil took Him to a very high mountain and showed Him all the kingdoms of the world and their glory; and he said to Him, "All these things I will give You, if You fall down and worship me." Then Jesus said to him, "Go, Satan! For it is written, 'YOU SHALL WORSHIP THE LORD YOUR GOD, AND SERVE HIM ONLY.'" Then the devil left Him; and behold, angels came and began to minister to Him.

Notice in these scriptures, Satan tempted Jesus with:

1. Food (he tried to get the Lord to break His fast).
2. Suicide (he tried to convince the Lord that He wouldn't die if He threw Himself off the pinnacle of the temple.
3. Power, Wealth, and Prestige (he offered the Lord what already belonged to Him).

The one we want to focus on is number three. Satan attempted to cause Jesus to fall into the same temptation he himself had been ensnared by. He offered Him the wealth of this world, along with power. However, Jesus rebuked him, thus causing the enemy to flee. Satan still tempts prophets and prophetic people with power, wealth, and notoriety till this day! And it works! Believe it or not, we have lost many leaders to lust and ambition. Ask any God-instituted leader; they can tell you about the many times they had been tempted to throw it all away in exchange for power and prestige. They can also tell you about the many people who've come into their churches or attempted to join their organizations that were driven by the pride of the eyes and the lust of the flesh. These people sat in the congregation and lusted after their leaders' platforms. Like Lucifer, they imagined themselves as being equal to or greater than their leaders. They then got up, joined a ministry within the organization, and from there, they started soul-tying themselves with other believers who'd volunteered. Nevertheless, they turned their noses up at the many souls who they felt were "nobodies" in the organization, all the while, chasing after the individuals who had power, privilege, and a measure of fame/notoriety within the organization. These broken souls often boast by saying things like, "I can't connect to just anybody," or "I feel like I'm called to do everything (insert leader's name here) is doing." These delusions of grandeur are often the evidence of their narcissism, but there's nothing wrong with knowing your worth, establishing boundaries, and being inspired by people you feel are doing great exploits in the Kingdom. So, when does it become narcissism? That's easy. When the individual attempts to evade the process of ascension and when the individual attempts to rush to a platform, totally disregarding standard protocol. For example, in my former church, any person who felt called to leadership could volunteer for a ministry in the church, after all, "The greatest among you will be your servant. For those who exalt themselves will be humbled, and those who humble themselves will be exalted" (Matthew 23:11-12). Servitude comes before elevation. However, narcissistic people are too prideful to serve anyone, and whenever they do volunteer, they are oftentimes rude, condescending, impatient, and controlling, especially to the people they feel are "nobodies." However, if you ever see them perusing the church, you will notice how friendly they are whenever they come in contact with the leaders within the organization. And whenever they serve, they oftentimes want to be seen, they will loudly boast about their progress, and they typically cause others within that team or ministry to quit because of their narcissistic abuse. In this, they hurt many people in their attempts to ascend in leadership, and if ever/whenever they are promoted, they use whatever power they have been granted to humiliate, intimidate, and dominate God's people, especially the ones who they feel pose as a threat to their agendas. This is why Satan loves ungodly ambition so much! This is why he seduces prophets and prophetic people with delusions of success and grandeur. He knows that if he can get ungodly ambition into a prophet's heart, he doesn't have to send Jezebel after that prophet because that prophet will become Jezebel! Yes, the Jezebel spirit loves to make its home in prophets/prophetic people! Why is this? Romans 11:29 answers this question; it reads, "For the gifts and calling of God are without repentance." In short, even if you don't adhere to the call of God that is on your life, even if you never submit and/or surrender yourself to the Most High God, the anointing on your life will still work, only it will be used by the enemy! Ungodly ambition is one of Satan's favorite bait, as it lures many prophetic types into witchcraft, perversion, and into madness! Our asylums today are filled with prophets and prophetic people who lost their minds because they chased after power, notoriety, and success, not realizing that God would have given them these things in due season. That is after they were healed enough, mature enough, and sober enough to host those realities. Funny thing is—when a prophet or prophetic person is sober and healthy enough to host the many riches and favors granted to us by God, they typically don't want it because they understand what comes with it, and that is a greater measure of responsibility.

The Sin Offering

Every deity requires an offering. First off, let's establish what we already know. YAHWEH is the one true and living God, and there is no other god besides Him. Sure, there are spirits that serve as deities, not because God has elected them as "gods," but because some people have erected them as gods. People worship things; they also worship other people, unclean spirits, feelings, and the list goes on. Everything has the potential to become an idol, including Heaven. There are a lot of believers who idolize Heaven; they want the house of God without the heart of God. They want the blessings of God without the burden of God. However, unbeknownst to them, if you worship anything other than the Most High God (YAHWEH), an unclean spirit will enter into your life and begin to seduce, manipulate, and attack you. It will then take the very thing that you are trying to acquire, whether that is a house, a car, a career, a relationship, or whatever it is that you want more than anything, and it will hold that thing over your head. Let me give you an example. A man goes outside the will of God and meets a woman, and by outside the will of God, I mean he introduces and exchanges numbers with a woman who isn't saved. The man in question is saved, so he knows what the Bible says about being unequally yoked with unbelievers, but he hasn't fallen yet, given the fact that the two have only exchanged numbers. Demons watch from up close and afar, hoping that the man will lust after the woman or he'll sin against God to be with the woman. In this, those demons may not have a legal right to attack him or they may not have the legal right to attack him with the intensity needed to bring him down, so the hosts of hell begin to plot against this young man. Please note that the man is financially stable, he genuinely loves and fears God, and his life has been nothing short of blessed for the last seven years. The enemies of his soul (demons) believe that it is his financial security that keeps him from sinning against God. Because of this, they plot and scheme to rob him of his wealth, but again, they can't find an open door. All the same, people are doors.

Being as it is that the woman is not saved or maybe she is not fully surrendered to God, the enemy decides to use her to tempt the man into sexual sin. This all started one night after the guy (let's call him Brad) got off work early. The woman (let's call her Brenda) happened to think about him after getting out of the shower. She'd forgotten that Brad told her that he had to work that night, but after his phone rang a couple of times, she'd suddenly remembered. However, to her surprise, Brad answered the phone. Three minutes into the call, Brad realizes he's made a big mistake because the woman of his dreams wants him to come to her house and dream next to her. He tries to reason with her, saying that he respects her and wants things to move at a healthy pace, but Brenda won't hear of it. "I just want to watch a movie with you and eat a little popcorn," she says in a lowered tone. She then appeals to Brad's ego by saying, "What are you afraid of?" In that moment, pride lifts up in Brad's heart as he boastfully replies, "I'm not scared. I'll be there in 35 minutes." Half an hour later, Brad pulls into Brenda's driveway. Forty minutes later, Brad finds himself in Brenda's bedroom staring at the ceiling fan as Brenda lies sound asleep next to him. What he doesn't realize is that Brenda is bound. In other words, she's jam-packed with unclean spirits that constrict her perspective of the world. This is how they essentially limit her movements. Those spirits didn't initially have a legal right to attack Brad because he was prayerful, intentional, and humble, but after Brad ignored every way of escape that God offered him, and entered into rebellion with Brenda, Brad found himself suddenly in bondage. The first spirit to enter him was Guilt, and then Guilt opened the door for Shame. (Yes, there is the human side of guilt and shame, but there are also demons called Guilt and Shame). After this duo entered his soul, they opened the door for Fear, and now Brad found himself being tormented by the fear of people finding out what he'd done, the fear of being rejected by God, the fear of Brenda being pregnant, the fear of potentially having a sexually transmitted disease, the fear that he'd fail God again, and the fear of being disqualified to lead God's people. As Brad lie next to Brenda, his soul was invaded with every ungodly thought. What Brad had done was he'd given the sin offering, and it was this offering that legalized the attack he'd find himself enduring for the next four years. Could he have repented? Yes, of course, but repentance doesn't cast out devils, nor does it eradicate the law of sowing and reaping. Think of it this way. What if Brenda was pregnant? Do you think that repentance would cast the baby out? What if Brenda gave Brad a venereal disease? Would repentance make it go away or stop it from spreading? Of course not! Repentance just puts you back on course, but it does rewind us back to the time when we were in right-standing with God, but it does help us to move forward. Refusing to repent, on the other hand, always ensures that we will be repeat offenders of whatever crimes we've committed. This is to say that Satan needs a sin offering to attack you in a major way; then again, all he needs is an open door (opportunity). Ephesians 4:26-27 reads, "Be angry and do not sin; do not let the sun go down on your anger, and give no opportunity to the devil." Read this carefully. Sometimes, Satan uses people to seduce, manipulate, and lure you back into sin; these people are "Delilahs." Yes, men can be Delilahs as well!

Another example of a sin offering is found in this very common scenario. Let's say that Donna meets a man named Jason. Donna loves the Lord. All the same, she met Jason at church, and Jason claims to love God as well. As a matter of fact, Jason plays the drums at their local assembly. The two exchanged numbers, and from there, their relationship began, but before it took off, Donna said to Jason, "I don't believe in sex outside of marriage, so are you okay dating me exclusively knowing that we won't be engaging in premarital sex?" Jason was silent for a few seconds. He then let out a chuckle before saying, "Of course." But Jason wasn't okay with the idea of a sexless relationship. As a matter of fact, Jason wasn't even sure if he ever wanted to be someone's husband. He would always tell women that he liked to take life as it came. He would often laugh as he exclaimed, "I love from moment to moment! I don't want to feel pressured to do or be anything I don't want to do or be." After this, he would go out of his way to extract the benefits of being someone's husband without undertaking the title or the responsibility. But Donna was different. She wanted to be accountable with their relationship, she wanted to remain abstinent until marriage, and she would always change the subject whenever Jason started love-bombing her. What's worse is—the news spread quickly around the church that Donna and Jason were a thing, and this was not welcomed news to Jason. After all, there were three more women at the church he'd been flirting with, and he liked to keep his options open. Needless to say, Jason began to rethink his relationship with Donna, but what kept him holding on for a few weeks was the fact that Donna was an incredibly shapely woman, and Jason was mesmerized by her body. He wanted more than anything to sleep with her. He would often think to himself how amazing she would look if she ditched the "church clothes" and started wearing form-fitting clothes. In other words, Jason had the heart of Satan towards Donna. He didn't see her as a potential wife for a good man. He saw her potential to be a freak, however, to get access to Donna's body, Jason knew that he needed to access her heart. He needed to establish a bond with her; this bond is what is commonly referred to as a soul tie, and to set the stage for this soul tie to form, Jason knew that he needed:

1. To establish a pattern with Donna. He would do this by texting her everyday around the same time, and then calling her every night around the same time.

2. To paint a picture in Donna's mind of a future together. This is what is referred to in the world of psychology as future-faking. In this, Jason would regularly ask Donna questions like, "How many children do you want?" or "Would you be okay with moving to Ohio if we were to get married?" His favorite statement to make was, "I need our daughter to have your eyes and your nose, but I hope that she gets my dimples." This type of dialogue would serve to get Donna invested in and excited about a potential future with Jason.

3. To mix some of his time and resources with Donna's time and resources. This is a marriage of sorts, and believe it or not, this accelerates the formation of a soul tie. All the same, it makes the soul tie far stronger than it should have been. In this, Jason begins to ask Donna to take his clothes to the cleaners from time to time, to shape his goatee, and to help him meal-prep every Saturday. He would also leave some of his personal items at her home, and he would encourage her to leave some of her personal items at his home.

4. To appeal to one or more of Donna's five senses repeatedly; this way, he could establish a craving or a longing within her soul. For example, Jason started cooking his mother's famous crème brulée for his new girlfriend. He also wore a specific cologne every time he went to visit her. He created a playlist of his favorite slow songs, and then he would play those

songs repeatedly every time he was around Donna. He even established three of those songs as "their" songs, and whenever these songs would play, Jason would insist that Donna dance with him. He'd also started mowing her lawn every two weeks, plus, he'd helped to rearrange her furniture. This is to say that Jason's fingerprints were all over Donna's heart as well as her house.

5. To get Donna to open up to him about her greatest fears, her insecurities, her desires, her plans, and her triggers. And through hours upon hours of conversation, Jason managed to extract every piece of information that he wanted from Donna. Before long, Donna found herself feeling like Jason was the man for her; she would often tell anyone who would listen that she was madly in love with Jason.

Everything took a turn for the worse on a Friday night. It was eight o'clock that evening and Donna was lying on her bed eating popcorn and watching television. That's when her phone rang. This was Jason's pattern, by the way. He would always call her at eight o'clock, and they'd talk for an hour or two. Donna quickly grabbed her remote, paused the show she was watching, and then answered her phone. Jason's normally upbeat voice was now dry. After the couple spoke for a few minutes, Donna asked Jason why he sounded so down. "Nothing," he said. "Just had a rough day. I could definitely use some company right now." Donna caught the hint, after all, Jason had been throwing out subtle hints ever since they'd exchanged numbers. "I understand," she said as she shoved a handful of popcorn into her mouth. The line was somewhat quiet for a while before Jason broke the silence. His loud sigh sent chills down Donna's spine. She could sense the coldness of his heart. She'd been there before; she'd been dumped by a man simply because she wouldn't have sex with him or give him any sexual favors. "Jason, remember that we talked about this. We said that we would share any disappointments, expectations, and upsets that we would have towards one another. We are going to keep our communication open and healthy." That's when Jason broke his silence. "I'm just tired of being alone," he said. "Like tonight, I wish I could lie next to you and hold you in my arms, but I can't because you don't trust me." Donna sat her popcorn on the stand next to her bed. She then grabbed her remote control so that she could turn off her television set. "What do you mean I don't trust you, Jason?" she asked, her tone revealing her slight annoyance. "I don't trust myself. I've been over to your house, just like you've been over to my house, but we agreed that we would not spend the night with one another, we wouldn't have sex outside of marriage, and that we wouldn't tempt one another. Do you remember that conversation, or have you had a change of heart?" Jason couldn't wait to speak up. "I remember that conversation, and not once did I say that I wanted to have sex with you. I simply said that I wish I could hold you. You see, that's why I don't open up to you about anything. You took what I said and twisted it, but no worries. I'm tired. I'll talk to you tomorrow." With those words, Jason hung up the phone. After he hung up the phone on Donna, he called his other girlfriend, Nadia. After Nadia agreed to come over to his house, he turned his ringer off and continued to play his video game until Nadia arrived. Donna, on the other hand, called Jason four times, and she'd gotten no answer. She'd left him three voicemails, sent him six text messages, and even messaged him on Facebook, but all to no avail. All of this caused Donna to panic, after all, Jason had once appeared to be the perfect man for her.

The next day, Donna checked her phone to see if she'd gotten her usual "good morning" text from Jason. Of course, he hadn't contacted her at all, not even to return her calls or her text messages. Throughout the entirety of that day, Donna regularly checked her phone, but Jason hadn't called. This caused her to experience agony, fear, and every negative emotion under the sun. Two days later, Jason would finally call Donna back, and he'd explained his absence as him simply needing time away from Donna and everyone around him. Fearing that he'd ghost her again, Donna would go on to lower her standards so that Jason wouldn't put her on punishment again. This led to them engaging in a sexual relationship, followed by the birth of their son, Tyson. It goes without saying, when Donna was around five months pregnant, Jason ended their relationship. He would then go on to date another girl at the church. Get this—once Jason managed to get Donna to give a sin offering in her attempts to hold onto him, that spirit in Jason no longer needed Jason to access Donna's soul (mind, will, and emotions). From there, Donna would experience guilt, shame, condemnation, and an ungodly amount of warfare. All of these would essentially drive Donna away from the church she once called home. She would also find herself growing more and more bitter. What Donna didn't know was this—Satan will send a narcissist or a narcissistic person into your life just so that the person in question can open the door for him to enter your life. Remember, the war is not against flesh and blood; it is against the powers, principalities, rulers of this dark world, and spiritual wickedness in high places. The objective here was to get Donna to marry the spirit of Jezebel. This way, every time Donna found herself in a relationship, she would attract Jezebel (the narcissist) because Jezebel and Ahab are married in the realm of the spirit. This is also to say that Jason managed to bag Donna, meaning, he'd successfully gotten her to open herself to the Ahab spirit.

The moral of this story is—demons will seduce, manipulate, and intimidate you to get what they want, but don't bite the bait! Don't give them a sin offering, otherwise, you'll legalize their presence in your life.

The Settlement Offer

Let's say that you were suing a popular cable company for $9.5 million. At first, they'd played hardball with you, refusing to give you back the money that they'd stolen from you. They'd tried to intimidate you, harass you, and to bully you into dropping the case, but you refused to back down. The day of court arrives, and the cable company's lawyer tries once more to get you to drop the case, but you wouldn't budge.

A few testimonies later, the cable company's lawyer turns to the person who'd been sent to represent the company. He then leans close to the individual and whispers something in his ear. During the court's recess, the cable company's lawyer approaches you and your lawyer. "I spoke with my client, and he's more than willing to be generous. He doesn't want to continue this circus, so if you will drop the case, he's willing to settle with you and give you $1.5 million and pay your attorney's fees. As you may know, if we win this case, you will get nothing, so to continue with it would be a huge gamble on your part." The plaintiff's lawyer turns to look at the plaintiff, and they both laugh hysterically. "Are you seriously offering my client $1.5 million?" the plaintiff's attorney asks. Did you guys really sit down and think this through, or are you that incompetent of an attorney that you thought it was a good idea to come over here and offer us an ice cube from the iceberg we're suing you for?" Offended, the defendant's attorney walks away. Moments later, he reemerges with a new offer. "Okay, this is our last offer. After this, we won't go up on our offer anymore. My client is more than willing to offer you $5.7 million, and again, we will pay the attorney's fees." This time, the offer sounds good; it's a settlement offer, and it almost feels foolish to not accept it. The plaintiff accepts the offer and later discovers that the judge was going to rule in his favor. This means that the settlement offer ended up costing the client $3.8 million in the end. That's a huge loss! Settlement offers are used by attorneys to play on both fear and doubt; they establish themselves on the "what if" questions that tend to form in our minds whenever we find ourselves at a crossroad. This is likely what happened to Ahab whenever he decided to make a treaty with Phoenicia. He saw the potential of the Phoenicians to wipe Israel off the face of this planet; this means that he did not consider the might of our God. He also looked at the other side of the equation. He thought about what he stood to gain by partnering up with Phoenicia. Because he did not trust the Lord, and because he allowed his lusts to consume him, Ahab took a settlement offer, not realizing that God had an army far greater than that of the Phoenicians, and His wealth is infinite.

To this day, the spirit of Jezebel goes about seeking out prophets and prophetic people who are willing to make a deal with the devil, and whenever the enemy wants to bargain with you, he first attacks you. What does this look like? I can answer this question through a brief story (I won't bore you with the details; I'll simply post the highlights).

The year was 2015, and three major storms were going on at once in my life:
  1. My Mom had just been diagnosed with cancer once again.

2. My business had slowed down to what felt like a screeching halt.
3. I had a little over two thousand dollars left in my account, all of which would be swallowed by my next month's bills.
4. My car started breaking down. I'm not talking about small, affordable, or even related issues. First, I had to replace the rotors on the tires. After I got the car back, the water pump went out a day or two later. I had to have it replaced. A few days later, one of the gaskets split. I had to have that replaced. After I got the car back, the gear shift got stuck. I had to hire a mobile mechanic to come out and fix that issue.

I was clearly under a demonic attack, and the fear, doubt, and depression was setting in, but I couldn't stop addressing how I felt because not only did I need to earn some money, I had to prepare for my mother's arrival. You see, she was going to be flying to Georgia because we'd successfully managed to get her into the Cancer Treatment Centers of America. This meant that I had another mouth to feed, and this wasn't a problem at all. I was honored to host my mother, but I was afraid of not being able to sustain us. All the same, how would I take her to the Cancer Treatment Center in Newnan, which was 45 minutes away from my house, given the fact that my car was breaking down every time I tried to drive it? Nevertheless, I knew that I was going to welcome my mother with open arms, but before she could arrive in town, I ended up getting an inbox message from an ex of mine. Here are three things that stood out about this encounter:

1. He was financially stable.
2. He matched a prophetic word I'd received a year earlier.
3. He was in the medical field.
4. He was still head over heels in love with the version of me he'd met some twenty odd years ago.

Of course, this was the enemy attempting to seduce me back into bondage. You see, I'd vowed to never entertain a married man again. The spirit of adultery ran heavy in my family, but Satan couldn't get me to outright engage myself with a married man, so:

1. I'd met my first ex in my early twenties. He was going through a divorce

and I justified our relationship by saying to myself, "It's not like I'm taking him from his wife. They are just waiting on the judge to sign their divorce papers."

2. When I met the second ex, I was going through a divorce. I justified my dealings with him by reminding myself that the previous ex had moved on.

During the second marriage, I'd made some major strides in not only maturing in the things of God, but also on my healing journey. I remember talking to God and repenting for the things I'd done in my past, and I vowed to Him to never engage in adultery or sexual sin anymore. Once that marriage ended, I had already fully surrendered myself to God (this is how I escaped that marriage; I essentially died my way out). My ex and I divorced amicably. Additionally, I'd led him in the sinners' prayer while we were going through a divorce. He got saved on my living room couch, and once the divorce was final, I waited a little over a year before moving to Georgia. After I moved to Georgia, the demonic attack began, and while in the midst of that attack, another ex of mine from well over two decades ago resurfaced. What's amazing is he appeared to be the answer to every single problem I was facing. He'd even said to me that he would take care of me financially, and please don't forget he was in the medical field. My mother had just been diagnosed with cancer. This man looked and sounded like a blessing until I observed the situation. As it turns out, he wasn't surrendered to God, even though he claimed to know the "man upstairs." And then, he said those words that let me know that he was not sent by God. He said, "My divorce should be final any day now." I was taken aback; flabbergasted even, but thankfully, I recognized it for what it was. The return of the unclean spirit. You see, you can cast a demon out by disowning and disobeying it. James 4:7 says it this way, "Submit yourselves therefore to God. Resist the devil, and he will flee from you." It was time for me to finally pass that test if I wanted to get off that level. So, I immediately rejected the guy, and on the third day, I finally obeyed God in totality by telling him to stop contacting me altogether. Was this easy? No, it wasn't because he appeared to be the answer to my prayers when, in truth, he was a part of the attack I was undertaking. This isn't to speak negatively about him, after all, he's just a soul in need of salvation; it is to show how strategic the enemy is. This is why the Bible tells us to be wise as serpents. In this, the enemy attacked me on so many fronts before sending me what appeared to be a solution and a false savior. I'm sharing this to say that whenever Satan sees that you are about to win and you're going to win big, he will often offer you a settlement. If you want to be married, he'll send you someone who appears to be a good fit for your life, but the problem is that the person is under his jurisdiction, plus, the individual is designed to fit your today, not your tomorrow. This is how the enemy uses Jezebel to constrict and limit the potential of God's people. And believe it or not, many prophets and prophetic people take the bait! Again, this is what Satan did to Eve. He destabilized her with lies before offering her what appeared to be the perfect solution, and like so many believers today, Eve bit into the lie. Another example of someone taking a settlement is found in the story of Abram, Sarai, and Hagar. Check out the following scriptures:

- **Genesis 15:2-4:** And Abram said, Lord GOD, what wilt thou give me, seeing I go childless, and the steward of my house is this Eliezer of Damascus? And Abram said, Behold, to me thou hast given no seed: and, lo, one born in my house is mine heir. And, behold, the word of the LORD came unto him, saying, This shall not be thine heir; but he that shall come forth out of thine own bowels shall be thine heir.

- **Genesis 16:1-4:** Now Sarai Abram's wife bare him no children: and she had an handmaid, an Egyptian, whose name was Hagar. And Sarai said unto Abram, Behold now, the LORD hath restrained me from bearing: I pray thee, go in unto my maid; it may be that I may obtain children by her. And Abram hearkened to the voice of Sarai. And Sarai Abram's wife took Hagar her maid the Egyptian, after Abram had dwelt ten years in the land of Canaan, and gave her to her husband Abram to be his wife. And he went in unto Hagar, and she conceived: and when she saw that she had conceived, her mistress was despised in her eyes.

- **Genesis 18:10-14:** And he said, I will certainly return unto thee according to the time of life; and, lo, Sarah thy wife shall have a son. And Sarah heard it in the tent door, which was behind him. Now Abraham and Sarah were old and well stricken in age; and it ceased to be with Sarah after the manner of women. Therefore Sarah laughed within herself, saying, After I am waxed old shall I have pleasure, my lord being old also? And the LORD said unto Abraham, Wherefore did Sarah laugh, saying, Shall I of a surety bear a child, which am old? Is anything too hard for the LORD? At the time appointed I will return unto thee, according to the time of life, and Sarah shall have a son.

Here, we see God making a covenant with Abram to give him a son, but because we prophesy in part, Sarai decided to make the prophecy come to pass. She could not conceptualize the fact that God was able to do exceedingly, abundantly, above all that we could ask or think. It was beyond her to imagine herself bearing a child, so she decided to create her own settlement. She could give her handmaiden over to Abram, and this way, they would conceive children for themselves to raise. The problem with this was—God was not planning to give "Abram" a son; His objective was to mature Abram until he walked into his true identity as "Abraham." The promise belonged to Abraham, not Abram. Galatians 4:1-2 reads, "Now I say, That the heir, as long as he is a child, differeth nothing from a servant, though he be lord of all; but is under tutors and governors until the time appointed of the father." This is to say that there is an appointed time and place for everything underneath the sun, but when you're impatient, you will settle for something or someone far less than what God had in store for you. All the same, when you settle, you will discover that you are like a sitting duck to Jezebel. After all, Jezebel is attracted to untapped authority; that spirit loves to rob prophets and prophetic people of their God-given authority, and while Satan does come to steal, kill, and destroy, the truth of the matter is that many prophets and prophetic people hand Jezebel their power, identities, and authority in exchange for love, acceptance, affirmation, opportunities, platforms, and the list goes on.

Understand that it will often look like you're about to lose in the courtroom of life. It will sometimes look as if sin is far better and far more promising than a life of righteousness. It will sometimes feel like God has rejected us when, in truth, God is perfecting us through His Son, Christ Jesus, and by perfecting, I mean maturing. And whenever God truly wants to use a prophetic vessel, He will often bankrupt the systems of fear, ungodly ambition, manipulation, perversion, rejection, idolatry, rebellion, and witchcraft in a prophet's life. He sometimes does this by allowing prophets and prophetic people to repeatedly experience disappointment, isolation, and loneliness until what's in the individual in question surfaces, and then resurfaces. This often provokes the prophetic individual to seek wise counsel, and this is where God wants him or her to be! In the safety of wise counsel! Proverbs 11:14 says it this way, "Where no counsel is, the people fall: but in the multitude of counselors there is safety." This is to say that prophets and prophetic people need community; yes, even if you consider yourself to be an introvert! Your gift comes to life in community! However, Satan wants you in isolation, so that (once again), he can play on whatever it is that you desire, you lust after, or you fear. From here, if he can get you in the courtroom without an attorney, he knows that he can get you to settle for less than what you're worth!

My Brother's Keeper

In this chapter, we will meet or revisit a few stories of narcissism at the hands of siblings.

Esau

Esau is a prominent figure in the Bible, appearing in the book of Genesis as the eldest son of Isaac and the twin brother of Jacob. Esau's story is one of great complexity and depth, with many lessons that can be gleaned from his life.

Esau is first introduced as a rugged hunter and a man of the outdoors, in contrast to his scheming and intelligent brother, Jacob. In Genesis 25:29-34, Esau returns from hunting to find Jacob cooking a pot of lentils. Exhausted and famished, he asks Jacob for some of the stew, to which Jacob replies that he will give him the stew in exchange for his birthright as the eldest son. Esau, in his hunger and exhaustion, agrees to the deal, selling his birthright for a bowl of soup. This act has come to symbolize Esau's impulsiveness and lack of forethought, a flaw that would haunt him throughout his life. Later on, as Isaac is nearing the end of his life, he calls Esau to him and asks him to go hunting and prepare a meal for him, after which he will bless him. However, Rebekah, Isaac's wife and Jacob's mother, overhears this conversation and devises a plan to secure the blessing for Jacob instead. Rebekah quickly prepares a meal for Isaac, dressing Jacob in Esau's clothes and covering his arms with goatskins to make them feel hairy like Esau's. Jacob presents himself to Isaac as Esau, and Isaac, unable to see well due to his advanced age, bestows the blessing upon Jacob rather than Esau. Esau returns from hunting to find that Jacob has stolen his blessing and, in his anger, resolves to kill him. Jacob flees, and the brothers are estranged for many years.

This story has come to symbolize the power of manipulation and deception, as well as the consequences of flesh-based decisions. Esau's impulsiveness and lack of foresight led to him losing his birthright, while Rebekah's scheming led to a rift between the brothers that lasted for years. However, Esau's story does not end there. In a touching scene in Genesis 33:4, the brothers are finally reunited after many years apart. Jacob is terrified of Esau's wrath and approaches him with much trepidation, but Esau runs to meet him, embracing him and weeping. Esau's forgiveness and compassion in this moment are a lesson in humility and the power of reconciliation. Esau could have easily held a grudge against Jacob for his deceitfulness, but instead chose to forgive and embrace him.

Miriam

Miriam was a woman of great courage and perseverance who played a vital role in the liberation of her people. Her story serves as an inspiration to countless people throughout history and highlights the importance of strong-willed individuals in the face of adversity.

Miriam was the older sister of Moses and Aaron; she was born in Egypt during a time when the Jewish people were enslaved by the Pharaoh. As a child, Moses, like many other Hebrew children, faced the threat of infanticide from Pharaoh's edict. However, her mother, Jochebed, managed to save her son by placing him in a basket and sending him down the Nile River, where he was found and raised by Pharaoh's daughter. Her story would intersect with her brother's story because of her dedication to watching over Moses. Exodus 2:1-8 tells the story; it reads, "And there went a man of the house of Levi, and took to wife a daughter of Levi. And the woman conceived, and bare a son: and when she saw him that he was a goodly child, she hid him three months. And when she could no longer hide him, she took for him an ark of bulrushes, and daubed it with slime and with pitch, and put the child therein; and she laid it in the flags by the river's brink. And his sister stood afar off, to wit what would be done to him. And the daughter of Pharaoh came down to wash herself at the river; and her maidens walked along by the river's side; and when she saw the ark among the flags, she sent her maid to fetch it. And when she had opened it, she saw the child: and, behold, the babe wept. And she had compassion on him, and said, This is one of the Hebrews' children. Then said his sister to Pharaoh's daughter, Shall I go and call to thee a nurse of the Hebrew women, that she may nurse the child for thee? And Pharaoh's daughter said to her, Go. And the maid went and called the child's mother. And Pharaoh's daughter said unto her, Take this child away, and nurse it for me, and I will give thee thy wages. And the woman took the child, and nursed it. And the child grew, and she brought him unto Pharaoh's daughter, and he became her son. And she called his name Moses: and she said, Because I drew him out of the water." As you can see, Miriam played a significant role in the safety of her brother; this tells us that Miriam wasn't just a prophet, she was an intercessor. And as Miriam grew older, she developed a deep-rooted faith in God and her prophetic mantle began to show up in her gifting. She became an accomplished singer and dancer who'd led a group of women in the singing and dancing of hymns and songs of praise, celebrating the freedom that God delivered to them from Egypt.

Despite her many accomplishments, Miriam would find herself falling into one of the most common prophetic traps ever set by the devil. In modern terms, it's called familiarity. She was so familiar with her brother's humanity that she began to focus more on it than she focused on his anointing or divinity. Numbers 12:1-2 gives us insight into the conversation that Miriam had with her brother Aaron. It reads, "And Miriam and Aaron spake against Moses because of the Ethiopian woman whom he had married: for he had married an Ethiopian woman. And they said, Hath the LORD indeed spoken only by Moses? Hath he not spoken also by us? And the LORD heard it." Believe it or not, this was a Jezebelic move on her part. Miriam was clearly in need of deliverance because she stopped thinking about what God wanted and started focusing on herself. She said to her brother, Aaron, "Have He not spoken also by us?" In other words, "We're anointed too! Why are we following this man?! Why can't we just launch our own ministries, instead of following his lead?!" Again, this is a common issue amongst prophets and prophetic people, because the maturation of the prophet is similar to that of the natural evolution of a child. It is common knowledge that whenever a child becomes a teenager, that child (in many cases) will begin to question his or her parents' choices, challenge their authority, and rebel against their instructions. Prophetic people tend to do this when they become comfortable prophesying or when they witness the power of God moving through them. They then start to say in their hearts, "Why am I following this pastor? I am just as anointed as him or her! Besides, he's not perfect, after all, he's got a divorce under his belt!" And it is those thoughts that typically lead the prophets of God into prematurely attempting to launch out on their own. Sadly enough, many of them become bitter in the process because they were so infatuated with the glitz and glam of ministry that they failed to see the responsibilities that came with it. All the same, many of them began to hurt God's children because of their immaturity, and this led to many prophets and prophetic souls being bound by Jezebel. Either the prophet would find himself or herself in major need of deliverance, or the prophet would find himself or herself standing at a courthouse altar, exchanging vows with Jezebel.

What happened to Miriam? God gave her leprosy because of her rebellion, and it was Moses who had to intercede on her behalf. Numbers 12:4-15 finishes this story. It reads, "And the LORD spake suddenly unto Moses, and unto Aaron, and unto Miriam, Come out ye three unto the tabernacle of the congregation. And they three came out. And the LORD came down in the pillar of the cloud, and stood in the door of the tabernacle, and called Aaron and Miriam: and they both came forth. And he said, Hear now my words: If there be a prophet among you, I the LORD will make myself known unto him in a vision, and will speak unto him in a dream.

My servant Moses is not so, who is faithful in all mine house. With him will I speak mouth to mouth, even apparently, and not in dark speeches; and the similitude of the LORD shall he behold: wherefore then were ye not afraid to speak against my servant Moses? And the anger of the LORD was kindled against them; and he departed. And the cloud departed from off the tabernacle; and, behold, Miriam became leprous, white as snow: and Aaron looked upon Miriam, and, behold, she was leprous. And Aaron said unto Moses, Alas, my lord, I beseech thee, lay not the sin upon us, wherein we have done foolishly, and wherein we have sinned. Let her not be as one dead, of whom the flesh is half consumed when he cometh out of his mother's womb. And Moses cried unto the LORD, saying, Heal her now, O God, I beseech thee. And the LORD said unto Moses, If her father had but spit in her face, should she not be ashamed seven days? let her be shut out from the camp seven days, and after that let her be received in again. And Miriam was shut out from the camp seven days: and the people journeyed not till Miriam was brought in again."

David

David, the future king of Israel, is widely regarded as one of the most important figures in Jewish and Christian history. He is renowned for his military prowess, his poetic talent, and his pivotal role in the establishment of the Kingdom of Israel. However, relatively little is known about his siblings, despite the fact that they lived in the same household and undoubtedly played a significant role in shaping his upbringing. In this section, we will explore what little information we have about David's brothers, assess their role in his life, and consider what impact they may have had on the future king's character.

The first mention of David's brothers in the Bible comes in 1 Samuel 16, when Samuel comes to Jesse, David's father, to anoint one of his sons as the future king. Jesse initially presents seven of his sons to Samuel, but none of them are chosen by God to be anointed. Only when David, the youngest of the brothers and the one who was tending to the flocks, is brought before Samuel does God reveal that he is the chosen one. This story has led to much speculation about David's relationship with his brothers. Was he overshadowed by them? Were they envious of him? Did they resent that he was chosen over them to be the future king? Was his father envious of him or did he despise him?

Unfortunately, the Bible provides only a handful of other references to David's brothers, and none of them shed much light on their character or relationship with David. We know that three of his brothers, Eliab, Abinadab, and Shammah, serve in Saul's army alongside David, but we learn nothing about their interactions. We also know that, following David's defeat of Goliath, his brothers come to visit him in the army camp, but their appearance is brief and unremarkable. Finally, in 2 Samuel 17, when David is fleeing from his rebellious son Absalom, he sends a message to the priests to consult with his friend Hushai, saying "If you return to the city, you shall say to Absalom, 'I am your servant, O king; as I have been your father's servant in time past, so now I will be your servant.' Then you will be able to thwart the advice of Ahithophel for me." "Are Zadok and Abiathar," asked Hushai, "not with you there? So it will be that whatever you hear from the king's house, you shall tell to Zadok and Abiathar the priest."

While these references are sparse, they do provide some insight into the possible personality traits of David's brothers. Firstly, their presence in Saul's army suggests that they were warriors themselves and may have shared David's love of battle. Secondly, their willingness to visit David in the army camp after his victory over Goliath may indicate that they were not envious of his success, at least not to the point of openly snubbing him. Finally, the Bible's silence on David's relationship with his brothers may suggest that he simply had a cordial, but not particularly close, relationship with them.

However, we can also speculate that David's relationship with his brothers may have been more complicated than the Bible lets on. After all, the story of Samuel anointing David over his older brothers suggests that there may have been some tension or jealousy between them. Additionally, we know that David's rise to power was not without enemies within his own family. After he becomes king, he is forced to fight a rebellion led by his eldest son, Absalom, who may have been motivated, at least in part, by resentment towards his father.

If we assume that there was some tension between David and his brothers, it raises the question of what impact this may have had on David's character. It is possible that, if his brothers resented him, David may have felt the need to prove himself to them and to the wider world. This could have contributed to his formidable ambition and his relentless pursuit of military glory, after all, the spirit of rejection often leads people to become incredibly ambitious. Alternatively, if his brothers were supportive but unremarkable figures in his life, it is possible that David developed his exceptional talents in literature and music as a way of standing out from the rest of his family.

Ultimately, we may never know the full story of David's relationship with his brothers. However, even the little information we have about them gives us a glimpse into the complex family dynamics that shaped one of the most important figures in world history.

Joseph

Joseph is one of the notable figures in the Bible, known for his remarkable story of resilience, faith, and leadership. As a young boy, Joseph went through a series of trials, including being sold into slavery by his own brothers, imprisonment, and unfair accusations. However, amidst all these adversities, he remained steadfast and became a prominent ruler in Egypt. This lesson delves into Joseph's life, examining his experiences, character traits, and significant life lessons that can be gleaned from his story.

Joseph's Early Life

Joseph was born to Jacob and Rachel, who had been barren for many years, and was his father's favorite son. Due to his parent's favoritism, Joseph's brothers did not like him. To make matters worse, Joseph had a dream that he would be a ruler one day, which angered his brothers even more (Genesis 37:5-8). Out of jealousy and resentment towards their younger brother, Joseph's ten older brothers sold him to a caravan of Ishmaelites, who took him to Egypt, where he was sold as a slave to Potiphar, an officer of Pharaoh.

Joseph's Time in Egypt and Imprisonment

Potiphar noticed Joseph's intelligence, diligence, honesty, and faithfulness and placed him in charge of his household (Genesis 39:4). However, Joseph's life soon took another turn when Potiphar's wife tried to seduce him. Joseph refused to sin against God and remained faithful, leading to false accusations and imprisonment. Nevertheless, even as a prisoner, he continued to exhibit qualities of leadership and integrity, which impressed the prison warden (Genesis 39:20-23).

Joseph's Promotion and Leadership Role in Egypt

It was not until Joseph interpreted Pharaoh's dream, predicting the seven years of abundance and seven years of famine, that he was promoted to the second in command in Egypt (Genesis 41:38-43). As the famine hit the land, Joseph planned ahead by storing surplus food, which ended up saving countless lives, including his father, his brothers, and their families. Joseph's leadership skills were evident in how he led the distribution of food and resources during the famine. He treated people with respect, generosity, and fairness.

Joseph's Forgiveness and Reconciliation with His Brothers

Joseph's brothers, who had sold him into slavery, later came to Egypt seeking food. Unlike the views of his brothers, Joseph did not harbor any grudges, hatred, or bitterness towards them. Instead, he chose to show them grace and kindness. Joseph's forgiveness and reconciliation with his brothers is a powerful testament to the importance of forgiveness, especially in situations where it is difficult to do so. He recognized that God had orchestrated his life to bring him to a place of leadership and influence, so he could provide for and protect his family, despite the painful experiences he had endured.

Joseph's life teaches us many lessons, including the importance of trusting God's plan even when we do not understand it, the value of resilience, perseverance, and faith in tough times, the need for forgiveness and reconciliation, the importance of humility, integrity, and diligence, as well as the necessity of wise leadership that benefits everyone. Joseph's life also illustrates the principle that when we obey God and do not compromise our values, he rewards our faithfulness.

Summary

In conclusion, Joseph's story is an inspiring story of overcoming adversity, forgiveness, and exemplary leadership. Joseph remained steadfast in his faith and grew to become a great leader in Egypt, making decisions that saved many lives. His forgiveness and reconciliation with his brothers exhibited true devoutness and empathy. Indeed, Joseph is an example for all of us to follow, no matter the trials we face in life, to keep living righteously and pursuing Godliness. Therefore, he will always stand as one of the most significant characters in the Bible.

Jezebelic Types and Shadows

What is the profile of a narcissist? First and foremost, as we discussed earlier, there are levels, ranges, and ranks in the spirit realm, so one man's Jezebel may not be as brutal or evil as another man's Jezebel. All the same, some narcissists are covert, while others are overt. Let's look at the definitions of "covert" and "overt" before we proceed. The following definitions were taken from Oxford Languages:

- **Covert:** not openly acknowledged or displayed.
- **Overt:** done or shown openly; plainly or readily apparent, not secret or hidden.

One easy way to remember the difference between the two is:

- **Covert:** Undercover.
- **Overt:** Over the top.

In this particular chapter, we will discuss a few biblical characters who embodied or displayed signs of being either narcissists or being incredibly narcissistic. After each character's story, you will find a profile of that particular individual. In this profile, I will share whether I believe the person is a narcissist or if the individual appears to be narcissistic.

Lot

This story begins with the destruction of Sodom and Gomorrah, two cities inhabited by wickedness and sin. Lot, a righteous man, along with his wife and two daughters, are commanded by the angels of God to flee from the city before its destruction. As they flee, Lot's wife disobeys the angels' commands by looking back, and is consequently turned into a pillar of salt. The family eventually settles in a cave in the mountains, and it is in this cave that the story takes a nasty turn.

Lot's daughters, fearing that they will never marry and have children, devise a plan to become pregnant by their own father. They get him drunk and have sexual relations with him on consecutive nights. As a result, they each became pregnant and gave birth to sons, who would become the ancestors of two nations.

This story, on its surface, is disturbing and raises many moral and ethical questions. How could a father have sexual intercourse with his own daughters? Why did the daughters feel justified in their actions? What was the purpose of this story in the biblical narrative? The simple answer is—to understand the story of Lot's daughters, we must first understand the historical and cultural context in which it was written. In ancient times, genealogy was incredibly important, and the preservation of one's family line was of utmost importance. The idea of marrying within one's own family was not unheard of, and may have been seen as a practical way to protect one's family line and ensure its continuity. Additionally, the story must be read in the context of the larger narrative of the Bible. In this sense, the story of Lot's daughters can be seen as a cautionary tale, showing the consequences of sin and the importance of placing one's trust in God. However, even when viewed in this broader context, the story of Lot's daughters remains unsettling. The idea of incest is repulsive to modern sensibilities, and raises questions about the moral and ethical frameworks of the characters involved.

It is important to note that the story does not portray Lot's actions in a positive light. He is shown to be a relatively immoral character who makes poor decisions, such as offering his daughters to be raped by a mob in Sodom. Lot's daughters, on the other hand, are portrayed as resourceful and determined, though their actions are certainly questionable, but ultimately, the story of Lot's daughters raises more questions than it answers. Was their behavior justified? Of course not! It was perverse, and it eventually brought about two nations of people who would ultimately become enemies of the Jews (Abraham's descendants). How should we interpret the actions of Lot and his daughters? It's simple. Their story denotes just how contagious perversion is. They'd just been delivered from a perverse place, but because they'd been in that world or atmosphere for an extended amount of time, they still carried the mindset and the residue of the season they'd just left.

Till this day, the story of Lot's daughters remains a haunting and thought-provoking narrative. It challenges us to consider the complexities of human behavior, the role of family in our lives, and the consequences of our actions. And perhaps most importantly, it reminds us that generational curses are oftentimes the results of one man's decision whenever he's faced with fear, tempted by perversion, or when he has lost his faith in God. All the same, it shows the domino effect of sin and rebellion, after all, it was Lot's decisions that led to his family's downfall, starting with his decision to go to Sodom and Gomorrah. Lot wasn't a prophet, but he knew God, so whenever Abram asked him which way he wanted to go, he should have consulted with God. He could have, at minimum, asked his uncle, Abram, to intercede on his behalf, but instead, he allowed his senses to lead him astray. This is why we can safely assume that Lot was relatively narcissistic, even though he wasn't a narcissist.

1. He had left with Abram, even after God told Abram to come from amongst his kin.
2. His herdsmen, not understanding rank or protocol, had gotten into an argument with Abram's herdsmen. Consequently, Abram asked to part ways with Lot and his crew, but instead of apologizing, taking accountability, or asking for prayer, Lot looked at the land and decided to chase what he believed to be a better blessing.
3. He'd been taken into captivity by four kings who'd overtaken Sodom and Gomorrah. Abram called upon 318 of his personally trained men, and they went out and pursued those kings until they had rescued Lot and taken the kings' possessions.
4. Abram found himself interceding on behalf of Sodom and Gomorrah after God warned him that He was about to destroy those cities.
5. When the men of the city tried to break into Lot's home to attack the angels of God who'd come to rescue Lot as a result of Abram's prayers, Lot offered his two daughters to these men to be raped and abused.

6. He'd gotten so drunk on two occasions that he allowed his own daughters to come into his space and sleep with him.

From what we can see, Lot was more of a low-ranking Jezebel; he was nothing more than a distraction, an inconvenience, and a nuisance to his uncle. Nevertheless, Abram loved his nephew, so he'd gone out of his way to protect Lot, not realizing that his seed and Lot's seed would ultimately be at war with one another.

Narc Profile	
Rendering	**Type**
Narcissistic	Covert

Ham

Ham, Noah's youngest son, is known for his role in the story of Noah's Ark and the Great Flood. The story of Ham begins with his birth to Noah and his wife, who were descendants of Adam and Eve. According to the Bible, Noah was a righteous man in the eyes of God. God chose him to build an ark and save his family and the animals from a great flood that He was going to send to cleanse the earth. Noah was instructed to build an ark and to take his family, his sons' wives, and a pair of every kind of animal on earth. In this, Noah employed the help of his sons: Shem, Japheth, and Ham. These young men helped their father build the massive ark as instructed by God. They had to gather wood, shape it, and use pitch to seal the boat's seams. Through Ham's committed labor to his father, he'd initially demonstrated the tenets of obedience, dedication, and hard work, but just like many narcissistic individuals, Ham was a ticking time bomb; it was only a matter of time before his narcissistic ways would make themselves known. This time, of course, was immediately after the flood.

When the flood came, it was only through the ark that Noah and his family survived. For a year, they stayed on the ark, caring for the animals and waiting for the flood to subside. When they finally left the ark, they were filled with hope and gratitude for God's mercy. Ham was instrumental in finding the means to restart their lives and reintroducing animals back into their natural habitats.

According to the Bible, after the great flood, Noah and his sons farmed. One day, Noah got drunk and passed out naked in his tent. Ham saw his father's nakedness and instead of covering him, he'd decided to expose him to his brothers. This is the mark of a true Jezebel. People with this particular spirit oftentimes make really good friends, companions, employees, coworkers, and the like; that is until they have something they can use against you to gain some form of leverage. By exposing his father, Ham was not only displaying dishonor, but his actions suggested that he was likely coveting his father's position in the family. After all, in times past, whenever one person wanted to overtake the throne or position of another person, the individual in question would either kill or humiliate the other person; this is why what Ham did was considered a power move. And this is one of the main reasons we can safely say that the spirit of Jezebel had managed to board the ark by hiding in Ham.

Narc Profile	
Rendering	Type
Narcissistic	Covert

Haman

Haman is a name that is synonymous with malice and wickedness. He is an incredibly narcissistic character in the Biblical story of Esther, a book in the Old Testament, where he serves as a villainous figure who conspired to annihilate the Jewish people. Haman was an official in the court of King Ahasuerus of Persia, who held a position of great influence and power. However, his craving for supremacy led him to plot against the Jews, resulting in his own downfall and eventual demise.

Haman was a proud and arrogant man who believed that his position in the court entitled him to unlimited power. He hated the Jews, and sought to destroy them because of their refusal to bow down before him. His encounters with Mordecai, whereas Mordecai repeatedly refused to bow down to him, led to an incredible narcissistic injury on his part. And just like any true narcissist, whenever Haman's pride was wounded, he simply could not let the matter go. Haman was a skilled manipulator and narcissist who used his cunning words and influence to turn the king against the Jews, convincing him to sign a decree that would lead to their extermination. This is why the story of Haman and Esther is a classic example of how narcissists manipulate and attempt to control even the people who serve as authority figures in their lives.

Esther, a Jewish girl, was chosen by King Ahasuerus to be his wife. When Haman saw an opportunity to have her people destroyed, it was Esther's bravery, quick thinking, and most of all, her prayers that thwarted his plans. She risked her own life by revealing her identity to the king and exposing Haman's treachery. In the end, Haman was hanged on the very gallows he had prepared for Mordecai. Mordecai, of course, was Esther's cousin and the man who'd helped to foil his evil plans. This is why Haman's legacy serves as a warning for those who seek power and authority at any cost. His desire for absolute control led him to disregard the basic principles of morality and justice, and ultimately resulted in his own downfall. The moral of his story is that pride and arrogance can lead to ruin, and that the pursuit of self-interest can blind us to the suffering of others. This story is also a testament to the resilience of the human spirit. The Jewish people found themselves in mortal danger, but through the bravery of Esther and the support of Mordecai, they were able to overcome yet another threat of extermination. The story has become a symbol of hope and a celebration of the triumph of good over evil.

Narc Profile	
Rendering	**Type**
Narcissist	Overt

Absalom

Absalom is one of the most fascinating characters in literature, both for his tragic story and his deep flaws. He is a figure of rebellion, a son who rises up against his father and becomes an outlaw. His tale is rich with themes of power, loyalty, and betrayal. Absalom's story continues to be relevant in modern times, reminding us of the pain and tragedy that can come from family disputes, unforgiveness, and civil unrest.

Absalom's story begins with his birth as the third son of King David. Despite his privileged position as a prince, Absalom grows resentful of his father's power and begins plotting against him. He is fueled by a fiercely competitive spirit, which is only intensified by his brothers' jealousies and rivalries. When one of Absalom's sisters (Tamar) is raped by their half-brother, Amnon, Absalom is consumed with rage and revenge. He bides his time, waiting for the right moment to strike. His rebellion against David began with a whispering campaign, in which he slowly turned the hearts of God's people against his father. He made promises of justice and fairness to those who felt forgotten or mistreated by the king. As he gained followers, he became bolder and more daring. Eventually, he declared himself king and he led a rebellion against David, who was forced to flee Jerusalem, not necessarily because he feared for his life, but more so because David did not want to kill his own son.

Although Absalom's cause seems just to some, he is not without fault. His ambition and pride blinded him to the true cost of his actions. He ignored the wisdom of his counselors and allies, leading his army into a disastrous battle against David's forces. In the end, he is killed by David's general, Joab, who disobeyed David's orders to spare him. Being a man of war, Joab understood that if left alive, Absalom would continue to come after his father until he'd successfully killed David or he himself was forced to give up the ghost. This is the nature of the Jezebel spirit, and any demon for that matter. When an unclean spirit has an assignment against an individual, it will stop at nothing to complete its assignment.

The tragedy of Absalom's story is that he was undone by his delusions of grandeur and his unforgiveness towards his father. He was a deeply flawed character, whose arrogance and ambition undermined his cause. He was a tragic figure whose death left a trail of destruction in its wake. His rebellion against David tore apart the kingdom and left a legacy of sorrow and pain. This is why Absalom's story is a reminder of the destructive power of family disputes and the tragic consequences of ambition and pride. Absalom's story is also a testament to the value of wise counsel and the danger of ignoring it. Ultimately, it is a warning about the dangers of misplaced loyalty and the importance of doing what is right, even in the face of overwhelming odds.

Narc Profile	
Rendering	**Type**
Narcissist	Covert

Potiphar's Wife

The story of Potiphar's wife is one of the most intriguing and fabled accounts from ancient Egyptian times. Potiphar was a powerful Egyptian official who gave Joseph, a Hebrew slave, charge of his household. Joseph was a man of wisdom and integrity who quickly rose to power and became a trusted servant of Potiphar. However, the real drama began when Potiphar's wife, a beautiful and seductive woman, repeatedly tried to tempt Joseph into sleeping with her.

The tale of Potiphar's wife has fascinated scholars and theologians for centuries, due to its complex and multi-layered themes. At its heart, the story is a moral lesson about the perilous nature of temptation and the strength of one's character in resisting it. It is also a tale of betrayal, as Potiphar's wife ultimately accuses Joseph of making advances towards her, leading him to be thrown into prison. This is the perfect example of a smear campaign, and this is what narcissists do to protect their secrets, their reputations, and most of all, their wounded egos. This is why we can safely say that the character of Potiphar's wife is an enigmatic one. She was undoubtedly as a villainous temptress, ruthlessly pursuing Joseph despite his repeated refusals. She is a symbol of lust and desire, willing to risk her marriage, reputation, and even her life for a fleeting moment of pleasure. Her seduction of Joseph has been interpreted by some scholars as a metaphor for the corruption and decadence of Egyptian society at that time.

The story of Potiphar's wife remains a timeless cautionary tale about the dangers of temptation and the importance of moral integrity. It reminds us that every decision we make has consequences, and that the choices we make define who we are as individuals and what we can expect to reap in life. May we all be guided by the wisdom and courage of Joseph, and resist the temptations that threaten to derail our lives and thrust us into the lap of Jezebel.

Narc Profile	
Rendering	**Type**
Narcissist	Overt

Delilah

Delilah is a Philistine woman whose story has been passed down through the ages. She is known for her beauty, her cunning, and her betrayal of Samson, the famed strongman of the Israelites.

Delilah is introduced in the Book of Judges, where she is described as a woman living in the valley of Sorek. She catches the eye of Samson, who is instantly smitten with her. Delilah, knowing that Samson is a man of great strength and power, sees an opportunity to profit off of him. She is offered a large sum of money by the rulers of the Philistines if she can discover the source of Samson's strength and betray him into their hands. Excited to be of service to her fellow Philistine brothers, Delilah agrees to the plan and proceeds to interrogate Samson, attempting to coax the secret out of him. She employs a series of tactics, including flattery, seduction, and outright deception, in order to extract the information she needs. Each time she tries, though, Samson gives her a false answer, leading Delilah to believe that she has found the secret to his strength.

Finally, after much cajoling, Samson breaks down and reveals the truth to Delilah: that his strength comes from his long hair, which has never been cut. Delilah immediately cuts his hair while he sleeps and turns him over to the Philistines. They blind him and put him to work grinding grain in a prison.

It is easy to see why Delilah is a type of Jezebel. She takes advantage of Samson's love for her and betrays him to his enemies for her own gain.

Narc Profile	
Rendering	**Type**
Narcissist	Covert

Athaliah

Athaliah was a significant figure in ancient Israeli history, known for her reign as queen over the Kingdom of Judah. She was the daughter of King Ahab and Queen Jezebel of Israel, and her marriage to King Jehoram of Judah cemented an alliance between the two kingdoms. After her husband's death, Athaliah became the queen regent of Judah, ruling for six years. And it was during her reign that she implemented policies that were influenced by her mother's worship of Baal and Astarte. This led to the destruction of the temple of Yahweh in Jerusalem and the promotion of idol worship throughout the kingdom. She also persecuted the Yahweh worshipers, killing off many of the high priests and prophets.

Despite Athaliah's oppressive rule, a small group of loyalists fought against her. One of these was the high priest Jehoiada, who helped to orchestrate a coup against the queen regent. With his backing, Prince Joash was crowned king of Judah after Athaliah's downfall.

Athaliah's reign is often remembered as a time of great strife and infamy, due to her heavy-handed policies and destruction of the temple of Yahweh. She was widely reviled among the Israelites, and her name became synonymous with tyranny and oppression.

Narc Profile	
Rendering	**Type**
Narcissist	Overt

Herodias

Herodias is a figure of historical and biblical importance, known primarily for her involvement in the execution of John, the Baptist. Her story is a tragic one, marked by political intrigue and personal ambition.

Herodias was a member of the Herodian dynasty, a family that ruled over the region of Judea in the first century CE. She was married to Herod Antipas, one of the sons of Herod, the Great, who was the king of Judea at the time. Herod Antipas ruled over a portion of Judea, including the city of Galilee, where he met John, the Baptist.

John, the Baptist was a controversial figure at that time who'd gained a following due to his boldness, his declarations of Christ's coming, and the prophesies he uttered. He had been critical of Herod Antipas and Herodias, claiming that their marriage was unlawful, as Herodias was the ex-wife of Herod Antipas's brother, Philip. Herod Antipas had divorced his own wife to marry Herodias, which John, the Baptist spoke out against. Angered by John the Baptist's criticism, Herodias plotted and planned his execution. She convinced her daughter, Salome, to dance for Herod Antipas at a banquet, after which she requested the head of John, the Baptist on a platter. Herod Antipas, fearing a rebellion if he refused, ordered the execution.

Herodias's desire for power and revenge led her to commit a heinous act, one that is still remembered today. This is why we can safely say that she was a narcissist to the core.

Narc Profile	
Rendering	**Type**
Narcissist	Covert & Overt

The Pharisees

The Pharisees were a Jewish sect that emerged during the Second Temple period, between the third century BCE and the first century CE. They were known for their strict adherence to the Torah, oral traditions, and interpretations, as well as their focus on personal piety and communal purity. Despite their dedication to religious practice and ethics, they were also one of the most criticized and controversial groups in Jewish history.

The term "Pharisee" comes from the Hebrew word "Perushim," which means "separated ones." This name reflects their belief that they were separate from the rest of society because of their commitment to Torah study and observance. They saw themselves as the faithful remnant of Israel, the heirs of the tradition of Moses and the prophets, and their religious practices were shaped by their interpretation of the Torah, as well as the oral tradition that accompanied it. They believed that the Torah contained not only ritual commandments but also ethical and moral teachings that should guide their behavior. They believed in the immortality of the soul, the resurrection of the dead, and the existence of angels and demons. They also believed in the coming of the Messiah, who would lead Israel to victory and establish the kingdom of God on earth. However, their strict adherence to the law and their focus on personal piety made them enemies of God. Don't get me wrong—they believed in the importance of prayer, fasting, and alms-giving, as well as the virtues of humility, compassion, and charity. They emphasized the importance of tithing, observing the Sabbath, and keeping the dietary laws. These practices were seen as a way of creating a holy community and bringing them closer to God. However, the Pharisees' strict interpretation of the Torah also made them religious guardians of traditions and lovers of power, rather than true men of God. They were a hypocritical, prideful, stubborn, and double-minded sect of saints who loved the idea of God but not the reality of

Him. They had a reputation for being legalistic, arguing about laws and regulations that seemed petty or trivial. Some saw them as a threat to the Temple cult and the authority of the High Priest, particularly after the Pharisees started to develop their own interpretations of the Torah that differed from those of the Sadducees.

The Pharisees also clashed with Jesus of Nazareth, also known as the Messiah, the Son of God, and the Word of God. Jesus criticized the Pharisees for their hypocrisy and legalism, accusing them of neglecting justice, mercy, and faithfulness. The Pharisees, in turn, accused Jesus of blasphemy and violating the Sabbath. Their conflicts ultimately led to Jesus' arrest and execution.

Narc Profile	
Rendering	Type
Narcissist	Overt & Covert

Egyptian Pharaohs

Pharaohs were the ruler-kings of ancient Egypt, a civilization that spanned over 3,000 years. They were regarded as divine beings with divine authority and power, which the ancient Egyptians believed stemmed from their unique ability to communicate with the gods. Their role was not only political but also spiritual, almost sacrosanct.

The rise of the pharaohs in Egypt dates back to the late Predynastic period, around 3100 BCE, when the country was split into Upper and Lower Egypt. The pharaohs were responsible for unifying the two regions into one empire, thus creating the first centralized government in ancient history. The first pharaoh of Egypt was Narmer, who is considered as the founder of the First Dynasty. Amazingly enough, Pharaohs were considered to be living gods, and it was their mandate to maintain order and balance, called Ma'at, in the universe. They were also believed to be the mediators between the gods and the people. The pharaohs played a significant role in the religious and spiritual life of the ancient

Egyptians. But that's not all. One of the major responsibilities of the pharaohs was to oversee the construction of massive architectural projects such as pyramids, temples, and monuments dedicated to the gods and the afterlife. These structures, built by skilled artisans and thousands of laborers, were a testament to the pharaohs' wealth, power, and influence. They also served as tombs for the pharaohs who believed that they would continue to rule in the afterlife.

The pharaohs were not only rulers but also judges. They were responsible for interpreting Ma'at and ensuring the proper administration of justice to their subjects. They had vast courts with scribes who recorded the legal proceedings. The pharaohs received reports and complaints concerning all matters, including crime, civil disputes, and matters of State.

The pharaohs were usually depicted holding the royal scepter, the flail, and wearing the uraeus, a symbol of kingship that represented divine protection. Some pharaohs were also portrayed wearing the double crown, the symbol of their unification of the Upper and Lower Egypt, while others wore the Nemes-headcloth. These symbols represented their authority as pharaohs. They were the heads of the administration and had a vast hierarchy of officials, including the viziers, who were second in command, and the high priests, who were responsible for the religious ceremonies. The pharaohs also had access to the finest scholars, artists, and craftsmen of the time, who worked for them as advisors and who assisted in performing their ceremonial duties.

Narc Profile	
Rendering	**Type**
Narcissist	Overt

Judas Iscariot

Judas Iscariot is one of the most infamous characters in the history of Christianity. He is known for one thing and one thing only: betraying Jesus Christ for 30 pieces of silver. This act of betrayal has cemented his name in history, and it has been used as a symbol of perfidy and treachery for centuries. It is impossible to talk about the story of Jesus Christ without mentioning Judas Iscariot. This is because Judas Iscariot was one of the twelve disciples of Jesus Christ. He was born in Kerioth, a small village in southern Judea, and he was the only non-Galilean among Jesus' twelve disciples. Not much is known about Judas' early life, but it is believed that he was a zealot, a revolutionary who wanted to overthrow the Romans and restore Israel to its former glory. Like most of Jesus' disciples, Judas was attracted to Jesus' message of hope and redemption, and he quickly became one of his closest followers.

Judas Iscariot's role in the story of Jesus Christ was pivotal. He was the treasurer of the group, and it was his responsibility to manage their finances. However, Judas was also grappling with doubt and disillusionment. He had hoped that Jesus would lead a revolution against the Romans, but instead, Jesus preached a message of love, forgiveness, and humility. This disillusionment was compounded by Judas' greed. He was tempted by the offer of 30 pieces of silver from the chief priests, and he saw this as an opportunity to profit from his association with Jesus.

On the night of the Last Supper, Judas left the table and went to inform the chief priests of Jesus' whereabouts. He identified Jesus with a kiss and Jesus was subsequently arrested, tried, and executed. Judas' betrayal of Jesus was a profound act of disloyalty. It was a violation of the trust that Jesus had placed in him, and a betrayal of the friendship that they had formed. Judas' actions were driven by greed, envy, and disillusionment, and they ultimately led to the death of Jesus Christ.

The legacy of Judas Iscariot is a complex one. On one hand, he is reviled as the ultimate traitor, an archetypal figure of disloyalty and perfidy. On the other hand, his betrayal of Jesus was necessary for the Easter story to unfold. Jesus was able to fulfill his redemptive mission because Judas played his role in the story. In this sense, Judas' legacy is one of paradox. He is simultaneously a villain and a necessary participant in the climax of the story of Jesus Christ.

Narc Profile	
Rendering	**Type**
Narcissistic	Covert

Goliath

Goliath is a well-known character in biblical history, who is described as a giant Philistine warrior who was defeated by a young shepherd boy, David. The story of Goliath has been retold and adapted in various forms throughout history and is considered to be an archetypal underdog story.

The biblical account of Goliath appears in the first book of Samuel, and it describes him as a man who was over nine feet tall and wore a coat of armor weighing over 125 pounds. Goliath was a champion warrior of the Philistines, who were at war with the Israelites. He challenged the Israelite army to send down a champion to fight him in single combat, with the victor winning the entire battle for their respective side. However, no Israelite was brave enough to accept Goliath's challenge until David, who was a young shepherd boy at the time, stepped forward and defeated him by simply putting his trust in God.

Narc Profile	
Rendering	**Type**
Narcissist	Overt

Herod

Herod ,the Great, also known as King Herod, was a towering figure in the history of ancient Judea, whose reign has been extensively studied and debated by scholars and historians. Born in 73 BCE, Herod was a member of the Idumaean dynasty, which was a mix of Jewish and Arab ancestry. Herod's father, Antipater the Idumaean, was a high ranking official in the Hasmonean kingdom of Judea, where he served as a governor and political advisor. Due to his father's connections and influence, Herod was able to rise up the ranks of the Judean aristocracy and eventually become the king of Judea, a title he held from 37 BCE until he died in 4 BCE.

Herod's reign was marked by great achievements, but also by brutality and tyranny. He was considered a skillful politician and an effective ruler, who managed to maintain Judea's autonomy and stability in a volatile region. One of his most notable accomplishments was the construction of the Second Temple in Jerusalem, which replaced the one destroyed by the Babylonians in 586 BCE. The temple was a colossal project that employed thousands of workers and artisans, and it became one of the most magnificent religious sanctuaries in the ancient world. Herod also undertook numerous infrastructure projects, such as building aqueducts, roads, and fortresses, that helped improve Judea's economy and security.

However, Herod's reign was marred by acts of violence and cruelty that earned him a reputation as a ruthless and paranoid despot. He was known for executing rivals, family members, and political opponents, often on flimsy or trumped-up charges. Herod's most notorious act of cruelty was the slaughter of innocent children in Bethlehem, which was ordered in response to a prophecy that a newborn king of the Jews would threaten his rule. This tragic event, which is known as the Massacre of the Innocents, was depicted in the Bible and other historical sources and has become synonymous with Herod's bloodthirsty nature.

Herod's character and actions have been the subject of much debate and interpretation among scholars and historians. Some scholars view him as a tragic figure who was driven by ambition and insecurity, and who resorted to violence as a means of maintaining power and protecting himself from threats, while others see him as a calculating and Machiavellian ruler who was willing to pursue his goals at any cost, even if it meant sacrificing innocent lives.

Narc Profile	
Rendering	**Type**
Narcissist	Overt & Covert

The Degenerative Prophet

Victim mentality is a state of mind that is characterized by a belief that one's problems and difficulties are the result of external factors beyond one's control. People with this mentality tend to see themselves as victims of circumstances or of the actions of others, and they often feel powerless and helpless to change their situations. This mindset has serious negative effects on a person's mental and emotional well-being and will prevent them from achieving their full potential in life. In this lesson, we will explore the causes and consequences of victim mentality and discuss strategies for overcoming it.

The causes of victim mentality are numerous and complex. It can be the result of past traumatic experiences or a negative upbringing, a sense of powerlessness due to systemic oppression or discrimination, or a lack of self-esteem and confidence. In some cases, it may also be due to a desire for attention or sympathy from others. Regardless of the cause, victim mentality can have serious negative consequences in a person's life.

One of the most significant effects of victim mentality is the cycle of self-pity and powerlessness that it creates. When people adopt this mentality, they tend to focus on their problems and difficulties, and they often feel sorry for themselves. This, in turn, can lead to a lack of motivation, a sense of hopelessness, and an overall feeling of powerlessness and defeat. Victims may begin to see themselves as helpless and dependent on others for support, perpetuating the cycle of self-pity and powerlessness. Another consequence of victim mentality is that it can lead to a lack of personal responsibility. In many cases, people with this mindset tend to blame external factors for their problems and difficulties rather than taking responsibility for their own actions. This can result in a lack of accountability and a reluctance to take necessary steps to improve their situations. It can also lead to a sense of entitlement and a belief that others should take care of them. In short, this mentality can lead to narcissism or, in many cases, it is the evidence of Narcissistic Personality Disorder.

Overcoming victims mentality is not an easy process, but it is possible with determination and effort. The first step is to recognize and acknowledge this mindset. People with victim mentality may not even be aware that they are in this state of mind and may need help to recognize and overcome it. Once the problem has been identified, the individual needs to take personal responsibility for their actions and focus on developing a sense of agency and control over their lives.

Another strategy for overcoming victim mentality is to develop a positive mindset. This often involves learning to focus on one's strengths and accomplishments rather than their weaknesses and failures. Positive self-talk and scripture reading can also be effective in shifting one's mindset from a victim to a survivor mentality. In addition, seeking support from friends, family, or a mental health professional can be helpful in addressing underlying emotional or psychological issues that may be contributing to the victim mentality.

In conclusion, victim mentality is a negative mindset that can have serious consequences in a person's life. It can lead to a cycle of self-pity and powerlessness, a lack of personal responsibility, and a sense of entitlement. However, it is possible to overcome this mindset with determination and effort. By taking personal responsibility for one's actions, developing a positive mindset, and seeking support when needed, individuals can break free from this cycle and achieve their full potential in life.

Some characteristics of a victim mentality include:
1. **Constant negativity:** Victims often have a negative outlook on life and tend to dwell on the negative aspects of situations.

2. **Blaming others:** They blame others for their problems and have difficulty taking responsibility for their own actions.

3. **Passive behavior:** Rather than taking charge of their life and making changes, a victim may feel hopeless and powerless.

4. **Constant fear:** They often feel powerless and helpless and have a constant fear of the unknown.

5. **Self-doubt:** Victims often doubt their abilities and worth and have low self-esteem.

6. **Refusal to seek help:** They may avoid seeking help, fearing rejection or feeling unworthy of support.

7. **Lack of boundaries:** Victims often have difficulty saying no and tend to put others' needs before their own.

8. **An ongoing sense of victimization:** They may continue to feel like a victim even after the situation has ended.

9. **Lackadaisical prayer life:** People with this mentality tend to pray only when they want something from God, but when their lives feel relatively stable or increasingly unstable, they often turn to other means for happiness, relief, and support.

10. **Biblical illiteracy:** People with this mentality are typically not avid students of the Word of God. Consequently, they don't have the Word to lean on when the storms of life come their way.

Prophetic Illusions

In its most basic definition, an illusion is a false or misleading perception of reality. The human mind is capable of creating illusions, and they often serve as a tool used to interpret the world around us. However, illusion can also lead to misunderstandings, delusions, and even dangerous consequences. One of the most common types of illusion is the optical illusion. Optical illusions are images that trick the brain and make the viewer see something that isn't really there. They can be created by changing colors, shapes, angles, or lines on the page in a way that causes the brain to misinterpret the image. Examples of optical illusions include the famous Ames Room illusion, which makes objects appear to change size as they move across the room, and the Necker Cube illusion, which causes the viewer to perceive a cube as shifting in perspective. Another type of illusion that often affects human perception is the perceptual illusion. These illusions trick the brain into misinterpreting sensations, causing us to perceive things in a way that is different from how they actually are. This can be caused by factors such as expectations, context, and attention. For example, the famous "Rubber Hand" illusion involves placing a rubber hand next to a person's real hand, then stroking both hands at the same time, causing the person to feel as though the rubber hand is their own.

One of the causes of illusions is our own internal biases and expectations. Our brains are wired to seek patterns, find meaning, and make sense of the world around us. As a result, when we encounter ambiguous stimuli, we often fill in the gaps with our own assumptions, interpretations, and expectations. This can lead to misinterpretations and illusions. For example, when we see a cloud that looks like a penguin, our brain fills in the details to create a complete picture, even though the image is just a collection of random shapes. This is why illusions can have both positive and negative effects on human behavior. On one hand, they can be a valuable tool for creativity, imagination, and problem-solving. Our ability to see things that aren't there can lead to breakthroughs in science, art, and engineering. On the other hand, illusions can also lead to dangerous delusions, cognitive biases, and irrational behavior. When we hold onto illusions too tightly, we can become blinded to the truth, and make decisions that are detrimental to ourselves and others. This is to say that optical and perceptual illusions can trick us, and our own internal biases and expectations can lead to misinterpretations of reality. While illusions can be a useful tool for creativity and imagination, they can also lead to dangerous delusions and irrational behavior. To avoid falling prey to illusions, we must remain aware of our own biases and constantly question our assumptions about the world around us. This is to say that illusions are often brought on by external stimuli, whereas delusions are brought on by internal stimuli. This is why it is important for prophets and prophetic individuals to be in environments and atmospheres that are conducive to their health and growth.

The Delusional Prophet

A delusion is a belief or perception that is contrary to reality, held with conviction even in the presence of contradictory evidence. Delusions can range from relatively benign beliefs, such as thinking one has special powers or abilities, to more dangerous beliefs, such as believing one is being persecuted or that a loved one is plotting against them. Unlike illusions, delusions are typically associated with mental illnesses such as schizophrenia, but they can also occur in individuals with other psychiatric disorders, neurological conditions, or substance abuse issues. Delusions can be categorized based on their content, with some common types including persecutory delusions, grandiose delusions, erotomanic delusions, and paranoid delusions. What's the difference between each?

- **Persecutory delusions** involve a belief that one is being targeted or threatened by others, often leading to a sense of paranoia and mistrust of others.
- **Grandiose delusions** involve an inflated sense of self-importance or superior abilities that are not grounded in reality.
- **Erotomanic delusions** involve the belief that someone is in love with the individual, often a famous person or authority figure, despite little or no evidence to support the belief.
- **Paranoid delusions** involve a belief that others are conspiring against them, often leading to extreme fear and anxiety.

Delusions can have a significant impact on an individual's thoughts, behaviors, and emotions. They can lead to isolation, fear, and anxiety, as well as an inability to distinguish between reality and fantasy. Furthermore, delusions can lead to dangerous behaviors, such as attempting to harm oneself or others based on false beliefs. An example of this is a common attack against prophets, especially prophetic women. What happens in these attacks is the woman may find herself playing or joking around with a male coworker, some guy at her church, a neighbor, or a male friend. She may find herself dreaming about this guy, whereas she will either see herself marrying the guy or the guy may approach her and declare his love for her. All of this is taking place in her dreams, or it could have taken place in a vision. This leads her to believe that he is the one sent by God to be her husband. When this happens, the woman will often find herself trying to be more approachable and friendly in hopes that the guy will finally feel confident enough to ask her on a date. This is typically the result of her thinking that she's too hardcore, masculine, or aggressive, and because of this, the man is intimidated by her. This delusional thinking is pacified by the guy in question's friendly or even flirtatious behavior, or his ability to seek her out in a crowded space. And when the guy still doesn't ask her out, the woman may then find herself trying to improve her appearance; she may do everything from going on a diet, cutting her hair short, getting hair extensions, wearing makeup, wearing more form-fitting clothes, or changing her wardrobe altogether. Again, this doesn't lead to a bite; it only leads to more jokes and conversations between the woman and her love interest. In the midst of this, she continues to have dreams, visions, and false confirmations. For example, let's say that the guy's name is Steve. The delusional prophet may find herself in the middle of a supermarket when, all of a sudden, another woman yells to her four-year old son, "Steve, put that down and get back over here!" To the delusional prophet, this may appear to be confirmation from God that Steve is set to be her future husband.

This delusional phase is often interrupted when the guy in question shows up to work, church, or at the supermarket with his long-term girlfriend, fiancé, or wife. Shocked and confused, the delusional prophetess will introduce herself to the woman she believes is standing in her place, and whenever she walks away, another voice will surface in her heart, saying, "He's the one. The woman he's with is a Jezebel sent to destroy him and ensure that the two of you don't get together. Pray for his deliverance from her." From there, the woman in question begins to slowly and subtly dabble in witchcraft by praying against the will of another human being. These delusional thoughts worsen over time, as the prophetess may constantly hear a voice or a set of voices telling her what to say, do, or believe. This is why wise counsel is important for the prophet! This is why deliverance is also an important factor in the life of the prophet!

Generalization

Generalization is a critical concept in many fields, including philosophy, logic, psychology, and linguistics. It refers to the process of drawing a conclusion about a set of things or events based on characteristics shared by some members of that set. Generalization is a powerful cognitive tool that allows individuals to reason and make predictions based on incomplete information. However, it also presents risks as it can lead to oversimplification and oversights in decision making.

- **In philosophy:** Generalization is related to the problem of induction, which asserts that it is not logically justified to infer a universal proposition from a finite number of observations. This implies that the generality of a statement is not guaranteed despite a set of observations is consistent with a hypothesis. However, the human mind has the predisposition to make causal generalizations, based on empirical observations, even though these inductive inferences raise epistemic difficulties.

- **In logic:** Generalization refers to the process of inferring a universal claim from a particular instance. For instance, if an individual has observed that all ravens they've seen are black, they might generalize and conclude that all ravens are black. However, it is vital to exercise caution when making such inferences, as they inherently contain some degree of uncertainty. Logical generalization ultimately rests on potential falsehoods and inexactness, since it leads to making statements about entire populations based on a limited number of observations.

- **In psychology:** Generalization is vital in the understanding of how humans learn and process information. The process of generalization helps individuals to extend the knowledge that they have acquired in one setting to other newer situations. Moreover, it enables people to develop schemas, or mental representations of patterns that they encounter in the world. Generalization in psychology is useful in allowing people to react more quickly to new situations, as they can use past experiences as the foundation for their responses. On the other hand, generalization can lead to stereotype formation, where individuals oversimplify complex issues by making assumptions based on their previous experiences and knowledge. For instance, an individual who has had negative encounters with dogs may generalize and develop an aversion or fear of all dogs, even if they've never had problematic interactions with them. In such cases, generalization can lead to inaccurate and unfair judgments.

- **In linguistics:** Generalization is significant in explaining language acquisition and the formation of linguistic rules. The process of generalization enables individuals to infer general rules about language use from specific examples and input, thus facilitating effective communication. For instance, a child learning a language may generalize linguistic rules by producing complex sentences in the future by incorporating simpler sentences and basic grammar rules.

However, generalization in language can lead to the formation of linguistic inaccuracies, colloquially known as "bad grammar," where the speaker applies the rule too broadly or incorrectly. In such cases, generalization can lead to confusion and inaccuracies in communication.

Now that we've learned what generalization is in scientific terms, let's get a grasp on what it means spiritually, especially as it relates to God's elect. To generalize a thing or a person is, simply put, to categorize that thing or person based on your experiences, what you've been taught, what you've consumed from the media, and your assumptions. In short, to generalize someone is to prejudge that person; in other words, it means to be prejudiced. Now, don't get me wrong—generalization can be beneficial at times. For example, if you are walking on a sidewalk and you notice a man heading your way and behaving suspiciously, you may assume that the guy is a dangerous character and respond appropriately. You may decide, for example, to reroute yourself by going to the other side of the street, walking into a nearby store, or stopping a group of strangers who happen to be in your area. This act could potentially save you from hurt, harm, or danger. Then again, generalization can work against you, whereas, your past experiences may cloud your judgment, and this is especially dangerous for the prophet or the prophetic person. Think of it this way: Rosie is a highly prophetic woman who has accepted her call to ministry. And like most prophetic people, Rosie has experienced a great deal of trauma in her past. One of the most traumatic events she's endured is the loss of two different relationships at varying stages in her life. First, there was Stanley, her high school sweetheart. The two had dated for four years, and just when Rosie thought that Stanley was about to propose to her, he ended up dumping her. She later discovered that Stanley had ended their relationship to be with another woman (Heather). Heather wasn't the classiest woman alive. As a matter of fact, she didn't seem to have much tact. She appeared to be a relatively wild woman, and not necessarily the type of woman a man would leave his girlfriend for. Three years later, Rosie met Nathan, and the two of them would go on to date for two years. History would seem to repeat itself once again when Nathan ended his relationship with Rosie to be with a girl named Christie. Like Heather, Christie wasn't in the least bit sophisticated. Instead, she left little to the imagination. All the same, Christie lacked tact as well as discretion. This was confusing to Rosie, as both of her exes appeared to be men of class, men who would ascend the ranks of success and make great names for themselves. Of course, this led to Rosie seeing well-put-together men a certain way. This also led her to hold prejudice towards women who didn't play by the same rules she played by. This discriminatory attitude would go on to negatively impact her prophetic gift. This is why healing is necessary; this is why therapy is necessary, and this is why accountability is necessary. Prophets who run past the therapist and straight towards a platform can be incredibly dangerous because their gifting will draw people to them, but their hurt and their hatred could cause them to hurt more people than they help. For example, Rosie would eventually hurt a bunch of women who'd walked into her church looking for God. She would also aid and abide in the destruction of a few relationships because of her assumptions towards men who appeared to be debonair. However, Rosie is a true prophet, but her mistake was that she didn't respect the process of ascension.

The highest expressions or manifestations of trauma are generalization and objectification. In generalization, the prophet makes the mistake of leaning to his or her own understanding as it relates to people. This causes the prophet or the prophetic person to become suspicious, distrusting, and distrustful. A great example of this would be someone who says:

- "All y'all women are …."
- "All men are …"
- "All Black men are …"
- "All White women are …"

These statements are often followed by a negative statement, suggesting that every person of a specific category is naturally and instinctively predisposed to certain behaviors. It's what I call lazy discernment, and it is often based on the individual's very limited experiences with the human race. All the same, whenever you've been hurt, for example, by a certain type of woman, you will find yourself noticing other people who've been hurt by people who've fit the mold of the individual who hurt you. This seems to strengthen your belief that women, for example, are naturally evil, promiscuous, distrustful, or narcissistic. This would not only impact your relationships with women in the future, but it would also limit you in ministry by limiting the amount of love you have to offer. Where there is no love, there will be no revelation.

Objectification

Objectification is a term that continues to gain attention in society as a means of describing the dehumanization of individuals or groups, often by reducing them to mere objects or parts of the body. The phenomenon of objectification is deeply concerning as it can lead to various negative outcomes such as harassment, discrimination, and violence. Therefore, it is important to understand the nature of objectification, its causes, and the ways through which it can be challenged and overcome. At its core, objectification involves treating human beings as mere things or commodities to be used or consumed. This can take many forms, such as sexual objectification, which occurs when individuals are reduced from complex human beings to mere bodies with sexual value. Objectification can also occur within professional settings, with individuals being reduced to their job titles or roles without consideration for their wider personality, experience, or background. In either scenario, the end result is the same: the dehumanization of individuals, which can lead to a range of negative consequences.

Objectification is often driven by a range of societal factors such as gender norms, advertising, and social media. In particular, women are often the target of objectification, with their bodies being reduced to mere objects of male desire in popular culture. This can have a range of negative outcomes such as harassment, discrimination, and assault, which can have long-lasting spiritual and psychological impacts on victims. Furthermore, the prevalence of objectification within advertising campaigns can further perpetuate harmful gender stereotypes, which can contribute to a wider culture of misogyny and sexism.

Overcoming objectification requires a multifaceted approach, which involves addressing both the societal and individual factors of the phenomenon. On an individual level, it is important to challenge negative beliefs and attitudes towards individuals, particularly those that center on objectification. This may involve actively challenging stereotypes, as well as promoting self-respect. However, at a societal level, it is crucial to address the root causes of objectification, such as sexism and misogyny. This can be achieved by promoting positive representations of diverse body types and backgrounds within popular culture, and holding individuals and institutions accountable for promoting objectifying attitudes and behaviors.

What a lot of people don't know is this—generalization leads to objectification, and objectification is the highest and most deadly form of prejudice. Most, if not all, serial killers manage to silence the voice of their conscious by objectifying their victims. The following information was taken from the website of Sam Vaknin, the author of Malignant Self-Love: Narcissism Revisited:

> "Serial killers and malignant narcissists share a lack of empathy, grandiose fantasies, and a sense of entitlement. Both objectify people and treat them as extensions of themselves. Serial killers seek to render their victims immobile to avoid abandonment or humiliation, and they believe they are improving their victims by killing them. The narcissist's life is a repetition

complex, and the serial killer's murders recreate earlier conflicts with meaningful objects. Both represent a dual failure of their own development and of the culture and society they grew in" (Source: Vahn Talks/Narcissistic Serial Killers and Mass Killers/Sam Vahn).

To objectify a person is to dehumanize that person, thus viewing the individual as nothing but a means to an end. In other words, the individual in question is only as valuable as what they do, how well they do it, and how fast they do it. This is what narcissists do. As a matter of fact, a narcissistic person could easily generalize a person, but a full-blown narcissist would objectify that same person. This is because a narcissistic person still has some measure of humanity left, whereas a narcissist is an individual who, quite frankly, has likely been turned over to a reprobate mind. And the more that individual descends into the darkness mentally and morally, the more psychopathic the individual's behavior will be. Can prophets and prophetic people fall into the trap of objectification? Yep, but this happens when the prophetic individual is no longer yielded to God, but has instead, turned to demonic and dark devices to get whatever he or she wants. A good example of this can be found in the story of Eli's sons.

- **1 Samuel 2:12-17:** Now the sons of Eli were sons of Belial; they knew not the LORD. And the priests' custom with the people was, that, when any man offered sacrifice, the priest's servant came, while the flesh was in seething, with a fleshhook of three teeth in his hand; and he struck it into the pan, or kettle, or caldron, or pot; all that the fleshhook brought up the priest took for himself. So they did in Shiloh unto all the Israelites that came thither. Also before they burnt the fat, the priest's servant came, and said to the man that sacrificed, Give flesh to roast for the priest; for he will not have sodden flesh of thee, but raw. And if any man said unto him, Let them not fail to burn the fat presently, and then take as much as thy soul desireth; then he would answer him, Nay; but thou shalt give it me now: and if not, I will take it by force. Wherefore the sin of the young men was very great before the LORD: for men abhorred the offering of the LORD.

- **1 Samuel 2:22-25:** Now Eli was very old, and heard all that his sons did unto all Israel; and how they lay with the women that assembled at the door of the tabernacle of the congregation. And he said unto them, Why do ye such things? for I hear of your evil dealings by all this people. Nay, my sons; for it is no good report that I hear: ye make the LORD'S people to transgress. If one man sin against another, the judge shall judge him: but if a man sin against the LORD, who shall intreat for him? Notwithstanding they hearkened not unto the voice of their father, because the LORD would slay them.

- **1 Samuel 2:27-36:** And there came a man of God unto Eli, and said unto him, Thus saith the LORD, Did I plainly appear unto the house of thy father, when they were in Egypt in Pharaoh's house? And did I choose him out of all the tribes of Israel to be my priest, to offer upon mine altar, to burn incense, to wear an ephod before me? and did I give unto the house of thy father all the offerings made by fire of the children of Israel? Wherefore kick ye at my sacrifice and at mine offering, which I have commanded in my habitation; and honourest thy sons above me, to make yourselves fat with the chiefest of all the offerings of Israel my people? Wherefore the LORD God of Israel saith, I said indeed that thy house, and the house of thy father, should walk before me forever: but now the LORD saith, Be it far from me; for them that honour me I will honour, and they that despise me shall be lightly esteemed. Behold, the days come, that I will cut off thine arm, and the arm of thy father's house, that there shall not be an old man in thine house. And thou shalt see an enemy in my habitation, in all the wealth which God shall give Israel: and there shall not be an old man in thine house for ever. And the man of thine, whom I shall not cut off from mine altar, shall be to consume thine eyes, and to grieve thine heart: and all the increase of thine house shall die in the flower of their age. And this shall be a sign unto thee, that shall come upon thy two sons, on Hophni and Phinehas; in one day they shall die both of them. And I will raise me up a faithful priest, that shall do according to that which is in mine heart and in my mind: and I will build him a sure house; and he shall walk before mine anointed forever. And it shall come to pass, that every one that is left in thine house shall come and crouch to him for a piece of silver and a morsel of bread, and shall say, Put me, I pray thee, into one of the priests' offices, that I may eat a piece of bread.

Eli's sons objectified God and they objectified women. The same was true for Eli because he'd repeatedly turned a blind eyes to the evils his sons were doing to God's people. And get this, when a leader begins to see the sheep of God as nothing but mere objects or a means to an end, that leader's downfall will typically be loud and quick. This is what ultimately happened to Eli.

- **1 Samuel 3:10-14:** And the LORD came, and stood, and called as at other times, Samuel, Samuel. Then Samuel answered, Speak; for thy servant heareth. And the LORD said to Samuel, Behold, I will do a thing in Israel, at which both the ears of every one that heareth it shall tingle. In that day I will perform against Eli all things which I have spoken concerning his house: when I begin, I will also make an end. For I have told him that I will judge his house for ever for the iniquity which he knoweth; because his sons made themselves vile, and he restrained them not. And therefore I have sworn unto the house of Eli, that the iniquity of Eli's house shall not be purged with sacrifice nor offering forever.

- **1 Samuel 4:12-18:** And there ran a man of Benjamin out of the army, and came to Shiloh the same day with his clothes rent, and with earth upon his head. And when he came, lo, Eli sat upon a seat by the wayside watching: for his heart trembled for the ark of God. And when the man came into the city, and told it, all the city cried out. And when Eli heard the noise of the crying, he said, What meaneth the noise of this tumult? And the man came in hastily, and told Eli. Now Eli was ninety and eight years old; and his eyes were dim, that he could not see. And the man said unto Eli, I am he that came out of the army, and I fled to day out of the army. And he said, What is there done, my son? And the messenger answered and said, Israel is fled before the Philistines, and there hath been also a great slaughter among the people, and thy two sons also, Hophni and Phinehas, are dead, and the ark of God is taken. And it came to pass, when he made mention of the ark of God, that he fell from off the seat backward by the side of the gate, and his neck brake, and he died: for he was an old man, and heavy. And he had judged Israel forty years.

This is what objectification looks like. To Eli's sons, Hophni and Phinehas, the offerings of God were just food that they could indulge in whenever they pleased; to them, the priests of God were nothing but mere men wearing costumes. Additionally, the women were nothing but objects to gratify their sexual appetites, and had Eli not silently agreed with their sins, he would have put a stop to their behaviors. Amazingly enough, you will find many stories in the Bible of people treating other people as mere objects. You should understand that any individual who uses or repeatedly takes advantage of other people is narcissistic; then again, they may be a full-blown narcissist. The same is true, for example, for promiscuous men who repeatedly take advantage of women for their own sexual gratification. These men are narcissistic. Of course, the same is true for women. Any woman who repeatedly uses men for sex, money, or power is a narcissistic female. Again, this doesn't mean that the people are full-blown narcissists. They are narcissistic, meaning they don't have much love to share with the world and, because of this, they have a habit of taking advantage of people to satisfy whatever desires or needs that they have. People, to them, are nothing but a means to an end. All the same, objectification is the last step before murder. This is to say that most murderers first objectified their victims before slaughtering them. So, as a prophet or prophetic person, it is your sole responsibility to test the spirit in everyone who attempts to connect with you in one way or another. You have to understand that the enemy is after your soul (mind, will, and emotions), and he will stop at nothing to get you to work for his kingdom. All the same, to him, you don't have an identity; you are just another soul he wants to use, and to get you on his side, he will almost always throw the narcissistic Jezebel at you, after all, Jezebel is one of his favorite darts. And Jezebel specializes in forming soul ties with people, and that demon uses those soul ties to drag people further and further away from God's will.

Jezebel and the Prophet

The Prophet's Reward

"He that receiveth a prophet in the name of a prophet shall receive a prophet's reward; and he that receiveth a righteous man in the name of a righteous man shall receive a righteous man's reward" (Matthew 10:41).

In this, we come to learn that there are benefits to receiving a prophet in the name of that person being a prophet. Let's look at some examples to get a better understanding of what this means.

- **Elijah and the Widow (1 Kings 17:8-22):** And the word of the LORD came unto him, saying, Arise, get thee to Zarephath, which belongeth to Zidon, and dwell there: behold, I have commanded a widow woman there to sustain thee. So he arose and went to Zarephath. And when he came to the gate of the city, behold, the widow woman was there gathering of sticks: and he called to her, and said, Fetch me, I pray thee, a little water in a vessel, that I may drink. And as she was going to fetch it, he called to her, and said, Bring me, I pray thee, a morsel of bread in thine hand. And she said, As the LORD thy God liveth, I have not a cake, but an handful of meal in a barrel, and a little oil in a cruse: and, behold, I am gathering two sticks, that I may go in and dress it for me and my son, that we may eat it, and die. And Elijah said unto her, Fear not; go and do as thou hast said: but make me thereof a little cake first, and bring it unto me, and after make for thee and for thy son. For thus saith the LORD God of Israel, The barrel of meal shall not waste, neither shall the cruse of oil fail, until the day that the LORD sendeth rain upon the earth. And she went and did according to the saying of Elijah: and she, and he, and her house, did eat many days. And the barrel of meal wasted not, neither did the cruse of oil fail, according to the word of the LORD, which he spake by Elijah. And it came to pass after these things, that the son of the woman, the mistress of the house, fell sick; and his sickness was so sore, that there was no breath left in him. And she said unto Elijah, What have I to do with thee, O thou man of God? Art thou come unto me to call my sin to remembrance, and to slay my son? And he said unto her, Give me thy son. And he took him out of her bosom, and carried him up into a loft, where he abode, and laid him upon his own bed. And he cried unto the LORD, and said, O LORD my God, hast thou also brought evil upon the widow with whom I sojourn, by slaying her son? And he stretched himself upon the child three times, and cried unto the LORD, and said, O LORD my God, I pray thee, let this child's soul come into him again. And the LORD heard the voice of Elijah; and the soul of the child came into him again, and he revived. And Elijah took the child, and brought him down out of the chamber into the house, and delivered him unto his mother: and Elijah said, See, thy son liveth. And the woman said to Elijah, Now by this I know that thou art a man of God, and that the word of the LORD in thy mouth is truth.

- **Elisha and the Widow (2 Kings 4:1-7):** Now there cried a certain woman of the wives of the sons of the prophets unto Elisha, saying, Thy servant my husband is dead; and thou knowest that thy servant did fear the LORD: and the creditor is come to take unto him my two sons to be bondmen. And Elisha said unto her, What shall I do for thee? tell me, what hast thou in the house? And she said, Thine handmaid hath not anything in the house, save a pot of oil. Then he said, Go, borrow thee vessels abroad of all thy neighbors, even empty vessels; borrow not a few. And when thou art come in, thou shalt shut the door upon thee and upon thy sons, and shalt pour out into all those vessels, and thou shalt set aside that which is full. So she went from him, and shut the door upon her and upon her sons, who brought the vessels to her; and she poured out. And it came to pass, when the vessels were full, that she said unto her son, Bring me yet a vessel. And he said unto her, There is not a vessel more. And the oil stayed. Then she came and told the man of God. And he said, Go, sell the oil, and pay thy debt, and live thou and thy children of the rest.

- **Elisha and the Shunammite Woman (2 Kings 4:8-17) Blessing #1:** And it fell on a day, that Elisha passed to Shunem, where was a great woman; and she constrained him to eat bread. And so it was, that as oft as he passed by, he turned in thither to eat bread. And she said unto her husband, Behold now, I perceive that this is a holy man of God, which passeth by us continually. Let us make a little chamber, I pray thee, on the wall; and let us set for him there a bed, and a table, and a stool, and a candlestick: and it shall be, when he cometh to us, that he shall turn in thither. And it fell on a day, that he came thither, and he turned into the chamber, and lay there. And he said to Gehazi his servant, Call this Shunammite. And when he had called her, she stood before him. And he said unto him, Say now unto her, Behold, thou hast been careful for us with all this care; what is to be done for thee? wouldest thou be spoken for to the king, or to the captain of the host? And she answered, I dwell among mine own people. And he said, What then is to be done for her? And Gehazi answered, Verily she hath no child, and her husband is old. And he said, Call her. And when he had called her, she stood in the door. And he said, About this season, according to the time of life, thou shalt embrace a son. And she said, Nay, my lord, thou man of God, do not lie unto thine handmaid. And the woman conceived, and bare a son at that season that Elisha had said unto her, according to the time of life.

- **Elisha and the Shunammite Woman (2 Kings 4:18-37) Blessing #2:** And when the child was grown, it fell on a day, that he went out to his father to the reapers. And he said unto his father, My head, my head. And he said to a lad, Carry him to his mother. And when he had taken him, and brought him to his mother, he sat on her knees till noon, and then died. And she went up, and laid him on the bed of the man of God, and shut the door upon him, and went out. And she called unto her husband, and said, Send me, I pray thee, one of the young men, and one of the asses, that I may run to the man of God, and come again. And he said, Wherefore wilt thou go to him today? it is neither new moon, nor sabbath. And she said, It shall be well. Then she saddled an ass, and said to her servant, Drive, and go forward; slack not thy riding for me, except I bid thee. So she went and came unto the man of God to Mount Carmel. And it came to pass, when the man of God saw her afar off, that he said to Gehazi his servant, Behold, yonder is that Shunammite: Run now, I pray thee, to meet her, and say unto her, Is it well with thee? Is it well with thy husband? Is it well with the child? And she answered, It is well. And when she came to the man of God to the hill, she caught him by the feet: but Gehazi came near to thrust her away. And the man of God said, Let her alone; for her soul is vexed within her: and the LORD hath hid it from me, and hath not told me. Then she said, Did I desire a son of my lord? Did I not say, Do not deceive me? Then he said to Gehazi, Gird up thy loins, and take my staff in thine hand, and go thy way: if thou meet any man, salute him not; and if any salute thee, answer him not again: and lay my staff upon the face of the child. And the mother of the child said, As the LORD liveth, and as thy soul liveth, I will not leave thee. And he arose, and followed her. And Gehazi passed on before them, and laid the staff upon the face of the child; but there was neither voice, nor hearing. Wherefore he went again to meet him, and told him, saying, The child is not awaked. And when Elisha was come into the house, behold, the child was dead, and laid upon his bed. He went in therefore, and shut the door upon them twain, and prayed unto the LORD. And he went up, and lay upon the child, and put his mouth upon his mouth, and his eyes upon his eyes, and his hands upon his hands: and he stretched himself upon the child; and the flesh of the child waxed warm. Then he returned, and walked in the house to and fro; and went up, and stretched himself upon him: and the child sneezed seven times, and the child opened his eyes. And he called Gehazi, and said, Call this Shunammite. So he called her. And when she was come in unto him, he said, Take up thy son. Then she went in, and fell at his feet, and bowed herself to the ground, and took up her son, and went out.

- Now, these were just a few examples of people receiving favor and miracles because of their decision to be a blessing to one of God's prophets. But please note that the prophet's reward works in reverse as well or, better yet, you can be punished with a prophet who happens to be in rebellion. How do we know this? Consider the story of Jonah.

- **Jonah 1:1-17:** Now the word of the LORD came unto Jonah the son of Amittai, saying, Arise, go to Nineveh, that great city, and cry against it; for their wickedness is come up before me. But Jonah rose up to flee unto Tarshish from the presence of the LORD, and went down to Joppa; and he found a ship going to Tarshish: so he paid the fare thereof, and went down into it, to go with them unto Tarshish from the presence of the LORD. But the LORD sent out a great wind into the sea, and there was a mighty tempest in the sea, so that the ship was like to be broken. Then the mariners were afraid, and cried every man unto his god, and cast forth the wares that were in the ship into the sea, to lighten it of them. But Jonah was gone down into the sides of the ship; and he lay, and was fast asleep. So the shipmaster came to him, and said unto him, What meanest thou, O sleeper? Arise, call upon thy God, if so be that God will think upon us, that we perish not. Then said they unto him, What shall we do unto thee, that the sea may be calm unto us? For the sea wrought, and was tempestuous. And he said unto them, Take me up, and cast me forth into the sea; so shall the sea be calm unto you: for I know that for my sake this great tempest is upon you. Nevertheless the men rowed hard to bring it to the land; but they could not: for the sea wrought, and was tempestuous against them. Wherefore they cried unto the LORD, and said, We beseech thee, O LORD, we beseech thee, let us not perish for this man's life, and lay not upon us innocent blood: for thou, O LORD, hast done as it pleased thee. So they took up Jonah, and cast him forth into the sea: and the sea ceased from her raging. Then the men feared the LORD exceedingly, and offered a sacrifice unto the LORD, and made vows. Now the LORD had prepared a great fish to swallow up Jonah. And Jonah was in the belly of the fish three days and three nights.

This is to say that God blesses and chastens His prophets, and if you follow the lead of God and you choose to be a blessing to one of His blessed ones, you will too be blessed. However, one not-so-known truth is this: prophets can and do rebel, and whenever you host a rogue prophet, your association with that prophet could lead you to the very same punishment. For example, we have discussed throughout this book how Jezebel, also known in the world of psychology as the narcissist, is after God's prophets. This spirit has been after the prophets of God from the beginning of time. Remember, it was the Jezebel spirit that led Cain to slaughter his brother, Abel. And nowadays, one of the most common prophets you will ever come across is the running prophet; this is the prophet or the prophetic person who keeps running away from his or her assignment. This is the prophet or prophetic individual who keeps procrastinating and promising God that they will surrender to His will in their own timing. This is the prophet or the prophetic soul who is caught up in the sin of idolatry. This is the 'me-first' prophet, the lust-stricken soul who wants a man or a woman more than he or she wants God. This is the prophetic vessel whose golden calf is money, notoriety, sex, relationships, or the applause of mankind. Last but certainly not least, this is the prophet who exalts his or her feelings and plans over the Word of God. These are the prophets and the prophetic individuals who repeatedly find themselves in the custody of Jezebel; these are the souls who cry, "Why do I keep attracting narcissists?" What they don't realize is that they are in Jezebel's boot camp learning how to become all-the-more narcissistic; they are being groomed by the spirit of Jezebel to become a Jezebel, an Ahab, or a Eunuch. What are the differences between the three?

1. **Jezebel:** This individual is narcissistic, rebellious, idolatrous, and incredibly self-centered. This spirit will lead prophets through the ranks from generalization to objectification, whereas the prophet or prophetic person will go through a series of rejections from other narcissistic individuals; that is until they become like their narcissistic counterparts: cold, calculating, perverse, and deceptive. In other words, they will not only date Jezebel, but the spirit of Jezebel will enter them and begin to drive them from one place to another—hurting, betraying, manipulating, and attacking others, from lovers to leaders; they will become venomous vampires sent out by hell to spread Jezebel's influence, and to open others up for the Jezebel spirit.

2. **Ahab:** This is a truly anointed individual who fears his or her own

authority, but is ambitious, self-centered, religious, and rebellious. The Ahab spirit loves to enter men and women who hate responsibility but love power, platforms, and notoriety. Additionally, Ahabs are slaves of comfort, which is why they love Jezebelic people; they want the blessings without the systems, wait times, and processes needed to get to the blessings. Make no mistake about it. This particular spirit is not only married to the Jezebel spirit, it often serves as a covert narcissist whenever Jezebel, the overt narcissist, is not around to do the devil's bidding.

3. **Eunuch:** This castrated soul is what is commonly referred to as the flying monkey. Often cut off from the body of Christ, this particular brand of prophet no longer serves the Most High God, but is instead a servant of whomever it is that is in power. If a true man or woman of God is in power, the Eunuch will serve that person; if an evil, satanic, and murderous soul is in power, the Eunuch will serve that individual. Think about Jezebel's eunuchs. 2 Kings 9:30-35 demonstrates this point; it reads, "And when Jehu was come to Jezreel, Jezebel heard of it; and she painted her face, and tired her head, and looked out at a window. And as Jehu entered in at the gate, she said, Had Zimri peace, who slew his master? And he lifted up his face to the window, and said, Who is on my side? Who? And there looked out to him two or three eunuchs. And he said, Throw her down. So they threw her down: and some of her blood was sprinkled on the wall, and on the horses: and he trode her under foot. And when he was come in, he did eat and drink, and said, Go, see now this cursed woman, and bury her: for she is a king's daughter. And they went to bury her: but they found no more of her than the skull, and the feet, and the palms of her hands." The point is—the Eunuch is self-serving and has no true allegiance to anyone besides himself or herself.

And because of their allegiance to Jezebel, they are given the same reward as Jezebel. Consider God's judgment of the Church at Thyatira. Revelation 2:19-23 details the judgment of God associated with tolerating Jezebel; it reads, "Behold, I will cast her into a bed, and them that commit adultery with her into great tribulation, except they repent of their deeds. And I will kill her children with death; and all the churches shall know that I am he which searcheth the reins and hearts: and I will give unto every one of you according to your works." To commit adultery with Jezebel is not limited to sleeping with someone who's hosting that particular spirit; it deals with anyone who empowers Jezebel's witchcraft, rebellion, and her evil ways. Keep in mind that when the book of Revelations was written, the woman, Jezebel, had been dead for well over two-thousand years. This is to say that the aforementioned scripture was not about the woman Jezebel, it was about the spirit of Jezebel and the system of Jezebel. A great example of this is a church that had a Jezebelic leader; this is a religious church that constricts its members using fear, false prophecy, and familiarity. Many of these churches sprang up in the 60's and 70's, and eventually, the Jezebelic soul who had been leading those churches passed away. However, the system of Jezebel was maintained by a board of trustees, and you'll notice that in those types of churches, the sick and shut-in list is always long. It is not uncommon in these churches for people to pass away prematurely. This is because they have a form of godliness, but they deny the power thereof. All the same, they keep tolerating Jezebel, even though many of them inwardly question the things that take place within the four walls of their churches. Consequently, they end up being punished alongside Jezebel for empowering that spirit, rather than casting it out. This is to say that Jezebel is the prophet's reward for idolatry. The same is true for the prophet who dates, marries, and/or has children with Jezebel. They typically find it difficult, if not impossible, to break the grasp that Jezebel has on their souls. This isn't because they truly love Jezebel; the problem is that many of them have been turned over to Jezebel like Jonah was turned over to the great fish (Leviathan) because of their rebellious and idolatrous ways, and their repeated refusals to repent and turn from their wicked ways. So they wake up next to Jezebel or they stop waking up altogether because of Jezebel. They are addicted to the love-bombing, the gaslighting, and the ups and downs associated with courting Jezebel. They go out and about looking for people to build strong relationships with; this way, they can boast about these people to Jezebel, and just when Jezebel's jealousy gets the best of him or her, they will then sacrifice those relationships on the altar of Jezebel. They do this in an attempt to appease their deity and prove to Jezebel that he or she is the most important person in the individual's life. This is what I call the fatted calf effect. It means that anytime you find yourself being flattered by a friend, a relative, a coworker, or anyone in your life who is desperate to either be in a relationship or hold onto a relationship, chances are, you are the calf that's being fattened up for the sacrifice.

The Fatted Calf Effect

Chances are, you've been the fatted calf at some point; you just didn't know it. How does this work? Let's say that you have a close friend who is married to a narcissist. Let's call your friend Rhonda to make this flow better. Rhonda is a newlywed, and her husband, Fred, has become her everything. But like many immature or broken prophets or prophetic people, Rhonda thinks she can talk a demon out of being a demon. This is to say that the way of escape had been opened to her by God, but she repeatedly chose her boyfriend over God; that is until she entered into a legality. She married the weapon that had been formed against her, thus giving that devil a legal right to her, so her relationship graduated from being a mere soul tie to a yoke. However, you've kept Rhonda around because she is always spoiling you with kindness, gifts, and quality time. She repeatedly and excessively boasts about you to Fred, and there's a reason for this, you're the calf; she's fattening you up for him and in front of him. In other words, she's increasing your value time and time again in preparation for what's to come. She does this so much that Fred begins to despise you. It starts off as a subtle complaint on his part. Believe it or not, this is a ritual and you are the sacrifice. You see, worship is an instinctual act. No one has to tell us how to worship; it's something we naturally and instinctively do. Sure, we have to learn how to worship the Lord, our God, in Spirit and in Truth, but for the most part, we know how to worship. This is to say that while Rhonda may be ignorant of what she's doing on the surface, inwardly, she knows what she's doing. Over time, Fred begins to complain about Rhonda's relationship with you. He complains about the time, money, and all the gifts that she pours into you. He then starts looking for issues in your character because he is her deity, and she's treating you like a greater deity. Because of this, Fred will eventually want you to get out of his way. He will see you as a threat and seek to sever ties between you and Rhonda. Again, Rhonda inwardly knows this, so she continues to fatten you up. She also continues to defend her relationship with you, reassuring her husband time and time again that he shouldn't be so intimidated by you.

Slowly, but surely, Fred grows more and more distant from his wife, and one day, he doesn't come home after work. Rhonda calls you day after day complaining about her failing marriage, and it is clear that she is confused and distraught. On one hand, she says that she will walk away from Fred, file for divorce, and reset her life. On the other hand, she says that the devil is attacking her marriage, and she's going to do whatever it takes to fix her marriage. This double-mindedness on her part leads you to jump in and offer your opinion. You tell her that she can do better than Fred; there's a man out there for her who will love her, not cheat on her, and treat her like the queen she is. The conversation continues until you find yourself admitting that you have never been a fan of Fred because of something he did or said at some point in their relationship. Rhonda listens intently, wiping the tears from her eyes, and seemingly agreeing with you. At some point in the conversation, Rhonda may yell at you, storm out of your house, or say something rude. Then again, she might not say a word. However, that night, Fred comes home to face the music or pack his bags, and it is then that she seduces him. The two find themselves in the bed together, and after they've completed their ritualistic sex (sex designed to appease their wayward emotions), Rhonda offers you up during pillow talk. She tells Fred everything you've said, all the mistakes you've made over the years, and she then brags about how she yelled at you for speaking against him. In this, Rhonda is offering your friendship as a sacrificial lamb in exchange for Fred's love. Every deity has the ability to accept or reject an offering. All the same, an offering can only appease a god for so long. Let's say that this works. Rhonda will cut ties with you, and Fred will stick around a little longer because he knows how valuable you are to her. He watched her sow gifts, time, and praise into you. Then again, he could reject her offering, and if or when this happens, Rhonda may find herself offering her own children to her narcissistic beau in an attempt to appease his demons. She may insist that the children go and live with their fathers; that is if Fred is not the dad. She may allow Fred to abuse them. Then again, she may give her children up for adoption in exchange for more time with Fred.

Again, worship is instinctual. Rhonda will continue to give up everything valuable to her until she has nothing left to give. After this, she will be discarded by Fred, and she will either lose the health of her mind all the more, find herself another narcissist to give offerings to, or attempt to repair the damage she's done to her relationship with you and others. If you open your life and your heart back up to her, she will sacrifice you to another Jezebel at some point in time but not before praising and spoiling you with gifts and words. This is because the fatted calf, to Jezebel, is nothing but a glorified Eunuch who exists simply to make her life easier.

Homospiritual Relationships

We all know what the word "homo" means, and if you don't know, it means "same." For example, a homosexual relationship is a relationship that consists of two people of the same gender. So, what then is a homospiritual relationship? It is a relationship between two people who are hosting the same spirit, for example, it is possible for someone with the Jezebel spirit to meet, marry, and procreate with another person who has the Jezebel spirit. In psychological terms, it is possible for two narcissists to meet, marry, and have children with one another. It happens more often than you think. All the same, it is possible for two people who are bound by the Ahab spirit to come together in not-so-holy matrimony. What typically happens in these relationships is pure chaos and, if I can be honest, pure comedy. For example, have you ever seen two elderly people screaming and yelling profanities at one another? The wife clearly wants to dominate her husband, but the husband is stubborn, prideful, and sick of his wife's abusive ways. Don't get me wrong! He's no saint himself. He's abusive like his wife, but he may not be as abusive as she is. This is to say that in these types of relationships, one demon often outranks the other. You see, there can be five people with the Jezebel spirit in a single room, and not all of their demons will have the same rank. In the midst of the beehive, there is always a queen bee. Going back to the example of the toxic wife and husband, you may find yourself feeling a little sorry for him, even though he's learned to be just as aggressive, loud, and stubborn as his wife. However, the truth of the matter is—he loves every moment of their fights. As a matter of fact, what if I told you the guy was likely married before to a healthy woman who'd tried relentlessly to submit to him, and he'd treated her far worse than he's treated his current wife? What if I told you that his current wife was the tow truck that God allowed Satan to send to tow him away from his first wife? What if I told you that he and his current wife are bound souls who reaped each other because of their narcissistic and unrepentant ways? Get this—the guy in question may be a covert narcissist, whereas his wife is an overt narcissist. Then again, the coin could be on the other side, whereas the wife is the covert narcissist while her husband is an overt narcissist. And, of course, they can both be covert narcissists or overt narcissists. And finally, they can both be bound by the Ahab spirit.

One of the lessons I soon learned is that the overt narcissist in a homospiritual relationship often serves as the Ahab in that relationship. It may not appear this way because the overt narcissist is known to be aggressive, domineering, loud, and filled with rage. However, anger is a handle. In short, people with anger issues are usually easy to control, and the covert narcissist typically uses his or her calm demeanor to charm and control their overtly narcissistic spouse. A great example of this is found in the story of King Herod and his not-so-charming wife, Herodias. Matthew 14:1-12 tells the story; it states, "At that time Herod the tetrarch heard about the fame of Jesus, and he said to his servants, 'This is John the Baptist. He has been raised from the dead; that is why these miraculous powers are at work in him.' For Herod had seized John and bound him and put him in prison for the sake of Herodias, his brother Philip's wife, because John had been saying to him, 'It is not lawful for you to have her.' And though he wanted to put him to death, he feared the people, because they held him to be a prophet. But when Herod's birthday came, the daughter of Herodias danced before the company and pleased Herod, so that he promised with an oath to give her whatever she might ask. Prompted by her mother, she said, 'Give me the head of John the Baptist here on a platter.' And the king was sorry, but because of his oaths and his guests he commanded it to be given. He sent and had John beheaded in the prison, and his head was brought on a platter and given to the girl, and she brought it to her mother. And his disciples came and took the body and buried it, and they went and told Jesus." As we can see from this story, both Herod and Herodias were incredibly narcissistic. I would dare to say that Herod was likely narcissistic, whereas, Herodias was a full-blown narcissist. While Herod was a tetrarch (Roman governor) who ruled Galilee and Peraea, Herodias ruled him. Knowing that her husband feared the people, Herodias devised a plan. We don't necessarily know if having her daughter dance in front of her husband and a bunch of men was a part of her plan, but we can all clearly see that whenever Herod was charmed or, better yet, under her daughter's influence, she utilized that opportunity to execute her evil plan. Remember, Jezebel has always been after the prophet. In this, we find that the covert narcissist, Herodias, is manipulating and dominating Herod without having to scream her demands at him, get violent with him, or threaten to leave him. No, like most covert narcissists, she simply waited for the perfect opportunity to manipulate her husband, Herod, and she'd used a legality to trip him up. They took oaths seriously during those times; this was especially true for men of notoriety because their reputations literally preceded them. Once Herod swore that he'd give Salome, Herodias' daughter, whatever she asked for, all the way up to half of his kingdom, Herodias knew she had her husband where she wanted him.

In a relationship or marriage where one party is an overt narcissist, while the other party is a covert narcissist, most people will automatically see the overt narcissist as the villain, even though the covert narcissist may have a higher-ranking Jezebel spirit. The covert typically has a baby face, an air of shyness about them, and the appearance of innocence but inside, they are ravenous wolves. Most people will see the overt as the problem. They may even go out of their way to rescue the covert narcissist from the overt narcissist, and the covert will play right into their deception. This has everything to do with the fact that most Americans and most people in the Western world are slaves to the storyline model, whereas, in every story, there is a villain, a victim, and a hero. It is incredibly hard for us to conceptualize the fact that villain-on-villain relationships do exist, just as victim-on-victim relationships exist. For example, let's create two characters: Craig and Yolanda. Craig has the Ahab spirit, but his wife, Yolanda, has the Jezebel spirit. First and foremost, we have to overcome the belief that Ahab is a victim. He is not! Ahab was trusted by God to lead His people. Ahab chose to partner with a pagan nation for his own selfish gain. He doesn't get to play the victim when, in truth, he is a villain. Getting back to the story, Yolanda is incredibly abusive; she says some of the cruelest things to her husband, she cheats on her husband, and she has no respect for the man she'd once exchanged vows with. Craig's problem is that he idolized her; he chose her over God repeatedly. Sure, he may go to church, read his Bible, and use Christian jargon, but the truth of the matter is that Craig worships himself. In other words, he is self-centered, and because of this, he has repeatedly chosen to satisfy and gratify his sinful desires; this is how he found himself in a relationship with Yolanda. You see, Craig is a prophet of God who, like Jonah, is running from his assignment, and his narcissistic ways led him straight into the arms of Jezebel. And despite being a prophet, Craig is also bound by the Ahab spirit.

One day, Craig's niece, Briana, decides to visit her uncle and his wife. As always, she finds Craig sitting on a chair with his head down while his wife scolds and abuses him with her words. She even picks up one of their dog's squeaky toys and throws them at her fear-filled husband. The toy hits Craig's chest, and then squeaks before falling to the ground. Despite his wife's latest episode of narcissistic rage, Craig doesn't move from his seat, nor does he utter a word. Ten minutes later, Yolanda leaves for church, thus allowing Briana to speak with her uncle. Briana uses this time to beg her uncle to leave his toxic, controlling, and spiteful wife. Craig refuses; he simply responds with, "All marriages have problems, and we're no different." Realizing that Craig is not going to change his mind, Briana starts talking to him about her single neighbor, Ms. Lydia. Now, we can end this story here, but what do you think would happen if Craig left his wife to be with the sweet, loving, soft-spoken Lydia? The answer is simple:

1. He'd cheat on her with someone who has the Jezebel spirit. He may even

cheat on her with his former wife.

2. He'd abuse and mismanage her every single day.
3. He'd leave her because he wouldn't find her as entertaining as Jezebel.

I warn people about this all the time because, once again, most people are only familiar with the storyline model, so much so that they spend a great deal of their lives trying to rescue villains from villains, not realizing that they have become the supply for one or both narcissists. This is why it is important to always pray and try not to take sides whenever you see two lovers spatting because they can be the equivalent of Satan playing with his dolls or demons having a live puppet show. This is to say that just because someone proclaims that their ex was a narcissist doesn't automatically mean that the person in question is a victim. Ask any therapist who's had the pleasure of counseling some of the victims of narcissistic abuse. Those therapists will tell you that they've had many one-on-one sessions with people claiming to be the victims of narcissistic abuse, but their choices, attitudes, and habits told the therapists that the men or women lying on their couches were narcissists or they were incredibly narcissistic. Again, this does not mean that the lovers or spouses of the people receiving therapy are victims; instead, it demonstrates just how blindly hypocritical we can be as humans.

Beelzebub and the Prophet

Baal worship is centered around self. It is the very "me-movement" that we see dominating the airwaves today, whereas there are droves of people who've popularized the concepts of:

*   Me-time
*   Self-Love
*   Isolation
*   Affirmations
*   Manifestation

In 2 Timothy 3:1-7, God warns us about this. It reads, "But understand this, that in the last days there will come times of difficulty. For people will be lovers of self, lovers of money, proud, arrogant, abusive, disobedient to their parents, ungrateful, unholy, heartless, unappeasable, slanderous, without self-control, brutal, not loving good, treacherous, reckless, swollen with conceit, lovers of pleasure rather than lovers of God, having the appearance of godliness, but denying its power. Avoid such people. For among them are those who creep into households and capture weak women, burdened with sins and led astray by various passions, always learning and never able to arrive at a knowledge of the truth." Today, it is common for people to refer to their parents as toxic or narcissistic, and then use these labels as a justification to dishonor their parents, totally disregarding what God says about honoring our parents. This doesn't mean that you have to place them on a pedestal, allow them to continue abusing you, keep their abuse private, or allow them a space in your life. In this, God is simply saying to place value on them. As a matter of fact, the Greek word for "honor," is "timaō," and according to Thayer's Greek Lexicon, it means:

- to estimate, fix the value
- for the value of something belonging to one's self
- to honor, to have in honor, to revere, venerate

For example, despite what I went through with my parents, I still choose to acknowledge the good that they did. I can testify about the things I endured under their care, but this does not take away those times, moments, and events when they actually got it right. By doing this, I avoid the snare of unforgiveness. And when I did not honor their sacrifices, I despised the idea of becoming a parent. I even attempted to kill my child when I thought I was pregnant some twenty odd years ago. In this, I was partnering with the hosts of hell unwittingly and unknowingly, and my attempt to murder a child was nothing short of Baal worship because I made everything about what I wanted, what I felt, and what I feared. Again, Baal worship centers itself around self-worship.

First and foremost, who was Baal? Baal is an ancient deity who was worshiped by various cultures throughout the ancient Near East. He was often considered to be the god of fertility, rain, and agriculture, and was linked with various aspects of nature, such as thunder, lightning, and storms. All the same, the worship of

Baal appears to have first emerged among the Canaanite peoples of the Levant, who inhabited the region that encompasses much of modern-day Israel, Lebanon, and Syria. However, this cult soon spread throughout the Mediterranean world and beyond, with evidence of Baal worship being found as far afield as ancient Egypt and Carthage.

The name Baal itself actually means "lord" or "master" in the Semitic languages spoken by the ancient Near Eastern peoples. However, it was often used as a specific name for this particular devil who was often depicted as a powerful and sometimes fearsome figure with the ability to control the forces of nature.

The worship of Baal seemingly declined over time, particularly with the rise of monotheistic religions such as Judaism and Christianity. However, the figure of Baal continued to hold a certain fascination for many throughout history, with some even attempting to revive his worship in modern times. Today, the name Baal is often used more generally to refer to any deity or figure seen as powerful and intimidating, and the modern concept of "Beelzebub" as a demonic figure is also derived from the original Baal. Who then is Beelzebub? Beelzebub, also known as the "lord of the flies," is a powerful and malevolent demon. As a matter of fact, he is one of the seven princes of Hell and is often associated with the sin of gluttony. The origins of Beelzebub can be traced back to ancient Semitic religions, where he was worshiped as a deity associated with the Philistine city of Ekron. In literature and popular culture, Beelzebub is often depicted as a fearsome and sinister figure, embodying the darker aspects of human nature. He is a tempter and a deceiver, luring people into sinful and destructive behaviors. The name "Beelzebub" itself is often used as a synonym for the devil or evil, emphasizing the character's dark and malevolent nature.

Again, Beelzebub or Baalzebub is referred to as the "lord of the flies." What do flies represent? Filth. A fly's diet consists of feces, rotting meat, decaying fruits, and pretty much anything filthy. Washington Monthly reported the following regarding Baal worship:

321

"Ritualistic Baal worship, in sum, looked a little like this: Adults would gather around the altar of Baal. Infants would then be burned alive as a sacrificial offering to the deity. Amid horrific screams and the stench of charred human flesh, congregants—men and women alike— would engage in bisexual orgies. The ritual of convenience was intended to produce economic prosperity by prompting Baal to bring rain for the fertility of 'mother earth'" (Source: Washington Monthly/Baal Worshipers/Steve Benen).

As you can see, these pagan, idolatrous rituals consisted of:

- An altar.
- The slaughtering of the innocent (babies).
- Perverted sex.

In short, Baal worship centers itself around human desire. That is the desire to have sex without restraints, rules, consequences, or limitations; the avoidance or evasion of responsibilities by slaughtering the children born as a result of their sexual exploits, and an attempt to worship a god that would accept their evil behaviors and reward them with rain, bountiful harvests, and prosperity. Make no mistake about it, Baal worship is still prevalent today, only it's not necessarily known as Baal worship. In modern day America, it's known as "freedom of choice." And while God has given us will, and the freedom to exercise our will howsoever we please, He has also given us His Word, and in the Word, He tells us how to conduct ourselves in the Earth. Additionally, let's not forget that with every choice comes a consequence.

Why is this chapter important? Because Baalzebub or, better yet, Beelzebub is one of the highest-ranking devils today; this is largely because the concept of Baal worship is to do as you please. Today, we see the worship of Baal through promiscuity, homosexuality, abortions, and the like. Any and everything you do with your body is worship, and anything you repeatedly and systematically do with your body is a ritual. And what a lot of prophets don't know or understand is—Jezebel is probably one of the least of their worries. There are spirits that outrank Jezebel, and if a prophet or a prophetic person is not careful, they may easily find themselves in a relationship with someone hosting the demon of Beelzebub. This is when you're no longer dealing with someone who's just narcissistic. Someone who is bound by Beelzebub can be and oftentimes is psychopathic. And believe it or not, a psychopath can be incredibly charming, immensely intelligent, and consistently calm, unlike their narcissistic counterparts. This is why many of us who administer deliverance on a regular basis warn people to not attempt to use deliverance as a shower between sins. Matthew 12:43-45 will help you to understand why we give this warning; it states, "When the unclean spirit is gone out of a man, he walketh through dry places, seeking rest, and findeth none. Then he saith, I will return into my house from whence I came out; and when he is come, he findeth it empty, swept, and garnished. Then goeth he, and taketh with himself seven other spirits more wicked than himself, and they enter in and dwell there: and the last state of that man is worse than the first." Let's establish this fact: the spirit of Jezebel comes in many ranks; there are low-ranking Jezebels, just as there are Jezebelic principalities. All the same, the Jezebel spirit never comes alone. In the ministry of deliverance, we know that if we come in contact with Jezebel, we also have to cast out:

- Pride
- Leviathan
- Control
- Witchcraft
- Fear

And this is just a short list! In most cases, there are many more unclean spirits that have to be addressed like Python, Rebellion, Deep Hurt, Religion, etc. Imagine all of these spirits being cast out, only to come back with seven more wicked than themselves! This is to say that prophets, prophetic people, and believers who repeatedly engage in witchcraft, fornication, adultery, and any sin that involves the body, that person is at a greater risk of picking up or attracting the spirit of Beelzebub to themselves, and please remember this—Jezebel is in submission to Baal. This is to say that the spirit of Baal is far worse than the spirit of Jezebel! It is far more diabolical than Jezebel, and yes, a man or woman who is hosting the Jezebel spirit can also be bound by Beelzebub!

Overturning the Tables of Jezebel

Matthew 21:12-14 reads, "And Jesus went into the temple of God, and cast out all them that sold and bought in the temple, and overthrew the tables of the moneychangers, and the seats of them that sold doves, and said unto them, It is written, My house shall be called the house of prayer; but ye have made it a den of thieves. And the blind and the lame came to him in the temple; and he healed them." In this powerful story, we find our Lord and Savior, Christ Jesus, displaying what we've come to know as righteous indignation. He overturned or, better yet, flipped over the tables of the sellers who were trying to fleece God's sheep. Know this, while this is a story of an actual event that took place, a lot of the facts in this story are symbolic of deliverance.

1. The temple can be likened to our souls.
2. The money-changers or marketplace sellers can be likened to demons.
3. The customers who were cast out of the temple can be likened to ungodly men and women.
4. Jesus is Himself; all the same, He can be used to represent believers who have enough faith to cast out demons.
5. The items being sold can be likened to the desires of our hearts.

In this, we can say that men and women were selling their souls (mind, will, and emotions) to demons in exchange for the desires of their hearts. Notice that after Jesus took the temple through deliverance, the blind and the lame came to Him, and He healed and set them free, thus restoring the temple of God to its original design and purpose: a house of prayer.

Think of this being your soul. As a prophet or a prophetic person, you have a purpose. You also have a sinful nature, a bunch of desires, and an addictive personality. And like many prophets, it is possible that Satan got you addicted to sin before you even knew who you were. So, while you desire to be used by God, something keeps holding you back or holding you down, making righteous living appear to be an impossibility for you. If this is your truth, you are in good company. All the same, it's worth mentioning that selling your soul isn't just having a ritual, cutting yourself, and selling your soul to the devil for wealth, fame, and the trappings of success. No, to sell your soul means to allow the thief, Satan, to enter your heart in exchange for something you want, whether that something be a spouse, a new home, a car, or wealth. This means you'd do anything or almost anything to achieve your goals. Again, this is idolatry, and anywhere you find idolatry, you will find the spirit of Jezebel lurking in the shadows, waiting for an opportunity to strike. To better understand this, consider the example I gave earlier—a woman who is desperate for marriage gives off a certain air about herself. She smiles slightly and allows her eyes to dance around shyly as she twists her feet and tries to find something to do with her hands. Her words are sweet, flirtatious, and maybe even playful; she is poised but nervous and self-conscious. A Jezebelic man who comes in contact with her would notice all of the signs and symptoms of idolatry:

1. Self hatred masking itself as low self esteem.
2. Fear masquerading as shyness.
3. Lack of confidence showing through her body language, inability to maintain eye contact, etc.
4. Overthinking displaying itself through clumsiness, nervous laughter, and through her nervously rubbing her hands together or trying to find something to do with her hands.
5. False confidence showing up as conceit.

The guy will then start the first part of the narcissistic mating ritual. In this, he will flirt with her, make a few comments to see how she will respond, and then ask to exchange numbers with her. His conversations with her will be calculating. He will try to see what type of woman she is, how desperate or confident she is, and how fast he can accomplish whatever agenda he has. In other words, he will count the costs associated with building a relationship with her. He will then begin to build a pattern, and that pattern may look like:

1. He sends her two text messages a day, at minimum. One in the morning at eight o'clock and the other in the evening at ten o'clock. His morning texts always reads, "Good morning, beautiful." His evening texts always reads, "WYD" which stands for "What you doing?" Of course, the not-so-dynamic duo will have spoken over the phone throughout the day, but these are the two patterns.
2. A second pattern is that he may start to call her every day during her lunch break.

After he's established a pattern and gotten his new girl addicted to or reliant on that pattern for her peace and happiness, he will move on to the second level of his attack, and that is to make an attempt to move in on her sexually. This may look like him asking to come over to her house, him inviting her over to his home, offering to go out of town with her (this way, they can share a hotel room), or by trying to get her alone. He may even make a few sexual innuendos. The goal of this behavior is to strengthen and solidify the soul tie he's already formed or is in the process of forming. If she resists his efforts by saying, for example:

*   "I don't believe in sex outside of marriage."
*   "I like you, but it's not a good idea for us to be alone."
*   "It's too soon for all that."
*   "I'm not that type of woman."

His response to these would depend on their initial conversation. For example, let's say that she told him that she was abstinent, and would remain that way until marriage on the first day that they'd exchanged numbers. If he'd initially pretended to be okay with this arrangement, he may say, "I'm not trying to sleep with you. I'm trying to get to know you better" or "So, you think that's all I want from you? Can a man simply want to hang out with his girl with no strings attached?" In other words, he will guilt-trip and gaslight her into thinking that she is overthinking his intentions. Narcissists love guilt-tripping people because guilt typically makes people feel like they owe the people they've allegedly misjudged more than an apology; instead, they have to do something to make up for their error. Let's say that the young woman in question says, "It's not like that. I just want us to use wisdom; I want us to be careful. I really like you, but I made a promise to God that I would remain abstinent, so while your intentions may be good, I don't trust the flesh." On the other line, he smiles, knowing that he's got her where he wants her. She's clearly lacks confidence because she's trying to soften her no to make it more palatable to him. "Who said you can't trust my flesh? You might not trust yours, but hey, I trust mine. I'm grown. Grown men know how to control themselves. I think you're used to grown boys." After these words, silence crowns the line for a minute. Realizing that the woman on the other end is not budging, he will then move to level three of the attack. In this, he will break the pattern of contacting her early in the morning, on her lunch break, and later in the evening. Broken patterns send prophets and prophetic people into a subtle panic that grows more and more chaotic throughout the day, and this panic continues to progress until it becomes full-blown anxiety. What the narcissist or narcissistic person is doing is testing the strength of the soul tie to see if the relationship is worth salvaging. A day or two later, the narcissist or narcissistic person will reemerge to test the waters. (Note: they can be gone for up to a week in many cases.) You see, after the prophet or prophetic person has experienced the fears, the anxieties, and the grief behind the narcissist's absence, in many cases, the prophet or the prophetic person will be ready to compromise. In other words, they are now ready to make a deal with the devil. And this deal does not sound like the woman calling her narcissistic beau, and telling him that she's ready to engage him sexually. While this can happen, in many cases, it may look like her agreeing to let him come over to her house late at night or her cranking up her car to go to his place. Either way, the narcissist will get what, spiritually and legally speaking, he needs to continue in her life, and that is the sin offering.

Once the soul tie is established, Satan will go out of his way to upgrade the soul tie to a yoke. What is the difference between a soul tie and a yoke? Practically put, it's the strength and the location of the tie. Unbeknownst to most people, you can have a financial soul tie with a person, just as you can have a platonic soul tie with someone who's romantically linked to you. The person may have a romantic or Eros soul tie with you, but this doesn't mean that you share the same type of tie with that person. A yoke, on the other hand, is legally binding, and it ties two minds or destinies together through the power of agreement. In short, it makes it more difficult to get away from an individual or a spirit. We build soul ties with non-believers all the time, but these soul ties are in the workplace, the marketplace, or just out and about. They are not romantic in nature; instead, they are surface-level. It simply means that we've developed a measure of familiarity with a person (and vice versa), and we have some insight and input into that person's life. But, God told us not to be *unequally yoked* with unbelievers; in other words, do not marry them, do not enter into any covenants with them, and do not enter into an intimate relationship with them platonically, romantically, professionally, or spiritually.

Once the soul tie has been upgraded to a yoke, the mask on the narcissist falls all the way off, and the man or woman who is in the narcissist's custody will begin to experience a great deal of confusion, loss, and abuse. This is when the Jezebelic mating ritual has been completed, and now the individual in question is a part of Jezebel's harem.

But how do you overturn the tables of Jezebel or, better yet, how do you turn the tables on Jezebel? There is no one collective Jezebel spirit, just like there is no one collective Robert, Donna, or Tasha on this planet. There are millions of people with each of these names. So the Jezebel spirit that was in Larry's ex is not necessarily the same one that was in his mother or father. The one in Larry's mother may be weaker than the one that's in his ex. This is why his mother and his ex fought with vigor, and his ex was able to stop him from contacting his mother. This is to say that there is rank in the spirit world, and how much rank a spirit has in your life represents the amount of success that spirit has had in times past, and how much authority it has managed to usurp from you and the people connected to you. So, to overcome the Jezebel spirit in your life may require more of a fight than your best friend, for example, may require to overcome the Jezebel spirit in his life.

Jezebel typically enters in through:
1.   A bloodline curse.

2. Idolatry.
3. Witchcraft.
4. Rebellion.
5. Unhealed trauma.
6. Fear and passivity.
7. Unforgiveness.

There are other doors, but these are the main ones. This is to say that casting Jezebel out without closing the door will always prove to be pointless. Sure, you can set up a deliverance session with a deliverance minister, and while I highly recommend that you do, you still have to do the work to overcome Jezebel's devices in your life. For example, if you have made marriage an idol, casting Jezebel out will only cause it to come back through a potential love interest. This is because the system of idolatry in your life has not been eradicated, so you'd want to address the system first before you attempt to address the demon that's benefiting from the system. If the issue is unhealed trauma, get therapy, and I'm not just talking about one to three sessions. You need to keep booking sessions until your trauma is a thing of the past. If witchcraft is the issue, you need to repent, renounce the witchcraft, and get back in the right posture with God. If it's a bloodline curse, it has to be addressed in deliverance, but the habits and strongholds have to be addressed in your day-to-day life through consistent Bible study, therapy, and obedience. So, if you love charming, manipulating, and taking advantage of people, you have to stop with this behavior, and start helping, interceding for, and loving people altogether. If rebellion is the issue, stop rebelling, get therapy, surround yourself with wise counsel, be accountable to that wise counsel, and commit to a lifestyle of obedience. The point is, overcoming Jezebel requires that you overcome the ungodliness that lurks within your heart. In simplistic terms, here are the steps to overcome the spirit of Jezebel once and for all:

1. Repent for your sins, the sins of your parents, and the sins of your ancestors; this is how you address the iniquity in your bloodline.
2. Seek ye first the Kingdom of God and His righteousness. In other words, your desires, your plans, your feelings, and your fears can no longer be

the fuel or the driving forces in your life. You have to chase God FIRST. I have to highlight the word "first" because religion blinds most people to the point where they are able to unconsciously cut out certain words while reading scriptures, and because of this, we have a nation of believers who are seeking God, but they are not seeking Him first. In other words, many believers today are unwittingly and unknowingly polytheistic.

3. Renounce all of the ungodly soul ties that you are a part of.
4. Forgive the people who've hurt and betrayed you, after all, unforgiveness is a soul tie.
5. No more rebellion! This includes sex outside of marriage.
6. Do not unequally yoke yourself with an unbeliever.
7. Pray and study your Bible daily, and do not forsake the gathering of the saints!
8. Say yes to the call and assignment on your life. Don't be like Jonah.
9. Grow up or, better yet, mature in the things of God. You do this by studying your Bible, being accountable to someone, and by putting your hands to your ministerial plow (assignment).
10. Establish, enforce, and solidify boundaries in your life, and do not allow Jezebel to talk, seduce, or bully you into changing or removing your boundaries.
11. Rid your life of anyone who does not respect your boundaries.
12. Don't rush in relationships; test the spirit by the Spirit to see if it is from God. And don't be so desperate for a relationship that you ignore the red flags. The red flags are signs that you are about to enter a circus.
13. Don't hold onto any expired relationships. Pray, close doors, have hard conversations, and let the Lord lead you in all of your doings.
14. Get therapy, and again, don't just sign up for a few sessions. Get therapy until your heart's health is restored.
15. Break up with the devil. You can't break up with the person of Jezebel, you have to break up, divorce, and cut ties with the spirit of Jezebel.

Breaking Up with Jezebel

I always tell people that the hardest breakup you'll ever have to go through is:

1. Breaking up with the old version of yourself.
2. Breaking up with the devil himself.

Ironically enough, the old you and whatever demons are cast out of you will stalk you in this event that we call life, but you have to remain 12 steps ahead of each enemy. You do this by chasing God day after day, moment after time, and time after time, regardless of what's going on in your life and how you feel. This means that your relationship with God and your pursuit of Him must remain consistent; it cannot be conditional or transactional. If your relationship with Him is based on what you want Him to do for you, you will find yourself amongst the many who cry "narcissist" whenever the paths they choose lead them into Jezebel's lair. For example, go on social media and you will find that the term "narcissist" is trending. You will find people telling traumatic stories about their narcissistic exes, you will find people asking for advice to deal with the narcissists in their lives, and you will find narcissists pretending to be victims of narcissistic abuse when, in truth, they were the villains in the stories they're sharing. And get this—the vast majority of these people are not victims, per se. They are people who repeatedly chose themselves over God, and what makes them feel like they are victims is the fact that they were faithful to their narcissistic lovers; they were good to the people who were horrible to them. They don't realize, however, that they reaped what they'd sown. How so? They weren't faithful to God. They cheated on Him with other deities, they exalted their plans above His plans, and they repeatedly sinned against Him in an attempt to get to the blessings without having to go the Kingdom route. Consequently, they sowed the seed of idolatry and reaped the harvest of adultery; this is because idolatry and adultery are the same crimes committed in different dimensions. And what the enemy does with many of these souls is—he teaches them to be masters of breaking up with people, but they lack discernment altogether. So, they boast and brag about discarding the narcissists in their lives; they tell their stories of defeat, victory, and reward, not once taking accountability for their wrongs because, get this—Satan uses the narcissist to make people all the more narcissistic. In other words, they do not realize that they are being groomed by a demon so that they too can be narcissistic by way of the Jezebel spirit, the Ahab spirit, or the spirit of the Eunuch. This is to say that if you have dated Jezebel more than once, chances are, you are being groomed or you have been groomed. The objective isn't always to turn you into a full-blown narcissist; Satan's goal is to bring you in subjection to the Jezebelic system; this way, God can't use you the way He wants to use you. In both systems, there are rewards, whereas, in the world's systems, the payout is faster, even though it is not longstanding. In the Kingdom's culture, the payouts can take more time than we want them to, but this is okay; God uses the delay to develop our patience, our character, and our trust in Him. Because most people are impatient, they lean to the world's system, but they go to church and sow a few seeds into the Kingdom's system; this is the equivalent of playing the lottery in the spirit. This is a gambling mentality, where people sow seeds into both systems, and then they wait to see which system will produce them an award. They then place their trust in the system that moved the fastest and appeared to be the most rewarding. This is almost always the systems of this world, but as the Bible tells us, when God blesses you, He will add no sorrow to it. This suggests that anything that comes from the enemy is laced with warfare.

This is to say that breaking up with Jezebel means to first break up with the systems of Jezebel. You cannot benefit from her systems and get rid of her altogether. This is similar to the example I gave earlier of some of the coaching calls I have had in the past, whereas, I've spoken with women who screamed, shouted, and pleaded with me to ask God to set them free from the ungodly soul ties they'd so willfully placed themselves in. The problem with this was the fact that they did not repent, nor had they even considered what they'd done wrong. Instead, they wanted to cancel out the laws of sowing and reaping, and this is impossible! In other words, they'd gambled with the devil and lost, and now, they were at Heaven's front desk asking for a refund. Of course, I helped them to understand that they had to forsake the systems of this world; this includes unequally yoking themselves with unbelievers, engaging in premarital sex, and putting God second to their own needs and desires. In other words, they had to relinquish their idols. And like the rich young ruler, they dropped their heads and drowned themselves in self-pity because they knew that they weren't ready to commit themselves fully to God. They still wanted to gamble with their souls a few more times because they were convinced that they were at the edge of their breakthrough, just not in God's Kingdom. This isn't to berate them, after all, I think most of us have been in that space at some point in our lives, and breaking up with a spirit wasn't something that we were taught. All the same, we weren't taught how to deal with the pain that came with severing soul ties; we weren't taught how to resist the devil. We were simply told that we were to live a certain way, and then, we were tossed into this world without a clue. This isn't to say that we are victims; it is to say that most of us have tried to fight a spiritual battle with no knowledge or understanding to undergird us.

Breaking up with the devil isn't as hard as it may appear; the hardest part is maintaining the breakup. Breaking up with the Jezebel spirit or any unclean spirit requires the following:
1. Putting God first.
2. Submitting to God.
3. Resisting the devil.
4. Keeping God first.

And get this—we have to repeat these steps every single day of our lives. How do you put God first? By pursuing Him daily, giving Him your plans, and accepting your assignment in Him. And this cannot be done in a transactional manner, otherwise, it's done in the wrong spirit. How do you submit to God? By following the Word of God. If God said that something is a sin or a crime against Him, don't do it. If God told you to do something, do it. How do you resist the devil? By ignoring and rejecting his many temptations. Follow the example that Jesus gave us when He was tempted in the wilderness by Satan. He kept answering the enemy with the Word. He didn't argue with His opinion, He didn't have an emotional flare-up, and unlike Eve, He didn't consider the devil's offer. He had a made-up mind, and please read this carefully—a made up mind is a wall that the devil can't get through; that is unless he finds a window (opportunity) or a door (legality). You also want to enhance your efforts by:

1. Getting into a good and Godly church.
2. Surrounding yourself with people who love and fear the Lord.
3. Asking the Lord to bless you with people who are smarter than you, more anointed than you, and more faithful than yourself; this way, they can serve as wise counselors in your life.
4. Addressing all unhealed trauma expediently.
5. Loving God with all of your heart, mind, and strength, and loving your neighbor as you love yourself.

If Satan can't get you to sin against God, you won't have to worry about Jezebel sharing a last name or a kid with you. Therefore, the key isn't getting rid of Jezebel; it's getting rid of sin, iniquity, and idolatry. This way, the devil won't be able to say that he has any place in you. In other words, he won't have any claims to your soul. Remember, we are multifaceted beings. You want to cast the enemy out of every dimension; this way, Jezebel won't find the weakest point of entry, and use that side of you to enter into your life. One last lesson is this—pay attention to the side of you that people try to connect to. You are like a spinning rack of faces, and some sides of you are illuminated because you have wisdom and revelation in those areas; then again, there are sides of you that are dark because you haven't invited God into those spaces. One thing you'll come to discover about narcissists (if you haven't discovered this truth already) is that they love to find those dark faces; they love to find the parts of you that are weak, undeveloped, guilt-ridden, and without wisdom, and they love to attach to you in those areas. This allows them to exalt themselves and pretend to be a needed fixture in your life. This is why you want to stay at the feet of Jesus, taking in His Word so that He can illuminate every part of you in due season. And it's okay to tell yourself that you are not ready to date just yet; instead, you are being developed as a prophet or a prophetic individual. To end this lesson, here are a few more pointers to help you end things with Jezebel once and for all:

1. Find a deliverance ministry, and set up an appointment so that you can go through deliverance.
2. Resist every temptation that the enemy throws your way. Yes, even those reemerging exes that seem to pop up during certain stages of your life.

3. Work on loving God, and work on loving yourself. When you love God, you won't let the devil enter your life. When you love yourself, you won't let the devil stay in your life.
4. Educate yourself about the Jezebel spirit.
5. Study books and watch videos about narcissism and Cluster B personalities. Learn as much as you can.
6. Learn to take yourself through deliverance.
7. Heal. Be intentional about it.

One more bonus: Ask the Lord for the gift of the discerning of spirits. All the same, ask the Lord for the gift of prophecy or to strengthen you in the prophetic. One thing I've learned is that if you stay in the Word of God and in the will of God, He will warn you about the people you attempt to connect with. He will give you a word of knowledge for the person seated across from you while you're on a date! He will give you wisdom and instructions designed to make a person's demon manifest while you are on the phone with them! I am a living witness to this. When you are no longer idolatrous or desperate for a relationship, it will become incredibly easy to identify Jezebel before the person hosting that spirit is able to part his or her lips to say hello.

Jezebel's Fall from Grace

2 Kings 9:1-11 reads, "And Elisha the prophet called one of the children of the prophets, and said unto him, Gird up thy loins, and take this box of oil in thine hand, and go to Ramothgilead: And when thou comest thither, look out there Jehu the son of Jehoshaphat the son of Nimshi, and go in, and make him arise up from among his brethren, and carry him to an inner chamber; Then take the box of oil, and pour it on his head, and say, Thus saith the LORD, I have anointed thee king over Israel. Then open the door, and flee, and tarry not. So the young man, even the young man the prophet, went to Ramothgilead. And when he came, behold, the captains of the host were sitting; and he said, I have an errand to thee, O captain. And Jehu said, Unto which of all us? And he said, To thee, O captain. And he arose, and went into the house; and he poured the oil on his

head, and said unto him, Thus saith the LORD God of Israel, I have anointed thee king over the people of the LORD, even over Israel. And thou shalt smite the house of Ahab thy master, that I may avenge the blood of my servants the prophets, and the blood of all the servants of the LORD, at the hand of Jezebel. For the whole house of Ahab shall perish: and I will cut off from Ahab him that pisseth against the wall, and him that is shut up and left in Israel: And I will make the house of Ahab like the house of Jeroboam the son of Nebat, and like the house of Baasha the son of Ahijah: And the dogs shall eat Jezebel in the portion of Jezreel, and there shall be none to bury her. And he opened the door, and fled." Then he opened the door and fled. " What's interesting about this story is the fact that Prophet Elisha put out the hit on Jezebel and, of course, it was the Lord who'd instructed him to do so. But originally, Prophet Elijah was supposed to be the one to orchestrate Jezebel's fall from grace, but after he'd been threatened by her, he'd gone on the run, thus Jonah'ing his assignment. What's alarming about his decision to run is the fact that he'd just witnessed God rain fire down from Heaven on the prophets of Baal, so he was no stranger to the miracle-working power of God. All the same, he'd been granted the grace by God to shut and open the Heavens. And let's not forget what he'd done to the captain and his army of fifty men in 2 Kings 1:10. He'd called down fire from Heaven on them. In 2 Kings 2:8, the prophet, through the power and grace of God, had even split the Jordan River by striking it with his cloak. And yet, he feared one woman. Because of this, God had him to anoint his replacement who, of course, was the prophet Elisha. And now, we find Elisha having a conversation with one of the prophet's sons. This simply meant that the men in question were a part of some type of prophetic school or guild. Also known as a "company of prophets," the sons of the prophets were likely:

1. Levites.
2. Leaders of the 7,000 Israelites who had not bowed down to Baal (1 King 19:18).
3. Prophetic messengers who carried out the instructions of the key prophets of that time. In other words, some of them were likely prophets in training, while others were likely the internet of their time; they helped prophets to deliver messages to the masses. For example, we know that a

company of prophets followed Elijah around; they were the ones who approached and instructed Elisha about Elijah's pending transition to Heaven.

He was told to go to Ramoth-Gilead; this is where Ahab was killed some ten years earlier. Ramoth-Gilead had been taken by Syria during the battles between Northern Israel and Syria. Initially a space and a place for the Levitical priests to dwell, Ramoth-Gilead, had also served as a city of refuge. What was a city of refuge? A city of refuge was a designated place where individuals who'd unintentionally committed manslaughter could seek asylum and protection from the vengeful relatives of the deceased. In the land of Israel, six cities were designated as cities of refuge: Kedesh, Shechem, Hebron, Bezer, Ramoth, and Golan. However, Ramoth-Gilead had been taken in battle, and Ahab had been determined to take it back. Ahab would be deceived by a lying spirit that had possessed the prophets of Baal, the false prophets in which he'd trusted, and he would be fatally wounded in the war against Ramoth-Gilead. Ten years later, we find Israel's military occupying Ramoth-Gilead, and Jehu was the commander of that army. The unnamed prophet had been instructed by the prophet Elisha to go and give a message to Jehu. This, no doubt, was a scary task, as Jehu and his men were considered blood-thirsty avengers who could kill a man, and then step over the man's body and commence with their day-to-day activities as if nothing had ever happened. So, Elisha advised the prophet to:

1. Get Jehu away from his army of men; he told him to take Jehu into an inner chamber.
2. To prophesy to Jehu that God had made him king of Israel; he would then give Jehu the instructions regarding the termination of Jezebel, along with Ahab's bloodline.
3. To not tarry; his next step was to flee the scene.

But first, Elisha told the unnamed prophet to "gird up his loins." What does this mean? In that time, the men would wear long tunics. These tunics would interfere with a man's leg movements if, for example, he were to do a lot of physical activity, go into war, or if he attempted to run or escape something. So, to prevent this, a man would pull up his garment and secure it with a belt; this would expose his legs, thus allowing him to have the full activity of his limbs. So, in this, the prophet was telling the other prophetic individual to prepare himself for a journey that could potentially be strenuous or even dangerous. In short, the man needed to prepare for his outlandish exit. He wasn't there to get familiar with the newly anointed king. His job was to deliver the word of the Lord, and then escape to safety; his assignment was to dodge familiarity. Again, Jehu and his men were brutish; these were not your ordinary men. They did not and could not be as empathetic as civilians. As a matter of fact, the kings and the priests of the Old Testament were the equivalent of modern-day apostles. An apostle is to Jezebel what Jezebel is to a prophet—cold, calculating, and relatively narcissistic. This isn't to say that apostles are bound by the Jezebel spirit; this is to say that apostles are wired to destroy. They are not wired to be super-sensitive and emotional. Don't get me wrong; true apostles are sensitive to God's presence or, in many cases, the Lord will prepare them for an encounter with Him, meaning, He will take them through a series of events to prepare their hearts for an encounter with Him, just like the priests of old would go through the Outer Court and Inner Court before they entered the Holy of Holies to have an encounter with the Most High.

Of course, the unnamed prophet was told to take some anointing oil with him. This is important because, even today, it is dangerous to approach the spirit of Jezebel without the oil of God, and by oil, I'm talking about the anointing of God. We see people do it all the time. They date Jezebel, marry Jezebel, reproduce with Jezebel, and then war with Jezebel in court, only to find themselves losing years of their lives and the soundness of their minds. Satan knows how destructive Jezebel is, and this is why he selected this particular demon to go after the prophets of God. Jezebel also comes after any and every move of God that hits the Earth.

The prophet did what he was told. He went to Ramoth-Gilead, had a meeting with Jehu, and then ran like his life depended on it, because it did. You see, prophets love to connect to people of power. This is because prophets and highly prophetic people are incredibly sensitive, and as such, they can become mesmerized by people of power and influence, so much so that an immature prophet can easily be led astray by ungodly ambition. The unnamed prophet was likely a student. Consider what happened to John of Patmos when he saw, in a vision, a woman riding a scarlet beast. He gives a testimony of this vision in Revelation 17:1-7 (NKJV); it reads, "Then one of the seven angels who had the seven bowls came and talked with me, saying to me, 'Come, I will show you the judgment of the great harlot who sits on many waters, with whom the kings of the earth committed fornication, and the inhabitants of the earth were made drunk with the wine of her fornication.' So he carried me away in the Spirit into the wilderness. And I saw a woman sitting on a scarlet beast which was full of names of blasphemy, having seven heads and ten horns. The woman was arrayed in purple and scarlet, and adorned with gold and precious stones and pearls, having in her hand a golden cup full of abominations and the filthiness of her fornication. And on her forehead, a name was written:

MYSTERY, BABYLON THE GREAT,
THE MOTHER OF HARLOTS
AND OF THE ABOMINATIONS
OF THE EARTH.

I saw the woman, drunk with the blood of the saints and with the blood of the martyrs of Jesus. And when I saw her, I marveled with great amazement. But the angel said to me, 'Why did you marvel? I will tell you the mystery of the woman and of the beast that carries her, which has the seven heads and the ten horns.'" Apostle John had walked with Jesus before His death and resurrection, and there he was in the middle of a prophetic encounter. While in the Spirit, he'd began to marvel at the woman riding the scarlet beast (this woman was likely Jezebel, but we can't say this for sure). Noticing that he was giving too much of his attention to the woman, the angel interrupted him, asking him, "Why are you marveling at that woman?" Was the Apostle attracted to her? Probably not. He was simply fascinated by her; this is what it means to marvel. The angel of the Lord had to get the apostle to turn his attention back to the rest of the vision. This is to say that if the Apostle John marveled at Jezebel or, at minimum, at the whore of Babylon, how much more will a prophet of God, especially an immature prophet or prophetic person, be intrigued by someone who has this spirit? The answer is evident today. Many prophets and prophetic people are in Jezebel's custody right now, and the ones who have escaped are yelling, "Narcissist! Narcissist!" from the four corners of the Earth. But do they learn their lessons? Most do not; this is because many prophetic people never get the education or the training they need to:

1. Better understand who God is.
2. Better understand who they are and how they are wired.
3. Better understand the demons that they are anointed to go up against and the demons that are assigned to take them down.

Consequently, they date the same demon in a different person time and time again. Many of their "best friends" are narcissistic people. All the same, many of them were born into families filled with narcissists and narcissistic people. This is to say that Jezebel has become a familiar spirit in their lives; they have come to be comfortable with Jezebel, all the while, terrified of change. And it is for this reason that many prophets and prophetic people remain in Jezebel's concubine quarters for the entirety of their lives. What's worse is that after going through hell on Earth, they still have to stand before the Lord and explain why they didn't do what they were designed to do on Earth; instead, they decided to spend their lives in bondage. They weren't just bound to Jezebel; they were bound to their lustful desires and to their fears. Jezebel was just the pimp who'd give them what they wanted in exchange for their silence and their service.

In the natural and in the spirit, there exists the concept of rank. Rank deals with hierarchy; it is a grading system of sorts, whereas some entities (spirits, humans, animals, and insects) are granted a certain measure of authority, and with that authority, they typically have a list of responsibilities, along with a certain number and/or group of entities that they must lead. Within the concept of rank, there exists leaders, co-leaders, sub-leaders, supervisors, and laymen. When dealing with spirits and with humans, there are rules of engagement. For example, God did not fight Satan and his angels; instead, in the book of Revelations, we find Michael, the archangel, along with his angels fighting with Satan and his angels. This has everything to do with rank because Satan is not equal in rank or authority to God. Like us, all of God's angels were created; this is why they are called creatures. As such, there is no entity that is more powerful than our God. So, to be fair, God allowed Michael and the angels under his command to fight against Satan and the angels under his command. When the Prince of Persia withstood the angel of the Lord who had been sent by God to deliver a message to the prophet Daniel, Michael, the archangel, came out and fought against the Prince of Persia, signaling that the Prince of Persia was his equivalent in rank (but not in power), spiritually speaking. The kings of old would send messengers to other kings, knowing that despite what the messages said, the other kings would likely not destroy the messengers because doing so could instigate an uproar amongst the other nations. This is where we get the idiom, "I'm just the messenger," signaling that we are not to incur any harm for delivering a message from one person to another or from one organization to another. This is to say that the prophet, Elisha, like his predecessor, Elijah, did not rank high enough to kill Jezebel. They needed a king to properly depose another ruler, so God instructed Elisha to give Jehu equal rank to Jezebel. This would allow him to legally and effectively remove Jezebel from power without having a bunch of people fighting over her throne. Of course, legally speaking, Ahab's sons would have a claim to the throne, so God told Elisha to kill them all off, after all, Ahab's bloodline was now accursed, and his sons would likely follow in his footsteps. God wanted to purge Israel of Jezebel's influence altogether. This is to say that coming against the spirit of Jezebel involves more than breaking up with a narcissist or a narcissistic person. It involves you breaking up with a demonic system, pattern or, better yet, stronghold. What is the layout of this particular stronghold?

1. Prophets tend to idolize themselves or, better yet, they tend to idolize how they feel; this is called self-worship. Another word for self-worship is selfishness, and another word for selfishness is sin. This is always the result of not putting God first (see Matthew 6:33).
2. Jezebel is an idolatrous woman, and the spirit of Jezebel is drawn to idol worshipers.
3. When and if a prophet or a prophetic person dates a narcissist or narcissistic person, what then happens is the narcissist or narcissistic

individual will accompany the prophet in worshiping himself or herself; this is what the world of psychology refers to as "love-bombing."

4. The narcissist will worship the prophet for weeks, days, months, or years; that is until a strong soul tie has formed. After the soul tie is solidified, the narcissist will then begin to play a bunch of mind games designed to get the prophet to give him or her the worship that the prophet typically gives himself or herself. In other words, there will be a switching of authority. In this, the spirit of Jezebel then begins to usurp the authority of the prophet or the prophetic person. This is the sin offering required to keep the individual who's bound by the Jezebel spirit.

5. Jezebel then seeks to get the prophet or prophetic person to graduate from being soul-tied to that demon to be yoked to it. Again, a yoke represents a legality. What demons want is to have a legal right to the prophet's soul; this way, they can have more uninterrupted control over the prophet or the prophetic person.

6. After this, the spirit of Jezebel will go out of its way to get the prophet or the prophetic person to go deeper and deeper into sin; that is, the prophet or the prophetic person will become more and more narcissistic by becoming more idolatrous. And, while this is happening, the prophet or the prophetic person will learn to repeatedly resist and ignore the instructions and warnings of God.

7. Next, the narcissistic prophet will slowly begin to lose the health of his or her mind, thus provoking the prophet or the prophetic person to go deeper into sin, and in many cases, into the depths of witchcraft.

8. After the prophet or prophetic person has repeatedly ignored the doors provided to them by God as ways of escape, and the prophet or prophetic person repeatedly rebels against the ordinances of God, they may likely be turned over by God to a reprobate mind.

Once the prophet or the prophetic person has been handed over to the enemy, Satan will continue to use the prophet's gifts, for the gifts and callings are without repentance. He will use these gifts to lead God's people astray, as many of God's people are drawn to signs, miracles, and wonders. They will see the gifts of God, but ignore the character of the prophets bearing those gifts. Why is this? Because many people don't have enough one-on-one encounters with God due to the fact that they don't read their Bibles often, nor do they pray as frequently as they should, so they are desperate for a God-encounter.

How does the story end? How is Jezebel defeated? 2 Kings 9:30-37 tells the story; it reads, "And when Jehu was come to Jezreel, Jezebel heard of it; and she painted her face, and tired her head, and looked out at a window. And as Jehu entered in at the gate, she said, Had Zimri peace, who slew his master? And he lifted up his face to the window, and said, Who is on my side? Who? And there looked out to him two or three eunuchs. And he said, Throw her down. So they threw her down: and some of her blood was sprinkled on the wall, and on the horses: and he trode her under foot. And when he was come in, he did eat and drink, and said, Go, see now this cursed woman, and bury her: for she is a king's daughter. And they went to bury her: but they found no more of her than the skull, and the feet, and the palms of her hands. Wherefore they came again, and told him. And he said, This is the word of the LORD, which he spake by his servant Elijah the Tishbite, saying, In the portion of Jezreel shall dogs eat the flesh of Jezebel: And the carcass of Jezebel shall be as dung upon the face of the field in the portion of Jezreel; so that they shall not say, This is Jezebel." Remember, eunuchs are loyal to power, not people. More than likely, the word had gone out in the land that Jehu had been anointed king, and Jezebel's eunuchs were probably exhausted by her narcissistic ways. I think that we can safely assume that they'd breathed a collective sigh of relief once they'd heard the news. And they'd probably spoke amongst themselves, detailing how they'd serve Jehu when and if the opportunity presented itself, so when Jehu approached the castle and told them to throw Jezebel out the window, they'd complied without hesitating. This is to say that the Jezebel spirit has to be confronted by someone with a certain measure of rank, and it is often tossed into the abyss or brought low by the very people who serve it. This is also to say that Jezebel's fall is often preceded by people taking their authority back. This essentially sets the stage for a narcissistic collapse. What is a narcissistic collapse? Very Well Mind reports the following:

"Narcissistic collapse happens when a person with narcissistic personality disorder (NPD) becomes unable to uphold their grandiose, confident image due to a perceived fatal blow to their reputation. This leads to a breakdown which manifests as angry outbursts, irritable or defensive behavior, and verbal or physical aggression. Internally the person with NPD feels a loss of sense of self along with perceived rejection and abandonment. It can result in harm to the person with NPD and those around them" (Source: Very Well Mind/Signs of Narcissistic Collapse and What to Do Next/What happens when a narcissist experiences a fatal blow to their ego?/Cynthia Vinney).

Eventually, the narcissist loses control. In many cases, they are repeatedly abandoned by their loved ones, especially as they age. Their children often go no-contact with them, and the children who stick around are oftentimes just as narcissistic as or even more narcissistic than they were. As the narcissist or the narcissistic person goes deeper and deeper into depression, the spirit of Jezebel will use the very people Jezebel once spoiled or traumatized to rob Jezebel of all that she has. Jehu had been a commander in Jezebel's army. While she was lying on the ground dead, he'd gone into the castle, and his first order of business was to get himself something to eat. So, as Jezebel was being eaten by wild dogs, Jehu, her former servant, was being served by the eunuchs who'd tossed her to her untimely demise. The same is true for Jezebel's children. The narcissistic ones will often fight over her possessions, all while Jezebel is in the other room wasting away. These are the same children who will happily tell Jezebel's doctors to pull the plug on Jezebel; this is so that they can stake claim to and eventually fight over Jezebel's insurance policy. In the end, Jezebel always falls. This isn't just referencing you breaking up with someone who has the Jezebel spirit; this deals more with you breaking up with the spirit of Jezebel itself by coming out of agreement with idolatry and self-worship. This is when you'll elect the King of kings to rule over your life, instead of allowing Jezebel to repeatedly rule over you. This is when the spirit of Jezebel will have no more claim to you. This does not mean, however, that narcissistic people won't attempt to enter or reenter your life. It does mean that you won't be a magnet for Jezebel anymore, nor will you tolerate Jezebel (unless you decide to rebel and return to Jezebel). Remember, in the end, Jezebel painted her eyes in an attempt to manipulate and seduce Jehu, but there was nothing about Jezebel that Jehu found alluring, so the voice of God that traveled through Elisha to the unnamed prophet to Jehu, and ultimately to her eunuchs will continue to go forth, commanding any and everyone who has tolerated Jezebel to toss her out of the window. Please don't take this literally. Don't toss a man or woman out of a window. Remember, a window represents an illegal entrance. Jezebel's entrance into and reign over Israel had been legalized by King Ahab, but once Ahab died and God's people had repented, Jezebel no longer had a legal right to rule over God's people. This is to say that if you have served as Ahab to Jezebel, you have to get delivered from and come out of agreement with the spirit of Ahab. In other words, you can no longer be passive, fearful, and non-confrontational. All the same, you can no longer be ambitious, impatient, self-reliant, and self-centered. Once you get rid of Ahab, Jezebel's fall is inevitable. Note: the judgment of God hits Ahab the hardest because God's trust wasn't in Jezebel, after all, she was the sub-leader of a pagan nation. God's trust was with Ahab, and Ahab violated that trust.

Soul Revival

Psalm 23:1-3 reads, "The LORD is my shepherd; I shall not want. He maketh me to lie down in green pastures: he leadeth me beside the still waters. He restoreth my soul: he leadeth me in the paths of righteousness for his name's sake."

What does it mean to restore or revive someone's soul? Earlier on, we talked about soul recovery; this is the retrieval of the soul after it has been shattered and spread out through ungodly soul ties, trauma, and having had your heart broken time and time again. However, soul revival is when God restores and renews the soul; this is when He breathes a fresh wind of restoration into the soul. Before we go further into this lesson, let's look at a couple of stories in the Bible so that we can get a deeper understanding.

- **Judges 19:1-30 (NIV):** Now a Levite who lived in a remote area in the hill country of Ephraim took a concubine from Bethlehem in Judah. But she was unfaithful to him. She left him and went back to her parents' home in Bethlehem, Judah. After she had been there four months, her husband went to her to persuade her to return. He had with him his servant and two donkeys. She took him into her parents' home, and when her father saw him, he gladly welcomed him. His father-in-law, the woman's father, prevailed on him to stay; so he remained with him three days, eating and drinking, and sleeping there. On the fourth day they got up early and he prepared to leave, but the woman's father said to his son-in-law, "Refresh yourself with something to eat; then you can go." So the two of them sat down to eat and drink together. Afterward the woman's father said, "Please stay tonight and enjoy yourself." And when the man got up to go, his father-in-law persuaded him, so he stayed there that night. On the morning of the fifth day, when he rose to go, the woman's father said, "Refresh yourself. Wait till afternoon!" So the two of them ate together. Then when the man, with his concubine and his servant, got up to leave, his father-in-law, the woman's father, said, "Now look, it's almost evening. Spend the night here; the day is nearly over. Stay and enjoy yourself. Early tomorrow morning you can get up and be on your way home." But, unwilling to stay another night, the man left and went toward Jebus (that is, Jerusalem), with his two saddled donkeys and his concubine. When they were near Jebus and the day was almost gone, the servant said to his master, "Come, let's stop at this city of the Jebusites and spend the night." His master replied, "No. We won't go into any city whose people are not Israelites. We will go on to Gibeah." He added, "Come, let's try to reach Gibeah or Ramah and spend the night in one of those places." So they went on, and the sun set as they neared Gibeah in Benjamin. There they stopped to spend the night. They went and sat in the city square, but no one took them in for the night. That evening an old man from the hill country of Ephraim, who was living in Gibeah (the inhabitants of the place were Benjamites), came in from his work in the fields. When he looked and saw the traveler in the city square, the old man asked, "Where are you going? Where did you come from?" He answered, "We are on our way from Bethlehem in Judah to a remote area in the hill country of

Ephraim where I live. I have been to Bethlehem in Judah and now I am
going to the house of the LORD. No one has taken me in for the night. We
have both straw and fodder for our donkeys and bread and wine for
ourselves your servants—me, the woman and the young man with us. We
don't need anything." "You are welcome at my house," the old man said.
"Let me supply whatever you need. Only don't spend the night in the
square." So he took him into his house and fed his donkeys. After they
had washed their feet, they had something to eat and drink. While they
were enjoying themselves, some of the wicked men of the city
surrounded the house. Pounding on the door, they shouted to the old
man who owned the house, "Bring out the man who came to your house
so we can have sex with him." The owner of the house went outside and
said to them, "No, my friends, don't be so vile. Since this man is my guest,
don't do this outrageous thing. Look, here is my virgin daughter, and his
concubine. I will bring them out to you now, and you can use them and
do to them whatever you wish. But as for this man, don't do such an
outrageous thing." But the men would not listen to him. So the man took
his concubine and sent her outside to them, and they raped her and
abused her throughout the night, and at dawn they let her go. At
daybreak the woman went back to the house where her master was
staying, fell down at the door and lay there until daylight. When her
master got up in the morning and opened the door of the house and
stepped out to continue on his way, there lay his concubine, fallen in the
doorway of the house, with her hands on the threshold. He said to her,
"Get up; let's go." But there was no answer. Then the man put her on his
donkey and set out for home. When he reached home, he took a
knife and cut up his concubine, limb by limb, into twelve parts and sent
them into all the areas of Israel. Everyone who saw it was saying to one
another, "Such a thing has never been seen or done, not since the day the
Israelites came up out of Egypt. Just imagine! We must do something! So
speak up!"

- **Ezekiel 37:1-9 (NKJV):** The hand of the LORD came upon me and brought
  me out in the Spirit of the LORD, and set me down in the midst of the

valley; and it was full of bones. Then He caused me to pass by them all around, and behold, there were very many in the open valley; and indeed they were very dry. And He said to me, "Son of man, can these bones live?" So I answered, "O Lord GOD, You know." Again He said to me, "Prophesy to these bones, and say to them, 'O dry bones, hear the word of the LORD! Thus says the Lord GOD to these bones: "Surely I will cause breath to enter into you, and you shall live. I will put sinews on you and bring flesh upon you, cover you with skin and put breath in you; and you shall live. Then you shall know that I am the LORD." So I prophesied as I was commanded; and as I prophesied, there was a noise, and suddenly a rattling; and the bones came together, bone to bone. Indeed, as I looked, the sinews and the flesh came upon them, and the skin covered them over; but there was no breath in them. Also He said to me, "Prophesy to the breath, prophesy, son of man, and say to the breath, 'Thus says the Lord GOD: "Come from the four winds, O breath, and breathe on these slain, that they may live." So I prophesied as He commanded me, and breath came into them, and they lived, and stood upon their feet, an exceedingly great army.

There is a lot that we can extract from the first story, but let's focus on the event itself. A woman was raped, and to communicate the horror of what he'd just experienced, the woman's husband decided to dismember her body. He then sent one of her body parts to every tribe of Judah. This was the equivalent, in that time, of him sending out a massive text message with gruesome pictures to an entire nation; this was comparable to him sending out a news blast about the crime he'd suffered through at the hands of other believers. He wanted the crime to be addressed, he wanted the men to be punished, but more than everything, he wanted every tribe to know what their Benjamite brethren were up to. All the same, the man was a Levite; this means that he was a part of the Aaronic priesthood. So, if the Benjamites could do such a wicked act to a priest or, at minimum, a priest's assistant, imagine how evil and immoral they were. However, the purpose of telling this story is to give you a picture of what soul ties do to the soul, even though this wasn't necessarily the intent of the author (believed to be Samson) when he shared this story. He intended to keep a record of the event so that the story would never be forgotten. Soul ties split and scatter the soul, and while this story was not a story detailing the dangers or the effects of soul ties, it does paint a picture of what a soul tie does. To finish off that particular story, the men of Israel summoned the Levite and had him tell his story. After this, they declared war against the Benjamites. During the war, it looked like the Benjamites were winning, but as the rest of the Israelites followed the instructions of God, they soon stood victorious against their rebellious and prideful brethren.

- **Judges 20:35-48:** The LORD defeated Benjamin before Israel, and on that day the Israelites struck down 25,100 Benjamites, all armed with swords. Then the Benjamites saw that they were beaten. Now the men of Israel had given way before Benjamin, because they relied on the ambush they had set near Gibeah. Those who had been in ambush made a sudden dash into Gibeah, spread out and put the whole city to the sword. The Israelites had arranged with the ambush that they should send up a great cloud of smoke from the city, and then the Israelites would counterattack. The Benjamites had begun to inflict casualties on the Israelites (about thirty), and they said, "We are defeating them as in the first battle." But when the column of smoke began to rise from the city, the Benjamites turned and saw the whole city going up in smoke. Then the Israelites counterattacked, and the Benjamites were terrified, because they realized that disaster had come on them. So they fled before the Israelites in the direction of the wilderness, but they could not escape the battle. And the Israelites who came out of the towns cut them down there. They surrounded the Benjamites, chased them and easily overran them in the vicinity of Gibeah on the east. Eighteen thousand Benjamites fell, all of them valiant fighters. As they turned and fled toward the wilderness to the rock of Rimmon, the Israelites cut down five thousand men along the roads. They kept pressing after the Benjamites as far as Gidom and struck down two thousand more. On that day twenty-five thousand Benjamite swordsmen fell, all of them valiant fighters. But six hundred of them turned and fled into the wilderness to the rock of Rimmon, where they stayed four months. The men of Israel went back to Benjamin and put all the towns to the sword, including the animals and everything else they found. All the towns they came across they set on fire.

The Benjamites were nearly exterminated, but the men of Israel grieved for them and pitied them. Because of this, they helped to restore Benjamin by helping some of the remaining men to attain wives from Shiloh. Again, this is a picture of restoration, but it is also a picture of devastation, especially for the Levite and his concubine. I know that some people would want to talk about how the woman's decision to be unfaithful to her husband, and then to leave her husband and return to her father, spiritually speaking, set the stage and opened the door for this demonic attack to take place, but realistically speaking, there are people who see this as "victim-shaming," who may find such an implication to be offensive. However, this does not minimize the fact that what we do in the natural is spiritual, and it will always have both natural and spiritual repercussions. The point of this story is—the woman was not restored, but she wasn't the bigger picture. The bigger picture was this—God saw that the men of Benjamin had fallen away from Him, and while He did not orchestrate this crime, He used it to circumcise or, better yet, prune the tribe of Benjamin. After this, they were restored to the fold.

The woman's body had been dismembered by her husband after she'd been raped and slaughtered by the men. The Levite then sent his wife's limbs to the other tribes. Understand this—whenever you soul-tie yourself to someone, you are essentially becoming one with that person. Once again, your soul is comprised of your mind, will, and emotions. Your mind, biblically speaking, is your heart; this is what God told you to guard. Whenever you give your heart to someone and you allow that person to mix and merge their soul with yours, the two of you become one through agreement. No, this doesn't mean that you will physically lose yourself, but it does mean that you will mentally and morally begin to share or lose snippets of yourself with that person. When that human being walks away from you or is ripped away from you, that individual will take a part of you with him or her, just like you will take a part of that person with you. Over the course of time, you may find yourself repeating this demonic transaction with other people, thus causing you to lose more of yourself and pick up traits, personalities, fears, insecurities, and demons that, quite frankly, do not belong to you. This is why we often say, "I'm finding myself," not realizing that we are all truly on a hunt to recover the pieces of ourselves that we lost in our failed friendships and relationships. Think about a used car that's been damaged. Sure, we can go and get the parts that the car needs from its manufacturer and we can even take it to the manufacturer to be repaired, but this could be expensive. So, what do we typically do? We find used parts that weren't made by the manufacturer; we then hire shade-tree mechanics to fix our vehicles for us. Sometimes, this works in our favor; at other times, we end up paying more for our frugal ways than we would have had we just gone back to the manufacturer. We do the same with our souls. When we lose pieces of ourselves, we tend to find the traits, qualities, and strengths that we need in other people. We then attempt to soul-tie ourselves with these people so that we can siphon what we need from them, not realizing that what God, our true Manufacturer, gave them won't work properly in us. This is why we have to recover ourselves, and then be restored to our original designs. Otherwise, we'll spend the rest of our lives connecting with and disconnecting from people in our attempts to get affirmation, acceptance, love, and understanding, only to lose more of ourselves in those relationships.

Let's talk about Ezekiel and the valley of dry bones. What's interesting about this story is the fact that he hadn't come across a bunch of flesh-covered corpses; he'd come across a valley filled with the bones of dead men. The Australian Museum reports the following, "Although an exposed human body in optimum conditions can be reduced to bone in 10 days, a body that is buried 1.2 m under the ground retains most of its tissue for a year" (Source: Australian Museum/ Decomposition - Body Changes). Wikipedia, on the other hand, reports the following, "In a temperate climate, it usually requires three weeks to several years for a body to completely decompose into a skeleton, depending on factors such as temperature, humidity, presence of insects, and submergence in a substrate such as water. In tropical climates, skeletonization can occur in weeks, while in tundra areas, skeletonization may take years or may never occur, if freezing temperatures persist" (Source: Wikipedia/Skeletonization). This is to say that the men had been dead no less than ten days when Ezekiel came across their bodies! This is way past the point of natural restoration. Chances are, they'd been dead for years! God restoring the flesh back to these soldiers, and then breathing life into them is a demonstration of His power, and it is a picture of revival!

How does this relate to you? You may have done the hard work to recover your soul, and that's admirable! Especially in this day and age where many prophets and prophetic people, despite knowing the truth, will continue to choose themselves over God, thus rejecting their God-given assignments. However, whenever a soul yields himself or herself fully to God, we start to witness miracles, signs, and wonders coming from that person. There's a reason for this. Imagine it this way. Raphael goes to the hospital, and once he is taken to the back, the nurse asks him to stand on the scale to his left. He weighs in at 350 pounds. At five foot, seven inches tall, Raphael is considered obese. His doctor says to him, "Sir, you need to lose 187 pounds, at minimum! Otherwise, your health will continue to decline, and you will be at a higher risk for heart disease, cardiac arrest, sleep apnea, and a host of other deadly diseases." Raphael takes the doctor's words seriously, so he decides to go on a diet and exercise journey. At one point in his life, Raphael weighed 150 pounds, but after getting married, he found himself having access to three full meals a day, plus, he didn't exercise or go out as much as he used to. But now, there he was 200 pounds heavier than he was when he'd met and married his wife. To get back to 163 pounds, which is the highest recommended weight for his height, he would have to scale back on the amount of foods he eats, along with calories, starchy foods, and sugars. And he wouldn't just go from 350 pounds directly to 163 pounds, he'd drop a pound at a time. This means that he'll be 349 pounds before he reaches 348 pounds. He'd continue to scale back and drop the weight until he reached his desired weight. Another example to help with this lesson is this—imagine that you've traveled from Arkansas to California. You had to pass through some states to get from your state of origin to your destination. Should you decide to return to Arkansas, you'd have to pass through some of those same states. This is to say that with soul revival, you're not just being restored instantly, there is a process that you must endure; there are some tests that you've failed, and these tests will likely be presented to you again. You must pass the test this time. I'm sharing this because I don't want to give you the idea that you can be passive during the deliverance and restoration process. No, you have to take it by faith! Matthew 11:12 says it this way, "And from the days of John the Baptist until now the kingdom of heaven suffereth violence, and the violent take it by force." Where is the Kingdom of Heaven? Is it above your head on the other side of the clouds? No, it is not. Jesus gave us the exact location of His Kingdom in Luke 17:20-23. It reads, "And when he was demanded of the Pharisees, when the kingdom of God should come, he answered them and said, The kingdom of God cometh not with observation: Neither shall they say, Lo here! Or, lo there! For, behold, the kingdom of God is within you." What does this mean? Potential is power locked in the womb. Your job is to tap into your potential by faith, and pull it out until you become potent or, better yet, powerful. This is to say that, like the man who'd cut up his concubine, you will have to open your mouth and share your testimony; don't allow the enemy to attack you in private and force you to reward him by keeping his secrets! "And they overcame him by the blood of the Lamb, and by the word of their testimony; and they loved not their lives unto the death" (Revelation 12:11). Next, like Israel, you will have to go to war with yourself; these are the parts of you that do not serve God. This includes you coming against negative self-talk, low self-esteem, breaking ungodly patterns, changing your eating habits, and the list goes on. This particular war can be long and drawn out, but you can make it much easier by getting therapy and wise counsel. This means that you have to be accountable to someone, and you have to be honest with them, otherwise, you will be wasting their time, along with your own. And finally, like Ezekiel, you have to learn to speak life into dead things. Remember what the Bible tells us in Proverbs 18:21; it states, "Death and life are in the power of the tongue: and they that love it shall eat the fruit thereof." The Bible also tells us, "Verily I say unto you, Whatsoever ye shall bind on earth shall be bound in heaven: and whatsoever ye shall loose on earth shall be loosed in heaven" (Proverbs 18:18). And again, you will find yourself being tempted again, but this time, let the outcome be different; this is how you take back whatever authority the enemy has stolen from you. Consider the story of Lot and his daughters.

- **Genesis 19:1-8 (NIV):** The two angels arrived at Sodom in the evening, and Lot was sitting in the gateway of the city. When he saw them, he got up to meet them and bowed down with his face to the ground. "My lords," he said, "please turn aside to your servant's house. You can wash your feet and spend the night and then go on your way early in the morning." "No," they answered, "we will spend the night in the square." But he insisted so strongly that they did go with him and entered his house. He prepared a meal for them, baking bread without yeast, and they ate. Before they had gone to bed, all the men from every part of the city of Sodom—both young and old—surrounded the house. They called to Lot, "Where are the men who came to you tonight? Bring them out to us so that we can have sex with them." Lot went outside to meet them and shut the door behind him and said, "No, my friends. Don't do this wicked thing. Look, I have two daughters who have never slept with a man. Let me bring them out to you, and you can do what you like with them. But don't do anything to these men, for they have come under the protection of my roof." "Get out of our way," they replied. "This fellow came here as a foreigner, and now he wants to play the judge! We'll treat you worse than them." They kept bringing pressure on Lot and moved forward to break down the door. But the men inside reached out and pulled Lot back into the house and shut the door. Then they struck the men who were at the door of the house, young and old, with blindness so that they could not find the door.

Like the Levite in Judges 19:1-30, Lot had found himself facing the same dilemma, only he'd experienced this dilemma almost nine hundred years earlier, and because he had an intercessor on his team by the name of Abraham, along with an obedient heart, Lot was rescued. His daughters did not have to be sexually assaulted; instead, the angels of God struck the men with blindness and were able to lead Lot and his daughters out of the city. Unfortunately for his wife, however, she turned into a pillar of salt, because like many prophets and prophetic types, she wasn't fully ready to let go of the life she was leaving behind. Lot left with his daughters in tow, and the sad news is, the spirit of perversion that was on that nation was now in him and his daughters. Their father had been willing and ready to hand them over to be raped, but the angels saved them. However, the spirit was now on them, and the daughters ended up taking turns getting their father intoxicated, and then sexually assaulting their father. This is important to note because if you are a parent, it is possible that a lot of the strongholds and demons you once wrestled with are now in your children. I've seen this many times—the mother, for example, will get saved, but her children will continue to love the world; this is a common story, believe it or not. But don't fret! You don't have to beat them over the head with the Bible or ridicule them. You simply need to demonstrate the love of God to them; you have to become a light, pray for them, and don't allow their ways to provoke you into cursing at them or doing something that could potentially ruin the reputation you are in the process of building. This is a realistic view of the journey, and not a rose-colored version of what this journey looks like. It can be hard, strenuous, and taxing, but it's worth it in the end! The more you chase, surrender, and submit yourself to God, the more He will restore and revive you. This is when you will show up as the prophet or prophetic soul He's designed you to be; this is when you won't just work miracles, but you will become a living and breathing miracle, which means that miracles, signs, and wonders will follow you wherever you go. This is also when you will find yourself experiencing a supernatural contentment that will transcend your imagination and everyone else's expectations. In other words, you will become the version of yourself that neither you or anyone else knew existed. This is when every facet of you will be illuminated as every false version of you is eliminated. All the same, this is when you will no longer be stalked by Jezebel; instead, that demon will flee from you whenever it sees you coming. You will also be able to help others get free from Jezebel because you will have become a living and breathing testimony, and your testimony will serve as a map for God's people. You got this because God's got you!

Broken for Such a Time as This

By now, you've likely read or heard of the story of the prodigal son. Nevertheless, let's look at the story in its entirety before we proceed.

"And he said, 'There was a man who had two sons. And the younger of them said to his father, 'Father, give me the share of property that is coming to me.' And he divided his property between them. Not many days later, the younger son gathered all he had and took a journey into a far country, and there he squandered his property in reckless living. And when he had spent everything, a severe famine arose in that country, and he began to be in need. So he went and hired himself out to one of the citizens of that country, who sent him into his fields to feed pigs. And he was longing to be fed with the pods that the pigs ate, and no one gave him anything. But when he came to himself, he said, 'How many of my father's hired servants have more than enough bread, but I perish here with hunger! I will arise and go to my father, and I will say to him, 'Father, I have sinned against heaven and before you. I am no longer worthy to be called your son. Treat me as one of your hired servants.' And he arose and came to his father. But while he was still a long way off, his father saw him and felt compassion, and ran and embraced him and kissed him. And the son said to him, 'Father, I have sinned against heaven and before you. I am no longer worthy to be called your son. But the father said to his servants, 'Bring quickly the best robe, and put it on him, and put a ring on his hand, and shoes on his feet. And bring the fattened calf and kill it, and let us eat and celebrate. For this my son was dead, and is alive again; he was lost, and is found.' And they began to celebrate.
Now his older son was in the field, and as he came and drew near to the house, he heard music and dancing. And he called one of the servants and asked what these things meant. And he said to him, 'Your brother has come, and your father has killed the fattened calf, because he has received him back safe and sound.' But he was angry and refused to go in. His father came out and entreated him, but he answered his father, 'Look, these many years I have served you, and I never disobeyed your command, yet you never gave me a young goat, that I might celebrate

with my friends. But when this son of yours came, who has devoured your property with prostitutes, you killed the fattened calf for him!' And he said to him, 'Son, you are always with me, and all that is mine is yours. It was fitting to celebrate and be glad, for this your brother was dead, and is alive; he was lost, and is found'" (Luke 15:11-32).

Regardless of whether you are a prophet or a prophetic person, you are still a vessel of God (if you have accepted Jesus Christ as your Lord and Savior). And get this, you've likely wandered away from Him at some point in your life. This is to say that you can likely relate to the prodigal son. He was impatient. He was immature. He lacked honor and understanding. He was foolish. He was self-centered. And, of course, he was narcissistic. Consider this—when he asked his father for his inheritance, he was essentially declaring his father dead because heirs did not fully take possession of their inheritances until their fathers passed away. This is why when Isaac realized that he was about to pass on, he summoned his son, Esau, so that he could impart the birth rite blessing to him and, of course, we know how that story ended. Jacob, who would later be known as Israel, disguised his appearance and his scent so that his father could give him the blessing instead. It would have been dishonorable for any of Israel's sons to ask him to give them their inheritances while he was still vibrant and full of life. It would have been the equivalent of them saying, "You're dead to me." This is evident in the fact that the entire time the prodigal son was away, he was not in contact with his father or his family. Instead, he partied hard, thinking of no one but himself. He didn't consider repenting until he was broke, hungry, broken, and homeless. In short, his world had to become too uncomfortable for him to thrive in, and just like Jonah had to lose his comfort, his peace, and nearly his life before he gave God a yes, the prodigal son had to lose everything before he returned to his senses, which led him to return to his father. Nevertheless, his father received him with open arms so much so that he turned the event into a feast. Get this—the prodigal son's return had nothing to do with him having a change of heart! He returned to his father's house because he was hungry and destitute! As humans, we would have likely turned our noses up at this behavior, however, God's love is insurmountable; this means that no one can overcome it, overrule it, or overturn it in your life! In short, His love is overwhelming! This is to say that, like the prodigal son, we often turn back to God when our idols begin to fall and break; this is especially true when we've made every last ditch effort available to piece our idols back together again. Nevertheless, how great is the love that God has for us that, even though our initial returns to Him are typically selfish and centered around our needs and wants, God still utilizes these opportunities to introduce us to the many facets of who He is. In this, God knows that if we stick around long enough, we'll likely learn to love Him in return. This is because we will soon come to discover that everything that we need and want is in Him! And even more than that, we also discover that when we truly put God first, many of our desires, plans, and preferences begin to evaporate because they are and were nothing but void-fillers that we believed were powerful enough to fill those God-sized holes in our hearts. The truth of the matter was, is, and always will be—it was Him all along! In other words, we unknowingly searched for Him in people and material things, and we tried to put ourselves back together again using all of the relationships we've built, all of the things we've purchased, and all of the information we've taken in. We were unwittingly searching for Him all along!

What does it mean to be a prodigal prophet or prodigally prophetic? The word prodigal, according to Oxford Languages, is defined as:

1. Spending money or resources freely and recklessly; wastefully extravagant.
2. Having or giving something on a lavish scale.

Get this, while the word "prodigal" deals with wealth, it's not just limited to tangible wealth. What do you give in exchange for money? Your time. Your time is an invaluable asset that you've allowed man to render as valuable. What does this mean? We have to work to eat; we should all know this, but I think that we can all agree that the amount of money your employer pays you for your time is simply not worth it. The only reason you discount your time is because you have bills to pay, mouths to feed, and a life of your own to live. In other words, you want to have your own house so you can make your own rules and stretch out your potential, your passion, and your perversion. What this means is you want and need space to be yourself, flaws and all! So you, in a sense, prostitute your time in exchange for the basic amenities in life. Then again, you may have a pretty decent career or hustle that pays you quite well; however, it's still not worth the time it takes from you, and if you have decided that it is well worth your time, this means that you have put a cap on your potential. The point of the matter is this—there is something that you have in your life that you have affixed a value to, and it is that thing that you are willing to lease or sell, whether it's a pair of earrings, a car, or your soul (mind, will, and emotions). However, there are some things in life that you render to be invaluable. But before we go any further, let's stop here. How does one sell their own soul? In short, you can't truly sell your soul because it's not yours to sell, but you can put it on the black market. In Mark 8:36-37, Jesus said, "For what shall it profit a man, if he shall gain the whole world, and lose his own soul? Or what shall a man give in exchange for his soul?" To lose one's soul is:

1. To lose your mind, since the soul is comprised of the mind, will, and emotions. The mind, biblically speaking, is the heart; again, this is what God told us to guard.
2. To lose yourself; this is when life overtakes and overwhelms you so much that you don't know who you are or Whose you are; instead, you live your life under an identity that God never assigned to you. This is when the peace of God evades you, while chaos, perversion, fear, insecurity, and pain settle into your life to become your reality.

To lose your soul means to give Satan your heart in exchange for something that you desire. However, when you go before the Living God to be judged, He will judge you based on who you loaned your soul to while you were here on Earth. This is why Jesus said in Matthew 16:25, "For whosoever will save his life shall lose it: and whosoever will lose his life for my sake shall find it." In this, what we discover is that because we are spirits living inside of the bodies God loaned to us, we are in constant interaction with the spirit world, and we have to create an account with one of the spiritual kingdoms, whether it's the kingdom of darkness or the Kingdom of Light. We are all on a journey, and the path of this journey looks like a spectrum. On this spectrum, we are either moving to the left or the right. If we go both ways, we are bi-spiritual, meaning we are polytheistic, double-minded, lukewarm, and unstable in all of our ways. If we go to the right, we are righteous, but if we go to the left, we at enmity with God. In James 4:4, the Lord declares, "Ye adulterers and adulteresses, know ye not that the friendship of the world is enmity with God? Whosoever therefore will be a friend of the world is the enemy of God." The word "adulterer" suggests that the people who God is referring to are believers. He uses the word "adulterer" because we can relate to this world more than we can understand idolater. However, to commit adultery with the world is to commit idolatry against God. This implies that we are not only in a relationship with YAHWEH, but we have a covenant with Him through His Son, Christ Jesus.

Chronology. I cannot emphasize this word enough. God is a God of order. He requests and requires to be the Head of our lives; He has to be first in our lives. As a matter of truth, we have to put Him above ourselves. Let's look at a few scriptures.

- ✓ **Genesis 4:4:** And Abel, he also brought of the firstlings of his flock and of the fat thereof. And the LORD had respect unto Abel and to his offering.
- ✓ **Matthew 6:33:** But seek ye first the kingdom of God, and his righteousness; and all these things shall be added unto you.
- ✓ **1 Corinthians 15:23:** But every man in his own order: Christ the first fruits; afterward they that are Christ's at his coming.
- ✓ **Exodus 20:3:** Thou shalt have no other gods before me.
- ✓ **Malachi 3:10:** Bring ye all the tithes into the storehouse, that there may be meat in mine house, and prove me now herewith, saith the Lord of hosts, if I will not open you the windows of heaven, and pour you out a blessing, that there shall not be room enough to receive it.

What does all of these scriptures have in common? They all deal with the order of a thing. Abel gave God the *firstlings* of his flock, God told us to seek the Kingdom of God *first*, Christ is the *first-fruit* of our faith, we are to have no other gods *before* YAHWEH, and we tithe or, better yet, give God the *first-fruits* of our increase. As I mentioned earlier, the average believer in the Western world and abroad is unknowingly polytheistic. This is because, while many of us are Christians, while others simply identify as Christians, we have chosen Jesus to be our Savior, but we refuse to let Him be our Lord. This is why Jesus said in Luke 6:46, "And why call ye me, Lord, Lord, and do not the things which I say?" This means that we choose God, we just don't choose Him FIRST. We love God, but we just don't love Him ABOVE ourselves. We want God, but we want something else MORE than we want Him. In short, we've been deceived into believing that just being Christian is enough; we've been deceived into thinking that just acknowledging God, going to church, and reading our Bibles is enough. And we treat the Word like a magic spell designed to abolish the laws of sowing and reaping when whatever it is that we're in place to reap does not match the harvests we've fantasized about in our states of delusion. For example, when our narcissistic lovers love-bombed us, we fantasized about marrying and having children with the individuals in question. We reasoned within ourselves that we could tow our broken lovers into one of our local churches, convince them to go to the altar for prayer, and once the folks at the altar were done kicking all of their demons out, we could go on and live happily ever after with our hand-picked idols. And we can reward God by attempting to save their souls AFTER they've chosen us BEFORE they chose God. We would then schedule a few counseling sessions with people who are unfamiliar with our satanic arrangements, and we would attempt to give them a rose-colored view of our relationships. In this, we try to control how we're counseled; we try to control the narrative and the direction of what comes out of the counselor's mouth. This is to say that while we worship God, we worship ourselves, our ideologies, our plans, our special interests, our feelings, and our preferences above God, and we often think that this is enough to pacify God's wrath. The more entitled folks among us believe that they are not only in right-standing with God, but they are God's special batch of believers who are somehow above God's correction and direction.

Order in the Court

What is the cure-all, be-all to this madness? The answer is in the text: PUT GOD FIRST! When we do this, we will see one of the greatest exoduses of our time; we will see God's people and His prophets returning to Him on a massive level. Don't get me wrong. I'm not talking about them returning to church because many of them are regular church-goers. I'm not talking about them turning away from the sins that they so openly commit. I'm talking about people returning to God in thought; in other words, people giving God back His place in their hearts. This is the first place, not the roped off VIP section that they've placed Him in. When He's first, He blesses everything that comes after Him, and anything that is not of Him must bow before Him and give up its spoil. This is to say that if you reside and remain in His will, anytime the enemy throws a dart at you, whether that dart is a word, a storm, or a person, that dart will have no choice but to bless you. Simply put, something that is not God's will for you will not be able to enter His will to harm you. Read that again. God has to be the first-place winner, and get this—you have to lose in order to win. What this means is, when you give God what He wants (which is you), it is within His will to give you what you want. This is to say that God's Will is a place; think of it as your own personal Garden of Eden, and within that space, there are sections called seasons. Within each season or section, there are two systems:

1. The Tree of Life (all of the fruits that God permits you to eat/ fruits of the Spirit).
2. The Tree of the Knowledge of Good and Evil (the pride of the eyes and the works of the flesh).

And while our gardens are replete with mostly good things that we can consume, the problem is that our forefathers ate the forbidden fruits, and they fed them to us, and now, we desperately crave the fruits from the forbidden tree. We don't just crave them, we fiend for them! However, the anti-venom, the cure, and the solution is as simple as it is complicated:

PUT GOD FIRST!

And let's be honest with ourselves. Most of us have never had anyone tell us how to put God first ... how to give the Lord back His throne in our hearts. Understand that you're more than likely not a victim. Jezebel, aka the narcissist, didn't come into your *adult* life and mess it up without your permission. Sure, you may have been raised by a narcissistic mother and/or father, but the moment you were healed enough to recognize that you were broken, your assignment was to get help. You then should have moved the people around in your life like checker pieces, bringing the healed and intentional folks closer, while pushing the toxic and narcissistic ones further away, all the while establishing and enforcing boundaries. You're more than likely not a victim. You're a harvester, a farmer, or better yet, a reaper. Let's look at a few scriptures.

- ✓ **Genesis 2:5:** And every plant of the field before it was in the earth, and every herb of the field before it grew: for the LORD God had not caused it to rain upon the earth, and there was not a man to till the ground.
- ✓ **Genesis 2:15:** And the LORD God took the man, and put him into the Garden of Eden to dress it and to keep it.
- ✓ **Genesis 3:17-19:** And unto Adam he said, Because thou hast hearkened unto the voice of thy wife, and hast eaten of the tree, of which I commanded thee, saying, Thou shalt not eat of it: cursed is the ground for thy sake; in sorrow shalt thou eat of it all the days of thy life; thorns also and thistles shall it bring forth to thee; and thou shalt eat the herb of the field; in the sweat of thy face shalt thou eat bread, till thou return unto the ground; for out of it wast thou taken: for dust thou art, and unto dust shalt thou return.
- ✓ **Galatians 6:7-9:** Be not deceived; God is not mocked: for whatsoever a man soweth, that shall he also reap. For he that soweth to his flesh shall of the flesh reap corruption; but he that soweth to the Spirit shall of the Spirit reap life everlasting. And let us not be weary in well doing: for in due season we shall reap, if we faint not.
- ✓ **Matthew 14:24-30:** Another parable put he forth unto them, saying, The kingdom of heaven is likened unto a man which sowed good seed in his field: But while men slept, his enemy came and sowed tares among the wheat, and went his way. But when the blade was sprung up, and brought

forth fruit, then appeared the tares also. So the servants of the householder came and said unto him, Sir, didst not thou sow good seed in thy field? From whence then hath it tares? He said unto them, An enemy hath done this. The servants said unto him, Wilt thou then that we go and gather them up? But he said, Nay; lest while ye gather up the tares, ye root up also the wheat with them. Let both grow together until the harvest: and in the time of harvest I will say to the reapers, Gather ye together first the tares, and bind them in bundles to burn them: but gather the wheat into my barn.

✓ **2 Corinthians 12:7:** And lest I should be exalted above measure through the abundance of the revelations, there was given to me a thorn in the flesh, the messenger of Satan to buffet me, lest I should be exalted above measure.

Dirt, in the scriptures, is symbolic of flesh, and while the story of Adam and Eve is a literal account of what took place in the Garden of Eden, there is still a lot of symbolism in the story. For example, God told Adam to "till the ground." In this, God is telling us to crucify our flesh so that the fruits of the Spirit can come forth. What was the purpose of tilling the ground? The following information was taken from Oregon State University's website:

"Tilling is the practice of aerating the soil to permit moisture and air to permeate, allowing seeds to germinate, encouraging root growth, controlling weed growth, and integrating fertilizers into the soil. One field may be tilled multiple times before planting for different reasons. Land without a history of recent annual crops is often tough and needs to be tilled to prepare it for planting. Primary tilling is done to uproot weeds and tough stubble, while secondary tilling makes the soil finer. The removal of weeds prevents them from going to seed (Manitoba), while stubble removal helps control some diseases by reducing the pathogen's ability to overwinter in a field (Anderson, 2009)" (Source: Oregon State University/Tillage and Cultivation).

The objective of tilling the flesh is to prepare the flesh for breakthrough, but the question stands, what should we expect to break through our flesh?

1. **Weeds.** These are the tares (demons and demonic people) who've managed to infiltrate our lives when we were unsaved, broken, rebellious, fearful, or just foolish. When these foreigners begin to show themselves in our lives, our job is to uproot and expel them from our lives.

2. **Fruits of the Spirit.** Of course, there are nine fruits of the spirit (see chart below).

Love	Joy	Peace
Patience	Kindness	Goodness
Faithfulness	Gentleness	Self Control

Our job is to grow these fruits so that they can continue to produce fruits, not just in our lives, but in the lives of the people we come in contact with.

From the Breaking to the Breakthrough

1. **The Breaking:** This is when God begins to toil the ground of your heart, and during this time, you will typically experience a grieving of sorts that is comparable to depression. During this space of time, you'll notice that your life still looks the same way it's looked for years, but you will feel many of the soul ties you've formed with people begin to stretch and ultimately break. Yes, this occurs while they are still actively a part of your life! Things just won't feel the same. In this season, you may find yourself experiencing feelings of rejection and the fear of rejection.

2. **The Breakout:** The breakout is when your flesh begins to make its demands. You see, when the ground of your heart is being tilled, everything that once safely resided in you will begin to surface. This is the first stage of your deliverance because most farmers don't till the ground while it is night. They wait until the morning to farm their lands, and there are some issues and things that cannot be exposed to light. This is the season of discovery! When the farmers start turning the ground, they find insects that would ordinarily eat their crops before they could even

begin budding; these insects are oftentimes hiding underneath the soil. These are the insects (demons) that cannot reside in the light, but must go underground or hide under the weeds in your garden to shield themselves from the light. During this phase, many of your demons and issues will start to surface, and I'm talking about issues you didn't know you had! It is during this phase that you may experience your greatest flesh-driven temptations! This is when you're on the edge of leaving your personal Sodom and Gomorrah (your place of perversion and comfort), not knowing where God intends to take you, what He plans to take from you, or what He intends to take you through. This is the beginning of your faith-walk, whereas, you are required to walk by faith and not by sight.

3. **The Breakup:** This is when the soul ties break, oftentimes violently and suddenly, and many of the people in your life begin to fall away, walk away, or be ripped out of your life because the demons you once had are no longer there to entertain theirs. This is the season of contention. During this phase of your development, it may start to feel like everyone is angry with you, and some of the people you once held dearest to your heart are now exiting your life in droves. This includes family members, friends, lovers, and spouses. You see, when you break up with an ideology, you are simultaneously ending your relationship with the people who entered or remained in your life because of that ideology. You may feel like you're contending with everyone, including God during this time because you won't understand why you're experiencing the pain, the rejection, the confusion, and the retaliation from others that you are experiencing.

4. **The Break-In:** Once Satan and his imps realize that you have started your deliverance journey, not just from demons, but from strongholds of the mind, generational curses, and demonic contracts, they will begin to come together to discuss how they can hold you back, drive you back, hold you down, or destroy you altogether. During this time, those demonic bullies will look for any window (opportunity) or door (legality) in your life that they can enter in through. This is so that they can enter in and chase you back into obscurity; this is the darkness that you once

grew used to. If they can't get in you, they'll find a way to get around you. This is when a few potential love interests, both new and familiar (including exes), will begin to take a liking to you or try to enter or reenter your life. During this season, pride and offense will often partner with the spirits of rebellion (often disguised as procrastination) and fear to herd you back into the darkness that God called you out of. This is when you'll be able to effectively identify the thorns in your flesh. Nevertheless, during this phase or season, it is important that you make sure you are surrounded by wise counsel and you are getting regular rounds of deliverance.

5. **The Breakdown:** During this phase, it can almost feel as if God has forsaken you. This is because your flesh is now on the cross being crucified, and it hurts! In this particular section of your reality, you will likely find yourself dealing with anger, vengeful thoughts, and you may even find yourself wrestling with suicidal thoughts. This is because your world, as you knew it, has come crumbling down around you. This is when you are effectively broken. During this season, it is absolutely imperative that you not only have wise counsel, but that you are attending therapy regularly (once a week or, at minimum, once every two weeks). This is when the fruits of the Spirit are about to emerge, and the breakdown (deterioration/decomposition) of your flesh and the relationships that have suddenly died in your life will serve to fertilize the ground of your heart. "And let us not be weary in well doing: for in due season we shall reap, if we faint not" (Galatians 6:9). Note: to exit this season, you have to fully surrender yourself to God, not just in deed, but in purpose (assignment). Surrendering in deed (obedience) is your reasonable service, but surrendering to your assignment forces that great fish called Leviathan to spit you out! Without Leviathan, Jezebel becomes weaker and weaker until that spirit has no ground or leg (legality) left to stand on.

6. **The Breakthrough:** This is the moment of rejoicing; this is the morning after the mourning! Now, you have stepped into the genesis of God's promises to you; this is your personalized Promised Land. It is your

Garden of Eden. In this, your world is now new, and your today looks nothing like your yesterday, not even in the slightest way. This is your birthing season; this is when everything you've been through starts to make perfect sense to you! This is your season of laughter and revelation. And the journey here has just begun because your Promised Land is far too big for you to explore in this lifetime. This is the season where your "yes" meets God's "yes" and creates an eternal echo that you and your children, along with their children, will be able to glean from over the course of your lives.

You Need a Break

There will be breaks between many of these breaks. These are seasons of rest that God has strategically placed on your life's timeline. Please do not forsake these breaks! You'll know when you're experiencing a break (season of rest) because:

1. The warfare may slightly lift or get easier; alternatively, it may seem to stop altogether.
2. You may experience weariness in these seasons, so you will likely find yourself resting quite a bit, not wanting to talk on the phone as much as you once did, and not wanting to leave your house. During this phase, you may think that you're experiencing depression when, in truth, you are simply experiencing mental exhaustion. You may find yourself sleeping longer than usual. All the same, you may even experience yourself eating more than you normally eat.
3. People who usually call you quite often will not call you as much as they once did or they'll stop calling you altogether. This is because this season of rest was divinely orchestrated by God so that you can prepare for the next leg of your journey.
4. Revelation. Every season is a void until it is met and illuminated by revelation; this is the great revealing of the mysteries that were once hidden in that season. This is when you will experience a lot of "wow" and "aha" moments, whereas, some of the events you've suffered

through or experienced will suddenly come to the forefront of your mind. In this, God is bringing it back to your mind so that you can process it properly. This is how you extract the revelation from each event, and some of the nutrients you will find in this revelation include: love, forgiveness, understanding, mercy, and peace.

Note: Never park in a season of rest for too long, otherwise, it will become another place of bondage.

The objective here is for you to rearrange your priorities and to give God back His rightful seat in your heart. In this, you grow from being a prodigal son or daughter to a prophetic prodigy. According to Oxford Languages, a prodigy is, "A person, especially a young one, endowed with exceptional qualities or abilities." In other words, God will be able to trust you all the more with signs, miracles, and wonders because you wouldn't be willing to misuse this powerful for your own selfish gain. Put God first. This is the chronology of true Christianity. God has to be FIRST and FOREMOST, otherwise, any and everything we place above Him will fail and falter. This is because everything you want, everything you touch, and everything you build needs His blessing to thrive. Outside of God, everything that you'll build will be centered around a bunch of worthless idols.

Jezebel is Defeated

In conclusion, the way to get rid of Jezebel once and for all is to put God first. When God is the (true) head of your life, Jezebel can't reside in your members, but when you make Him Lord in title but not in deed, Jezebel will lurk behind the shadows because you summoned her with your idolatry.

I won't share the entirety of these dreams, but they occurred in late 2013 or early 2014. In one of those dreams, I was in a bedroom with a very frail guy; he was incredibly skinny and he looked weak. I was sitting next to him on the bed, and I didn't want to be there. I knew that I had been kidnapped, but I didn't know what to do. A very wicked woman entered the room, along with her husband. I identified that the woman was the ruler of that household, and she was more wicked than her husband. The husband was assertive; he was incredibly wicked as well, but he was submissive to his wife. And the guy sitting next to me on the bed was their son. I was terrified! At one point, the woman told her son to go and do something (I don't remember what it was), so he got out of the bed and left the room. The woman and her husband waited before leaving the room. Not long after this, the husband returned to my room, sat next to me, and demanded that I remove my clothes. I was terrified! In the dream, I was incredibly worried about his wife walking in and blaming me for her husband's indiscretions. He shouted at me to remove my clothes once again, so I pulled down the strap to the tank top I was wearing, and just as I'd feared, the evil wife reentered the room, but to my dismay, she didn't appear to be mad at me. Instead, she demanded that her husband follow her. After they left the room, I heard the sounds of chariots and horses approaching and I instinctively knew that I was about to be rescued. The dream then transitioned to me being with the horsemen, but I couldn't see them. I could only see the evil woman from an aerial view as me and the army came upon her. I remember that she was screaming, and after that, I woke up. The next dream I had, I was in a room getting my hair and makeup done when I decided to get up and peep out the door. I saw a teenage girl (around 12 or 13), and two young boys (one looked to be around nine-years old, while the other was maybe between 3-5 years old). The trio passed the room with the young girl giving me one of the most sinister and hateful looks I've ever received. I somehow knew that I couldn't leave that room and they couldn't come in. The Lord ministered to me, letting me know that the three children represented the evil woman I'd seen in the first dream, along with her wicked husband and wicked and frail son. In the second dream, they were smaller and they no longer had access to me. Why were they smaller? The answer is, I now outranked them, so what was once a giant to me was now under my authority. All the same, that spirit no longer posed a threat to me. Around two years later, God blessed me to start casting that spirit, along with other demons, out of His people. You see, I had to overcome it with the blood of the Lamb and the Word of my testimony. Matthew 7:3-5 reads, "And why beholdest thou the mote that is in thy brother's eye, but considerest not the beam that is in thine own eye? Or how wilt thou say to thy brother, Let me pull out the mote out of thine eye; and, behold, a beam is in thine own eye? Thou hypocrite, first cast out the beam out of thine own eye; and then shalt thou see clearly to cast out the mote out of thy brother's eye." This is a deliverance principle! You see, I couldn't just cast Jezebel out of the folks I had surrounded myself with; I had to cast whatever it was that attracted me to Jezebel out of myself before I could effectively address Jezebel. In other words, I had to repent for idolatry. I had to start walking with God, and get this, I had to give Him a "yes" that I could not take back. Was it easy? No, but the warfare associated with serving myself was way harder! I'd finally learned to love God enough to deny myself! When I denied myself, every Jezebel in my life had no choice but to flee! "Submit yourselves therefore to God. Resist the devil, and he will flee from you. Draw nigh to God, and he will draw nigh to you. Cleanse your hands, ye sinners; and purify your hearts, ye double minded. Be afflicted, and mourn, and weep: let your laughter be turned to mourning, and your joy to heaviness. Humble yourselves in the sight of the Lord, and he shall lift you up."

Of course, we know that Jezebel was defeated over two-thousand years ago when Jesus went to the cross, but the spirit of Jezebel still makes its way to and fro in the Earth, seeking someone to devour: preferably a prophet or, at minimum, a prophetic person. However, Jezebel has no control over a believer who has self-control. Read that again. Proverbs 25:28 (ESV) says it this way, "A man without self-control is like a city broken into and left without walls." The Bible tells us to guard our hearts; we know this. The walls referenced in the aforementioned scripture represent boundaries; what the author (YAHWEH) is saying is that a person who lacks boundaries or a person who does not guard his or her heart has no protection from the enemy. Satan and his henchmen can enter that person's heart at will. So, when Satan goes about like a roaring lion seeking whom he may devour, he is looking for cities (people) without walls (guards; boundaries). And whenever he finds prophets and prophetic people who repeatedly or routinely exalt themselves and their feelings over the Word and the will of God, Satan sends a demonic spy to find out what those prophetic vessels esteem. He then sends them a customized Santa Claus in the form of a narcissist to offer, promise, or give them those things, and after the narcissists have effectively soul-tied themselves to these prophetic souls, they will then use those soul ties in the same manner that a tow truck uses a chain to repossess a stolen vehicle. He will use those soul ties to drag God's prophets and prophetic vessels further outside of God's will, so the way to steer clear from Jezebel is to give up your plans and preferences, and put God first! There is no way around this. Every step that God has placed in front of you is a season filled with the information, the healing, and the revelation you'll need to go to the next level. On each of these levels, you may find something or someone that you've been wanting and praying for. All the same, you may lose something or someone you thought you needed. Just stay the course, and you will eat the good of the land.

Jezebel is defeated. Your assignment is to stay within the will of God, wherein lies your victory; this way, you won't step outside of God's will and into a wilderness season that God didn't usher you into. In the wilderness, you'll meet wild animals, and one of those animals is Jezebel, the narcissistic predator who preys on lost, immature, broken, and rebellious prophets and their prophetic counterparts. I can share with you a thousand prayers to defeat Jezebel, I can teach you all I know about narcissistic abuse, but as long as you reign as lord in your life or you allow someone or something to take God's place in your life, you would be praying in vain. This is because your prayers will only be centered around getting the person free from the Jezebel spirit, but it won't be a prayer addressing the root cause of the issue: idolatry. James 4:3 confirms this; it reads, "Ye ask, and receive not, because ye ask amiss, that ye may consume it upon your lusts." In this, God is saying that your prayers are not coming from a Godly place; they are selfish and immature, and because of this, He is not answering them, after all, YAHWEH will never ride shotgun to an idol. He will not polish an idol, nor will He repair it. Consider the story of Dagon, a false god worshiped by the Syrians.

- ✓ **1 Samuel 5:1-5:** And the Philistines took the ark of God, and brought it from Ebenezer unto Ashdod. When the Philistines took the ark of God, they brought it into the house of Dagon, and set it by Dagon. And when they of Ashdod arose early on the morrow, behold, Dagon was fallen upon his face to the earth before the ark of the LORD. And they took Dagon, and set him in his place again. And when they arose early on the morrow morning, behold, Dagon was fallen upon his face to the ground before the ark of the LORD; and the head of Dagon and both the palms of his hands were cut off upon the threshold; only the stump of Dagon was left to him. Therefore neither the priests of Dagon, nor any that come into Dagon's house, tread on the threshold of Dagon in Ashdod unto this day.

The Philistines took the ark of God and placed it in the same room as their demonic deity, and early the next day, they found the statue of Dagon fallen prostrate before the ark of God. James 2:19 states, "Thou believest that there is one God; thou doest well: the devils also believe, and tremble." Additionally, Philippians 2:10 says, "That at the name of Jesus every knee should bow, of things in heaven, and things in earth, and things under the earth." In short, there is no power greater than God's power, and there is no name above the name of Jesus! All the same, anything or anyone that you exalt above God will serve as an idol in your life, and the closer you get to God, the more you will witness the breaking of relationships, in addition to the breaking of your own heart. That is until you fully align your heart with God's heart, and get this—the broken and idolatrous heart that you may be hosting now won't be able to stand before God. This is why He said in Ezekiel 36:26, "A new heart also will I give you, and a new spirit will I put within you: and I will take away the stony heart out of your flesh, and I will give you a heart of flesh." After you've received your new heart, God will then give you the desires of that heart, and not your former heart. Please note that by heart, the Lord is referring to the spirit of your mind; this has everything to do with generational iniquity, demonic strongholds, and ungodly systems that form the rhythm (patterns) of your heart; these patterns form your habits. Your habits form your environment or, better yet, habitat. Your habitat is the reality that you inhabit as a result of whatever it is that you've stored in your heart. Your reality is what's real to you. You see, you can exist in the same house with a person, and have experienced the same events over the course of your life, but the two of you can have totally opposing realities, even though you're constantly looking at the same furniture, driving around the same neighborhood, and sharing the same experiences. How you process a thing will determine your perspective of the event and life in general; the same is true for the other person involved. Nevertheless, anything that takes God's seat in your heart will be forced to bow before Him.

The Philistines did not heed the warning. They simply took Dagon and stood him back up. On the next day, the Philistines found their handmade god fallen prostrate once again, but this time, his head had been severed from his body and his hands were both broken off. The head represents authority; a severed head represents the destruction of an authority or, in this case, the pulling down of a principality. The hands represent strength and ability. The severing of Dagon's hands was God making that spirit impotent. In this, Dagon was defeated and put to shame before the very people who worshiped him. This is exactly how God treats our gods. If you idolize a relationship, God will dry out that relationship, meaning He won't bless it, and without the water of His Word, anything that we build becomes fragile and weak. This is why so many relationships fail today. The following information was taken from Wilkinsin & Finkbeiner's website:

1. Almost 50 percent of all marriages in the United States will end in divorce or separation.
2. Researchers estimate that 41 percent of all first marriages end in divorce.
3. 60 percent of second marriages end in divorce.
4. 73 percent of all third marriages end in divorce.

Source: https://www.wf-lawyers.com/Divorce Statistics: Over 115 Studies, Facts And Rates For 2024

According to statistics, one out of every two hundred people have Narcissistic Personality Disorder. This does not count the people who are narcissistic, meaning they don't necessarily have the disorder, but they relatively higher on the spectrum of narcissism than most people. All the same, the principality over the United States of America is Baal, and Baal employed Jezebel as a ruling spirit over this name. Furthermore, Leviathan works as an armor bearer for Jezebel.

This is to say that a lot of people in the United States are narcissistic, so it's not uncommon to find yourself entangled with a person who is a slave to the Jezebel spirit. This is why God employed the law of first. We have to seek Him FIRST and place no other gods BEFORE Him.

Jezebel-Proofing Your Heart

If you remember and apply these facts and truths, you will become immune to Jezebel's venom. "And these signs shall follow them that believe; In my name shall they cast out devils; they shall speak with new tongues; they shall take up serpents; and if they drink any deadly thing, it shall not hurt them; they shall lay hands on the sick, and they shall recover."

1.	Put God first. This is something you'll have to intentionally do every single day of your life because your flesh will wrestle to take His place.
2.	Remember that a curse without a cause cannot come. Satan looks for an opportunity to ensnare your soul. If you stay within the confines of God's will, you're safe. If you go into sin or wander outside of God's will, you are being led astray by your flesh and seducing spirits. When Satan goes about like a roaring lion seeking whom he may devour, he will come after you because lions eat flesh.
3.	Satan loves to use the people around you to lead you astray. He doesn't need a big wide open door in your life to come in. All he needs is a cracked door or window. This is to say that if you want to Jezebel-proof your life, you have to mind your connections. 1 Corinthians 5:11 warns us this way, "But now I have written unto you not to keep company, if any man that is called a brother be a fornicator, or covetous, or an idolater, or a railer, or a drunkard, or an extortioner; with such a one no not to eat."
4.	Don't tempt yourself! As a single woman, I have vowed to God to not participate in fornication, nor will I kiss a man before our wedding. Why is this, you ask? I always say this—kissing is foreplay. Why would I heat up the oven if I don't plan to put anything in it?! Understand that the Bible expressly tells us to flee fornication. To do this, one thing you have to

	remind yourself of repeatedly is this—your flesh is not Christian. Your flesh is not saved, nor does your flesh love the Lord. So, it doesn't matter what you tell yourself, if you put yourself in a position where you can easily be tempted and you can easily give into that temptation, you will likely fall into the lap of Jezebel through sexual immorality. In this, you will give that devil a legal right to your soul (mind, will, and emotions) through the ungodly soul tie that you form with that person.
5.	In Psalm 32:7, King David song to the Lord, "Thou *art* my hiding place; thou shalt preserve me from trouble; thou shalt compass me about with songs of deliverance. Selah." God does the same for His people. He surrounds us with songs of deliverance, so why do we turn our radios on and listen to songs of bondage? Listen, each kingdom has its own music; both kingdoms have their own artists! So, why are believers listening to songs that encourage them to be bound; I'm talking about songs that glorify rebellion, pride, witchcraft, seduction, and self-worship? Music enters into the heart through the emotional realm, and a song is nothing but a chant put to a beat. What are you chanting every day? Jesus said in Matthew 15:11, "It is not what goes into the mouth that defiles a person, but what comes out of the mouth; this defiles a person."
6.	There is a season for everything underneath the sun and the Son; this includes marriage, money, and all of the things that we, as humans, tend to idolize. Be patient with God and chase Him until you are content with Him. If you put your preferences first, you will make that thing greater in your life than God, thus making it your god. And it doesn't matter how long you've been going to church, serving your pastor, or serving in any ministry, you can still fall into the many pits of idolatry, thus landing in Jezebel's territory. Philippians 4:6 (NIV) says, "Do not be anxious about anything, but in every situation, by prayer and petition, with thanksgiving, present your requests to God." In Matthew 6:34, the Lord told us, "Take therefore no thought for the morrow: for the morrow shall take thought for the things of itself. Sufficient unto the day is the evil thereof." This is to say that you ABSOLUTELY have to cast down imaginations and every high

thing that exalts itself against the knowledge of God, and bring every thought captive to the obedience of Christ (see 2 Corinthians 10:5). So, when those fantasies of marriage, babies, and riches start auditioning for your attention, cast them down! This is a form of warfare that does not look, nor does it feel like warfare; consequently, many believers welcome this brand of warfare with open arms and open hearts. That is until the devil settles in and begins to do what he does best: steal, kill, and destroy.

7. Read, apply, and reread this scripture until it penetrates your heart and your reality. "Beloved, believe not every spirit, but try the spirits whether they are of God: because many false prophets are gone out into the world" (1 John 4:1). Additionally, 2 Corinthians 11:14 tells us why we need to test the spirits that come into our lives; it reads, "And no marvel; for Satan himself is transformed into an angel of light." Lastly, Matthew 7:21-23 reads, "Not every one that saith unto me, Lord, Lord, shall enter into the kingdom of heaven; but he that doeth the will of my Father which is in heaven. Many will say to me in that day, Lord, Lord, have we not prophesied in thy name? And in thy name have cast out devils? And in thy name done many wonderful works? And then will I profess unto them, I never knew you: depart from me, ye that work iniquity." Not every person who identifies himself or herself as a Christian is Christian. Everything that God creates, Satan goes out of his way to create a counterfeit of it. Don't get overly excited just because someone says Jesus, speaks in tongues, dances during worship, or falls out every time someone touches them. People can and do fake worship; they also fake deliverance, tongues, and everything that we do as believers. This is why God told us that we will know them by their fruits; this is how we discern them. What fruits should we look for, you ask? The fruits of the Spirit.

8. Heal and forgive. Unforgiveness, unbeknownst to most believers, is actually one of the many soul ties that you can form with a person. You see, if you're unforgiving, what your heart is telling you is that the individual that you're angry or disgruntled with owes you something, whether that debt is money, an explanation, an apology, or to give you

back the seat you once held in that person's life. It essentially causes you to lord yourself over that individual. All the same, in this, you are disregarding the blood of Jesus by exalting that person's crimes against you over your crimes against the Most High God; yes, the very crimes that Jesus went to the cross for. This is to say that you make the cross of Jesus null and void, and of no effect in your life. Matthew 6:14-15 (NIV) says, "For if you forgive other people when they sin against you, your heavenly Father will also forgive you. But if you do not forgive others their sins, your Father will not forgive your sins."

9. Come out of victimhood! Unforgiveness is one of the many paths to victimhood. Again, victimhood is a state of mind; it is a neighborhood of thinking, whereas, you see yourself as either the victim of someone else's evil, or you see yourself as being so anointed that the devil has placed a special mark on you, causing you to become a target for the enemy. In this, you begin to see yourself as one of the few "chosen ones." While we do know that many are called, but few are chosen, the Bible tells us in Romans 12:3, "For I say, through the grace given unto me, to every man that is among you, not to think of himself more highly than he ought to think; but to think soberly, according as God hath dealt to every man the measure of faith." People who see themselves higher than they should are typically bound by the spirits of Jezebel and Leviathan, and they are often driven by their pain. They essentially become kings and queens of the lower realms of thinking, meaning they become leaders of the blind who lead other blind folks into ditches, pits, and sewers with their anger, bitterness, and the demonic perspectives they've settled into when their pain met and married their potential. What this does is it causes people who are fueled by vengeance-driven thoughts of success to be arrested by ungodly ambition. What does this look like? It looks like a person who chases platforms, money, and people with titles, all the while imagining how the people who hurt, betrayed, rejected, abandoned, persecuted, and robbed them would regret losing them once they became successful. These types of thoughts are not only demonic, but they are commonly found in victimhood. The victim's hood is where Jezebels are trained and

	developed. See yourself the way that God sees you. How? By taking accountability for your role in your own adult-sized pain and getting therapy for the issues that happened when you were young, all the way up to now.
10.	Remember this—most of us LOVE to be love-bombed. This is especially true for people who are prophetic. Love-bombing does not usher in true love; it ushers in obsession. Another word for obsession is idolatry. So, while we love being flattered, listening to people future-fake with us, and being pursued by people who we are mutually attracted to, never forget that love-bombing is designed to get you to open your heart; this means that you have to stop guarding your heart and let whatever it is that is posing as love to enter your heart. This false love is responsible for every relationship that you had trouble letting go of; it is responsible for the suicidal thoughts that followed the breaking down of those relationships. It was and is not from God; it is counterfeit love. Again, God told us in 1 Peter 5:8, "Be sober, be vigilant; because your adversary the devil, as a roaring lion, walketh about, seeking whom he may devour." Whenever you "fall in love," you are not in true love; instead, you have simply lost your sobriety. To make this clear, understand that witches cast spells on people. The word "spell" is where we get the word "spelling," and it has everything to do with words. According to the Galatians 5, witchcraft is one of the works of the flesh. This is to say that it is (fallen) human nature to cast spells using words; we do this without realizing what we're doing. For example, a lot people have friends who laugh and call them stupid whenever they say or do something funny; we've made a culture and a habit of calling ourselves crazy. We even refer to the miracles of God as "crazy." So, it goes without saying that whenever you open your life for another person to enter into it, that person may start speaking things that you have to cast down, and if the individual sees a huge benefit in having you around, that person may begin to love-bomb you. Love-bombing is an attack, not a shower of affection. Keep your conversations sober, and make sure that the man or woman that's pursuing you remains sober as it relates to you.

11.	Don't run the stop signs, the red flags, and the speed bumps, and do not run the speed limit of God's will!
12.	Don't give someone access to your heart who has trouble guarding their own. Be quiet. Let the other person speak, after all, out of the abundance of the heart, the mouth speaks (see Luke 6:45). The problem isn't that you lack discernment (if you do, ask for it in prayer by name). The problem oftentimes is that you are so impatient that you try to rush into relationships by telling your insignificant other everything there is to know about you. By doing this, you create a culture of you speaking, while the other person listens and learns everything there is to know about you. In other words, you start handing over your power to the narcissist the moment you decide that you like the individual. Be quiet and listen more than you speak. Let the individual tell you who he or she is; let them express their concerns, share their goals, and spell out their expectations. When you do this, you can effectively and soberly execute Luke 14:28-30, which reads, "For which of you, desiring to build a tower, does not first sit down and count the cost, whether he has enough to complete it? Otherwise, when he has laid a foundation and is not able to finish, all who see it begin to mock him, saying, 'This man began to build and was not able to finish.'" Practically speaking, whenever you are sober-minded, you can see what the person is hosting and what he or she is bringing to the table, both good and bad. From there, you will be able to part ways from people who do not have God's heart. Let the individual speak! Tell them to turn off any music that they may be playing while speaking to you. Jezebel loves to seduce and entice her victims. Keeping the conversations sober is a form of gray-rocking.
13.	People who have little to no self-control will always specialize in people-control. If you don't see self-control in a person's life, run for your life! It is only a matter of time before the individual in question starts making demands, either overtly or covertly. And every demand isn't shouted; all too often, demands are "suggested," but make no mistake about it. Jezebel always demands her way! This typically happens after the soul tie

	has been formed or when it has turned into a yoke (legally binding).
14.	If someone tries to make you choose between themselves and God, choose God! Let Him be 5-0 in your life! As a matter of fact, choose Him first right now so that whenever the enemy throws his fiery darts at you, you will be sober and cognizant enough to recognize that those people were not sent to you by God; they are on demonic assignments. In this, you won't allow them to soul-tie themselves to you, and then drag you out of the God-established churches, partnerships, friendships, or covenants that you've made with others. Remember that narcissists love to separate their supply from the people who care about them and the people who have their best interests at heart. Read between the lines. Jezebel will rarely, if ever, directly tell you what he or she wants. Someone hosting this spirit will hint around as to why they are upset with you, putting you on punishment, or threatening to discard you. They want you to figure it out, and this is because they know that what they're thinking and wanting is insane. They can't come out and say, for example, "I don't want you going to the church you attend anymore because your pastor is making it hard for me to seduce and control you. I'm having to work extra hard because of that church of yours; plus, I don't like your mother because she loves you, and I hate that she's looking at me with a sober set of eyes. I could not bewitch her with my flattery, so I don't want her around. As for your close friends, they are way too confident, and I know that their confidence has been rubbing off on you. This makes it harder for me to look like the hero I want to portray myself as. I want to break you, take you around some of my friends who, by the way, are worse off than me; this way, I can look like a catch to you, and whenever I hurt or abuse you, you will excuse my behavior by telling yourself that it could be worse. So, I need to isolate you so that I can break you down; this way, you'll need me and I will become your everything." They can't come straight out and say this because it would sober you up. So, they need to put a spell on you by speaking intoxicating lies that are designed to make you believe that you are the problem; they will go out of their way to convince you that you are the narcissistic one in the relationship, while

they are anointed, chosen by God, and the victims of your foolish antics. This is why it is imperative that you stay in the will of God and choose God first. If you do this, every narcissist that manages to get past your boundaries will find themselves being discarded by you the moment and the minute that you see that fork in the road; this is the end of any given season. This is when God is calling you to go right, while they are trying to get you to make a left turn. This is when you'll know that your relationship with that person has come to an end; that is unless you follow them down the yellow brick road of idolatry and straight into the witch's trap.

15. Throw away your fake ID! You're not an empath, even though you may be highly empathetic to others. You are (more than likely) a prophet or a prophetic person! Being an empath suggests that you are an emotional, naive, and sensitive victim of the narcissists that once exposed your idolatry. You're none of those! You were an idol worshiper who reaped what he or she sowed; then again, you can be the product of a generational curse, but the moment you perpetuated that curse, you were no longer a victim. You simply became a practitioner of it. Satan wants you to see yourself as an empath; he uses witches to describe the very wiring that God gave His people. In this, Satan is simply giving away his playbook in exchange for your attention and your loyalty, however, your true power is found in your calling and identity! Again, you may not be called to the office of the prophet, but you may very well be prophetic. This is why you're sensitive, and yes, this is why you are a narcissist magnet. But the problem isn't that you attract Jezebel; the problem lies in the fact that you have been attracted to Jezebel; it's a two-way street, not a dead end. Your identity is found in your "yes" to God; it's located a few smiles behind your surrender (by this, I mean that God loves a cheerful giver). It's when you count all of the suffering as joy; it's when you stop chasing the created things of this world and start chasing the Creator, Himself. Embrace who you are in Christ, and stop embracing the victim-status that Satan is using to pacify your perversions and your procrastination. Simply do what God has already instructed you to do. You are more than a conqueror in Christ Jesus, so act like it! And anytime you

find yourself at a fork in the road, follow God, no matter who and what you have to leave behind to do so!

In the next chapter, you will find a glossary for the world of psychology. Be sure to familiarize yourself with every term and definition; this way, you can readily identify a narcissist whenever he or she attempts to enter your life. After the glossary, be sure to fill out your prophetic profile. This will help you to get a better view of who you are in Christ.

The World of Psychology (Glossary)

Welcome to the World of Psychology's Glossary. In this glossary, you will find terms associated with narcissism and narcissistic abuse. While this library is not an exhaustive or a completed list of terms, you will find the majority of largely used terms in this glossary, and they can help you to identify the symptoms of narcissism, the signs of narcissistic abuse, and the many behaviors of Jezebel, the narcissist.

Abuse Amnesia

Abuse amnesia, also known as dissociative amnesia, is a psychological condition in which an individual represses or blocks out memories of past abuse or trauma. This phenomenon can occur as a coping mechanism, allowing the individual to function in their daily lives without being overwhelmed by the traumatic memories.

In many cases, individuals may not even be aware that they are experiencing abuse amnesia. They may have little to no recollection of the abusive events, or they may have fragmented memories that are difficult to piece together. This can lead to confusion, emotional distress, and difficulty in forming healthy relationships.

Abuse amnesia can have long-lasting effects on the individual's mental health and well-being. Without proper treatment and deliverance, the repressed memories of abuse can resurface in the form of flashbacks, nightmares, or sudden triggers that bring back the traumatic memories. This can lead to a cycle of repressed memories, emotional distress, and an inability to move on from the past.

It is important for individuals who suspect they may be experiencing abuse amnesia to seek professional help and support. Therapy and counseling can help individuals process and heal from the trauma of the past. By addressing and working through the repressed memories, individuals can begin to regain control over their lives and move forward in a healthy and positive direction.

Attachment Trauma

Attachment trauma is a type of psychological injury that occurs when a person experiences a disruption or deprivation of the normal bonds and relationships with primary caregivers during early development. This can occur as a result of neglect, abuse, or a sudden separation from primary caregivers, and it can have long-lasting effects on a person's emotional and psychological well-being.

Research has shown that attachment trauma can lead to a range of cognitive, emotional, and behavioral difficulties, including depression, anxiety, low self-esteem, and difficulties in forming and maintaining healthy relationships. In addition, individuals who have experienced attachment trauma may have difficulty regulating their emotions and may exhibit impulsive or self-destructive behaviors as a result.

It is important to recognize the impact of attachment trauma and to provide appropriate support and interventions for individuals who have experienced it. This may include therapy to address underlying attachment issues, as well as support in developing healthy coping mechanisms and building secure relationships.

By understanding attachment trauma and its effects, we can work to create more nurturing environments for children and provide the necessary support for individuals who have experienced trauma in their early years. Through this awareness and support, we can help individuals heal and thrive despite the challenges they have faced.

Baiting

Baiting is a manipulation tactic employed by individuals with narcissistic personality disorder to provoke a desired response from their victim. This form of abuse is insidious, as it involves the deliberate provocation of the victim in order to elicit a reaction that can then be used against them.

One common way that narcissists bait their victims is through the use of passive-aggressive behavior. This can take the form of subtle insults or criticisms disguised as jokes or off-handed remarks. The goal is to make the victim feel uneasy or insecure, and to provoke them into defending themselves or reacting emotionally. Once the victim has responded, the narcissist can use their reaction as evidence of their supposed irrationality or over-sensitivity.

Additionally, narcissists may use gaslighting techniques to bait their victims into feeling confused or doubting their own perception of reality. By gaslighting, the abuser can make the victim feel as though they are overreacting or being paranoid, thus undermining their confidence and making them more susceptible to further manipulation.

It is important for victims of baiting to recognize these tactics and seek support from trusted individuals or professionals. By doing so, they can begin to break free from the cycles of manipulation, witchcraft, control, and intimidation so that they can regain control over their own well-being.

Blame Shifting

Blame shifting is a common tactic used in narcissistic abuse. This behavior is characterized by the narcissist shifting the responsibility for their actions onto their victim, often leaving the victim feeling confused, guilty, and at fault for the problems in the relationship.

Narcissists are skilled manipulators who use blame shifting as a way to maintain control over their victims. By making the victim feel responsible for the problems in the relationship, the narcissist is able to avoid taking any accountability for their own actions. This can lead to the victim feeling isolated, confused, and questioning their own reality.

Blame shifting can take many forms, including gaslighting, projection, and denial. Gaslighting involves the narcissist manipulating the victim into doubting their own thoughts and feelings, while projection involves the narcissist attributing their own negative qualities onto the victim. Denial is another common tactic in which the narcissist refuses to acknowledge their own behavior but instead insists that the victim is overreacting or exaggerating the situation.

It is important for victims of narcissistic abuse to recognize the signs of blame shifting and seek support from trusted individuals or professionals. By understanding the manipulative tactics of the narcissist, victims can begin to reclaim their own sense of reality and break free from the demonic cycles of blame and control.

Coercive Control

Coercive control is a form of domestic abuse that involves a pattern of controlling, dominating, and coercive behaviors aimed at exerting power and control over a victim. This can include isolating the victim from friends and family, monitoring their every move, controlling their finances, and manipulating them through emotional and psychological abuse.

This type of abuse is often subtle and insidious, making it difficult for victims to recognize and escape from. It is a form of psychological abuse that can have long-lasting and damaging effects on the victim's mental and emotional well-being. It is important to recognize the signs of coercive control and to seek help and deliverance if you or someone you know is experiencing this type of abuse.

Coercive control is now recognized as a criminal offense in many countries, and there are laws and support services in place to help victims escape from this type of abuse. It is important for believers to educate themselves about coercive control and to offer support and resources for victims who are struggling to break free from the cycle of abuse.

Breadcrumbing

Breadcrumbing is a term that has gained popularity in the realm of modern dating and relationships. It refers to the act of giving someone just enough attention or communication to keep them interested, without actually committing to a relationship or making any real effort to pursue things further. This behavior can be extremely frustrating and hurtful for the person being "breadcrumbed," as it can lead to feelings of confusion, disappointment, and insecurity.

Breadcrumbing is often characterized by sporadic and inconsistent communication, mixed signals, and the withholding of true emotional investment. It can leave the recipient feeling emotionally drained and confused about where they stand in the relationship. This pattern of behavior can also have a negative impact on one's self-esteem and sense of self-worth, as it can lead to feelings of inadequacy and rejection.

The concept of breadcrumbing reflects the changing dynamics of modern dating and the impact of technology on interpersonal relationships. With the rise of dating apps and social media, it has become easier for people to engage in breadcrumbing behavior, as they can easily maintain a connection with someone without fully committing to them.

Overall, breadcrumbing is a hurtful and manipulative behavior that can have lasting emotional effects on the recipient. It is important for individuals to be aware of this pattern and to prioritize open and honest communication in their interactions with others.

Cognitive Dissonance

Cognitive dissonance is a psychological phenomenon that occurs when an individual holds contradictory beliefs, attitudes, or behaviors. When faced with this internal conflict, the individual experiences discomfort and seeks to alleviate it by either changing their beliefs or justifying their actions.

One classic example of cognitive dissonance is the smoker who is aware of the health risks associated with smoking. The individual may experience discomfort because their behavior contradicts their belief in the importance of good health. To reduce this dissonance, the smoker may either change their behavior by quitting smoking or justify their actions by downplaying the health risks.

Cognitive dissonance is a powerful force in shaping behavior and beliefs. It can lead individuals to rationalize unethical behavior, resist changing deeply held beliefs, or even experience physical symptoms of stress. Understanding cognitive dissonance is essential in fields such as psychology, sociology, and marketing, as it can influence decision-making, persuasion, and conflict resolution.

By recognizing cognitive dissonance in ourselves and others, we can better understand the motivations behind certain behaviors and beliefs. This awareness can lead to more empathetic and effective communication, as well as more thoughtful decision-making. Ultimately, acknowledging and addressing cognitive dissonance can lead to personal growth and positive change.

Dark Triad

The Dark Triad is a term used in psychology to describe three distinct but related personality traits: narcissism, machiavellianism, and psychopathy. These traits are characterized by a lack of empathy, a focus on self-interest, and a tendency to engage in manipulative and exploitative behavior. Individuals who exhibit traits of the Dark Triad may be charming and charismatic, but they often lack genuine concern for others and are willing to use deceptive and coercive tactics to achieve their goals.

Narcissism is characterized by a grandiose sense of self-importance, a need for excessive admiration, and a lack of empathy for others. Machiavellianism is marked by a willingness to manipulate and exploit others for personal gain, as well as a tendency to be distrustful and cynical. Psychopathy involves a lack of remorse or guilt, callousness and a disregard for the rights and feelings of others, and impulsive and irresponsible behavior.

Individuals with high levels of these traits may be more likely to engage in behaviors such as cheating, lying, and manipulation in order to achieve their desired outcomes. They may also have a higher likelihood of engaging in criminal or unethical behavior.

It is important to note that while the Dark Triad traits are associated with negative outcomes, not all individuals who exhibit these traits will engage in harmful behavior. However, understanding the characteristics and potential risks associated with the Dark Triad can help in identifying and managing individuals who display these traits in various personal and professional settings.

Devaluation

Devaluation is a common tactic used in narcissistic abuse, and it can have long-lasting and damaging effects on the victim. This form of psychological abuse involves the narcissist belittling, demeaning, or degrading the victim in order to undermine their sense of self-worth and power. The narcissist may use tactics such as gaslighting, invalidation, and criticism to constantly chip away at the victim's self-esteem and confidence.

Devaluation serves several purposes for the abuser. It allows them to maintain a position of power and control over the victim by eroding their sense of self-worth and independence. By constantly devaluing the victim, the narcissist can ensure that the victim remains reliant on them for validation and approval, thereby perpetuating the cycle of abuse.

The effects of devaluation can be profound, leading to low self-esteem, feelings of worthlessness, and even depression or anxiety in the victim. Over time, the constant devaluation can erode the victim's confidence and make it difficult for them to trust their own discernment, perceptions, and emotions.

Discard

Narcissistic discard is a term used to describe the abrupt and often cruel ending of a relationship by a person with narcissistic tendencies. This type of discard can leave the other person feeling devalued, confused, and emotionally devastated. The narcissist, in their quest for validation and control, may use this tactic as a means of asserting their power and superiority over their partner.

During the discard phase, the narcissist may suddenly and without warning, cut off all communication, show little to no concern for the other person's feelings, and may even move on to a new relationship or interest without a second thought. This can leave the discarded individual feeling betrayed, abandoned, and questioning their self-worth.

Narcissistic discard is a particularly harmful form of emotional abuse, as it can deeply impact the individual's sense of self and their ability to trust in future relationships. It is important for those who have experienced narcissistic discard to seek support and therapy to heal from the emotional trauma inflicted by the narcissist.

Ego

Ego plays a central role in narcissistic abuse, as the abuser's inflated sense of self often leads to manipulation and exploitation of others. The narcissist's ego is fragile and dependent on external validation, leading them to seek out targets who can provide them with the admiration and attention they crave. However, this constant need for validation often leads to a cycle of abuse, as narcissists will go to great lengths to maintain their grandiose self-image, often at the expense and the well-being of those around them.

The narcissistic abuser's ego drives them to exert control and dominance over their victims, using psychological manipulation, gaslighting, and other forms of emotional abuse to maintain their perceived superiority. This exploitation is a result of the narcissist's overwhelming need to have their ego constantly fed, leading them to devalue and mistreat those who do not meet their expectations or challenge their inflated self-image.

Please understand that the ego of the narcissistic abuser is at the root of their destructive behavior, driving them to seek out and exploit others for their own validation and self-aggrandizement. Recognizing the role of ego in narcissistic abuse is essential for understanding and addressing the dynamics of this harmful and often traumatic relationship dynamic.

Fauxpology

Fauxpology, a portmanteau of the words "faux" and "apology," refers to a disingenuous or insincere apology that is intended to manipulate or deceive others. While genuine apologies are rooted in feelings of remorse, accountability, and a genuine desire to make amends, fauxpologies often lack these qualities and are typically used as a tactic to avoid consequences or to manipulate the perceptions of others.

Fauxpologies can take many forms, including shifting blame onto the offended party, using conditional language that minimizes the offense, or making excuses for the behavior in question. Fauxpologies can also be characterized by a lack of empathy or understanding of the harm that has been caused, further indicating insincerity.

The use of fauxpology can be damaging to relationships, as it undermines trust and creates a sense of invalidation for the offended party. It can also perpetuate a pattern of dishonesty and manipulation that erodes the integrity of communication and interaction.

Flying Monkeys

Flying monkeys are individuals who, often unknowingly, enable the behavior of a narcissist and assist in perpetuating their abuse. These individuals may be friends, family members, or even colleagues who serve as allies to the narcissist, either willingly or out of coercion or manipulation.

The term "flying monkeys" originates from the Wizard of Oz, in which the Wicked Witch of the West uses her army of flying monkeys to carry out her bidding. In the context of narcissistic abuse, flying monkeys may fulfill various roles, such as spreading rumors, gaslighting the victim, or acting as intermediaries between the narcissist and their targets.

Flying monkeys are often unaware of the harm they are causing, as they may have been manipulated or deceived by the narcissist into believing that their actions are justified. In other cases, flying monkeys may willingly participate in the abuse due to their own underlying issues, such as a desire for power or control, or a lack of empathy towards the victim.

Recognizing the role of flying monkeys in narcissistic abuse is crucial for understanding the dynamics of the situation and for those seeking to break free from the cycle of abuse. By addressing the behavior of flying monkeys and setting boundaries, victims can begin to reclaim their own agency and work towards healing from the trauma inflicted by the narcissist and their enablers.

Future-Faking

Future-faking is a term used to describe the deceptive practice of making promises or commitments about the future in order to manipulate or control a person in the present. This behavior is commonly seen in relationships where one partner may lead the other to believe that they have long-term intentions or plans, only to later renege on those promises.

Future-faking can take many forms, such as making grandiose statements about the future, making long-term plans, or expressing deep emotions and investment in the relationship. These promises are often used as a means of gaining the trust and loyalty of the other person, while avoiding any real commitment or accountability.

This behavior can have damaging effects on the individual who is being manipulated, as they may invest time, energy, money, and emotions into a relationship that ultimately proves to be insincere. It can also lead to a sense of betrayal and mistrust, as the person realizes that they have been deceived and manipulated.

In order to prevent future-faking, it is important for individuals to be aware of the signs and patterns of this behavior, and to maintain healthy boundaries in their relationships. Open and honest communication is also crucial in order to build trust and ensure that both partners are on the same page regarding their intentions and commitments. By being vigilant and aware of future faking, individuals can protect themselves from being manipulated and hurt in their relationships.

Gaslighting

Gaslighting is a psychological tactic that has been used for decades to manipulate and control individuals. The term "gaslighting" originates from a play in the 1930s called Gas Light, where a husband tries to convince his wife that she is losing her mind by purposely dimming the gas lights in their home and then denying that any changes had been made. Gaslighting is a form of psychological abuse in which the abuser convinces their victim that their thoughts, feelings, and experiences are invalid or untrue.

Gaslighting can occur in various settings, such as personal relationships, the workplace, or even in religious and political environments. The abuser may use gaslighting to maintain power or control over their victim, to deflect blame, or to cover up their own wrongdoing.

Gaslighting can take on many forms and is often a gradual process. The victim may not recognize the behavior as abusive or manipulative and may even start to question their own sanity. The abuser may use tactics such as denial, lying, projection, and minimization to convince their victim that their perception of reality is inaccurate.

What are some gaslighting tactics that narcissists and narcissistic people use?
- One of the most common tactics of gaslighting is denial. The abuser may deny that certain events have occurred or that they have said or done certain things. They may also deny the victim's emotions and experiences, making them question their own feelings and perceptions.
- Another tactic is lying, where the abuser may tell falsehoods to the victim, sometimes making themselves out to be the victim in the situation. This is done to confuse the victim and make them less likely to trust their own judgment.
- Projection is also a common tactic of gaslighting. An abuser may accuse their victim of doing something wrong or having a certain emotion, when in fact it is the abuser who exhibits these behaviors. This serves to shift the blame onto the victim and make them feel guilty for the abuser's behavior.
- Minimization is yet another tactic of gaslighting. The abuser may downplay the severity of a situation or belittle the victim's feelings, making them feel as if their emotions are invalid or overblown.

Gaslighting can have long-term effects on a victim's mental health and well-being. Victims may experience anxiety, depression, and other mental health issues as a result of the abuse. They may also struggle with trust and self-doubt, making it difficult for them to form healthy relationships or trust their own judgment.

Grey Rock Method

Grey rock is a term that has been gaining increasing popularity in recent years, particularly among individuals who have experienced emotional abuse. The term refers to a specific method of dealing with difficult and toxic people, whereby an individual seeks to become as emotionally neutral and uninteresting as possible. Despite its simplicity, the grey rock technique has helped countless people to deal with difficult situations in a healthy and effective manner.

The term "grey rock" was popularized by a blogger named Skylar, who originally coined the term in 2012. The concept is based on the idea that when dealing with someone who is trying to manipulate or control you, the best approach is to become as uninteresting and unresponsive as possible. The goal is to deprive the other person of the emotional response they are seeking and to minimize the power dynamic between the two parties. Essentially, the grey rock method teaches individuals to become emotionally neutral when interacting with toxic people.

One of the main benefits of the grey rock method is that it allows individuals to remain in control of their emotions and responses. When someone is trying to manipulate or upset you, it can be all too easy to become defensive or reactive. By practicing the grey rock technique, individuals can remain calm and composed, which can help to deescalate the situation and prevent it from getting worse. Additionally, the method can help to minimize the long-term emotional impact of dealing with difficult individuals.

Applied in practice, the grey rock method involves several key principles. Firstly, the individual must seek to become as uninteresting as possible. This can involve avoiding topics of conversation that are likely to trigger emotional responses or simply providing monosyllabic responses to questions. Secondly, the individual should avoid engaging in conflict with the other person. This means avoiding arguments, not responding to insults, and generally keeping interactions as brief and to-the-point as possible. Finally, the individual should focus on their own emotional well-being, seeking support and self-care whenever necessary.

While the grey rock method is not a panacea, it can be an effective tool for dealing with difficult people. That being said, there are some situations where the method may not be appropriate or effective. For example, if someone's behavior is genuinely dangerous or abusive, it may be necessary to seek outside help or remove oneself from the situation entirely. Additionally, if someone is displaying aggression or violence, the grey rock method may not be enough to ensure the safety of oneself or others.

Hoovering

Hoovering, in the context of interpersonal relationships, refers to a manipulative technique used by individuals, often those with narcissistic or abusive tendencies, to try and regain control over a person they have previously abused or discarded. This term draws its inspiration from the Hoover vacuum cleaner, as the abuser attempts to literally "suck" the victim back into the relationship.

Hoovering typically occurs after the victim has ended the relationship or distanced themselves from the abuser. The abuser may use various tactics such as apologies, promises to change, or grand gestures of love to lure the victim back into the relationship. This behavior often creates confusion and emotional turmoil for the victim, as they may feel a mix of hope, guilt, and fear.

Hoovering is dangerous because it perpetuates the cycle of abuse and can prevent the victim from fully breaking free from the toxic relationship. It is important for individuals to recognize hoovering for what it is and seek support from trusted friends, family, or professionals to resist these manipulative tactics.

Hypervigilance

Hypervigilance is a state of being constantly on edge, alert to potential threats and dangers. When this state is a result of narcissistic abuse, it can be particularly distressing. Narcissistic abuse is characterized by manipulation, gaslighting, and emotional or psychological manipulation by a person with narcissistic personality traits.

Those who have experienced narcissistic abuse often find themselves in a state of hypervigilance, constantly monitoring their surroundings for potential threats or signs of danger. This is a result of the constant psychological warfare inflicted by the narcissist, which leaves the victim in a state of heightened sensitivity and fear.

Hypervigilance in the context of narcissistic abuse can have severe effects on the victim's mental and emotional well-being. It can lead to constant anxiety, difficulty in focusing, and a sense of being constantly on edge. It can also lead to long-term physical effects such as fatigue, insomnia, and other stress-related health issues.

In order to heal from hypervigilance caused by narcissistic abuse, it is essential for individuals to seek therapy and support from mental health professionals. It is also important to practice self-care and develop healthy coping mechanisms to manage the effects of hypervigilance. By addressing the root cause of the hypervigilance and working through the trauma of narcissistic abuse, individuals can begin to heal and reclaim their sense of safety and well-being.

Idealization

Idealization is a common tactic used by individuals with narcissistic personality disorder to manipulate and control their victims. This process involves the abuser projecting an idealized image onto the victim, which can manifest as excessive praise, intense admiration, and the portrayal of the victim as perfect or flawless.

This idealization serves to create a strong emotional bond or, better yet, soul tie between the victim and the abuser, as the victim feels valued, special, and unique in the eyes of the narcissist.

However, this idealization is often short-lived and is ultimately used as a tool for the abuser to gain power and control over the victim. Once the victim has been sufficiently idealized, the abuser will then devalue and discard them, leaving the victim feeling confused, hurt, and unworthy.

This idealization and subsequent devaluation cycle is at the core of narcissistic abuse and can have a profound impact on the victim's mental and emotional well-being. The constant shifting between idealization and devaluation can lead to feelings of insecurity, low self-worth, and emotional trauma for the victim.

Idealization is a manipulative tactic used by narcissists to establish control and power over their victims, ultimately leaving the victim feeling emotionally and psychologically traumatized.

Intermittent Reinforcing

Intermittent reinforcement is a type of operant conditioning in psychology that involves providing rewards or punishment at irregular intervals. This method is known to be highly effective in shaping and maintaining behavior, as it creates a sense of unpredictability and anticipation in the individual being conditioned.

One of the key characteristics of intermittent reinforcement is that it can result in stronger and more persistent behavior compared to continuous reinforcement. This is because the individual is not able to predict when the reward or punishment will be delivered, leading to a heightened sense of motivation and persistence in seeking the desired outcome.

Intermittent reinforcement is commonly seen in everyday situations, such as gambling, where the occasional big win keeps individuals coming back for more, despite the overall loss. It is also prevalent in relationships, where occasional positive reinforcement from a partner can lead to increased devotion and investment.

However, while intermittent reinforcement can be highly effective in shaping behavior, it can also lead to addictive and compulsive behaviors, as individuals become conditioned to seek out the reward or punishment at all costs. In other words, intermittent reinforcement is a powerful tool in shaping and maintaining behavior, but it also has the potential to lead to negative consequences when used inappropriately. It is important for individuals and practitioners to be mindful of the effects of intermittent reinforcement and to use it judiciously.

Love-Bombing

Love-bombing is a manipulative tactic often used in relationships where one person showers their partner with excessive affection, attention, and praise in order to gain control over them. This tactic is typically used by individuals with narcissistic tendencies or a manipulative nature.

Love-bombing can be effective in creating a sense of euphoria and excitement in the beginning stages of a relationship, as the receiving partner feels adored and cherished. However, as the relationship progresses, the love bomber may begin to use this excessive affection as a way to manipulate and control their partner. They may become possessive, jealous, and demanding, using the threat of withdrawing their affections to keep their partner compliant.

In the long run, love-bombing can have damaging effects on the recipient's sense of self-worth and autonomy. It can create a cycle of dependency and emotional manipulation that is hard to break free from. Recognizing the signs of love-bombing early on in a relationship is crucial in order to protect oneself from falling victim to this harmful tactic.

Mask

The narcissistic mask is a term used to describe the facade that individuals with narcissistic personality disorder present to the world. Behind this mask lies a deep sense of insecurity, vulnerability, and fear of being unlovable. The narcissistic mask is a defense mechanism that allows individuals to hide their true emotions and insecurities from others, while projecting an image of confidence, superiority, and grandiosity.

The narcissistic mask serves as a shield to protect the fragile self-esteem of the individual with narcissistic traits. It allows them to maintain an image of perfection and superiority, while avoiding any criticism or rejection that may threaten their fragile ego. This carefully crafted persona often includes traits such as charm, charisma, and a sense of entitlement, which are used to manipulate and control those around them. Behind this facade, however, lies a deep sense of emptiness and a constant need for validation and admiration from others.

Living behind the narcissistic mask can be exhausting and ultimately damaging to both the individual and those around them. It creates a barrier to authentic and meaningful relationships, as the true self is hidden behind a facade of false confidence and grandiosity. It is important for individuals with narcissistic traits to seek professional help and deliverance in order to address their underlying insecurities, their demons, their strongholds, and to develop healthier ways of relating to themselves and others.

Mirroring

Mirroring is a concept that pertains to the behavior of mimicking or imitating another person's gestures, expressions, and speech patterns. This phenomenon can occur consciously or unconsciously and is often associated with building rapport and connection with others.

One of the primary functions of mirroring is to establish a sense of familiarity and likeness between individuals. When one person mirrors another, it sends a signal that they are in sync and can create a sense of mutual understanding and trust. In addition, mirroring can be used as a nonverbal communication tool to convey empathy and validation. For example, a therapist may use mirroring to show understanding and solidarity with their client's emotions.

From a psychological perspective, mirroring is believed to activate the mirror neuron system in the brain, which is responsible for understanding and interpreting the actions and emotions of others. It is also thought to play a role in the process of social learning and the development of empathy.

Overall, mirroring serves as a powerful tool in building relationships and fostering understanding between individuals. While it may be used consciously as a communication strategy, it also occurs naturally in social interactions, contributing to the nuances of human connection.

Monkey Branching

Monkey branching is a term used to describe the behavior of some individuals who transition from one romantic relationship to another without fully ending their current relationship. This behavior is unethical and hurtful to all parties involved.

The term "monkey branching" is derived from the way that monkeys swing from one branch to another without letting go of the previous one. In the context of relationships, it refers to the act of seeking out a new partner while still being involved with someone else, essentially using the current partner as a safety net until a new relationship is secured.

This behavior can be emotionally damaging for the person being monkey branched, as they may feel used and betrayed by their partner's lack of commitment. It also creates a sense of distrust and insecurity in the new partner, knowing that the person they are involved with is capable of such disloyalty.

Monkey branching can also have long-term negative effects on the individual who engages in this behavior, as they may develop a pattern of avoiding dealing with their own emotions and communication issues in relationships. This can hinder their ability to form genuine and healthy connections with others in the future.

Narcissistic Collapse

Narcissistic collapse is a phenomenon in which individuals with narcissistic personality traits experience a sudden deterioration of their self-esteem and identity. This collapse typically occurs when their inflated sense of self is threatened or when they are unable to uphold their grandiose self-image. This can be triggered by a variety of factors such as a major life event, rejection from others, or a failure in achieving their goals. What does a narcissistic collapse look like? During a narcissistic collapse, individuals may exhibit symptoms of depression, anxiety, and intense shame. They may struggle to maintain their self-image and may become emotionally unstable, unable to cope with their feelings of inadequacy. This can lead to a loss of interest in activities that were previously sources of validation and support for their self-esteem. All the same, it is important to note that narcissistic collapse is not a recognized clinical diagnosis, but rather a concept based on observations of individuals with narcissistic tendencies. However, it is a topic of interest in the field of psychology and has been studied in the context of narcissistic personality disorder.

Dealing with narcissistic collapse can be challenging, as these individuals may resist seeking help or fail to recognize their own patterns of behavior. Therapy and support can play a crucial role in helping individuals navigate through their collapse and work towards rebuilding a healthier sense of self.

Narcissistic Fog

Narcissistic fog is a term used to describe the clouded and distorted perception of reality experienced by individuals with narcissistic personality disorder. This fog encompasses a range of behaviors and thought patterns that are indicative of a deeply ingrained sense of superiority, entitlement, and a lack of empathy for others.

Those affected by narcissistic fog often exhibit traits such as grandiosity, arrogance, and a constant need for admiration and validation. They are often unable to see beyond their own needs and desires, and may manipulate or exploit others in order to maintain their inflated sense of self-importance.

This fog can have a profound impact on the relationships and interactions of those affected by it, as they are often unable to truly connect with others on a genuine and empathetic level. They may struggle to recognize the needs and feelings of others, and may engage in behaviors that are harmful or destructive to those around them.

Addressing narcissistic fog requires a combination of therapy, self-reflection, and a willingness to change. By recognizing the impact of their behaviors and thought patterns, individuals affected by narcissistic fog can begin to work towards a healthier and more balanced understanding of themselves and the world around them. However, this process can be difficult and may require long-term support and intervention, along with deliverance counseling.

Narcissistic Rage

Narcissistic rage is a term used to describe the explosive anger and aggressive behavior exhibited by individuals with narcissistic personality disorder (NPD). This disorder is characterized by an inflated sense of self-importance, a need for constant admiration, and a lack of empathy towards others. When individuals with NPD feel that their sense of self-importance has been threatened or challenged, they may respond with intense anger and aggression.

Narcissistic rage is often triggered by perceived threats to the individual's self-worth and an inflated sense of superiority. For example, a narcissistic individual may become enraged when someone criticizes their ideas or actions, challenges their authority, or suggests that they are not as important as they believe themselves to be. This rage is characterized by explosive outbursts of anger, verbal abuse, and sometimes even physical violence.

One key feature of narcissistic rage is the lack of empathy displayed by the individual. They may not show concern for the feelings or well-being of others, even if their aggressive behavior causes harm. This lack of empathy can make it difficult for others to understand why the individual is so angry, and can also make it challenging to reason with them or deescalate the situation.

Another feature of narcissistic rage is the intensity of the emotional response. Individuals with NPD may display a disproportionate level of anger and frustration in response to minor or even perceived slights. This is because their sense of self is closely tied to their self-image and any perceived attack on that image is seen as a direct threat to their sense of self-worth.

There are several potential causes of narcissistic rage. One is the individual's upbringing, particularly if they experienced significant trauma or neglect in childhood. This can lead to feelings of inadequacy and a need for validation that manifests as narcissism. Additionally, some experts believe that a genetic predisposition may also contribute to the development of NPD.

The effects of narcissistic rage can be significant and far-reaching. Individuals who experience narcissistic rage may damage relationships with family members, friends, and colleagues, and may also struggle to maintain stable and fulfilling romantic relationships. In some cases, this anger can lead to aggressive or violent behavior that poses a risk to the individual and those around them. Additionally, episodes of rage may lead to feelings of guilt and shame, further exacerbating the individual's sense of inadequacy.

Ultimately, with proper treatment and support, individuals with NPD can learn to manage their emotions in healthier, more constructive ways.

Narcissistic Supply

Narcissistic supply is a concept within the field of psychology that refers to the attention, admiration, and validation that a narcissist seeks from others in order to maintain their inflated sense of self-worth. This supply can come in various forms, including praise, adoration, compliments, and even fear or envy from others.

Narcissists often rely on this external validation to bolster their fragile self-esteem and mask their deep-seated insecurities. They may go to great lengths to ensure that they are constantly receiving the attention and admiration they crave, manipulating, and exploiting others in the process.

The pursuit of narcissistic supply can have harmful effects on both the narcissist and those around them. For the narcissist, their relentless quest for validation can lead to shallow and superficial relationships, as they only value those who provide them with the desired supply. For those in the narcissist's orbit, their manipulative and self-serving behavior can lead to emotional and psychological abuse.

It is important for individuals to recognize the signs of narcissistic behavior and to protect themselves from being used as a source of narcissistic supply. By setting boundaries and refusing to enable a narcissist's manipulative tactics, individuals can safeguard their own well-being and avoid contributing to the destructive cycle of narcissistic supply.

Narcissistic Wound

Narcissistic wound is a term used to describe a psychological injury that occurs when a person experiences a threat or an insult to their self-esteem or self-worth. This term was coined by the psychoanalyst Heinz Kohut, who was the first to identify and describe narcissistic personality disorder.

The narcissistic wound occurs when an individual's self-esteem is threatened or diminished. This can happen in a variety of ways, such as criticism, rejection, or failure. The result of the narcissistic wound is a sense of shame, humiliation, and vulnerability.

A narcissistic person typically has a grandiose sense of self-importance and an inflated self-image. They believe that they are special, unique, and deserving of admiration and attention. They often have an entitlement complex, where they expect others to cater to their needs and desires.

When a narcissistic person experiences a narcissistic wound, their sense of self is threatened, and they may respond in a variety of ways. Some may become aggressive and lash out at others, while others may retreat and avoid any further criticism or rejection.

One of the ways that a narcissistic wound can be observed is through the behavior of the person experiencing it. They may become defensive, angry, or argumentative when their sense of self-worth is challenged. They may also engage in behavior that is designed to bolster their self-esteem, such as boasting or seeking out admiration.

In addition to the behavioral responses, the narcissistic wound can also have a significant impact on the person's internal world. They may experience feelings of shame, worthlessness, and insecurity. They may also struggle with a sense of identity, as their previously held beliefs about themselves have been called into question.

While the term narcissistic wound is often used to describe the experience of individuals with narcissistic personality disorder, it is important to note that anyone can experience this type of psychological injury. It is a common experience for many people, especially in situations where they are vulnerable, such as a job interview or a romantic relationship.

Treating narcissistic wound can be a challenging process, as it requires the person to confront their vulnerabilities and face the reality of their self-worth. Therapy is often a useful tool in helping individuals with narcissistic wounds to develop healthy coping mechanisms and strategies for building self-esteem and resilience.

No Contact

No contact is a strategy that many people use when dealing with difficult or toxic relationships. It involves intentionally cutting off all communication and contact with the person causing distress. This can be a difficult decision to make, but it is often necessary for one's mental and emotional well-being.

No contact serves as a form of boundary-setting, allowing individuals to protect themselves from further harm or manipulation. It also provides the space needed for healing and self-reflection. By removing oneself from the toxic environment, individuals can focus on their own needs and well-being without the constant stress and negativity that the other person brings.

While no contact may seem extreme, it can be an important step in creating a healthier and safer environment for oneself. It allows individuals to regain a sense of control and regain their independence. Additionally, it can help individuals to establish new, healthier relationships and boundaries based on mutual respect and understanding.

It is important to note that no contact is not always possible for everyone, especially in cases where the individual is dealing with a family member or co-parent. In these situations, seeking support from a therapist or counselor is important to navigate the complexities of the relationship while still setting and enforcing healthy boundaries.

Object Constancy

Object constancy is the ability to maintain a stable emotional connection with a person, even when they are physically absent. This concept is particularly significant in the context of narcissistic abuse, wherein the abuser lacks object constancy and struggles to maintain consistent, empathetic behavior towards their victim.

In narcissistic abuse, the victim often experiences intense emotional highs and lows as the abuser vacillates between love-bombing and devaluation. The abuser's inability to maintain object constancy leads to erratic and unpredictable behavior, leaving the victim feeling confused, anxious, and constantly on edge. The victim may also struggle with their own sense of self-worth and emotional stability as the constant onslaught of abuse creates a state of emotional turmoil.

Additionally, the lack of object constancy in the abuser can lead to gaslighting and manipulation, as they may deny or invalidate the victim's experiences and feelings. This further exacerbates the victim's sense of confusion and emotional distress.

Overall, object constancy in the context of narcissistic abuse is essential for maintaining a stable and healthy emotional connection. Without it, the victim is left vulnerable to the abusive tactics of the narcissist, unable to establish a sense of safety and security in the relationship. Awareness of this dynamic is crucial in understanding and addressing the complexities of narcissistic abuse.

Parentification

Parentification is a form of emotional and psychological manipulation in which a narcissistic parent places the burden of their emotional needs onto their child. This can include the child taking on the role of caretaker, confidante, or emotional support for the parent, often at the expense of their own emotional well-being.

The narcissistic parent may use guilt, manipulation, and emotional blackmail to compel the child to fulfill their needs, while neglecting the child's own emotional needs. This can result in the child feeling overwhelmed, anxious, and constantly seeking validation and approval from the parent.

This form of abuse can have long-lasting effects on the child, often resulting in feelings of inadequacy, low self-esteem, and difficulty forming healthy relationships in adulthood. The child may also struggle with setting boundaries and asserting their own needs, as they have been conditioned to prioritize the parent's needs over their own.

It is important for individuals who have experienced parentification to seek therapy and support in order to process the trauma and learn healthy coping mechanisms. Understanding the dynamics of narcissistic abuse and the impact it has had on their lives can be the first step toward healing and reclaiming their own emotional well-being.

Projection

Projection is a common and destructive behavior seen in narcissistic abuse. It occurs when the abuser projects their own negative traits, actions, or feelings onto their victim, often blaming the victim for things they themselves are guilty of. This can create confusion and self-doubt in the victim, as they are made to feel responsible for the abuser's behavior.

Narcissistic abusers use projection as a way to avoid taking responsibility for their actions and to maintain their own sense of superiority. By projecting their faults onto their victim, they can maintain their façade of perfection and control. This behavior also serves to manipulate the victim into feeling inadequate and dependent on the abuser, further cementing the power dynamic in the abusive relationship.

Victims of narcissistic abuse may struggle to recognize and address the projection being directed at them, as the constant blaming and gaslighting can cause them to question their own perceptions and experiences. This can lead to a cycle of self-blame and emotional turmoil as the victim attempts to meet the unrealistic expectations of the abuser.

In order to address projection, it is essential for the victim to seek support and validation from trusted sources outside of the abusive relationship. By recognizing and exposing the manipulation and projection at play, the victim can begin to reclaim their own sense of agency and self-worth. Understanding projection is a crucial step in breaking free from the cycle of narcissistic abuse.

Rage Baiting

Rage baiting is a manipulation tactic used by individuals with narcissistic personality disorder to provoke anger and frustration in their victims to maintain control over them. This form of abuse exploits the victim's emotional vulnerabilities and triggers them into a state of rage, which the narcissist can then use to further manipulate and gaslight their victim.

Rage baiting often involves deliberately pushing the victim's buttons, provoking them into a reaction, and then using that reaction to justify their own abusive behavior. This can create a vicious cycle of abuse, where the victim is constantly on edge and walking on eggshells to avoid triggering the narcissist's rage.

It is important for victims of rage baiting to recognize the signs and seek help. This may involve setting boundaries, seeking therapy, and ultimately removing themselves from the toxic relationship. By understanding the manipulation tactics used by narcissists and learning to assert their own boundaries, victims can begin to break free from the cycles of abuse and regain control over their own lives.

Reactive Abuse

Reactive abuse is a dynamic that occurs within interpersonal relationships, particularly in situations of conflict, where one individual responds to the antagonistic behavior of another with their own abusive behavior. This kind of abuse is often a result of feeling provoked, threatened, or overwhelmed by the initial abusive behavior of the other person.

Reactive abuse can take various forms, including verbal, emotional, and even physical abuse. It is important to note that while reactive abuse is a response to the initial aggression, it does not excuse or justify the abusive behavior of the responding individual. Both parties are responsible for their actions, and reactive abuse perpetuates a cycle of violence and harm within the relationship.

It is essential for individuals to recognize and address reactive abuse in their relationships, as it can have detrimental effects on the well-being and safety of both parties. Seeking help from a therapist or counselor can be beneficial in understanding and managing reactive abuse, as well as learning healthy communication and conflict resolution skills.

Smear Campaign

A smear campaign is a form of psychological manipulation and control used by narcissists to discredit and undermine their victims. This type of abuse involves spreading lies, rumors, and false information about the victim in an attempt to tarnish their reputation and destroy their relationships with others. This insidious behavior is designed to isolate the victim and make them feel powerless and alone.

The narcissist behind the smear campaign may use various tactics to accomplish their goal, such as gaslighting, manipulation, and charm to convince others to believe their lies and turn against the victim. They may also use triangulation to involve others in the abuse and create further distress for the victim.

The impact of a smear campaign can be devastating for the victim, leading to feelings of betrayal, shame, and helplessness. It can damage their personal and professional relationships, and erode their self-esteem and mental well-being. Victims may experience anxiety, depression, and even post-traumatic stress disorder as a result of the relentless attacks on their character.

It is important for victims of a smear campaign to seek support from trusted friends, family, and mental health professionals. By speaking out and seeking help, victims can begin to reclaim their power and heal from the trauma of this form of abuse.

Stonewalling

Stonewalling is a communication behavior characterized by a refusal to engage in dialogue or cooperate with another person. This behavior often takes the form of completely ignoring the other person, refusing to acknowledge their presence, or giving short, noncommittal responses.

Stonewalling can be incredibly damaging to interpersonal relationships, as it effectively shuts down any chance of resolving conflicts or reaching a mutual understanding. It can leave the other person feeling frustrated, unheard, and dismissed, leading to resentment and a breakdown in communication.

Psychologically, stonewalling can be a form of emotional manipulation or control. It may be used as a way to avoid taking responsibility for one's actions, or as a means of maintaining power and control in a relationship. It can also be a way of avoiding uncomfortable conversations or emotions.

Stonewalling has been identified as one of the "Four Horsemen" of the apocalypse in relationships, as coined by relationship researcher John Gottman. When stonewalling becomes a regular pattern in a relationship, it can lead to a breakdown in trust and intimacy.

In order to address stonewalling in a relationship, it is important for both parties to communicate openly and honestly about their feelings and needs. Seeking the help of a professional therapist or counselor can also be beneficial in addressing and resolving this harmful communication behavior.

Trauma Bond

Trauma bonding is a psychological phenomenon that occurs when an individual develops a strong emotional attachment to someone who has inflicted trauma upon them. This bond is often observed in abusive relationships, where the victim becomes deeply attached to their abuser despite the harm they inflict. This can be attributed to a variety of factors, including the sense of dependency and control that the abuser cultivates in the relationship, as well as the intermittent reinforcement of positive experiences amidst the negative ones.

The trauma bond is reinforced by the victim's belief that the abuser is the only one who can provide them with validation, love, and security, creating a cycle of hope and disappointment. The victim may prioritize the abuser's needs and well-being over their own, believing that they are responsible for the abuser's behavior and are the cause of their suffering.

Breaking free from a trauma bond can be incredibly challenging, as the victim may experience intense feelings of guilt, shame, and fear at the thought of leaving the relationship. Additionally, the abuser may manipulate and gaslight the victim, further entrenching the bond.

It is crucial for individuals in trauma bonds to seek support from trusted friends, family, or mental health professionals who can provide them with the necessary guidance and resources to safely extricate themselves from the abusive relationship. Ultimately, recognizing and understanding the dynamics of a trauma bond is a crucial step towards healing and breaking free from the cycle of abuse.

Triangulation

Triangulation is a common tactic used in narcissistic abuse, where the abuser manipulates and controls their victim by involving a third party in the abuse dynamic. This third party can be anyone, including a friend, family member, or even another romantic partner. Triangulation serves as a way for the narcissistic abuser to further their power and control over their victim while also bolstering their own sense of superiority.

In this dynamic, the abuser may use the third party to create feelings of jealousy, insecurity, or competition in their victim. By doing so, the victim is constantly in a state of anxiety and mistrust, which makes them more susceptible to the abuser's manipulation and control. This tactic can also be used to undermine the victim's self-esteem and make them feel unworthy or inferior.

Additionally, triangulation can be used to shift blame and responsibility away from the abuser by creating a divide between the victim and the third party. This allows the abuser to avoid accountability for their actions and further manipulate the victim's perception of reality. This is why triangulation is a powerful tool in the arsenal of a narcissistic abuser, and it is important for victims to recognize and understand this tactic in order to break free from the cycle of abuse and regain their autonomy.

Trickle Truths

Trickle truths are a common phenomenon in the realms of communication and interpersonal relationships, and they occur when an individual reveals information gradually rather than all at once. This can occur for a variety of reasons, such as a desire to avoid confrontation, guilt, or a fear of the potential consequences of sharing the entire truth.

Trickle truths can have significant impacts on the dynamics and trust within relationships. When one person is perceived as withholding information or deliberately revealing it in a piecemeal fashion, it can create feelings of suspicion and doubt in the other party. This can erode the foundation of trust and lead to breakdowns in communication and intimacy.

Furthermore, trickle truths can lead to a cycle of distrust and further deceit, as the withholding of information can drive the other party to seek out the truth through other means. This can create a toxic cycle of dishonesty and hurt, which can be difficult to repair.

In order to navigate trickle truths within relationships, it is important for individuals to prioritize open and honest communication. This means being upfront about information rather than revealing it gradually, and being willing to address any concerns or conflicts that may arise as a result. By prioritizing transparency and trust, individuals can work towards building and maintaining healthy and strong relationships.

Word Salad

Word salad is a psychiatric term that describes a jumble of words that are seemingly nonsensical and disconnected from each other. This symptom is most commonly associated with schizophrenia and other psychotic disorders, but it can also occur in other neurological conditions such as dementia or brain injury.

People experiencing word salad may speak in a way that is disorganized and difficult to follow. Their speech may be filled with nonsensical or unrelated words and phrases, making it challenging for others to understand and engage with them. This can be distressing for both the individual experiencing word salad and those around them.

The underlying cause of word salad is not fully understood, but it is believed to result from disturbances in language processing and thought organization in the brain. It is often a manifestation of the disordered thinking and communication patterns that are characteristic of psychosis.

Treatment for word salad typically involves addressing the underlying psychiatric or neurological condition. Speech therapy may also be beneficial in helping individuals improve their communication skills and language processing abilities.

Overall, word salad is a complex and challenging symptom that can have a significant impact on an individual's ability to effectively communicate and interact with others. It is important for healthcare professionals and caregivers to be aware of this symptom and provide appropriate support and intervention for those experiencing it.

Your Prophetic Profile

First Name	Middle Name	Surname

List Your Gifts and Talents Below		
Example: Singing, Helps Ministry, Cooking, Comedy, Etc.		

List Your Strengths Below		

List Your Weaknesses Below		

List Your Spiritual Gifts Below		

Were either of your parents narcissistic?	
Mother	**Father**

Were any of your grandparents narcissistic?			
Paternal Grandfather	**Paternal Grandmother**	**Maternal Grandfather**	**Maternal Grandmother**

Are any of your siblings narcissistic?		
Yes	**No**	**I'm Not Sure**

Are you narcissistic?		
Yes	**No**	**I'm Not Sure**

Do you possess any of the Gifts of the Spirit below?			

Check the box below that fits your answer next to each gift.

Gifts of the Spirit	Yes	No	I'm Not Sure
Word of Wisdom			
Word of Knowledge			
Faith			
Gifts of Healing			
Working of Miracles			

Gifts of the Spirit	Yes	No	I'm Not Sure
Prophecy			
Discerning of Spirits			
Divers Kinds of Tongues			
Interpretation of Tongues			

How old were you when you first tapped into your prophetic abilities?

How often to you dream?

Check the box under the correct answer.

Daily/Nightly	Weekly	Bi-Weekly	Infrequently	Not Sure

How many of your dreams have come to pass?

0	1-5	6-10	10-25	26-50	50 +	N/A

Which of the following do you identify mostly with?

Please circle your answer.

Introvert	Extrovert	Ambivert	Not Sure	None

Do you identify with any of the major and minor prophets?

Check the box to the left of any prophet below that you identify with.

Isaiah	Obadiah
Jeremiah	Jonah
Lamentations	Micah
Ezekiel	Nahum
Daniel	Habakkuk
Hosea	Zephaniah

Joel		Haggai	
Amos			

How many narcissists and narcissistic people have you been romantically involved with?						
0	1	2	3	4	5	6+

Are you currently involved with a narcissist or a narcissistic person?		
Yes	No	I'm Not Sure